ESSAYS ON SOCIOLOGY, PHILOSOPHY AND AESTHETICS

RESEARCHES IN THE SOCIAL, CULTURAL AND BEHAVIORAL SCIENCES

EDITED BY BENJAMIN NELSON

Alfred Adler: PROBLEMS OF NEUROSIS, edited by H. L. Ansbacher. TB/1145

Gladys Bryson: *MAN AND SOCIETY: *The Scottish Inquiry of the Eighteenth Century.*

Kenelm Burridge: *MAMBU: *A Melanesian Millennium.*

Hadley Cantril: *THE INVASION FROM MARS: *A Study in the Psychology of Panic.* New introduction by the author.

Allison Davis and John Dollard: CHILDREN OF BONDAGE: *The personality development of Negro youth in the Urban South.* TB/3049

Emile Durkheim, et al.: ESSAYS ON SOCIOLOGY AND PHILOSOPHY, *with appraisals of Durkheim's life and work,* edited by Kurt H. Wolff. TB/1151

Leon Festinger, Henry W. Riecken and Stanley Schachter: WHEN PROPHECY FAILS: *A social and psychological study of a modern group that predicted the destruction of the world.* TB/1132

Herbert Fingarette: THE SELF IN TRANSFORMATION: *Psychoanalysis, Philosophy and the Life of the Spirit.* TB/1177

Raymond Firth, editor: MAN AND CULTURE: *An evaluation of the work of Bronislaw Malinowski.* TB/1133

Alvin W. Gouldner: WILDCAT STRIKE: *A Study in Worker-Management Relationships.* TB/1176

J. L. Hammond: *THE RISE OF MODERN INDUSTRY. Introduction by Max Hartwell

J. L. and Barbara Hammond: *THE TOWN LABORER.
*THE VILLAGE LABORER.

David Landy: TROPICAL CHILDHOOD: *Cultural Transmission and Learning in a Rural Puerto Rican Village.* TB/1235

Kurt Lewin: FIELD THEORY IN SOCIAL SCIENCE: *Selected Theoretical Papers,* edited by Dorwin Cartwright. TB/1135

David Lockwood: *THE BLACK-COATED WORKER. Introduction by Ralf Dahrendorf

Robert K. Merton, Leonard Broom, Leonard S. Cottrell, Jr., editors: SOCIOLOGY TODAY: *Problems and Prospects,* Vol. I, TB/1173; Vol. II, TB/1174

Roberto Michels: FIRST LECTURES IN POLITICAL SOCIOLOGY. Translated with an Introduction by Alfred de Grazia. TB/1224

Barrington Moore, Jr.: POLITICAL POWER AND SOCIAL THEORY: *Seven Studies.* TB/1221

Barrington Moore, Jr.: SOVIET POLITICS—THE DILEMMA OF POWER: *The Role of Ideas in Social Change.* New Introduction by the author.

John H. Rohrer and Munro S. Edmonson, editors: THE EIGHTH GENERATION GROWS UP: *Culture and Personalities of New Orleans Negroes.* TB/3050

Henri de Saint-Simon: SOCIAL ORGANIZATION, THE SCIENCE OF MAN, *and other writings,* edited by Felix Markham. TB/1152

Kurt Samuelsson: RELIGION AND ECONOMIC ACTION: *A Critique of Max Weber's* The Protestant Ethic and The Spirit of Capitalism. TB/1131

John H. Schaar: ESCAPE FROM AUTHORITY: *The perspectives of Erich Fromm.* TB/1155

Muzafer Sherif: *GROUP RELATIONS AT THE CROSSROADS.
*THE PSYCHOLOGY OF SOCIAL NORMS.

Georg Simmel, et al.: Essays on Sociology, Philosophy and Aesthetics, edited by Kurt H. Wolff. TB/1234

Ernest Lee Tuveson: MILLENNIUM AND UTOPIA: *A Study in the Background of the Idea of Progress.* TB/1134

Edward A. Tiryakian, editor: *SOCIOLOGICAL THEORY, VALUES AND SOCIOCULTURAL CHANGE.

W. Lloyd Warner: A BLACK CIVILIZATION: *A Study of an Australian Tribe.* TB/3056

W. Lloyd Warner and Associates: DEMOCRACY IN JONESVILLE: *A Study in Quality and Inequality.* TB/1129

Florian Znaniecki: *THE SOCIAL ROLE OF THE MAN OF KNOWLEDGE. Introduction by Lewis Coser.

---

* *In preparation*

ESSAYS ON SOCIOLOGY, PHILOSOPHY AND AESTHETICS

EDITED BY KURT H. WOLFF

GEORG SIMMEL

HOWARD BECKER
HUGH DALZIEL DUNCAN
LORE FERGUSON
KURT GASSEN
PAUL HONIGSHEIM
GERTRUD KANTOROWICZ
DAVID KETTLER
DONALD N. LEVINE
MATTHEW LIPMAN
HEINZ MAUS
ARTHUR SALZ
MASAMICHI SHIMMEI
F. H. TENBRUCK
E. V. WALTER
RUDOLPH H. WEINGARTNER
KURT H. WOLFF

HARPER TORCHBOOKS *The Academy Library*
Harper & Row, Publishers, New York

ESSAYS ON SOCIOLOGY, PHILOSOPHY, AND AESTHETICS

Printed in the United States of America.

This book was orginally published in 1959 by The Ohio State University Press under the title *Georg Simmel, 1858–1918*. It is here reprinted by arrangement.

First HARPER TORCHBOOK edition published 1965 by
Harper & Row, Publishers, Incorporated
49 East 33rd Street
New York, New York 10016

Library of Congress catalog card number: 59-10168

CONTENTS

Preface vii

Analyses

Preface to Georg Simmel's *Fragments, Posthumous Essays, and Publications of His Last Years* 3
GERTRUD KANTOROWICZ

The Structure of Simmel's Social Thought 9
DONALD N. LEVINE

Form and Content in Simmel's Philosophy of Life 33
RUDOLPH H. WEINGARTNER

Formal Sociology 61
F. H. TENBRUCK

Simmel's Image of Society 100
HUGH DALZIEL DUNCAN

Some Aspects of Simmel's Conception of the Individual 119
MATTHEW LIPMAN

Simmel's Sociology of Power: The Architecture of Politics 139
E. V. WALTER

The Time and Thought of the Young Simmel 167
PAUL HONIGSHEIM

A Note on Simmel's Anthropological Interests 175
PAUL HONIGSHEIM

Simmel in German Sociology 180
HEINZ MAUS

Georg Simmel's Influence on Japanese Thought 201
MASAMICHI SHIMMEI

On Simmel's *Philosophy of Money* 216
HOWARD BECKER

CONTENTS

A Note from a Student of Simmel's — 233
ARTHUR SALZ

Translations

Letter from Simmel to Marianne Weber (*with a facsimile of the original*) — 239

The Adventure — 243

The Ruin — 259

The Handle — 267

The Aesthetic Significance of the Face — 276

On the Nature of Philosophy — 282

The Problem of Sociology — 310

How Is Society Possible? — 337

Bibliography of Writings on Georg Simmel — 357
KURT GASSEN

Bibliography of Simmel's Books in German and His Writings Which Are Available in English — 376
KURT H. WOLFF

Notes on the Contributors — 382

Index — 385

PREFACE

This volume illuminates facets of an inexhaustible human being. It follows that there are many aspects of Georg Simmel that are not represented here. However, the book will at least acquaint the reader with the catholicity and originality of his intellect.

An even more modest aim of this volume is to introduce the reader to the many areas that Simmel explored. It is unfortunate that—particularly in the United States—he is known chiefly as a sociologist, or more narrowly as the inventor of "formal sociology." The papers that follow should broaden this view. Three of them—Donald N. Levine's, F. H. Tenbruck's, and Hugh Dalziel Duncan's—will correct and deepen our understanding of Simmel the sociologist. Matthew Lipman's paper shows that because of his interest in social phenomena—and not in spite of it—the individual was one of Simmel's primary concerns. E. V. Walter articulates Simmel's conception of power and demonstrates the importance of this conception. Howard Becker's exposition of *Philosophie des Geldes* conveys the significance of Simmel's analysis of money as a socioeconomic phenomenon, and its importance as a basis for his diagnosis of our time. Rudolph H. Weingartner discusses Simmel's philosophy of life, which—abroad more than here—has been the occasion for granting Simmel fame (and giving him a too restrictive label). Mr. Weingartner also shows that the dichotomy of form and content which is central to Simmel's sociology pervades all areas of his interest. Gertrud Kantorowicz' Preface to a collection of Simmel's essays, which was published posthumously, also addresses itself to his philosophy of life. The high tone of her essay may serve the reader to form high expectations of both Simmel and the treatment he receives in this volume; he may wish to read it first to form these expectations, and then to read it once more to test them, after he has inspected the remaining analyses and the translations.

Other essays in the volume include discussions of Simmel's

time and place by Paul Honigsheim, his position in German sociology by Heinz Maus, his influence on Japanese social thought by Masamichi Shimmei, and his relation to anthropology, also by Mr. Honigsheim. Arthur Salz's reminiscences introduce us to the Berlin in which Simmel worked, as well as to Simmel the teacher.

The translations[1] offer Simmel's mature views on philosophy and sociology and present his treatment of the Kantian question "How Is Society Possible?" Four other translations are what might be called phenomenal explorations of everyday matters—the adventure, the ruin, the handle, and the human face. Perhaps these essays show Simmel at his most spontaneous, in his most "beginning" mood. Consequently, a few remarks concerning three of them—"The Adventure," "The Handle," and "The Ruin"—may be helpful.

Simmel's new readers—and some of those who are reading him again—may well feel puzzled when they try to ascertain whether what they read brings them to an extraordinary mind or to changes this mind works on the world it contemplates, whether they are impressed by an attitude or the discoveries made by virtue of having it. They may even be intrigued by the question whether such alternatives are simply inapplicable to the unique thinker that is Simmel, whether these and other contrasts and conflicts between reality taken as a fact and reality apprehended as a process do not actually rise out of our sense of life as we catch ourselves in the act of sensing it. No thinker was as conscious of such dualities as was Simmel. In his last, consummate book, *Lebensanschauung,* he states that man is the only being who, recognizing that he is bounded, transcends the boundaries: life is characterized by the immanence of its own transcendence.

"The Adventure" is only one of several hundred entries in Simmel's bibliography. It is, however, one of his fundamental essays. It seems as novel to us today as it must have been to those who first read it nearly half a century ago. Its significance lies, not in its subject, but in the way in which that subject is transformed, by him who meditates on it, into a symbol of the inexhaustibility of the creative consciousness. "Everything could not become an adventure if the elements of adventure did not in some measure reside in everything, if they did not belong among the vital factors by virtue of which a happening is designated a human experience." We really do not know the world, including ourselves, but we do know that the wind bloweth where it listeth and that it touches us too, and so makes us adventurers.

"The Adventure" is an example of Simmel's ability to account for and mediate—in one process—an object to which he turns his attention. He is a master at both. In performing them, he often uses analogies, which may present difficulties to the reader and translator. He often introduces these analogies by such expressions as "so to speak," "as if," and "as it were," and by the verb "seems." "The Handle" contains some eighteen instances of this use, "The Ruin" about half as many. Most of them can be translated literally, and they are so translated in this volume. Here is the first instance in "The Handle":

> ...The vessel stands in two worlds at one and the same time: whereas reality is completely irrelevant to the "pure" work of art and, as it were, is consumed in it, reality does make claims upon the vase as an object that is handled.

Not quite "consumed," only "consumed, as it were." Such expressions reveal the writer's awareness of his need for analogy; without them, he could not say what he must say.

The function of analogy is to mediate between that which is being discussed and the person discussing it. Again the first paragraph of "The Handle" furnishes a good example.

> ...The real object interacts with everything that surges past or hovers around it, but the content of a work of art cuts off these threads, fusing only its own elements into a self-sufficient unity.

The German text reads:

> ...Der reale Gegenstand in Wechselwirkungen mit allem steht, was um ihn herum flutet oder beharrt, der Inhalt des Kunstwerkes aber diese Fäden abgeschnitten hat und nur seine eigenen Elemente zu selbstgenugsamer Einheit verschmilzt.

A more literal translation of the passage is:

> ...The real object stands in reciprocal effects with all that floods or perseveres around it, but the content of the art work

> has cut off these threads and melts only its own elements into self-sufficient unity

The analogy derives from two worlds: that of the web of objects and that of the single work of art. The web is surging, flooding, hovering, remaining; but these very liquidities and suspensions are, at the same time, threads that are cut by the work of art as it makes its own unity, a unity which it does not receive from without, from the world of objects.

As Simmel moves (to paraphrase one of the distinctions he liked to use) from the *terminus ad quod* to the *terminus a quo,* he seems to be in a hurry; he rushes to come more nearly to a point, so that it often seems as though (to use a Simmelian analogy) he does not hunt for ideas, but is hunted by them. For the reader, therefore, it is often impossible to distinguish between the scholar and his prey.

Another means of mediation lies in the choice of objects: Simmel's selections are characterized by many "superficial" and "unpretentious" topics like those treated in the essays translated for this volume. There are others: coquetry, the Alps, fashion, the picture frame, caricature, the portrait, and so on. The reasoning which lies behind Simmel's use of apparently insignificant and inconsequential objects for his investigations may be reflected in "The Problem of Sociology" where he argues passionately that this new science must not confine itself to the large, "as it were, official social formations." If it were to do so, it would resemble

> the older anatomy which limited its study to the major, definitely circumscribed organs such as heart, liver, lungs, and stomach, and neglected the innumerable, unnamed or unknown tissues without which these more obvious organs could never make up a living body.

The metaphor of the organism suggests the ahistoricity of Simmel's sociology—it was, after all, invented by a man whose approach was predominantly ahistorical. Since it is placed inevitably in history, however, the work has import as an expression of its time—which is also ours. The comments which I have ventured here more or less follow Simmel's ahistorical procedure, a procedure which might be called intrinsic analysis.

But as a complement to this, there exists a need for extrinsic, historical and sociological, analysis—a mode of interpretation to which Simmel's work with its freedom from the confines of a single age and with its lack of dependence on a particular school offers an unusually rigorous challenge. Before it can even be undertaken, a great deal more systematic reading and intrinsic interpretation of his writings must be done. However they are classified, they are also a work of art, one which has yet to find its exegete and its critic. In the meantime, Simmel's "method" may help to teach that exegete what to search for and that critic how to interpret. Some of the essays that follow, informed by Simmel as they are, may also be of help.

The facts of Simmel's life and reputation are interesting because they set the boundaries of his own "adventure." He was born on March 1, 1858, in Berlin, to Jewish parents who had been converted to Protestantism. He attended the humanistic Gymnasium and later studied at the University of Berlin (history with Mommsen, Droysen, Sybel, and Treitschke; psychology with Lazarus, Steinthal, and Bastian; philosophy with Friedrich Harms and Zeller). He received his doctorate in 1881 with a dissertation on Kant and a "minor" paper on Petrarch. Four years later he became a *Privatdozent,* a position which he held for a decade and a half before being promoted to professor extraordinarius, the rank at which he remained for fourteen years. Altogether he was twenty-nine years at his alma mater, receiving little or no salary—only student fees—and living mainly on his private income. In 1914, he accepted a regular professorship at the University of Strasbourg. At these institutions, he taught logic, the history of philosophy, metaphysics, ethics, philosophy of religion, philosophy of art, social psychology, sociology, and courses on Kant, Schopenhauer, and Darwin. In addition, he dealt with many other phenomena on which he found occasion and necessity (the two were one for him) to meditate. Four years after he went to Strasbourg, near the end of the First World War, on September 26, 1918, Simmel died, harassed to the end by the re-emergence of the sort of chauvinism to which he was constitutionally alien.

Although Simmel created impressive works in aesthetics, ethics, epistemology, philosophy of history, and sociology; and although he enjoyed great fame during his life as both a speaker and writer, he was often condemned as too critical, relativistic, and formalistic. This condemnation was probably one of the reasons for his unusually slow advancement in academic rank. The attitude of the eminent Dilthey, who held the chair of philosophy at Berlin, may have been another, though in his general disapproval of that newfangled enterprise, sociology, Dilthey exempted Simmel's version of it. Had Simmel lived longer, the Nazis would surely have considered him a decadent Jewish intellectual.

In the post-Nazi world of today, where other forms of totalitarianism continue to tyrannize vast numbers of people, we may well regret the almost total absence in Simmel of a political consciousness, such as that of his friend, Max Weber. Simmel's several observations on socialism, for example, are certainly brilliant, but they are the remarks of the formal sociologist. He began his career by puzzling over the nature of history, and he wrote on the subject throughout his life, but he consistently veered away from it toward the "individual law"—the term which he used as the title for the last chapter of his last book. He resolved the issues of his own life, but he was apparently unaware of the power of his thought to illuminate the issues of our age, of the degree to which it is the product and the manifestation of the symptoms that are characteristic of our difficult time in history. We need to expose ourselves to his extraordinary mind, to be enchanted and instructed by its journeys. We must not fear to travel the erratic road along which he would lead us, nor do we dare to turn away from him because he was different. We would suffer by such a rejection, and he would suffer too; he needs us, as we need him.

This volume is a collective enterprise beyond the obvious meaning of the term. Everett Walters, dean of the Graduate School and chairman of the Editorial Board of the Ohio State University Press, enthusiastically received the idea of the book when it was first suggested, and has supported it faithfully throughout its long period of preparation. Edith C. Rinehart, co-ordinating editor, and Weldon A. Kefauver, editor, have worked indefatigably and with extraordinary competence at improving the manuscripts and seeing them into print. Several of my friends and colleagues have helped greatly in editing both the analyses and the translations; these include, above all, Professor Roy Harvey Pearce (English), and Professors John W. Bennett (Anthropology), Virgil G. Hinshaw, Jr., and Anthony Nemetz (Philosophy), Melvin Seeman (Sociology), and Claude M. Simpson, Jr. (English), all of the Ohio State University.

The usefulness of the book has been greatly increased by the Index prepared by Marcia O'Kelly.

Else Simmel, M.D., Simmel's daughter-in-law, and Hans Broermann, owner of the publishing house of Duncker und Humblot, have generously permitted the use of materials for translation. The University of Chicago Press gave permission to quote from Simmel's "The Sociology of Sociability," translated by Everett C. Hughes in the *American Journal of Sociology;* and the Free Press of Glencoe, Illinois has approved the use of quotations from *The Sociology of Georg Simmel,* translated, edited, and with an Introduction by Kurt H. Wolff.

It is obvious that without this help, completion of this volume would have been impossible. The reader will be as grateful as is the editor.

KURT H. WOLFF

Department of Sociology and Anthropology
Ohio State University
Columbus, Ohio
April 21, 1959

1. Only the last two exist in earlier versions; see *The Sociology of Georg Simmel,* trans., ed., and with an Introduction by Kurt H. Wolff (Glencoe, Ill.: Free Press of Glencoe, Illinois, 1950), Nos. 12 and 13, pp. lviii-lix.

ANALYSES

PREFACE TO GEORG SIMMEL'S *FRAGMENTS, POSTHUMOUS ESSAYS, AND PUBLICATIONS OF HIS LAST YEARS*[1]

GERTRUD KANTOROWICZ

Beyond their particular substantive concerns, Simmel's last essays show the applications and ramifications of his central metaphysical idea. Not only, however, do the sweep and fertility of this idea thus become apparent; not only does it become clear that here we have the conception of a world view which is capable of focusing on the whole variety of appearance: the profundity of the idea itself comes more clearly to light.

The essence of it is that the concept of life includes both open flux and closed crystallization; both the process of life incessantly newborn and the entities which emerge out of life (in the one-sided sense of the word) are lifted out of the flux, and are even pitted against it. They reach from the individual solidity of organisms to the objective forms of the spirit, the timeless existence of a world of values as such. The connection of these two elements must not, however, be thought of as merely causal, as if the world of ideas were rooted in life without being of the stuff of life (like a tree and the ground it stands in): it must be thought of as real, essential likeness. If life is viewed sufficiently in the large, it *is* both the dynamic rhythm of its course and its immobile opposite; it is "more-life" and "more-than-life" just because it is *more*-life. The concept of creativity is taken as absolute—of creativity which is both the dissipation and the culmination of its own force and the reach beyond itself, the putting-forth of the work as it is separated from its creator.

What is the fertility of this concept of life? What is the significance of the formula? Something in it, it seems to me, has not been wholly appreciated or recognized in its consequences, namely, that in this concept a synthesis or, better, a germinal point has been gained in which the great, fundamentally contrasting views, the old poles of being and becoming, can meet and fuse. In doing so, neither of them is in the least degraded or compromised: contrasted, they maintain their absolute character. Becoming preserves its pure dynamics—in the degree of intensification given it by the modern image of the world, with its rarification of all substance into subtle relation. But beside it stands fast the unchangeability of eternally valid structures of timeless being. These poles, however, are revealed as of the same kind. Not only are they complementary sides of the same metaphysical entity, not only are they born in the same breath, they simply are one and the same, *are* the one identical creative power. "The transcendence of life," life's turning upon itself: this very transcendence is, at the same time, life's inborn drive, its immanent necessity. Life brings forth, as an identical function, movement infinitely becoming and its transformation into being.

"All that is perfect in its kind goes beyond its kind"—all of Simmel's ultimate syntheses rest on the courage with which the unconditional development of a thought is pursued until, reaching for the "other" within it, it transcends itself and performs that turn of the axis in virtue of which the opposite poles meet and a new whole emerges through the tension of their opposition. Thus, unit-pairs hitherto unknown arise: de-subjectification of the individual; individuality and totality of life; eternity of the temporal; movement of the timeless; life of the idea.

But the point is—as might appear—by no means a mere interpretation of the world of spirit. What is conceived in a new way, rather, is man's position in the totality of being—and hence the whole extrahuman sphere. That which seemed the innermost essence of man—his capacity to fashion and know objective forms and norms, valid worlds separate from psychological becoming—no longer stands in contrast to unconscious, numb, nature-like being, but rests embedded in its great order. Spirit is only the strongest expression of the same metaphysical power which led to the formation of organisms; it is mere symbol or embodiment of total cosmic reality. What seemed to set man off from the sphere of things and non-human beings—the fact that he confronts himself as a conscious mind—becomes, precisely, affirmation and interpretation of the very world-essence; precisely *this* gives man his place, renders him necessary for the whole which becomes word (as it were) in man: "Self-consciousness, that is, the subject which makes itself into its own object, is the symbol, or the real self-expression, of life."

However strange it may sound in the face of this flowing image of the world which eternally gives birth to itself anew, it nevertheless permits the possibility of a cosmos to appear again, as for the first time. This is a cosmos, certainly, not as the Greeks conceived of it: their notion of a harmony of the elements in a round-shaped world without contradictions is denied to modern times. But in constant tension and in the militant contrast of the basic currents, emerges, from processual life in the narrower sense and its counterplay of persistent forms, the wholeness of life at large, including being and becoming. Each part of it is done justice; not one of them is dissolved into soulless elements so that it may be somehow "incorporated." For every single particle is utterance, embodiment, crystallization of the ultimate principle which pervades the world. In its uniqueness, it carries, repeats, embodies the whole—*because* the ultimate principle is life; as becoming or as form, each particle must *be* the whole. But this occurs by clearly distinguishable measures of power and clarity, so that myriad being-like wholes form a hierarchy of values, of superordination and subordination, which allocates to every component its particular position, serving or dominating, but fixed, at any rate, within reality.

Perhaps a simile and a more detailed comparison as regards ancient opinion on these matters would clarify the right by which the force to form a unified cosmos can be asserted of this image of the world. It is the essence of Simmel's idea of "life" to revert (while always remaining in flux), to turn against itself, to "transcend" itself. It may thus be represented by the symbol of a circle, of movement regressing into itself, of self-contained, living infinity. But in this lies a profound affinity, beyond all difference, with the Greek world, whose enigmatic wealth—namely, the revelation of life *being,* the fixation of *becoming* in perfect form—has been missed, over and over again, only because the modern period has not been able to grasp, with its shattered concepts, a dynamics which becomes formed into a pattern that, while growing, rests in itself.

Clearly, the special fields of knowledge can be enriched by a philosophy which has no need for forcing the single item into ready schemata or for dissolving it into shapeless elements, but which comprehends it as form becoming, and becoming formed. Simmel himself could no longer work this out. But his last statements, and particularly his fragmentary notes, allow one to visualize the great extent to which specific branches of knowledge can be illumined by the metaphysical core of his view. At the same time, it becomes understandable why certain fields again and again occupied Simmel above all others: they are those phenomena in which the metaphysical character of life—the polar duality in which it reveals itself and the one root force on which this duality is grounded—becomes visible as if at one stroke.

Art interpretation and philosophy thus are conceived of in a new light. For in art, indeed, a point is reached in which the contrast between becoming and being finds rest: art is entirely life-formed, form become life, "living content." On the other hand, its empirical origin in the artist shows the opposed directions with full clarity: the artist, most alive, caught most deeply by life, is at the same time driven to creative formation, that is, to the production of the permanent work which, in its growth beyond all life, is no longer tied to its psychological origin.

In this connection, the art of the actor attains a significance of its own. For the miracle of art becomes most astonishing—a symbol at once enigmatic and clarifying—where the body itself is the organ of the work of art, where man himself, acting and agitated, *is* the objective work of art.

Perhaps it is possible only from such a vantage point to appraise contemporary tendencies in art or even, more generally, to find value standards for different artistic styles. Thus, Simmel does justice to expressionism by conceiving it as the will to pure dynamics, as the will to complete documentation of inner life in its flux, in its unfalsified factuality. But measuring expressionism by the larger concept of life-and-art, he sees in this very will a deep estrangement from art. The external distance of expressionism from nature does not deceive one into missing it as an inverted naturalism. For it renounces the unity of the counterforces of life which characterizes all art, the union, in one creation, of psychological process and valid form. One might express it thus: the over-all metaphysical sense of *life* is forgotten before life's appearance as *experience*.

Simmel's conception of history rests on the same basis. History, too, presents itself to him as the unifying point where life and form meet. In history, science achieves something otherwise denied to intellectual cognition as it works with particular elements lifted out of life. For in history, life remains preserved in the form of experience. Even more than this, life not only forms the particular content of history but operates as the force which connects it, and by means of which alone the particular facts of the historical process become an understandable order, become history. That is, science, serving pure interest in knowledge, here, within itself, preserves life. What has become spirit is shot through with the life process with whose co-operation alone it can emerge. Or to express it otherwise, history offers us an interpretation of life which is an altogether living interpretation.

Herein, too, lies, finally, the essential significance for Simmel's philosophy of the problem of love. Love appears to be most deeply embedded in the biological teleology of the life flux. At the same time, however, in love the separation from this teleology of the species—a separation which alone transforms general drive into love—becomes most clearly manifest. The turning against life, inherent in all life, operates most powerfully in that phenomenon which at once is the root and crown of life, more-life and more-than-life. Certainly, the polarity which everywhere characterizes life (and which in art is uniquely in equilibrium), in love again becomes shockingly evident *because* its two elements are so closely intertwined—but also, perhaps, because the possibility of its resolution at the highest stage of human existence is manifested here. All Simmel's hints at "erotic nature," and his ever renewed efforts at grasping it, can mean only that the conflict between being and becoming comes to a resolution where love, torn from blind life and become sovereign, again becomes *life*.

Yet such a vista (such respite, as it were) is not intended to diminish the polar absoluteness of the conflict. The essence of life as a metaphysical principle is necessarily tragic. If life's counterforces are not sought beyond life, but inhere in life itself, then life and life, life's Yes and No, must clash with equal strength in the same arena. There is no evasion, even in the sense in which flight or liberation from the tragic might be possible for man. For man, who himself is life in every form, whose essence actually stands and falls with the embodiment of these counterforces and their oneness (because he alone, as a being which *becomes* through living, is capable of envisaging and creating the timeless world of spirit)—for him, there is only the way of affirmation. For the tragic is nothing negative: it is intensification, wealth, the *more*—redemption from becoming and redemption from rigidity, exuberance and the greatness of the cosmos, its passing and its eternity. And yet, the tragic remains. But if the immense is given us only in the form of the tragic, then there is nothing but to accept it and exhaust it to its limits. This courage and this humility are what are demanded of man.

In this fashion, Georg Simmel's last fragmentary words open the way to the application of his metaphysics to active life in the everyday world. There are only some allusions, a thinker's criteria and guidelines for his task as a man. But goal and way are clear: the perfection of man through growth and self-containment; his rootedness in the dark power of the shapeless and his elevation into the clear world of form; readiness for existence and deed, and readiness for sacrifice and destruction. It is affirmation in every form: "Perhaps one must have set life into the center of one's world view and must have valued it as I have to know that one may not preserve it, but must give it away."

Translated by Kurt H. Wolff

1. "Vorwort" to Georg Simmel, *Fragmente und Aufsätze aus dem Nachlass und Veröffentlichungen der letzten Jahre* (Munich: Drei Masken Verlag, 1923), pp. v-x. Used by permission of Else Simmel, M.D.

THE STRUCTURE OF SIMMEL'S SOCIAL THOUGHT

DONALD N. LEVINE

During the first two decades after the death of Simmel, the center of professional sociology shifted away from Continental Europe. In the United States a prosperous economy and an increased interest in science favored the support of sociological research on an unparalleled scale. With the redoubtable exception of Karl Mannheim and the British social anthropologists, the most significant sociological writing after the First World War was done by Americans.

The character of sociology in the New World, however, was notably different from what it had been in Simmel's milieu. It was marked chiefly by the desire to record the diversity of contemporary life by means of responsible techniques of observation. American sociologists developed the questionnaire and the interview, "content analysis" of personal documents and publications, participant observation, and statistical procedures, and came to conceive of social scientific method as the application of these instruments and operations to areas that had been the traditional concern of novelists and journalists. The "Gold Coast" and the slum, the ghetto and the street corner, the classes which number and the classes which count, criminals, sectarians, and immigrants—all these became in turn the object of empirical scrutiny and the subject of new books.

The practitioners of this method had cheerfully abandoned the armchair theorizing of their predecessors. They set about building a science of society that would begin with controlled observations of conditions and events, and whose progress would depend on the refinement of empirical techniques and the accumulation of observations. In so doing, they nearly worked themselves into a theoretical vacuum.

For this reason, the publication in 1937 of *The Structure of Social Action*, by Talcott Parsons, may be regarded as a turning point in the history of American sociology. In that monument of didactic scholarship, Parsons sought to integrate the chief theoretical contributions of the major European sociologists of Simmel's generation and therewith to demonstrate the importance of systematic theory in directing and lending meaning to empirical research. The results of that study provided a matrix within which Parsons was to develop a highly differentiated and systematic conceptual scheme in the ensuing decades, a development of great importance for the status of sociological theory in the United States. Indeed, it may be said that Parsons' "theory of action" is, in respect to complexity, scope, elegance, and refinement, the most advanced body of sociological theory available today.

In the book which laid the foundation for this imposing structure of sociological theory, the work of Simmel is curiously neglected. Of the generally acknowledged major minds of his generation, Simmel is the only sociologist not treated in *The Structure of Social Action*. Curiously so—because he was deeply concerned with interpreting "some of the main features of the modern economic order,"[1] and it was on the basis of this concern that Parsons claimed to have brought together the writers who were considered forerunners of the "theory of action." What is more, Simmel's was, as Parsons himself stated, "perhaps the first serious attempt to gain a basis for sociology . . . as a special science."[2] For when Simmel was starting to write, sociology was generally conceived of as a master science: either a grand melting pot in which the knowledge obtained by special sciences of society was to be combined, or else the most abstract social science, responsible for the most general laws of social statics and dynamics. One of Simmel's first tasks was to stake out a particular area of investigation which would give sociology a distinctive mission and a distinctive competence.

Simmel's definition of the nature and scope of sociology remains a challenge to this day. Besides delimiting the province of sociology, moreover, he cultivated many of its special areas, with results that leave a powerful impression on each new generation of readers. It is surprising, then, that Simmel is not incorporated in what may be regarded as the mainstream of contemporary sociological theory.[3]

Simmel's status in other intellectual traditions in which he felt at home is similar. Throughout his work appear incisive propositions concerning the psychology of the ego which are not the common property of professional psychologists. His original studies of Michelangelo, Arnold Böcklin, and Rodin are not well known by art historians and critics. His highly relevant chapters on the philosophy of history are little heeded by historians. His competent treatment of Kant, Schopenhauer, and Nietzsche, as well as his books on ethics and metaphysics, receive less than their due attention from philosophers.

Though much of what I have to say in this essay applies also to Simmel's writings in these other fields, I shall limit myself here to an account of Simmel's *social* thought taken as a whole, thereby suggesting another direction in which contemporary sociological theory might proceed, as well as providing an introduction to some of Simmel's more important works.

The presentation of a coherent account of the whole of Simmel's social thought is complicated by the fact that coherence is generally not considered to be one of the hallmarks of Simmel's writing. With few exceptions, sociologists have either praised his work as highly sensitive, suggestive, and full of insight, or else damned it as too oblique, intellectually playful, and lacking system. Whether he is viewed as the author of seminal hypotheses or as one who is not to be taken too seriously by hardheaded sociologists, the tendency is to regard Simmel primarily as a precocious man of letters, one who turned an agile mind from topic to topic, offering assorted *aperçus* on the way, but in whose work a consistent, coherent approach to things is lacking.

Support for such an image of Simmel is not entirely wanting in his own attitudes. He does not explicitly relate everything he says to a basic idea or set of ideas. He nowhere defines what might be distinctive of his thinking as a whole. He speaks again and again as one struck by a new idea or absorbed in some matter of the moment, and conspicuously fails to transcend the moment by acknowledging influences or detailing references. At the end of his life, moreover, he observed that he was leaving behind no school, no disciples, and rightly so; for his contribution to posterity was analogous to the bequest of cash, whereby the successors may do with what is left them as they please, each according to his own disposition.

Nevertheless, careful examination of Simmel's treatment of a wide variety of problems has led me to see a significant unity in Simmel's social thought. This unity reveals itself in his choice of subject matter, principles, and method of inquiry, and in his special kind of insight. These four aspects of Simmel's thought will be reviewed in turn in the pages which follow.

One way of expressing the unity in Simmel's subject matter is to note the recurrent categories of subjects which dominate his work. A complete list of the problems considered by Simmel in his various sociological writings falls readily into three categories. One category is suggested by such topics as subordination and domination, competition, secrecy, gratitude, and reconciliation. These topics all represent *social processes,* relatively stable patterns of social behavior which may be found in the most diverse times and places. In discussing a social process, Simmel tells what goes into it, what processes it resembles or contrasts with, and what variety of shapes it may assume; and he illustrates its workings through examples drawn from experience and history. Part of what Simmel has to say about the process of fashion, for example, may be summarized as follows.

Fashion is a process which combines both imitation and individualization. Fashion satisfies the individual's need for being different from others by successively adopting a variety of contents and by marking the domain of a special class. In this latter respect, fashion is similar to honor, another form which imparts a common character to the members of a particular group and at the same time distinguishes them from those who stand outside the group.

That both imitation and differentiation are indispensable components of fashion is shown by the following cases. In isolated, homogeneous, primitive societies there is little interest in differentiation, and so no show of fashions. Similarly, fashion was not in evidence among the Venetian nobles, who wore black in order not to draw attention to their small numbers, and thus could not express any need to differentiate themselves in public. On the other hand, it is said that there was no ruling fashion in Florence toward the end of the *trecento* since everyone adopted a style of dress of his own. Fashion was not present because the disposition to fuse with the collectivity was absent.

The fashionable individual derives the satisfaction of knowing that he represents something special and striking, while he feels inwardly supported by a set of persons who are striving for the same thing. He is envied as an individual, approved of as a member of a group. Fashion is thus an ideal preoccupation for individuals who are dependent, yet who demand a certain prominence.

As soon as any vogue becomes widely accepted within a collectivity, it begins to die out as a fashion. Much of the charm of fashion lies in the fact that it is at once novel and transitory. At its height, a fashion imparts a peculiarly strong sense of the present, an emphasis which likewise accentuates the sensation of change. One reason for the hold of fashions on the modern mind is that the great, permanent, unquestionable convictions are continually losing strength, with the result that the transitory elements of life acquire more room for their activity. Fashion has thus acquired increasing influence over taste, over theoretical convictions, even over the moral foundations of life. Yet despite the transiency of particular fashions, the fashionable objects of the moment seem to promise a certain permanency. This is because fashion itself, as a social process, is immortal; some fashion or other is always with us.[4]

The second category into which the subjects treated by Simmel fall is that of *social types*. Whoever engages in a particular relationship takes on certain characteristics, and sometimes these characteristics come to be essential qualities of the person, independent of the particular relationship. The types analyzed by Simmel include the miser, the modern cynic, the non-partisan, the poor man, the coquette, and the stranger. The following summary of some paragraphs from his *Soziologie* illustrates what Simmel has to say about one social type: the aristocrat.

The sociological form distinctive of aristocracies derives from a unique relation between the general social content of the group and the individual existence of each of its members. Each member of an aristocracy participates in, and avails himself of, whatever is most valuable in all the members of the group. It is as though a substance of lasting value ran through the blood of the various members of an aristocracy, generation after generation.

The importance of the family tree for aristocracy lies in its indication that the substance which forms the individual concerned is, indeed, the same substance which has passed through the whole line of noble stock. This preoccupation with maintaining oneself intact may explain the aristocrat's aversion to work, which, after all, demands a submergence of the self in behalf of an object. Characteristic aristocratic activities such as war and hunting involve the predominance of the subjective factor. The work of the artist, which seeks to articulate the inner motion of a subject, bears the closest resemblance to the aristocratic type of activity; but in this instance it is an individuality, not a common substance handed down by family and class, which comes to expression.

The most crucial thing about aristocracy is that the whole constellation of accumulated and traditional values which confront the noble-born has no objective, superindividual significance. These values come into their own, rather, in the self-reliant, self-contained existence of individual aristocrats. Aristocracy thus represents a peculiar synthesis of two extreme conditions—in the one, the individual is swallowed up by his group; in the other, he stands independent, in opposition to it. The weight of tradition the aristocrat must bear calls for strength and independence as well as responsibility. When the personalities involved are too weak, the mere execution of traditional forms results in decadence. The fusion of aristocrats into their collectivity "finds (more than any other superindividual structure) its meaning and purpose in the existence of individuals, in their might and meaning, in the freedom and self-sufficiency of their lives."[5]

The label I have applied to the third category of social phenomena explored in the work of Simmel is *developmental patterns*. This term refers to historical processes, processes of genesis or transformation. The items under this heading are relatively complex, and cannot be rendered by single familiar words. The sense of a few developmental patterns may be indicated by these formulas: the splitting of group G into factions g_1 and g_2, which are able to unite into G again by relegating their doctrinal differences to the realm of individual preference; the differentiation of a unified state of things into one part which bears characteristics of the original whole, and other contrasting parts; the development from a local basis of social organization to a functional one. A better idea of the kind of subjects involved in this category may be obtained by following what Simmel has to say about one of them: the expansion of the group and the development of individuality.

As the size of a group increases, its members become more unlike one another. This correlation of individual differentiation with sociological expansion appears in the most diverse areas of social life. The powerful, extended family is replaced by wider political groupings, on the one hand, and individuals and their nuclear families, on the other. Corporate guilt and the blood feud are succeeded by justice, in the name of the larger society, and individual responsibility. Unspecialized production for small markets gives way to production for large markets by means of considerable specialization on the part of producers.

The narrower group constitutes a sort of mean between the expanded group and individuality; that is, the second and third offer separately the same possibilities for social life that are offered in combination in the first. Whichever case obtains, a balance between individual and social tendencies is maintained. The narrower the group, the less individuality its members have, but the more distinct the group itself is; in larger groups the individuals have more room to differentiate themselves, but the groups as wholes tend to resemble each other. Individual uniqueness is attained at the cost of social uniqueness.

This correlation (which obtains synchronically and in alternation, as well as in linear developmental patterns) is illustrated in ante-bellum American political life. The New England States were originally composed of small townships which absorbed and regulated much of the individual's life. The Southern States, on the other hand, were populated mostly by adventurous individuals with no inclination for local self-government. They formed large, colorless counties as administrative units, and their real political unity lay in the state. The independent, almost anarchistic, temperament of the Southerners was complemented by this abstract (state) political structure, while the more strictly controlled citizens of New England created strongly individualized and autonomous local communities.[6]

The larger number of subjects dealt with by Simmel fall into the category *social processes;* the rest, into the categories *social types* and *developmental patterns.* These categories, in turn, are part of a more general class fundamental to all Simmel's thought: *form.* This concept will be discussed in the next section, but here we may mention one of its essential features. Forms are interesting and recognizable because they appear in the most unlikely assortment of contexts. Fashion is found in the use of pet terms by the members of a small clique and in the adoption of clothing styles by an entire social class. There have been aristocrats in the widest variety of groups—in ancient Rome, under the Normans, in the *ancien régime,* and among the "aristocracies" of such smaller collectivities as labor groups, large family circles, and the clergy. The pattern of group expansion attended by increased individuation of members is found, we have already seen, "in the most diverse areas of social life."

If the concept of *form* provides the key to the unity of Simmel's subject matter from a logical point of view, the problem of freedom underlies its unity from the point of view of content. Just as the whole of Max Weber's writing may be viewed as an extended commentary on the question, What is distinctive of the modern capitalist order?; and just as it may be said, as Lewis Coser has put it, that "all of Parsons' work, beginning with *The Structure of Social Action,* is an extended commentary on the Hobbesian question, How is social order possible?"[7]—so a large part of Simmel's output may be related to the question, How does freedom increase with the development of society? Extensive discussions of freedom and individualism appear in each of four books by Simmel specifically devoted to sociology.[8] Indeed, the crowning achievement of his life's work was to have been a comprehensive treatment of the concept of freedom, including an interpretation of its significance in history. One can but deeply regret that all that was completed at the time of his death was a scant thirty pages of notes.[9]

Of the many aspects or kinds of freedom which Simmel mentions, three are of special relevance to sociology. There is freedom in the sense of liberation from obligations to others, freedom in the sense of the development of personality according to the demands of one's own nature, and freedom in the sense of power to express one's will. Because the adoption of a money economy increases freedom in all three senses, Simmel devotes a good part of his *Philosophie des Geldes* to an examination of the relationship between money and freedom.[10]

Widespread enjoyment of freedom in the sense of liberation from constraints imposed by external objects results, above all, from the numerical expansion of the group. The small group is narrow in its restrictive control of the individual as well as in size. Expansion of the circles of social relationship increasingly frees the individual from the guardianship of community and church, from the demands of class and economic groups. Liberation from such connections was the great ideal of eighteenth-century individualism.

Money advances this ideal in a number of ways. By providing a means of condensing and mobilizing economic values, money extends the effective range of economic intercourse; larger markets are "larger circles." Furthermore, money frees the subordinate from extensive obeisance to his master because it permits him to discharge his obligations by transmitting an object which may be acquired in any way he chooses. Finally, as the perfect medium for impersonal relations among people, money helps to create a situation in which the individual is dependent on a host of other people for their services but free and independent of them as particular persons; any extension of impersonality in social life involves a corresponding increase in individuality.

Freedom in the sense of the unhampered development of personality according to one's inner nature is especially favored by the transition from organization based on propinquity to organization based on interest. In a society which contains a large number of interest groups, the individual may find a collectivity within which to realize each of his several aspirations and at the same time enjoy the advantages of group membership. Despite the amount of association this implies, his individuality is assured by virtue of the unique constellation of groups to which he belongs. This idea of individualism—that the individual should realize what is unique in himself and thereby distinguish himself from all others—was expressed in the nineteenth century, in theory by the romantic movement, in practice by the division of labor.

This situation is encouraged by money, for money promotes the formation of groups on a purely functional basis. But money furthers differentiation not only as a by-product of differentiation in society but within the individual directly. It does this by providing an effective means of distinguishing between the subjective center and the objective achievement of a person. The individual's performance may be paid for while his person remains outside the transaction. Or else the person, as such, may be supported (by contributions from many individuals), his specific performances remaining free from financial considerations.

Money also plays an important role in increasing freedom by extending the individual's power over things. As a possession, money frees the individual from the responsibilities which usually attend possession of less mobile objects. Of all objects, money offers the least resistance to an agent. It is the most possessable of all things, and hence completely submissive to the will of an ego. It can be come by in countless ways. The amount of it that one can possess can be indefinitely increased, and its uses are without number.

The increase of freedom is not the only direction taken by society in its historical development, nor is freedom the only value to be realized in society. Human beings require a certain balance of freedom and constraint in order to live well. Just as, for example, the widespread diffusion of secret societies usually indicates a condition of regimentation and political oppression—that is, represents a reaction stemming from the need for freedom—so, conversely, ritual regulation within secret societies reflects their relative freedom from the larger society—that is, provides a condition in which human nature is kept in equilibrium through the establishment of norms which compensate for the rejected norms of the larger society.

The substantive unity that may be attributed to much of Simmel's work by reference to the problem of freedom marks the area in which he functioned as a social philosopher. His strictly sociological writings, on the other hand, comprise a unified subject matter primarily by virtue of the recurrent categories into which his subjects fall. Other characteristics of these categories of subjects will be presented after his principles and method have been examined.

Logically, all that Simmel wrote about society rests upon three assumptions. These assumptions or starting points in Simmel's thought may be viewed as answers to three questions: What is the nature of society? In what kind of structures is society to be described? How are these structures constituted?

Simmel's answer to the first question should be viewed against the background of an age-old controversy which had reappeared when he began to write: whether society is a real entity or a fictitious abstraction. The former viewpoint, called "sociological realism" by historians of ideas, dominated French and German social thought in the nineteenth century. It conceived of society as a great being, with a nature to express or a mission to fulfill, and as the author of such things as law, custom, religion, and language. Simmel's criticism of this position derives from the empiricist emphasis of the natural science of his day—that this great being can nowhere be experienced directly and so may not legitimately be conceived of as real.

The alternative viewpoint, called "sociological nominalism," assumes that society is a fiction, that individuals alone are real, and hence the only proper objects of scientific attention. Yet individual persons are themselves composites, Simmel insists; the only true unit is the ultimately indivisible material atom. A consistent adherence to this mode of argument would thus involve a reductionism that is impossible in practice and, Simmel adds in a later treatment of the same problem, metaphysically unsound.

To resolve this dilemma, Simmel proposes that the selection of objects for scientific study be based on the perspective of the observer rather than on the nature of absolute units in reality. Still, he maintains, there must be something in reality that corresponds to the categories of the observer if inquiry is to be at all meaningful. At this point he enunciates his first principle: This "something in reality" is always an interaction of parts. Society, then, is for Simmel neither a collective being nor a fictitious entity; rather, it exists in the processes of interaction among individuals and groups.

The principle of interaction is of the greatest importance in all of Simmel's thought. It is invoked by Simmel to explain a variety of phenomena. The structure of law, for example, exhibits a radical reciprocity: every legal precept is valid only in relation to another. Similarly, economic value does not inhere in any quality of an object but derives exclusively from the "reciprocal relation which is set up among several objects by virtue of these qualities, each defining the other, and each giving back to the other the meaning which it receives from it."[11] Again, the problem of the dramatic actor is seen to be that of realizing a character born of the creative interaction between the role in the text and his own personality. And so on, in many of the problems Simmel touched.

The answer to the first question, What is the nature of society? leads abruptly to the second, In what kind of structures is society to be described? For if interaction among social units (individuals or groups) is the locus of society, and if, as Simmel says, every unit stands to some degree in interaction with every other one, how is one to find order in this manifold flux? Simmel replies that the main criterion for studying one interaction rather than another is the frequency with which it occurs, so that its study may yield propositions about regularities in human behavior. To express this principle of order, Simmel employs the concept of *form.* A form indicates the way some finite selection of processes from the infinite potentialities of life has been organized when it has attained such stability that the structure remains the same though a variety of contents embody it. Forms emerge as appropriate modes of channeling the life process; once emerged, a form confronts the vital process which created it with an independence and a development—or rigidity—that follows from its own nature. Simmel defends the scientific utility of this concept by demonstrating its basis in reality. The same forms of behavior, such as competition, representation, or the formation of parties, are found in the most diverse groups imaginable—a band of conspirators, an art school, or a family; while interests of identical content—a particular economic interest or religious belief—can be realized in very different forms, such as liberal or centralized forms of association.

Concerning the variety of forms in social life, Simmel provides no explicit classification. In practice, however, he often distinguishes among different kinds of forms. One distinction has already been given: the differences among interactive processes, social types, and developmental patterns. Another distinction is between forms still close to the processes of life and those which have attained greater distance and independence. The former are illustrated by spontaneous processes, such as exchange and imitation. The latter (*Gebilde*) include the more obvious, persisting structures, like business organizations and churches. Forms are further distinguished according to the degree of reciprocity they involve. At one extreme are interactions in which the effect of one on the other is barely perceptible, as in the case of a man dominating his subordinate. At the opposite extreme are instances where thoroughgoing reciprocity is an essential aspect of the form in question: personal adornment, looking into one another's eyes, economic exchange, and crowd behavior illustrate this purity of interaction. Simmel also distinguishes "play forms," like sociability and coquetry, in which interaction expresses the form of the association itself rather than the interests that are being realized through it.

The question of the inner articulation of the forms of interaction is answered by the third principle underlying Simmel's social thought: the concept of dualism. The assumption is that the subsistence of any aspect of human life depends on the coexistence of diametrically opposed elements. Simmel asserts this frequently, and in his final book he wrote:

> Man's position in the world is defined by the fact that, in every dimension of his being and his behavior, he finds himself at every moment between two boundaries. This appears as the formal structure of our existence, manifesting itself in continually new content in the manifold provinces, activities, and destinies of human life. We feel that the content and value of each hour stand between a higher and a lower, every thought between a wiser and a more foolish, every possession between a more extended and a more limited, every deed between a greater and a lesser measure of meaning, adequacy, and morality.[12]

It is no wonder, then, that the principle of dualism is typically employed by Simmel to define particular forms of interaction. It is used in two main ways. In the one, a form is defined as the synthesis of opposing tendencies. Thus, conflict involves a synthesis of antagonistic and solidary tendencies. In the form of subordination, needs to be dominated and to oppose one's ruler are present together. Jealousy combines the polar sentiments of love and hostility. Related to this sort of analysis is Simmel's use of expressions like "both more than and less than." Intellectual possessions differ from economic possessions in that the former can be taken from an individual "on the one hand, much more thoroughly, on the other hand, much less so" than the latter. The characteristic inadequacy of private welfare has to do with its giving "not only too little, but also too much."

Otherwise, dualisms are employed by Simmel as heuristic constructs which enable us to allude to what is in reality some "inner unity." In this mode, one defines a form, not as a synthesis of opposites, but as a mid-point between them. Thus, confidence in another person is a hypothesis about his future behavior which lies between knowledge and ignorance of him. Likewise, the middleman performs a single role, but we can only articulate it as a combination of connecting and separating functions. It is not far from this sort of analysis to setting up continua bounded by opposite concepts, and defining a phenomenon in terms of its position in the continuum; and Simmel does this repeatedly. In a continuum from establishment to wandering, for example, the stranger represents a mid-point which combines both traits, so to speak: actually, to be a stranger is to experience a specific position whose unity cannot be directly expressed.

The identification of these principles suggests the theoretic framework underlying Simmel's thought. It likewise makes clear certain aspects of his choice of subject matter. For one thing, nearly all of his problems concern "subinstitutional" phenomena. Such favorite sociological topics as the analysis of bureaucracy, the professions, and religious organizations, not to mention whole societies, never command the center of his attention. In preferring subjects like secrecy, conflict, and fashion, Simmel devotes his attention, rather, to the labile and "interstitial" aspects of social organization. It is clear that this preference has to do with his interest in interaction, for these matters represent what goes on in person-to-person processes, whereas an emphasis on institutions presumes greater preoccupation with symbols and purposes in social life.

Another consequence of Simmel's principle of interaction is the importance of the dimension of *distance* in his thinking. For Simmel, the truly "social" begins when individuals face one another, directly or in fantasy. This means that society, or social interaction, depends on the distance between individuals in relation to each other. Conflict is considered a kind of social interaction because the individuals concerned are, despite their antagonism, relatively close. When individuals grow so far apart that they are indifferent to one another, they are no longer in conflict. (This view may be elucidated by referring to an alternative conception that the presence of common values is what defines society or social life. Simmel rejects this view, for he considers norms to be a "mere by-product" of interaction. Thus, a social party, Simmel says, doubtless presumes the existence of a number of common values to regulate the behavior of its participants, but it is a party in the true sense of the term "only when there is reciprocal pleasing, stimulating, and cheering.")[13]

The assumption that distance is the main dimension in social life accounts for a great many of Simmel's choices of topics. For one thing, Simmel wrote a pioneering and penetrating account of the influence of physical distance on human relations.[14] Furthermore, nearly all of the social processes and social types treated by Simmel may readily be understood in terms of social distance. Domination and subordination, the aristocrat and the bourgeois, have to do with relations defined in terms of "above" and "below." Secrecy, arbitration, the poor man, and the stranger are some of the topics related to the inside-outside dimension.

Another attribute of Simmel's subject matter is the fact that his topics are not localized and time-bound. We never find him selecting a particular locale, as in *Middletown,* or a historic change, as in *French Canada in Transition,* or a problem in a special context, like that of *An American Dilemma.* This peculiarity of Simmel's writings may be understood in the light of his emphasis on the concept of *form,* which makes the object of his sociological inquiry something that must be abstracted from any given phenomenon or situation. Not fashion in Italian dress, for example, but the general form of fashion, is what interests Simmel; knowledge of the former is of use only in so far as it bears on the latter.

The principle of dualism, finally, leads Simmel to the study of a number of social processes that have been relatively neglected in contemporary sociology—those having to do with conflict, not in the sense of strains or disruptions, but as a normal and necessary part of everyday social life. Simmel's dualistic conceptions draw him to the study of processes by which individuals continue to associate in spite of, and because of, antagonisms between them. These include such phenomena as envy, competition, rivalry, lying, secrecy, and the unification of hostile parties through common aversion toward a third. Similarly, when Simmel examines the state of things in the modern world, it is in those respects in which polar qualities establish the structure of things—be they subjectivity versus objectivity or spontaneous life versus established form.

Throughout Simmel's writings one may observe a characteristic trend of thought representing what I have called the method of *causal resolution*. This method may perhaps best be described by first stating what it is not, in terms of the other methods generally employed in sociology and anthropology.

One of these has already been mentioned: the method, prominent in modern American sociology, which organizes inquiry chiefly around the application of observational techniques and the refinement of those techniques. Another method, more common in cultural anthropology and cultural history, seeks to connect any phenomenon with all the other phenomena in its universe by formulating basic configurations which run throughout and unify a society or a period. Ruth Benedict's *Patterns of Culture* is the archetype of this method. There is, finally, the method incorporated in the work of Parsons, which aims primarily at constructing a scientific theoretical system, a system that will conceptualize the variables of empirical systems and represent the relations among those variables by the interrelations among the concepts representing them.

In the method of causal resolution, by contrast, the course of inquiry is not determined by the elaboration of techniques to be executed, by the interrelation of a phenomenon with all the other phenomena in some integral whole, or by the application of universally valid analytic concepts. The course of inquiry depends, rather, on the particular perspective and interests of the investigator, and on the cause or causes of whatever he happens to isolate as a problem. These causes may be of various kinds—indeed, any or all of the "four causes" listed by Aristotle. A phenomenon may be studied in order to learn what changes in the preceding situation brought it into being; or of what "material" it is composed; or what end or functions it serves; or what comprises its form or essence. The dominant method in Simmel's work is based on the last approach, in which the investigator moves from subject to subject, ascertaining the meaning of each by disclosing its form.

This is what Simmel explicitly proposes as the method appropriate to a science of sociology. The problem of sociology is to identify the "pure forms of association." On the basis of observations drawn from the most diverse provinces, the sociologist is to intuit forms of interaction which are constant or recurrent. "That which is similar among complex phenomena is lifted out of them, as if by taking a cross-section, while what is dissimilar, that is, the contents, the interests, is ignored."[15] Then the sociologist is to determine just what that form of relationship means in social life by defining its essential characteristics and derivative properties and examining its range of variability: how it arises and develops, what modifications it undergoes because of particular contents it may embody, and under what conditions it increases or decreases.

This method may be illustrated afresh by citing another of its applications in Simmel's work. The dyad, or relationship between two, may be abstracted as a form from such diverse phenomena as a pair of playmates, a teacher and student relationship, a doctor and patient relationship, a duo of musicians, or a couple of friends or lovers. The following summary shows how Simmel has isolated this form as a problem, defined the essence of the form, and determined its derivative properties.

The characteristic features of the dyad result from the plain fact that each member is affected by its interaction with one other member, as contrasted with two or more. The condition that each member of a dyad has but one person with whom to deal eliminates the possibility of a superindividual structure, that is, a structure that might persist despite the withdrawal or death of any of its members.

This formal condition—immediate reciprocity of action without any structure transcending the interaction—gives rise to some specific sociological features: the chance for intimacy, the threat of triviality, a check on irresponsibility, and the promotion of individuality.

Intimacy is a condition wherein whatever distinguishes a relationship from all others is made the heart of that relationship . Intimacy presumes that the participants in a relation see only one another. Third parties nearly always introduce something which distracts two people from interaction revolving about what is distinctive of "us." The dyad is thus the chief locus of intimacy in human life.

Because the dyad has no superpersonal existence, no "immortality of the group," its members perceive it to be unique and irreplaceable. This condition peculiarly exposes it to the possibility of being felt as trivial. For triviality connotes the frequent repetition of some process or situation, unrelieved by value or meaning. It sets in when something uniquely meaningful is deprived of its meaning. A dyadic relation is meaningful only so long as its members enjoy genuine interaction. When this fails, "the tone of triviality frequently becomes desperate and fatal."

The absence of a superindividual structure further implies that there is no "they" upon whom the individual can project sins of omission and commission. Each party to the relation knows exactly what he and the other are responsible for, and each knows that he is co-responsible for all actions undertaken in the name of the dyad.

Finally, the dyad also provides maximum room for the individuality of its members. The expression of personality is not inhibited by a third person or by transcendent frameworks. A member of a dyad need never fear being outvoted by a majority, nor does his individuality have to be sacrificed to any average level. The most decided individualists (as contrasted with "strong" personalities) thus tend to restrict their social relationships to that of friendship.[16]

Simmel's method, as described here, is by no means restricted to his *Soziologie*. It is typical of nearly all he has written with the purpose of demarcating some problem and reaching for its essential form, whether in the study of great figures like Goethe, Kant, and Rembrandt or in the exploration of miscellaneous topics such as adventure, Rome, and the problem of the portrait. In his monumental *Philosophie des Geldes,* Simmel devotes an entire book to the consideration of the form of money. He defines its nature, its variability, its emergence, and its relations with many other aspects of life. The method of resolving the formal causes of things thus underlies and contributes to the fundamental unity of Simmel's thought.

The passages in Simmel's writing which convey a flavor uniquely his own, the passages which kindle the excitement of first encountering Simmel—and perhaps account for the tedium of reading too much of him—need not be left in the realm of "inscrutable personality." They, too, may be analyzed; they, too, may be shown to possess a definite structure and a distinctive cast. I have analyzed what appears to me to be typical of Simmelian insight into three separate characteristics.

First, Simmel tends to disclose the subjective aspect of superpersonal structures. That is, although he deals with interactive processes, processes which cannot be understood by studying individual psychology, he often discusses those processes in terms of what it feels like, from the point of view of an individual involved, to be participating in them. Thus, as we have seen, in giving an account of the dyad as a form in social life he talks largely about subjective aspects—intimacy, triviality, the sense of responsibility. Again, gratitude as a relation is immensely important in the organization of social life, but Simmel chooses to describe the very sensations of the individual who feels gratitude. (This procedure is in marked contrast to that of Parsons, who likewise deals with the psychology of social interaction, but whose contribution to our insight lies rather in giving objective accounts of subjective structures, that is, an analysis in generalized and sociological terms of the dispositions and orientations of "actors.")

A second characteristic of Simmel's interpretations is their tendency to disclose formal entities and analogies. One does not readily suspect, for example, that there is a developmental form common to almost all parties (particularly political). During the initial period, when the idea of the party is fresh, the party tends to be small, decisive, and compact; but as it expands its program and increases in size, it tends to lose this compactness and become indecisive. Nor would one normally appreciate the common formal structure underlying the phenomena of fashion and honor, as mentioned previously.

An interesting formal entity and series of analogies are presented in Simmel's treatment of religion. On the one hand, religion (or "religiosity," as Simmel prefers to call it in this sense) constitutes one of the all-embracing categories by means of which the totality of things can be experienced. This formal category cannot be directly defined, but must be described, rather, as a complex of psychological polarities, as a unique mixture of such feelings as surrender of self and realization of self; humility and passion; fusion with, and distance from, the highest principle; tension and peace; danger and consecration. Indeed, on one occasion Simmel considers the religious mood as the form in which all the contrasts within the soul converge, as it were, at a single point.[17]

Religiosity is a reality prior to and independent of religious organizations; thus there are thoroughly religious people who take no part in formal religion. As there are sensualist natures or artistic natures, so there are religious natures—individuals whose experience is dominated by this form, whose every thought and deed are colored by the religious hue. Rembrandt was one of these: a man who rejected all religious dogma but whose painting reveals a profoundly religious mode of experiencing reality. In this first sense, then, religion is a form which organizes the whole of existence for the religious man, or for man qua religious.

On the other hand, religion consists of aspects of experience organized in a religious way, of life contents drawn out of practical, intellectual, artistic, or other contexts, and recast in the religious mold. Three areas of life are particularly susceptible of being "transposed into the religious key": man's relations to nature, to fate, and to his social environment. Considering primarily the last relationship, Simmel lists a number of analogies between religious experience and the forms of social interaction.

Certain social relations carry tensions and meanings which predestine them to become prototypes of the forms of religious experience. They involve a simultaneous mixture of humility and exaltation, of sensuous immediacy and non-sensuous abstraction, accompanied by "a certain tension of feeling, a specific inwardness and stability of inner relationship, and a transposition of the subject into a higher order that is at the same time felt by him to be something internal and personal." These relations include the individual's devotion to, and dependence on, his social group; the offering and accepting of gifts; belief in another person; duty or moral obligation; forgiving; and unity. The forms of religious experience consist in good measure of the more abstract and purified versions of these social forms. Thus, giving and receiving are hardly ever experienced by sensitive people without quasi-religious shades of meaning above and beyond the substantive value of the gift. In elaborated religions this formal component appears in the phenomenon of sacrifice to a deity.[18]

The third form of strategy in Simmel's writing is to contradict the principle of contradiction. As the second characteristic of Simmel's insight follows from his principle of form, so this one is the consequence of his principle of dualism. Simmel is continually showing how something is both more than and less than, nearness and at the same time distance, surrender of self and repossession of self, truth and falsehood. The aphorisms quoted by Kurt H. Wolff in the Introduction to his translations from Simmel abound in examples of this technique: "Objectivity toward people often hides the most boundless solipsism." "I don't know which of these two shows man's vulgarity more: when he gets accustomed to ugliness or when he gets accustomed to beauty."[19]

One of the most elaborate instances of this sort of insight appears in Simmel's discussion of the effects of a money economy.

Money serves to decrease the distances in life by enabling foreign products, strange peoples, and alien styles to be assembled with relative ease in urban centers. At the same time, money increases the distances in life. It increases the distance between men and things by causing a man's fortune to be considered a means of production instead of a basis for consumption, and by inclining one to consider the price of an item before arriving at a judgment about its nature. It increases the distance between persons by enabling members of the same family to pursue their several incomes in separate ways and by eliminating the personal factor in human relations. Likewise, money is the great agent for advancing objective culture (the cultivation of things and objective knowledge) and is equally powerful for the advancement of subjective culture (the cultivation of individuals). It promotes the former by making possible the autonomous system of production based on a complex division of labor. It favors the latter by making possible a kind of abstraction from immediate concerns that is the prerequisite for a high development of the inner life of man.

It is thus no accident that Simmel's social thought strikes time and again upon matters of immense human interest. He exposes the personal experiences of people caught up in everyday social relations; he documents intimate connections between happenings taken from the most unrelated moments of life; and he shocks common sense by asserting something to be true, and just as quickly asserting the reality of its opposite.

More than this, his method leads him to topics that are the portion of, and in proportion to, *human* cognition. His topics are not chosen because they are appropriate objects for the exercise of a special measuring technique, or by reason of the deductive requirements of a theoretic system, or because they are part of the whole picture of some community or society. They are chosen, rather, on the basis of the *interest* of some knower in a problem and the *existence* in reality of some corresponding, meaningful complex.

It is not surprising that this method is seldom adopted by contemporary social scientists. Professional status is likely to depend on the mastery of certain research techniques, competence in the intricacies of a particular system of theory, or familiarity with data pertaining to a certain society, period, or civilization. None of these valuable achievements acquired in customary professional training prepares or inclines one toward the kind of inquiry carried on by Simmel, which demands a certain intellectual independence and an imagination capable of discovering or creating significant formal problems. Such qualities can be promoted or destroyed by the organization of higher learning; they can scarcely be trained. Perhaps this is one reason why Georg Simmel is so rare, so worthy of attention in our time.

1. Talcott Parsons, *The Structure of Social Action* (2nd ed.; Glencoe, Ill.: Free Press of Glencoe, Illinois, 1949), p. vi.

2. *Ibid.*, p. 773.

3. Elsewhere I have tried to show why Parsons' approach leads in a direction different from that indicated by Simmel. See Donald N. Levine, "Simmel and Parsons: Two Approaches to the Study of Society" (Doctoral dissertation, University of Chicago, 1957).

4. Georg Simmel, "Fashion," *International Quarterly*, X (October, 1904), 130-55; reprinted in the *American Journal of Sociology*, LXII (May, 1957), 541-58.

5. Georg Simmel, *Soziologie. Untersuchungen über die Formen der Vergesellschaftung* (Leipzig: Duncker und Humblot, 1908), pp. 732-46.

6. *Ibid.*, Chap. x.

7. *The Functions of Social Conflict* (Glencoe, Ill.: Free Press of Glencoe, Illinois, 1956).

8. *Über sociale Differenzierung. Sociologische und psychologische Untersuchungen* (1890); *Philosophie des Geldes* (1900); *Soziologie. Untersuchungen über die Formen der Vergesellschaftung* (1908); and *Grundfragen der Soziologie* (*Invidiuum und Gesellschaft*) (1917).

9. Georg Simmel, "Über Freiheit: Bruchstücke aus dem Nachlass von Georg Simmel," *Logos*, XI (1922), 1-30.

10. *Philosophie des Geldes* (2nd ed.; Leipzig: Duncker und Humblot, 1907), Chap. iv.

11. *Ibid.*, p. 61.

12. *Lebensanschauung. Vier metaphysische Kapitel* (Munich and Leipzig: Duncker und Humblot, 1918), p. 1.

13. "Zur Methodik der Sozialwissenschaft," in *Jahrbuch für Gesetzgebung, Verwaltung und Volkswirtschaft im Deutschen Reich*, XX (1896), 222-37.

14. *Soziologie,* Chap. ix, "Der Raum und die räumlichen Ordnungen der Gesellschaft" ("Space and Spatial Orderings of Society"). Only two passages from this long chapter are available in English: "Sociology of the Senses: Visual Interaction" and "The Sociological Significance of the Stranger," in Robert E. Park and Ernest W. Burgess, *Introduction to the Science of Sociology* (Chicago: University of Chicago Press, 1921), pp. 256-61, 322-27. The second passage has been newly translated as "The Stranger" in *The Sociology of Georg Simmel,* trans., ed., and with an Introduction by Kurt H. Wolff (Glencoe, Ill.: Free Press of Glencoe, Illinois, 1950), pp. 402-8. See also Part IV, especially pp. 317-29.

15. *Soziologie,* p. 13.

16. *Ibid.,* Chap. ii; translated in Wolff, *op. cit.,* Part II.

17. "Die Gegensätze des Lebens und der Religion," *Das Freie Wort,* IV (1904), 305-12.

18. Cf. Georg Simmel, *Die Religion* ([1906] 2nd rev. ed.; Frankfurt am Main: Rütten und Loening, 1912).

19. Wolff, *op. cit.,* p. xx.

FORM AND CONTENT IN SIMMEL'S PHILOSOPHY OF LIFE[1]

RUDOLPH H. WEINGARTNER

Georg Simmel wrote about morality, history, society, money, religion, art, and philosophy. By the time of his death at the age of sixty he had written some twenty books and countless articles on these subjects and on such artists, writers, and philosophers as Rembrandt, Goethe, and Kant. It is easy to conclude that Simmel was an energetic, many-sided thinker who turned from one field to another as his interests led him.

Yet this conclusion would be hasty. However great the diversity of subjects to which Simmel devoted himself, a central theme unifies them all. He was concerned with man, his life, and his creations: Simmel's world was the world of culture.

Simmel was impressed—if not depressed—by the bewildering number and variety of human products which in the contemporary world surround and unceasingly impinge upon the individual. He is encircled by, and to various degrees involved with, different objects of art and artifact, scientific theories and religious dogmas, philosophical systems and interpretations of history, legal systems and social institutions, moral codes and conventions of behavior. Of these, some are creations of his own time or of his immediate past; others are products of every period of recorded history. All are present and clamor for attention. They demand to be understood, appreciated, employed, or adhered to; or they call for rejection, refutation, repudiation, or destruction. Whatever the particular situation requires, the individual is asked to locate his position amidst this array of human products, to discover and establish relations between himself and the objects of culture.

It is to this problem that Simmel addressed himself. He was above all a *philosopher* of culture. His primary interest in the various cultural disciplines in which he worked was philosophical. At one point he called his enterprise *Sinngebung*:[2] he sought to give meaning or significance to the products of culture, to render them intelligible and accessible.

This undertaking involves two ultimately inseparable tasks. The first is the discovery and articulation of a network of relations holding among the elements of culture. It calls for analyses in which similarities and differences are discerned and particulars are subsumed under more general principles—analyses, in short, which establish order out of chaos. But this is not enough. If the world of culture is to be meaningful, it must be so to *someone*. The task Simmel sets himself would not be complete (indeed, it would not have been begun) if the world of culture were not somehow brought into a significant relationship to the lives and experiences of men. And the fulfillment of this requirement, in turn, presupposes a conception of life and a philosophy of experience.

Both these sides of Simmel's enterprise make use of the concepts of form and content. First of all, distinguishing between the form of an object, institution, behavior pattern, or norm and its content is one of Simmel's favorite procedures for establishing order among the products of culture.

> There is perhaps no necessity of thought which is so hard to cast off as the analysis of things into content and form. . . . In countless modifications, . . . this division cuts across our image of the world. It is one of the organizers and flexible instruments with which the mind gives structure to the mass of all that is, a mass which, in its immediate unity, is structureless.[3]

The form-content distinction is an instrument, a tool of analysis, which Simmel applies over and over again in every field he discusses.

However, Simmel is not too scrupulous about attaching the same meanings to these terms whenever he uses them. Early in his career he remarks that

> the category of content and form is one of the most relative and subjective in the entire area of thought. What is form in one respect is content in another; and, upon closer scrutiny, the conceptual antithesis between the two dissolves into a merely gradual [opposition], having a determinateness which is between the general and the specific.[4]

It would seem that Simmel took great pains to live up to this dictum: the meanings of "form" and "content" shift and change, almost with every use he makes of this analytic tool. Nevertheless, it would be a worth-while job—though a difficult and painstaking one—to collect all the relevant passages in Simmel's far-flung writings and, by means of a kind of inductive process, arrive at a statement of the general meanings of these terms.[5]

Our concern will be with a second role played by the form-content distinction. It is the function associated with that aspect of Simmel's enterprise which proposes to relate the world of culture to the lives and experiences of human beings. When the distinction is regarded from this point of view, it is revealed to be more than an analytic instrument. Form and content function as elements in Simmel's philosophical doctrine; indeed, they are key terms in his philosophy of experience. This fact gives the philosophical interpretation of the form-content distinction a privileged status, one having priority over all of its uses as a means of analysis. Needless to say, to the extent to which the whole of Simmel's work is coherent it must be possible to subsume the particular uses of form and content under their general philosophic meaning.

Since we shall be occupied in this paper with the privileged meanings of "form" and "content" in Simmel's work, we must determine their place in his philosophical position. In his writings, Simmel never makes his position fully explicit. He seldom addresses himself directly and in detail to the philosophical problems he touches upon or to those that are raised implicitly. Our procedure, therefore, will be to reconstruct the framework of Simmel's philosophy of experience, primarily upon the basis of his later writings, although we shall not hesitate to search elsewhere for ways of bridging gaps in our construction. In the light of this plan, we shall make our beginning with the keystone of Simmel's philosophy, his conception of life.

In somewhat paradoxical language, Simmel defines life with "two complementary definitions: it is more-life and more-than-life."[6] The two characteristics are understood as interdependent. Only the first, however, will be taken up here. The discussion of life as more-than-life must be postponed to the last section.

By saying that life is more-life, Simmel declares life to be a process. Life is a motion; specifically, it is a motion which constantly reproduces itself, pushes beyond itself. Unlike mechanical changes, life is truly continuous; it "is an irreversible current in which every moment dissolves in the next."[7] In contrast with the mechanical motions of inorganic things, life is fully temporal.

Simmel's conception of time is very close to Bergson's.[8] Time is protracted and only therefore is it time. The present moment of an inorganic object marks the intersection of a past that is no longer and a future that is not yet. Accordingly, since it is an unprotracted moment, it is no more time than the point of intersection of two lines is space. For a living being, on the contrary, the present moment is "always composed of a small segment of the past and a smaller segment of the future."[9] Here time is protracted and motion continuous.

The present moment of a living being contains a part of its past and anticipates its future. For a life endowed with mind,[10] memory is the most obvious way in which the past is brought into the present. When we remember, we know *now* our experience of the past and we know it to be *of* the past. At that moment, "our present . . . is, so to speak, stretched backwards. In such moments we live beyond the moment into the past."[11] But the past is also present to us in a much wider sense. What I am at any present moment is a product of my past. The habits I have contracted, the skills I have learned, the knowledge I have acquired, and the emotions I have felt, all serve to make up my present constitution. " . . . Every present moment is determined by the entire previous course of life; it is the result of all preceding moments."[12]

As the present moment "reaches beyond"[13] itself into its past, so it reaches out and makes a part of the future a component of its present. No single goal regulates or describes an entire career, but at any given point the process of life has a determinate direction. In Simmel's theory of volition, for example, willing is not a psychological act that is separate and distinct from the "external" action willed, but simply the psychic reflection of an action already begun. In other words, willing and acting are part of the same complex process in which the end of the action is present and functioning from the beginning.[14] We may initiate a sequence of actions, to give a second example, with a view to deriving pleasure from the achievement of our goal, but the pleasure actually enjoyed does not merely accompany the successful outcome of the series. "In striving and attempting, a psychological anticipation of the goal takes place; there is enough of the latter in [the striving] to arouse a part of the pleasure which properly belongs only to [the goal]."[15] Such examples are readily multiplied and may be analyzed in much greater detail. Each case, however, will indicate the same conclusion: "The present of life consists of its transcending the present; . . . in [the present] moment the future is reality."[16]

No moment of life is a discrete scene, cut off from its past and its future. When an action is singled out by means of a descriptive concept, life's continuity is arbitrarily fragmented. An action must rather be considered a "pulsebeat of immediate life,"[17] a metaphor which does justice to the continuous character of the movement of life. With the expression "life is more-life," Simmel indicates the complex fact that at every moment life transcends its present, that it is a process whose motion is continuous.

> The mode of existence which does not limit its reality to the present moment, thus pushing past and future into unreality, but whose peculiar continuity remains . . . on this side of this separation, so that its past really exists into the present and the present into the future—this mode of existence we call life.[18]

Putting aside for a moment what has been said about life as more-life, we turn, in this section, to Simmel's understanding of content, and, in the next, to a general interpretation of form. A preliminary grasp of these three concepts—life, content, and form—will subsequently make it possible to develop Simmel's philosophy of experience.

Despite the importance and difficulty of the concept of content, Simmel is very sparing in his explanations and discussions. His meaning must consequently be approached by a circuitous route. Within any mental act, such as believing, doubting, desiring, or fearing, two components may be distinguished. First, there is a mental activity or attitude of the sort indicated by verbs of this kind. In addition to this, the quality of the act, there is *that which* is believed, doubted, or feared, the material of the act.[19]

Any mental act considered as a whole is clearly a psychological event; an individual's believing something, doubting it, or affirming it is a segment of his career. Whatever is believed must, in some way, be present to the mind of the believer. Hence, when we look at that something as represented in consciousness, it is seen to have a psychological dimension. But to represent something to oneself (to entertain an idea, as we say), even without believing, doubting, or fearing it, is *also* a mental activity of a certain quality. If, therefore, we wish to make our distinction quite clear, we must abstract the fact of its being represented from that which is being represented. When this "whatness" of an act has been isolated, we obtain an "objective mental *content* which is no longer anything psychological."[20] A start has been made in understanding what Simmel means by "content."[21]

Before the nature of content is further investigated, it must be noted that qualities and contents are understood as logically independent of each other. Given any act quality, there can be nothing about this mental attitude which requires that it have any particular, or particular kind of, content. Nor is any content ruled out from being grasped in a given way. In other words, anything *may* be believed or feared, affirmed or desired, but nothing *must* be. Still more important to us here is the equally true converse of the relationship. If we begin with a content, we have no ground for saying that it must be grasped in some particular way, say affirmed or denied. Nor is any content so constituted that some particular mental attitude, say desiring, *cannot* be directed to it.[22]

A content, then, is the objective element of a mental act which is independent of the quality of the act. We must not, however, go too far in stressing this independence, for it is also true that in time and space we shall never find a content all by itself. A content is always grasped in some way; it always functions in a mental act of some quality.

The consequences of this fact, as Simmel understands it, are very significant. No amount of analysis of whatever kind will enable us "to get at" the content, to isolate it as it is by itself. Analysis, after all, is a mental operation; however carefully we proceed, the content we seek to isolate is always *somehow* present to the mind. We can refrain from affirming or denying it, but we cannot help representing it to ourselves in some way. It is therefore futile to instigate a difficult and complex phenomenological analysis in order to determine the nature of contents more specifically. Contents "cannot . . . [be] grasped in their purity."[23]

Simmel is anxious to distinguish his concept of content from the Kantian *Ding an sich*. When a *content* is grasped, "all of it is contained in each [act] and not on credit from a more independent existence."[24] Kant's *Ding an sich,* by contrast, is not itself grasped but only its appearance. Nevertheless, Kant's influence is not altogether shed. Like Kantian "things-in-themselves," Simmel's contents cannot be experienced as they are. Something *does* happen as the content is grasped, for we cannot know the content outside a mental act, as it is by itself. Accordingly, the difference between Simmel and Kant would seem to be little more than verbal: the *Ding an sich* stands behind the act, as it were, while the content is contained within it. But, like the Kantian *Ding an sich,* Simmel's contents are not found but posited. They are only approached, *not arrived at,* by an analysis of experience. They constitute assumptions in Simmel's philosophical doctrine.

Contents are so conceived that they cannot be factored out of their contexts, the mental acts of different sorts. This position allows Simmel to enlarge indefinitely the kinds of mental acts by which contents can be grasped. Contents, for example, may be grasped religiously, morally, artistically, philosophically, or cognitively—to name only a few of the possibilities. Subsequently, much will have to be said about this grasping; here it must only be pointed out that in each case it may be assumed—though it cannot be demonstrated—that the same content is contained in many acts, whereas the attitudes toward it change completely.[25] It is worth while to quote in full the only example Simmel ever gives in his scattered discussion of content:

> When . . . we represent the color blue, it is perhaps an element of the sensibly real world which is the seat of our practical life. The picture in our imagination, where we have only detached

the color from the accompanying circumstances with which the world of reality has interwoven it, probably belongs to this significance of the color. Within the abstractness of the pure world of knowledge, however, "blue" is meaningful in quite another sense: there it is a particular oscillation of ether waves or a particular position in the spectrum or a particular physiological or psychological reaction. It signifies something else again as an element of the subjective world of feeling—in the lyrical feelings we might have in the face of a blue sky or the blue eyes of our beloved. It is the same blue, and yet, by its contextual meaning, it is oriented in a completely different way, when it belongs to the religious sphere, perhaps as the color of the Madonna's cloak or, more generally, as a symbol of a mystical world.[26]

Contents have "real" existence only when they function in a mental act. They can find no place in the temporal and spatial world unless they are in some way grasped. Contents, as they are by themselves, however, enjoy an "ideal" existence, an existence *sui generis*.[27] There is a realm of contents, a *Weltstoff*[28] which consists of the contents of all actual and possible mental acts. A particular psychological manifestation of a content may be new; the content may never before have been grasped, and thus brought into the temporal world and made real. However, when such an event is viewed from the standpoint of the realm of contents, the grasping of a content is never more than its discovery. It had existed in the realm of contents, and it will continue to exist there, ready to enter into an indefinite number of mental acts. Platonic ideas[29] are objects only of the intellect; Simmel's contents may be grasped in many different ways. However, like Platonic ideas (at least in one of the traditional interpretations), Simmel's contents constitute a realm which exists outside time and space, and which remains untouched by the processes of life and change.

Yet when the term "realm" is used to describe the world-stuff, its ordinary meaning is not strictly adhered to. No order reigns among the contents; no content is related to any other. Each content is what it is, discrete from all the rest. The "realm" is merely an immense aggregate. Each of its elements is structurable and hence relatable, but until it functions within a mental act, no content possesses an identifiable structure. Structure and relation come to contents in an act of grasping. And, by being grasped, contents are given form.

Speaking of contents, Simmel asserts that "the mere sum . . . [of] disconnected . . . elements is mere material."[30] Form, therefore, can best be recognized by the task it performs. First, form relates a number of contents to each other in such a way that they constitute a unity. "In any forming, a multiplicity of elements is synthesized into a unity."[31] Second, as a number of contents are given form, they are separated from other contents. Third, but not as an operation that is distinct from the others, form imparts a structure to the contents it relates.

Forms can be looked upon as principles which are brought to the contents, and by means of which contents are selected and gathered into a whole. The simplest example of a form is a descriptive concept. A concept (and let us suppose we are in possession of an explicit definition) will constitute a "circumference" within which a particular set of contents "merges into a unity."[32] As a result, the chosen collection of contents becomes a *thing,* the components of which are intimately related in (ideally) specifiable ways. In turn, the unity so composed is cut off and set apart from all other contents which are either unformed or formed differently.

A form shapes a number of contents into a unity, for it is itself the principle of unification. The unity is established by stipulation. No independent general criterion of unity exists; each form constitutes such a criterion. What holds for *all* cases of unity is merely the feeling of coherence, the feeling that this set of contents belongs together.[33]

Summing up, Simmel says:

> In short, what we call form is, from the point of view of the function it exercises, the unification of material: it overcomes the isolated separateness of its parts. The totality, as a unity which is made up of these parts or is imposed upon them, is now placed in opposition to other material, either unformed or differently formed.[34]

But form does at least one thing more: it provides the structure which makes it possible for contents to be related. Simmel himself never made this role of formal principles fully explicit. Nevertheless, what he does say requires us to conclude that forms fulfill this function. The contents, on the one hand, are discrete elements about the structure of which nothing can be said. Formed contents, on the other hand, stand in determinate relations to each other, and must hence be structured. Forming, therefore, must be structuring.

With so general an understanding of the nature of form, it will come as no surprise that there are many kinds, levels, and degrees of form. Simmel permits the grasping of contents in a great variety of ways which involve various principles that, at one and the same time, structure contents differently and relate them to each other in different ways. The same contents can be organized according to cognitive, artistic, religious, and philosophic principles, among others. Each constitutes a different way of looking at the realm of contents; each makes use of a different *kind* of organizing principle.[35]

There must also be different *levels* of form. A formal principle is required to unify a number of contents into what we call a "thing." Analogous forms are needed to shape contents into a graphic composition, a melody, a religious symbol, or a proposition in science. Generalizing on Kant's position, Simmel sometimes calls a "lower-level" principle of form an "a priori."[36] Yet a unit which is established by an a priori is not, in turn, an isolated entity, unrelated to anything else. Styles of art, religious doctrines, entire sciences, metaphysical systems, and so on, are structures that relate many such units (formed contents) to each other. Finally, there are art, religion, knowledge, philosophy, of which these latter are in a sense component parts. Each of these further levels (neither sorted out nor carefully examined by Simmel) involves principles of form.[37] Like the simple form of a concept, they unify some contents into a coherent system; that is, they connect them by a network of relations. On all levels, the forms function as criteria of adequacy, sorting out what does and does not belong. At the same time, they set off the chosen contents from others differently formed or altogether unformed.[38]

The content which is shaped by a formal principle need not be a content in the sense sketched in the previous section. Contents that are already formed are subject to further forming by another principle. The components of a formed unit, in other words, may themselves already be "wholes" according to some formal principle. Thus, for example, a thing, constituting a unified collection of contents in virtue of a particular principle, may be again formed by an artistic principle. This work of art may in turn become the content of a third forming, say religious. It is possible, then, to have different *degrees* of form, since contents already formed by a principle of one kind may serve as a content for a form of another kind. At no point can we rule out the possibility of further forming; for Simmel, it is entirely a matter of contingent fact whether a given object—of art, science, religion, and so on—does or does not serve as a content in another context.[39]

When formal principles are classified into different kinds, levels, and degrees, the categories used are clearly not totally independent of each other. However, since Simmel himself does not work out the relationships that hold among them, no attempt will be made here to trace their highly abstract interrelations. Instead, some aspects of this problem will be touched upon in an investigation of the origin and nature of form in experience.[40]

The definition of life as more-life constitutes a formal characterization of life. It indicates that life is a certain kind of motion, a cumulative process that pushes on without cessation. Contents, on the other hand, are not "real" unless they are in some way formed by being grasped. *Both* process and contents are abstractions from the unity of life as it is actually lived.[41] Life "exists only as bound up with some contents or other."[42]

The real starting point of Simmel's philosophy is that state which contains "process and content undifferentiated."[43] Simmel calls this state *Erleben,* "experience."[44] *Erleben* designates the condition in which "the self and its objects still remain undifferentiated, in which impressions or representations fill up consciousness, while the bearer of these contents has not yet separated himself from the contents."[45] It is a state of complete and immediate satisfaction: there is but the dumb absorption of the stream of contents as it comes to us. As long as it persists, needs that arise are fulfilled before there is any awareness of them; desires are satisfied before they are felt as desires; before they can mature, acts of the will are extinguished in enjoyment. Thus every act "is completely unified. We have a feeling which contains neither a consciousness of an object as such, standing apart from us, nor a consciousness of a self which is distinguished from its present state."[46] There is neither a self having a sweet taste, nor is there sugar; there is only sweetness.

In the state of *Erleben,* "our life . . . is . . . interwoven with the world of reality, and all of its functions are carried out like the breathing of a sleeper."[47] But so happy—if unconscious —a state cannot long persist, for our lives are not so well integrated with the course of reality. The world is no Land of Cockaigne: our impulses are seldom fulfilled immediately. More often than not, they meet with obstacles and frustrations. Then, in a situation where satisfaction fails to occur automatically, the undifferentiated process of *Erleben* cannot maintain itself. Its unity disintegrates; a gap is opened between the impulse and its fulfillment.

Prior to the stimulus of frustration, there was a stream of contents only as a stream of satisfactions. In a sense, the contents were grasped, for they became the sequence of contents of experience; but in the full sense, they were not grasped, for they were not given shape.[48] Now, when impulses do not issue in immediate fulfillment, awareness arises of something desired but not had, of something other than the self. At the same time, *self*-consciousness is born: the self comes to experience itself as desiring and as distinct from that which it desires. In Simmel's favorite metaphor, a *distance*[49] is interposed between two poles that had been fused in *Erleben*: "Subject and object are born in the same act."[50] The dissolution of *Erleben* is at the same time the beginning of objectification. We have reached the moment at which form is born in experience. Contents become objects in virtue of the forming activity of experience.[51]

So far, there has been no need to allude to the complexity of experience. *Erleben* designates a primitive unity which is prior to all distinction and differentiation. Now, however, as we observe the decomposition of that whole, we must begin to consider experience in its complexity.

Human beings function in a great variety of ways. They have different drives and impulses, native and acquired; they are endowed with numerous physical and psychic energies that press for release and expression. What is more, there can never be an exhaustive list of human needs and capacities, for they are conditioned by the fact that men are connected in numerous and changing ways with other men and groups. Moreover, needs and abilities change as men change, individually or as a species that is subject to evolutionary development.

This, briefly, describes the being that is brought to consciousness when its impulses are not automatically satisfied. The obstacle, in other words, which leads to the disintegration of *Erleben* stands in the way of a *particular* human function. It prevents the fulfillment of a certain lack, or it blocks the expression of a particular kind of energy. In every case, a gap is opened between subject and object, but the relation between them may vary from case to case. Depending on the impulses and capacities involved and on the character of the stimulus, the contents of which the subject becomes aware are "felt" in different ways, the "attitude" toward them varies, the subject "presents" contents to itself differently.[52] As the unity of *Erleben* breaks up, contents are experienced in different modes.

The disintegration of *Erleben* marks the birth of form in general. But since the complexity of human functioning (and of the world) results in the experiencing of contents in different modes, it is necessarily the genesis of the different *kinds* of form. The forming principle is contained in the reaction of the individual to the stream of contents. Depending on the conditions, the psyche imposes on the contents different ways of structuring, different principles of unification. In this way, artistic experience will unify a number of contents into an artistic object; philosophical experience will shape contents into a philosophic object; cognitive experience will give rise to a scientific object. And so, for every distinguishable way of experiencing, a different kind of object is created.

In this process of subject-object differentiation, the pole of the experiencing subject does not suffer a similar fragmentation. Simmel opposes not only a faculty psychology but any theory which understands experience as a purely mental activity. It is "the *entire* man . . . who thinks, feels, desires."[53] The entire individual is involved in each of his acts. Accordingly, as the objects created by him increase in number and kind, the experiencing subject becomes more aware of itself as subject and more fully developed in the functions appropriate to the different types of objects.

We have briefly traced the career of a life, from the unconscious process of *Erleben* in which subject and object remain fused, to the dissolution of *Erleben* and the precipitation of an experiencing subject, on the one hand, and the different types of objects, on the other. The lesson to be drawn from this sketch is that the *primary* sense of form is form as an "objective power, an operative reality within us."[54] Before it is an explicit principle, having logical status, it is a part of our experiential equipment which "lies deeply entangled in the . . . fabric of our knowing"[55] and of all the other modes in which we experience.

Conscious experience, in which contents are shaped by one or another principle, is brought into being when the hand-to-mouth existence of *Erleben* breaks down. The satisfactions of needs become goals that are more or less consciously set. Human needs, to be sure, must be understood in the widest sense. Among them are not only the stilling of hunger and thirst but also "the release of an energy, the realizing . . . of inner tendencies, the self-expression of [one's] being."[56] Nevertheless, whatever experience and activity is brought into play, it originates and exists only to serve the demands of the process of life. Cognition, for example, is

> to that extent nothing else than a scene of life itself, [one] which prepares another scene and which thus serves the vital intention of the whole. . . . The categories, by which the conscious picture of things is produced, are mere tools within the vital chain.[57]

Accordingly, the formal principles embodied in experience emerge out of the undifferentiated stream of *Erleben* and once more disappear in it when they have fulfilled their function.

This is the *teleological* or pragmatic stage of life: all experience can be understood in terms of goals set by the process of life itself and of the means devised to achieve them.[58] The various modes of experience are brought into being for the sake of the purposes of life and stand at their beck and call.

Experience on this level is still "ordinary" experience. Formal principles are in operation, but they are not sorted out, not sustained. They lead to knowledge, but that knowledge is limited to whatever is necessitated by primitive practical life. There is artistic activity, but artistic shaping goes no further than the whittling of a piece of wood or the expression of feelings in primitive song. There is religiosity, but it gives rise only to the rudiments of religion. In all areas, the formal principles embedded in experience are not yet full-fledged forms. They are *preliminary forms.*[59] Their existence is precarious; they are still impure, being so interwoven with each other as to prevent their explicit formulation.

The preliminary forms are brought forth out of the "teleological necessities [of life]";[60] they function merely as instruments of life. Nevertheless, all traces of the operation of these forms do not disappear when their job is done. Propositions, though they arise merely as directives for action, may nonetheless be uttered, possibly even recorded in some way. Primitive song and wood carving are given an existence independent of the process that shaped them. Religious symbols, moral judgments, patterns of social behavior—all become products that have a career transcending the experience which brought them forth.

These structures are not yet the elements which compose the various realms of culture. But despite the fact that they came into being solely to serve the needs of life, they outlast the needs which produced them, and they accumulate. The principles of form that are embodied in them are merely preliminary forms; the structures themselves might best be called the elements of proto-culture, more specifically, of proto-science, -art, -religion, -ethics, and so forth.[61] The manner in which the transition from preliminary form to form, from proto-culture to culture, is achieved will be the subject of the next section.

When the process of *Erleben* disintegrates, life must resort to setting conscious goals. It enters upon the teleological phase. In Simmel's use of the term, this means not merely that human activity is directed toward ends but that these ends have their locus within the career of the individual. "Teleology" means "teleology of life": all action in *this* sense purposive is instituted to serve, directly or indirectly, a need of life.[62]

However, man is able to break the bonds of the teleology of his life and emancipate himself from the rule of his needs. He is capable of acting for the sake of goals which are not, either directly or indirectly, for his own benefit. More accurately, men can act from motives which aim at something completely outside the individual and his career. Action which is in this sense non-teleological Simmel calls *free* action.[63] "Freedom signifies precisely the potentiality for breaking through teleology."[64] Life has a level of freedom.[65]

To this point, free action has been characterized only negatively. It is *non*-teleological, it is *not* pursued for the sake of the subject. Instead, the goal of free action is something objective, standing outside and independent of the self. Previously, we have seen that in the teleological phase of life structures are created—namely, the elements of proto-culture—which become independent of their creators. These formed contents constitute experience objectified and embody the formal principles which Simmel calls preliminary forms. It is preliminary form—and through it form—which becomes the object of free activity.

From the teleological stage of life there occurs a *turning* to the level of freedom.[66] The possibility of such a turning depends, on the one hand, on the human ability to act for the sake of something other than the ends of life itself, that is, on the capacity to change the direction of human impulses. On the other hand, it depends on the presence of structures that have an existence independent of life. While their origin is in life, once such structures exist, life can serve *them* and integrate its contents into a form.[67]

Looked at in one way, the turning to activity for the sake of form is a historical event, taking place at different times for each form.[68] The progress of a preliminary form is gradual; at some point, perhaps never precisely specifiable, the form is "ready" to become the object, rather than the instrument, of human activity. The necessary independence is gained, and the turn occurs: " . . . The forms stand forth as autocratic ideas and themselves determine life and its value."[69]

Clearly, the turning can be regarded in a second way. It is also an occurrence, indefinitely repeatable, in the careers of some, if not all, individuals. Usually (that is, in the teleological phase), men see in order to live. Artists, however, come to live in order to see and create works of art.[70] " . . . At first men know in order to live; but then there are men who live in order to know."[71] And so for all the areas of culture, there are moments in the lives of individuals when the nature of the action is determined, not by the needs of the individual, but by the requirements of a form. Men turn to act for the sake of a form.[72]

Those who rise above a life in which all energy is devoted to the pursuit of ends that are set by life itself are engaged in a twofold task. First, action for the sake of a form requires that the form itself be refined. Second, the realm of contents formed in a particular way must be enlarged.

"Ordinary" experience leaves only the elements of proto-culture in its wake. The formal characteristics of such objects are only incidentally artistic, cognitive, religious, or whatever. Since they are products of the teleological level, the forms by means of which contents are given shape are developed only to the very limited extent required for the fulfillment of immediate life needs. The formal principles embodied in experience constitute only preliminary form which is confused, unstable, and surrounded by a penumbra of formal principles belonging to other modes of experience.

This is the situation that must be rectified. The artist, scientist, or metaphysician must purify the formal principles with which he produces the objects of his field. He must refine the mode of experiencing that pertains to his specialty. This does not mean that the artist is called upon to write treatises on the formal principles of art; nor is it the scientist's special task to make explicit the criteria of scientific truth. Not even the philosopher need be conscious of the principles which shape the realm of contents into a metaphysical system.[73] In every case, the analysis and explication of the formal principles operative in an area of culture are the job of the philosopher as epistemologist.[74]

Instead, the practicing artist is required to look upon the

world artistically and attempt to shut out all other ways of experiencing. Regardless of what he makes the content of his work, the principles which control its shaping must be as purely artistic as is possible for him. The principles which must be operative in the experience of a scientist and which must govern the construction of the propositions to which he gives utterance must be exclusively those which pertain to, and are developed in, the realm of science. Thus in every field of culture, action for the sake of a form demands attention and obedience to the formal requirements of the area of culture in question.

The second task of those who change the direction of their impulses and make a form the end of their action is a more obvious one. Equipped with the ability to experience in a mode from which, to a large measure, the impurities have been removed, the individual uses his ability to give shape to some part of the realm of contents. Each contributes to the already existing store of objects that embody the formal principles relevant to his specialty. More particularly, the artist proceeds to experience contents artistically and gives overt expression to that experience by creating works of art. The scientist makes contributions to his field by integrating new contents into the system of science. The historian is concerned with ordering some part of the realm of contents by means of the forms of historical writing. Each, according to his vocation, enlarges the treasure of objects of culture.[75]

Among the forms operative in human experience, Simmel singles out what may be called "world-forms" for special attention.[76] A world, in Simmel's sense of the term, is more than the mere collection of all things and events. It is the totality of contents unified into a single comprehensive system in such a way that every single content has its precise and determinate position. A world-form, therefore, is a form which is capable of giving shape to the entire realm of contents and of transforming its aggregate into a world.

There is no definitive list of world-forms. Simmel lists reality or the world of practice, knowledge, art, religion, value, and philosophy or metaphysics as the categories capable of creating worlds.[77] There is no reason to suppose, however, that it might not be possible to isolate still other world-forms from experience.

Viewed ideally, no content can escape being assigned to its place in each of the possible worlds. Moreover, looked at *ideally,* each content *is* assigned to its place in each world generated by a world-form. Once a world-form comes into existence in human experience, it implicitly transforms the entire realm of contents into a world. Just as the contents are endowed with an ideal existence outside time and space, so there are ideal domains which are genuine systems of formed contents. Each of them "has a self-sufficient subsistence that is held together from the inside . . . [in virtue of] an inner logic."[78]

The ideal worlds may be regarded as languages, each of which is adequate to refer to all contents. Each world-form constructs out of the totality of contents a self-consistent whole which excludes nothing. Each is an autonomous perspective which is sovereign precisely because *all* contents can be seen from their vantage point. There can be "no mixing, no overlapping, no crossing"[79] of worlds; one can in no way interfere with another. Art, science, metaphysics, or religion is each a way of realizing all contents. Each is equally adequate to that task; no perspective may be subjected to criticism from the view afforded by another.[80]

"For the naïve man," reality or the world of practice has a privileged status.[81] He calls it *the* world. At the same time, he relegates the other worlds to inferior positions as superstructures.[82] Common sense commits an error here, although it is one that can easily be understood and forgiven. Reality, after all, is that world "which must be the basis of our acting in a beneficial, life-preserving way, according to the peculiarity of the psychobiological organization of our species."[83] In our daily lives and occupations we must deal with the world of contents by means of the form of reality. And since most of our lives and occupations are conducted on the teleological level, it is not surprising that we attach special importance to the world of practice.[84]

What is ideally true of world-forms can never be historically realized. "What exists is not knowledge as such, art as such, religion as such. No determinate representation is any longer connected with these concepts in their absolute generality."[85] These forms, in other words, "are never operative in abstract purity and absolute perfection."[86] Instead, we have "the arts, artistic means, and styles of the culture of a period . . . [which] suffice to give artistic shape only to certain contents . . . . We have . . . only historical religions, each of which permeates only a certain part of the contents of the world, the soul and destiny."[87] In sum, the forms which actually function in human experience and which have given and continue to give shape to the objects of culture we find around us are always historically determined specifications of world-forms.

Besides the world-forms which, ideally at least, organize every element in the realm of contents, there are numerous forms which, even ideally, are not so powerful.[88] Among limited forms Simmel explicitly names law (making use of the concept of justice), economy (organizing contents in terms of economic value), and practical morality.[89] But clearly there are many more such forms, though they are not readily identifiable. Given the fact that in any historical context world-forms can never live up to their title, no empirical mark distinguishes them from forms that are limited even ideally. Accordingly, it is not clear whether history[90] and pedagogy,[91] for example, are world-forms or more limited ones. At any rate, it would seem to be true that the particular sciences and, perhaps, the individual arts are limited forms of the kind here meant.

The difference between world-forms and other, weaker ones is not of the greatest importance to Simmel, for even a limited form succeeds in organizing the contents over which it holds sway into a unified whole. Such a form gives some—not all—contents "a compactness, in virtue of a pervasive meaning, an autonomy and inner solidarity, . . . which converts each of these worlds into a formal analogy, on a smaller scale, with the all-inclusive ones."[92]

The difference between world-forms and limited forms derives exclusively from their scope. Both have their origin "in the contexts of life [and are] brought forth by its organic forces."[93] In the case of both, "a highest concept carries out . . . the function of unification."[94] The structure created by world-forms and by limited forms both "emancipate themselves [from life] . . . and now absorb the energies and contents as they pulsate in the rest of life."[95] It does not matter, in other words, whether or not a form can ideally master the entire realm of contents. In either case, it becomes a fit object of free activity. Its goals can be pursued by him who has liberated himself from the bond of the teleology of his life.

In the preceding reconstruction of Simmel's philosophical position we have pursued two interwoven paths. We attempted to state what meaning Simmel attaches to the concepts of form and content and to show how these concepts function in Simmel's philosophy. To achieve the latter goal, we traced the natural history of human experience as Simmel understands it. Now, finally, we are ready to close the circle and make the connection between form and content in experience and Simmel's conception of life.

Life as more-life expresses the fact that life is a self-perpetuating process. " . . . As long as life exists at all, it produces something living,"[96] namely, more of itself. But life's productivity does not end with its creation of more life. It creates and sets free from itself something that is not life but "which has its own significance and follows its own law."[97] Because of this attribute of life, Simmel adds a second defining expression: "life is more-than-life."[98]

This "more-than-life" refers to the objects which life creates by virtue of the formal principles implicit in experience. Whether we consider contents only as they are shaped *in* experience, whether we focus upon an ideal world that is implicitly *generated by* experience, or whether we attend to a human work as a material *embodiment of* experience, the structure in question "possesses its own meaning, a logical coherence, some kind of validity or stability, independent of its having been produced and being borne along by life."[99] The very formal principles which are the conditions of the creation of objects by life, guarantee, at the same time, the emancipation of the created from the creator.

It is not an accidental attribute of life that it creates something which is not life or, as Simmel puts it, which is more than life. The process of life is that of experiencing. In the most general terms it is the constant absorption of contents. But, as we know, the passivity implied by this expression is deceptive: experience is structured and structuring. In their being experienced in some mode, contents are formed in one of many possible ways. In being formed, they become objects and independent of the process of life itself. Looked at in one way, an event is merely a fleeting phase in an individual's career; but regarded in another, that same event "is something logical, . . . something that is in principle fully definite and definable."[100] If life is an experiential process, it cannot help but be creative.

We have already begun to clarify the relationship between Simmel's two "definitions" of life. To say that life must be creative means that the property designated by "more-life" necessarily produces the one referred to by "more-than-life." Furthermore, if the process of life is to perpetuate itself, it must go outside itself and create objects that will serve as instruments for its maintenance: life as more-than-life is a necessary condition of life as more-life.

The converse of this holds as well. Objects of art, knowledge, or metaphysics—one manifestation of what is meant by "more-than-life"—are, as it were, experience crystallized. They come into being and are what they are by virtue of the forming power of experience and hence of life. Life as more-life is a necessary condition of life as more-than-life.

Life is defined by means of two interdependent essential attributes[101] because it is a process that is both complex and single. Life is a complex process because it is an activity which, in two ways, continually pushes beyond itself. It moves beyond the present moment with *its* content to another with its *different* one; it moves beyond itself by producing worlds that are free from the motion of life. The expressions "more-life" and "more-than-life" define life by saying that life is what life does.

In spite of its complexity, however, life is a *single* process. Both expressions—"more-life" and "more-than-life"—are needed to define life, but each of the attributes to which they refer is a condition of the existence of the other. With his dual definition of life, Simmel seeks to convey that "the dualism, retained in its full acuteness, does not only not contradict the unity of life, but is precisely the way in which its unity exists."[102]

The objects of culture which surround men are crystallizations of human experience. The content of cultural products is that which is experienced by their creators; the formal character of such objects is a function of the structuring power of human experience. The concepts of form and content, as understood in Simmel's philosophy and as related to his conception of human life, become powerful tools of analysis in Simmel's examinations of various areas of culture and in his effort to bring the products of culture into significant relationship with men. Upon his philosophy of life and experience, Simmel builds his philosophy of culture.

1. My appreciation goes to the Social Science Research Council for an appointment in their Political Theory and Legal Philosophy Program which made it possible for me to devote the year 1957-58 to a study of Georg Simmel.

2. *Philosophische Kultur. Gesammelte Essais* ([1911] Leipzig: Kröner, 1919), p. 5.

3. *Hauptprobleme der Philosophie* ([1910] Berlin: de Gruyter, 1950), p. 15. (See the translation in this volume, p. 288.)

4. *Einleitung in die Moralwissenschaft. Eine Kritik der ethischen Grundbegriffe* ([1892-93] Stuttgart and Berlin: Cotta, 1911), II, 309.

5. In a modified but interesting way, this was done for Simmel's sociology by Maria Steinhoff in her article, "Die Form als soziologische Grundkategorie bei Georg Simmel," *Kölner Vierteljahrshefte für Soziologie,* IV (1925), 215-59.

6. *Mehr-Leben* and *Mehr-als-Leben.* See Georg Simmel, *Lebensanschauung. Vier metaphysische Kapitel* ([1918] Munich and Berlin: Duncker und Humblot, 1922), p. 20.

7. *Fragmente und Aufsätze aus dem Nachlass und Veröffentlichungen der letzten Jahre,* ed. Gertrud Kantorowicz (Munich: Drei Masken Verlag, 1923), p. 185.

8. Bergson is never discussed in Simmel's last book, *Lebensanschauung.* Nevertheless, in writing it, Simmel was very much under the influence of the French philosopher. See, for example, the essay, "Henri Bergson" in George Simmel, *Zur Philosophie der Kunst. Philosophische und Kunstphilosophische Aufsätze,* ed. Gertrud Simmel (Potsdam: Kiepenheuer, 1922), pp. 126-45.

9. *Lebensanschauung,* p. 8.

10. While Simmel writes as if he meant life in general, he is, in fact, concerned only with human life.

11. *Lebensanschauung,* p. 9.

12. Georg Simmel, *Rembrandt. Ein Kunstphilosophischer Versuch* ([1916] Leipzig: Wolff, 1919), p. 2.

13. *Lebensanschauung,* p. 13.

14. See Georg Simmel, "Skizze einer Willenstheorie," *Zeitschrift für Psychologie und Physiologie der Sinnesorgane,* IX (1895), 206-20. See also *Lebensanschauung,* pp. 9-10.

15. *Moralwissenschaft,* I, 250. See also Georg Simmel, *Schopenhauer und Nietzsche. Ein Vortragszyklus* (Leipzig: Duncker und Humblot, 1907), pp. 76-78.

16. *Lebensanschauung,* p. 10.

17. *Ibid.,* p. 171.

18. *Ibid.,* p. 12.

19. For purposes of exposition, I am borrowing the quality-material distinction from Edmund Husserl. See his *Logische Untersuchungen,* Vol. II, *Untersuchungen zur Phänomenologie und Theorie der Erkenntnis* (4th ed.; Halle: Niemeyer, 1928), Part I, p. 411.

20. *Soziologie. Untersuchungen über die Formen der Vergesellschaftung* (Leipzig: Duncker und Humblot, 1908), p. 559.

21. See *Moralwissenschaft,* I, 1 ff. See also Georg Simmel, *Philosophie des Geldes* ([1900] Munich and Leipzig: Duncker und Humblot, 1922), p. 10.

22. This is expressed in various ways, but it is insisted upon from the first. See, for example, *Moralwissenschaft,* I, 9-11; "Beiträge zur Erkenntnistheorie der Religion" (1902), in *Brücke und Tür. Essays des Philosophen zur Geschichte, Religion, Kunst und Gesellschaft,* ed. Michael Landmann (Stuttgart: Koehler, 1957), pp. 108-9; *Philosophie des Geldes,* pp. 5 f.; *Soziologie,* pp. 557-59; and *Lebensanschauung,* pp. 31-32. In spite of this insistence, Simmel is not always consistent on this point. See, for example, "Erkenntnistheorie der Religion," p. 114, and pp. 50-53 in this paper. Nevertheless, I think it can be successfully argued that the position here presented is the definitive one.

23. *Lebensanschauung,* p. 30. It is at this point that Husserl's and Simmel's positions diverge. Simmel's position might be located somewhere between the Kantian and that of phenomenology. See the following paragraph.

24. *Ibid.*

25. *Hauptprobleme,* pp. 15-16. (See pp. 288-89 in this volume.)

26. *Lebensanschauung,* p. 30.

27. *Ibid.,* pp. 30-31.

28. Literally, "world-stuff." *Lebensanschauung,* pp. 29, 30, 31.

29. *Philosophie des Geldes,* p. 7; *Hauptprobleme,* pp. 105-11; *Lebensanschauung,* p. 31.

30. *Kant. Sechzehn Vorlesungen gehalten an der Berliner Universität* ([1904] Munich and Leipzig: Duncker und Humblot, 1924), p. 64.

31. *Ibid.,* p. 63.

32. *Lebensanschauung,* p. 169.

33. That there is no criterion of unity in general which is more stringent does not prejudice the possibility of stricter criteria applicable to different kinds of forms. Of several discussions of this topic, the following is useful: Georg Simmel, *Die Probleme der Geschichtsphilosophie. Eine erkenntnistheoretische Studie* ([1892] Munich and Leipzig: Duncker und Humblot, 1922), Chap. i, *passim.*

34. *Kant,* p. 64.

35. See pp. 50-53 of this paper.

36. *Kant,* pp. 30 ff.

37. See, for example, *Hauptprobleme,* pp. 15-18 (pp. 288-91 in this volume).

38. Henceforth the term "form" will be reserved for formal principles of the "highest" level, that is, for art, religion, science, and so on. The more general term "formal principle" will be used for "lower" level forms and for all formal principles when the level of generality is irrelevant.

39. The discussion of religious art in *Rembrandt,* pp. 141-95, is an excellent example.

40. There are different kinds, levels, and degrees of form. The contents need not be elements of the realm of contents as set forth on pp. 37-41 of this paper. This state of affairs goes a long way toward explaining the bewildering variety of uses of the form-content distinction in Simmel's analyses of cultural phenomena.

41. "Aus Georg Simmels nachgelassener Mappe 'Metaphysik,'" with an Introduction by Gertrud Simmel, in *Aus unbekannten Schriften. Festgabe für Martin Buber zum 50. Geburtstag* (Berlin: Schneider, 1928), p. 222.

42. *Lebensanschauung,* p. 183.

43. "Metaphysik," p. 222.

44. *Ibid.* See also *Fragmente und Aufsätze,* p. 150. Since *Erleben* is not used to designate experience in general, the German term will be retained to avoid confusion.

45. *Philosophie des Geldes,* p. 9.

46. *Ibid.,* p. 11.

47. *Lebensanschauung,* p. 52.

48. Because of its process-character, life itself, that is *Erleben,* may be said to be a form. This issue, however, will not be discussed here. See

Lebensanschauung, pp. 119-25, 150-239. A related discussion can be found in Georg Simmel, "Das Problem der historischen Zeit" (1916), in *Brücke und Tür,* pp. 43-58.

49. *Hauptprobleme,* pp. 36-37. (See pp. 304-6 in this volume); *Philosophie des Geldes,* p. 11; Georg Simmel, *Grundfragen der Soziologie (Individuum und Gesellschaft),* (Berlin and Leipzig: Göschen, 1917), p. 10, translated by Kurt H. Wolff, ed., in *The Sociology of Georg Simmel* (Glencoe, Ill.: Free Press of Glencoe, Illinois, 1950), p. 7.

50. *Philosophie des Geldes,* p. 11. See also "Vom Subject und Object" (Chap. iii), *Hauptprobleme,* pp. 86-112.

51. Note the similarity of this position with the role of the "problematic situation" in the philosophy of John Dewey.

52. See *Moralwissenschaft,* I, 7-8; *Kant,* p. 118; *Schopenhauer und Nietzsche,* p. 136; *Lebensanschauung,* pp. 35, 83; "Erkenntnistheorie der Religion," p. 105; Georg Simmel, *Die Religion* (Frankfurt am Main: Rütten und Loening, 1912), pp. 41-43; Georg Simmel, *Schulpädagogik. Vorlesungen, gehalten an der Universität Strassburg,* ed. Karl Hauter (Osterwieck/Harz: Zickfeldt, 1922), p. 3.

53. *Lebensanschauung,* p. 206; italics added.

54. *Kant,* p. 30.

55. *Ibid.,* p. 34.

56. *Lebensanschauung,* p. 51.

57. *Ibid.,* p. 52.

58. *Ibid.,* pp. 37-44. See also pp. 47-49 of this paper.

59. *Vorformen.* See Georg Simmel, "Vorformen der Idee. Aus den Studien zu einer Metaphysik," *Logos,* VI (1917), 103-41. Most of the material in this article was included in Chap. ii, "Die Wendung zur Idee" of *Lebensanschauung,* pp. 27-95. There, too, the term is used; see, for example, p. 60.

60. *Lebensanschauung,* p. 93.

61. In this context, Simmel uses both *Form* and *Vorform* ambiguously. They stand both for the formal principles and for the collection of objects formed by a principle; for example, both for the preliminary form of art and for proto-art.

62. *Lebensanschauung,* pp. 37-39.

63. The discussion here concerns only one of several uses Simmel makes of the concept of freedom.

64. *Lebensanschauung,* p. 40.

65. *Ibid.,* pp. 39-44. Note that nothing has been said about the *source* of the impulse of free action. This conception of freedom touches only

on the *terminus ad quem.* The causal energy which propels men toward whatever end has its source in the process of life. As one moves from the teleological to the free stage, *only the direction* of the impulses changes. The impulses are sublimated.

66. Simmel variously calls it *Wendung zur Idee, Drehung, Achsendrehung des Lebens.* See, above all, the chapter, "Die Wendung zur Idee," of *Lebensanschauung,* pp. 27-95, especially pp. 37 ff.

67. *Lebensanschauung,* p. 37.

68. *Ibid.; Hauptprobleme,* pp. 86-87.

69. *Lebensanschauung,* p. 93.

70. *Ibid.,* pp. 63-64.

71. *Ibid.,* p. 55.

72. This *turning* must not be confused with action for the sake of any end-in-itself. There is no turning when a person takes to living for the sake of eating. The goal, eating, is still to be located within the individual. Here, there is no action for the sake of a form.

73. *Hauptprobleme,* p. 12. (See p. 286 in this volume.)

74. "Epistemology" is here understood in an extended sense: it pertains to the analysis of *all* forms, their logic, and their functioning in experience, and not to cognition alone. It comes close to including much of Simmels conception of philosophy of culture. See *Geschichtsphilosophie,* pp. 197-98, n. 1.

75. It is difficult to cite specific passages in Simmel's writings in support of the position developed here. In a sense, whenever Simmel writes about one of the spheres of culture, he makes these points. For some general statements, see the essays, "Der Begriff und die Tragödie der Kultur," in *Philosophische Kultur,* pp. 223-53, and "Vom Wesen der Kultur" (1908), in *Brücke und Tür,* pp. 86-94. The first chapter, "Vom Wesen der Philosophie," of *Hauptprobleme,* pp. 7-43 (see pp. 282-309) in this volume), is an analysis of what it means to be working for the sake of the form, philosophy.

76. *Lebensanschauung,* pp. 27-36; *Hauptprobleme,* pp. 15-18 (see pp. 289-90 in this volume).

77. *Lebensanschauung,* pp. 27-36; *Hauptprobleme,* pp. 15-18 (see pp. 289-90 in this volume).

78. *Lebensanschauung,* pp. 29, 30.

79. *Ibid.,* p. 29.

80. *Hauptprobleme,* pp. 36-39. (See pp. 304-7 in this volume).

81. *Religion,* p. 10.

82. *Ibid.*

83. *Ibid.,* p. 11.

84. See also *Lebensanschauung,* pp. 27-29. Broadly speaking, Simmel arrives at his theory of world-forms by way of a generalized Kantianism. From a basis that is essentially phenomenological, Alfred Schuetz reaches a position which, in some respects, is strikingly similar to that of Simmel. His article, "On Multiple Realities," *Philosophy and Phenomenological Research,* V (June, 1945), 533-76, focuses primarily on "The Reality of the World of Daily Life" (pp. 533-51)—Simmel would say, "The World of Reality, of Daily Life"—and "The World of Scientific Theory" (pp. 563-75). Here, as well as in Schuetz's view of relations *among* the worlds (see especially pp. 553-54, including n. 19), much can be found that is in fundamental agreement with Simmel.

How a position such as Simmel's can be put to work is shown (though without explicit reference to Simmel) by Kurt H. Wolff in "The Sociology of Knowledge: Emphasis on an Empirical Attitude," *Philosophy of Science,* X (1943), 104-23. The concepts of "central attitude" and "typical central attitude" (pp. 111-21), developed there as instruments of analysis in the sociology of knowledge, might be regarded as extensions of Simmel's world-forms *as they function in experience.*

85. *Lebensanschauung,* p. 32.

86. *Hauptprobleme,* p. 16 (see p. 289 in this volume).

87. *Ibid.,* pp. 16-17 (see p. 289 in this volume).

88. Simmel's position is that contents are neutral with regard to all structuring, that form and content are logically independent of each other (see pp. 37-41 of this paper). When, now, he claims that there are forms which cannot structure *all* contents, he cannot escape the charge of inconsistency.

89. *Lebensanschauung,* p. 86.

90. See especially "Die historische Formung," in *Fragmente und Aufsätze,* pp. 147-209.

91. See *Schulpädagogik.*

92. *Lebensanschauung,* p. 86.

93. *Ibid.*

94. *Ibid.*

95. *Ibid.*

96. *Ibid.,* p. 20.

97. *Ibid.,* p. 24.

98. *Ibid.,* p. 20.

99. *Ibid.,* p. 23.

100. *Ibid.,* pp. 22-23.

101. Simmel prefers to call them two complementary definitions; *ibid.,* p. 20.

102. *Ibid.,* p. 25.

FORMAL SOCIOLOGY

F. H. TENBRUCK

From the very beginning, the reception of Simmel's sociology has been marked by a peculiar blend of lively interest and severe criticism. Most commentators have been ready enough to give Simmel credit for brilliant insights, but they have denied him the status of a systematic sociologist. The niche in the history of sociological theory in which Simmel has come to rest bears rather securely, and all too conspicuously, the inscription "innovator of ideas and theoretical leads."[1] This paper attempts to show that the niche is inadequate for Simmel. It will be maintained that his work provides little basis for the criticisms which are usually leveled against him. It should be noted, however, that we shall concern ourselves with the inner consistency of Simmel's sociology, rather than seeking any transcendent or objective justification.

Two accusations have become almost standard in criticisms of Simmel. One is directed against his program of formal sociology; the other, against his concrete sociological investigations. The program is deemed classificatory, formalistic, and altogether too narrow to accommodate sociology. Preston and Bonita Valien write that "few would agree today with the limitations that Simmel placed on sociology."[2] Their verdict is only a late one in a long series of similar statements.[3] We shall refer to this type of criticism as the formalistic view, interpretation, or misunderstanding. What precisely is meant by that will be seen later.

The second standard accusation is that Simmel's particular investigations persistently violate his own program of formal sociology. Referring to his analyses of concrete situations, Theodore Abel characterizes his method as "a procedure which is completely at variance with the requirements of Simmel's theory," and concludes that "the refutation of the theory by Simmel's sociological analyses becomes an established fact."[4] This, too, has been a persistent argument against Simmel's sociology.[5]

It is important to notice the logical connection between these two major criticisms. Given the character of Simmel's sociological investigations, the second charge becomes inescapable once the formalistic interpretation is accepted. The two are almost certain to appear jointly: "Few would agree today with Simmel's insistence upon confining sociology to the study of social forms —and Simmel himself was a conspicuous offender of this principle."[6] Indeed, the violations of the program, as viewed by the formalistic interpreters, are truly obvious, gross, striking, and persistent.

However, the very crudeness and continuance of the alleged transgressions should have cautioned against the formalistic interpretation. Was it not at least possible that Simmel's program had been misunderstood? Such a misunderstanding results in a vicious circle: Formal sociology confines its investigation to a classification and analysis of the general aspects of society; hence it is a mere "catalogue of human relations";[7] hence Simmel's investigations violate the program; hence Simmel's sociology lacks unity and system; hence his program is of little value to systematic sociology; hence it is useless to search for a better understanding of this program.

How could such a misinterpretation originate and become accepted? It cannot be denied that Simmel's writings readily lend themselves to a formalistic misconstruction. The lack of systematic and disciplined procedure; the rather careless terminology; the obvious presence in his work of many residual traces from different stages in the gradual evolution of his sociology;[8] the unique combination of Kantianism and *Lebensphilosophie* which, in a way, provides the setting—all these combine to obscure the true focus which gives unity and coherence to his sociology. In addition, there are extraneous factors, on some of which I shall briefly touch. Formal sociology was soon overshadowed by Max Weber's emerging system of *verstehende* sociology and came to be interpreted largely in the light of von Wiese's system.[9] In America, two other conditions were unfavorable to an understanding of Simmel's intentions and contributions: The available translations were mostly renditions of early drafts of his essays; and, unfortunately, formal sociology was from the beginning intimately connected with the issue over sociology as a "general," as opposed to a "special," social science.[10]

On the whole, however, it might be more fair to seek an explanation of the formalistic misunderstanding, not in any shortcomings on Simmel's part, nor in any failures on the part of his interpreters, but in more general conditions. It might be suggested that when Simmel was writing, the social sciences did not have available the conceptual tools which he needed to express his thought articulately. He had to work mainly with such non-specific concepts, illustrations, and images as the "cultural" sciences of his day could offer him. To wrest meaning from his text—or as Kant, in genuine deference to the achievement of an author, put it, "to understand an author better than he understood himself"—is a task that can be met only to the extent that there has been progress in conceptualization and methodology. While early followers and defenders of Simmel's sociology often showed a remarkable grasp of his intentions and views, it seems to me that the beginning of a correct and distinct understanding of them has come into being—and could have come into being—only lately.[11]

The key to the comprehension of Simmel's program and, consequently, to his entire sociology is a correct understanding of the "forms of sociation" which he designated as the object of sociology proper. "Despite the relatively numerous discussions of the 'forms,' the concept has yet to be specified in a satisfactory manner. To do so requires a painstaking collection and juxtaposition of all passages in which Simmel employs the term, and the subsequent formulation of a definition which does justice to all of them."[12] This proposal calls for a monograph on formal sociology, and, ideally, on Simmel's entire work,[13] and can therefore not be taken up on the present occasion. Existing efforts to arrive at an understanding of Simmel's key concept by classifying "forms" and making subsequent generalizations concerning them display a danger to which such a procedure is liable: A classification which would eventually reveal the meaning of the forms of sociation depends, in part, on an adequate grasp of the notion to begin with.[14] Within the scope of this paper, it seems proper, therefore, to follow Simmel's programmatic discussions of "forms," drawing on his investigations into concrete forms for further information and confirmation.[15] As preparation for this, I shall suggest a general view regarding the significance of the idea "forms of sociation."

Upon introducing the distinction between form and content in the programmatic essay "The Problem of Sociology," Simmel warns his readers

> that this is here properly only an analogy, for the sake of approximately designating the elements to be distinguished. This antithesis should be understood immediately in its peculiar sense, without prejudice to the provisional names from remoter meanings of the terms.[16]

Whenever interpretations have overlooked the significance of this explicit warning, the results have been devastating. Sorokin's relentless criticism, for example, is a learned commentary on the historical meanings of "forms," but it utterly disregards Simmel's usage of the term.[17] Recently, interpreters have come to realize the importance of its "provisional" character.[18] Analogy is perhaps a legitimate element and device of science, but it is certainly unusual for an author to set forth his key notion by mere analogy. The fact that Simmel does so permits only one interpretation, which careful reading of the passage corroborates: He admits his inability to explain his idea in detail. Although it shows a lack of concern for terminology on Simmel's part, this admission should not be construed as the result of a flippant attitude toward scientific precision or as evidence that the program is merely the hasty experimentation of a versatile mind with sociological theory, rightly to be dismissed by posterity. Rather, the admission indicates only that Simmel lacks the proper tools for an adequate conceptualization of a new perspective that he has discovered, a perspective which, he assures his readers, is capable of explaining the puzzling paradoxes of social life. He can explain only by analogy and illustration, relying on the reader's empathic understanding and trusting that he will extract the "peculiar sense" from the analogy.

In the face of the complexity and elusiveness of Simmel's writing, interpreters have often sought refuge in his dictum about "the personal attitude toward the world," and have expected "a personal equation" to reveal the unifying bond of his ideas.[19] But whatever the significance of the dictum or its worth for the task of interpretation may be, Simmel certainly did not mean to renounce his claim to the objective unity of his sociology. In the Preface to his *Soziologie* he admonished his reader "to hold on, uninterruptedly, to this one method of asking questions, as it is developed in the first chapter (since otherwise these pages might impress him as an accumulation of unrelated facts and reflections)."[20] He strikes a similar note when he concedes the "wholly fragmentary, incomplete character of this book"; but he insists simultaneously that "if this character should strike one as a defect, this would only go to prove that I have not been able to clarify the fundamental idea of the present volume."[21] Simmel was unable to articulate his fundamental idea programmatically and thus, in order to illuminate it, he had to rely on its illustrative applications in concrete analyses.[22] Indeed, on the surface, these analyses exhibit little consistency and have to be read in the light of "the fundamental idea" of the programmatic essay.[23] However, these admissions of an inability to "objectify" his thoughts[24] are only meant to impress upon the reader his concern with the central idea. What is of foremost importance is not the analysis of concrete phenomena nor the various insights into the specific aspects of such phenomena that might be gained thereby. The most important thing is to have an adequate grasp of the fundamental idea. Simmel emphatically rejects the role he is so often assigned in both favorable and unfavorable accounts—that of the "brilliant" man who freely lavishes "leads" and "insights" but fails to expound a coherent and systematic conception.[25]

It is extremely difficult to give here a general but brief indication—let alone exposition—of Simmel's fundamental idea. Such an indication should emphasize, not any substantive differences by which Simmel's sociology can be contrasted with earlier systems, but the basic difference in level or perspective. Simmel was the first, or among the first, to uncover for sociology a specific "layer" of reality, its "social dimension." His writings reflect his fascination with this novel perspective and the world of new phenomena it opened up. Viewed from this perspective, adornments are not sufficiently described by their objective qualities and an individual's appreciation of them, but gain significance only through an intricate social interplay; superordination is not simply a matter of superior power but presupposes and entails a web of intricate orientations of ruler and ruled; the poor are characterized not so much by an objective lack of money as by their attitudes and by those of others toward them; the secret is not merely knowledge restricted to an individual or group; a stranger is not just a person with few connections and little local information. In brief, the most general characterization of Simmel's fundamental idea would seem to be that objects and phenomena reveal their full significance only when questioned in respect to their social dimension, a dimension which possesses an order of its own.[26]

The originality and novelty of this idea have been obscured for us by subsequent advances in sociology, psychology, and social psychology. Today, we take Simmel's basic perspective for granted, no matter how much his particular insights may still impress us. We are used to exploring the social presuppositions and implications of phenomena. But in Simmel's time, things in general were conceived from the standpoint of their objective qualities; actions in particular, from that of the individual ends pursued in them. This must be remembered if we would justly appraise Simmel's contribution.

Simmel advanced his theory in pointed opposition to previous attempts at accounting for social life. These attempts were based either on a supra-individual entity (such as the *Volksseele* or similar organismic notions) or on instincts, drives, and other strictly individual properties.[27] Simmel submitted that it is interaction which sustains society. Modern sociologists have rightly given him credit for this insistence on "functionalism." But functionalism does not suggest the peculiar character of interaction as it unfolds in Simmel's analysis.

What is perhaps the most commonly agreed upon conception of interaction can be described as follows: Given two actors, A and B, and two respective action systems,[28] a and b, interaction consists of a series of changes occurring in these action systems. (The term "action system" refers to the totality of drives, motives, ends, and other psychological characteristics which are the causes, potential and sufficient, of actions.) The changes that occur in the action system of A are in some way correlated with the changes that occur in the action system of B. A will modify his ends and means upon perceiving B's course of action, and vice versa. Thus, b changes to b′ as, or after, a changes to a′. The entire interaction process thus consists of two sequences (a, a′, a″, a‴, . . . , and b, b′, b″, b‴, . . .). They are related so that every state of an action system (b″, for example) is considered a modification of its earlier state (b′), which is induced, at least partially, by the earlier state of the action system of the other actor (a′).

It is precisely this common understanding of interaction which Simmel rejects. He does not consider it incorrect as far as it goes; for certain purposes or disciplines (psychology, for example), it is legitimate, if not unavoidable, to conceive of interaction in this manner. Nor does Simmel level his criticism against theories which regard the individual as the true and only bearer of interaction. On the contrary he says: "The data of sociology are psychic occurrences which, in their immediate reality, are the proper object of psychological categories." This concept is not, however, a properly *sociological* conceptualization of interaction. Sociology does not aim at investigating such psychic occurrences,

> although they are indispensable for a description of the facts. Rather, it is concerned with the objectivity of sociation . . . . That people influence one another, that they act or suffer, change or do not change, because others exist, express themselves, act or feel—all these are, of course, psychic phenomena.[29]

The occurrence of such phenomena can be understood or described only psychologically. But with regard to the sociological form, these phenomena, as they occur in the two actors, are of no direct interest.

In his rejection, Simmel is not proposing to disregard in particular the dependence of every state of an action system on its previous state (that is, the sequence a, a′, a″, a‴, a⁗, . . .) while concentrating on actions in so far as they are changed or modified by the actions of co-actors (that is, for A, the dependence of a′ on b, of a″ on b′, of a‴ on b″, and so on). Rather, he rejects the entire approach, because what is sociologically relevant in interaction cannot be found by an analysis which explains individual actions by reference to the action systems of individual actors and co-actors; that is, by reference to individual ends, conscious or unconscious. This means that, logically, interaction is not necessarily social action.

To convey its significance, two implications of this position must be brought out. In the first place, Simmel's rejection of the psychological interpretation of interaction signifies his rejection of sociology as a general social science, in that acceptance of this interpretation would make sociology indistinguishable from social psychology. If actors decide on courses of action by orienting themselves to their individual action systems, it follows that social life must be conceived and explained as a system of combinations or compromises of individual ends. An explanation of society by a general social science would have to draw on the totality of mental objects and psychic mechanisms.

In the second place, Simmel objects to such an idea of interaction on other than methodological grounds. He considers it substantively incapable of accounting for societal facts. Society, after all, exhibits stable and persistent relationships. The psychological model of interaction leaves the actors isolated; their deliberations evince the ultimate independence of individual action systems. While each individual must take cognizance of the actions of his co-actors, he eventually decides on his own actions by exclusively orienting himself to his individual ends. Such a situation could never produce those behavioral regularities which we observe in society.

In order to confirm this interpretation of Simmel's basic position and to demonstrate the consistency of his program with the method he applies in his concrete investigations, we can draw on these investigations. For example, Simmel refuses to regard strictly physical submission as an object of sociology;[30] and, throughout his writings, he objects to identifying what he calls "parallel" or "statistical" or "average" phenomena—mere "side-by-sideness"—as social phenomena.[31] Such phenomena do not represent social action because they result from purely individual action systems. We might describe Simmel's fundamental position in the following manner: Strictly speaking, the psychological understanding of interaction reduces all societal phenomena to distributive phenomena which ultimately originate in individual action systems. Sociology deals with phenomena only in so far as they are truly collective phenomena, which cannot be reduced to individual action systems. Interaction is more than a series of reactions.

This brings us to Simmel's positive conception of interaction as social action. Most of the time he characterizes it as having a certain "unity" or as being a certain "synthesis." "Unity" is used by Simmel in a double sense, however. It may refer to the manifest unity which actions of members of a social group can be said to possess as observable behavioral regularities—this manifest unity is, of course, what sociology endeavors to explain. Or it may refer to a unity or synthesis which is *not* the observed unity of the actions themselves but which is needed by interaction if it is to be social action. In the second sense, the term designates some quality which the actors must have for their actions to display certain patterns: the actors must be "sociated."

Simmel makes it unmistakably clear that the unity of social action rests with the individual actors. They "experience the synthesis which gives them the unity of a society only through processes of the mind which relate one existing individual to the other in certain forms and according to certain laws."[32] Sociation is not a quality of the actions but has its locus in the individual actors.[33] To look for sources of this unity outside the individual is "a mysticism" because it is an attempt to locate psychic phenomena outside a psyche.[34] Simmel formulates pointedly: "The unity which is in question in society is nothing but this being conscious of forming a unit with others."[35]

Simmel has tried to describe this "unity" or "sociation" of individuals in ever new and varying formulations; he returns constantly to this central point of his sociology throughout his writings, stressing different aspects of it depending on the context.[36] He offers no standard formula, but familiarity with his writings makes it clear beyond any doubt that basically he is concerned with the actors' fundamental reciprocal orientations.

A paradox seems to arise here: If these reciprocal orientations are located in the individuals, if they are components of the individual consciousness, why do they not form part of the individual action systems? Or, if they do, how can Simmel reject the idea that social action results from individual action systems? Clearly, there is only one possible solution, and it is precisely the one Simmel offers: The reciprocal orientations represent (as we shall see) a special layer or level of consciousness which is not a part of the individual action systems proper.

It is to these reciprocal orientations that Simmel refers when he speaks of "forms of sociation." The reciprocal orientations are the conditions which account for stable patterns in interaction and for the regularities of overt behavior (collective phenomena).

It should be noted that the distinction between interaction and social action is an analytical distinction. As Simmel sees it, interaction is almost bound to result in the sociation of the actors, except in extreme cases. The distinction is not meant to exclude interaction from the subject matter of sociology. Rather, it reveals that quality of interaction which makes it truly social, but which is overlooked in the common view of it as a sequence of reactions.

The foregoing is intended to be a systematic restatement of the frame of reference for the study of society which Simmel proposes in his programmatic essay "The Problem of Sociology." Actually, this essay contains only a sketchy exposition, and for a systematic understanding the reader must draw on the whole of his writings, as Simmel urges him to do. The inarticulateness of Simmel's exposition reflects no disregard for systematic procedure nor a lack of talent for analytical precision. There is a systematic reason for the spotty and incomplete character of the exposition, to which we shall turn later.

First, however, we must relate the understanding of social action gained in the previous analysis to Simmel's controversial use of the terms "form" and "content." We see immediately that "content" is what we have called "individual action systems":

> Everything present in the individuals (who are the immediate, concrete data of all historical reality) in the form of drive, interest, purpose, inclination, psychic state, movement—everything that

> is present in them in such a way as to engender or mediate effects upon others or to receive such effects, I designate as the *content,* as the *material,* as it were, of sociation.[37]

From this we see that it is the reciprocal orientations which Simmel designates by the term "forms of sociation." It must be noted, however, that Simmel, for the sake of convenience, often makes the overt behavioral regularities, rather than the underlying orientations, the referent of the term—especially when he discusses highly crystallized or institutionalized behavior patterns. Nevertheless, behavior patterns are never the ultimate referent and criterion of the "forms"; these are always the reciprocal orientations.

Having distinguished between form and content, Simmel proceeds[38] to designate the forms as the object of sociology proper, that is, of formal sociology. Strictly speaking, however, the distinction remains a mere hypothesis. The methodological argument that only a formal sociology would fulfill the unique purpose which is required of a special social science does not constitute a factual proof of the validity of the distinction. It does not demonstrate conclusively that collective phenomena (social action) cannot result from an interplay of reactions among individual action systems. The notion that a specific "content," or a certain combination of "contents," in a multitude of actors inevitably produces a specific reciprocity or unity of action is not disproved. However, the distinction can be validated empirically if—and only if—the same content can actually be shown to exist in various and different forms, and if the same forms can be found to contain different contents. There would be no justification for establishing sociology as a separate social science of the forms of sociation if these forms were merely derivatives of their contents. Simmel shows, though in summary fashion, that the facts prove his claim and establish the legitimacy of the distinction and provide a subject matter *sui generis* for sociology. The forms of sociation are not derivatives of individual action systems, and they must be treated by a special science.

However, the evidence that there is a factual basis for the analytic separation of form and content must not be construed as evidence that each has a separate existence.

> In every given social situation, content and societal form constitute a unified reality. A social form can no more attain existence detached from all content than a spatial form can exist without a material of which it is the form. Rather, these are in reality inseparable elements in every social situation and occurrence.[39]

Although they cannot be derived from the individual action systems, the forms exist in the minds of the individual actors.[40] This brings us back to the paradox mentioned above. The forms have their locus in the mind; the individuals are "conscious of forming a unity." Does this not make the forms part of the individual action system? Are they not then identical with content, after all?

Simmel answers that being conscious of the unity

> does not, of course, signify a consciousness of forming an abstract unity, but rather a feeling and apprehension of being in many single relationships in which one influences another and is influenced by him.[41]

Later he says:

> The individuals are not *in abstracto* conscious of forming a society, but everyone knows the other as sociated, even though this knowledge of the other as sociated, this apprehension of the total complex as a society, may be consummated only in separate, concrete contents.[42]

We are given to understand that the forms of sociation have a peculiar mode of existence. Although they inhere in the individual action systems and perform a function for them, they differ in origin and function from their contents. The content bears a relation to actions which is such that the latter correspond materially to the former. Emotions, feelings, beliefs, interests, dispositions, instincts, and similar individual qualities can each be considered an adequate cause for action. This is not true for reciprocal orientations. Generally speaking, they are not and cannot become individual ends. This can be illustrated by a reference to Simmel's essay "Superordination and Subordination" where he points out that the societal form of superordination designates, among other things, a readiness on the part of the superordinate to be bound by his own dictates. This is not an end of the superordinate, however, nor is the allegiance and obedience which he owes his master an end of the subordinate. These are "moments" of their relation or interaction which are rooted in their reciprocal orientations. They do not explain particular actions—in the way in which love, hunger, or other contents do—but they are operative in the interaction process.

What Simmel had in mind when he made the distinction between form and content can be clarified, perhaps, by a paraphrase of his arguments. Analysis of an action can ascertain certain causes which lie behind the act. The friendly act of a person toward another may be found, for instance, to stem from love. But love, Simmel would insist, can at best explain why the act was a friendly (and not, for example, an unfriendly) one, for love can express itself in a large variety of actions. If we study the actual behavior of people, we recognize that not all content that could be actualized, is actualized. And what does become actual does not find expression at random from the totality of potential actions which are adequate as far as content is concerned: the action displays a pattern. People do not choose their ends from the full theoretical potential of expressions. Contents are a priori limited in their expression, for they find expression only "in or through"[43] forms, that is, through reciprocal orientations. In contrast to content, forms cannot be found by analyzing a single action. Simmel speaks of a "synopsis"[44] of the course of events as yielding the forms of sociation. Thus he advises us to inspect the sequence of paired states of action systems (a-b, a′-b′, a″-b″, . . .), not for some common quality they possess distributively, but for a pattern or structure which reveals the stable reciprocities in their interaction.

Simmel has been severely criticized for his form-content terminology. It is undoubtedly awkward, but this must not obscure the fact that, in a way, it very aptly sums up the core of the distinction to which he wishes to call attention. It is the contents that seek expression and realization. They are, so to speak, the force or energy which receive their direction and structure in and through the reciprocal orientations. Both are located in the individual mind, but in entirely different ways.

If forms and contents constitute an inseparable entity in reality, the problem arises of how the forms can be studied. Simmel discusses this methodological problem in his program.[45] His first point in this discussion is that there exists, at present, no teachable method, no set of rules, for separating form from content. His second point is to recommend the use of what might be called the method of comparison: he suggests the comparative study of the forms in complexes of widely different content. Our interest here is not in either of these points but in his third and basic thesis: that the forms must be "abstracted" from reality.

It is at this point that what we have called the formalistic interpretation of Simmel's sociology launched its attack, led conspicuously and effectively by Sorokin. In Sorokin's view, the program of Simmel's formal sociology must result in "a purely scholastic and dead science, a kind of almost useless catalogue of human relations."[46] It "studies the most general characteristics of social phenomena."[47] Another critic, Abel, writes: "Form is identical then with the generalized aspects of society."[48] This interpretation which sees formal sociology as a classificatory and merely analytic science is based on Simmel's assertions that the forms must be "abstracted" from reality. And the belief that they are merely abstract and generalized aspects must inevitably result in the standard reproach that Simmel's program places undue limitations on sociology that cut from it "its other more vital parts."[49]

However, Simmel is not understood by such hasty interpretation. When he speaks of abstracting the forms of sociation from reality, he does not plead for the establishment of categories of a high degree of abstractness (all concepts are, of course, abstract in varying degrees). His emphasis is not on the abstract character of the forms of sociation but on the process of abstracting them. It is this which poses a peculiar problem. The forms inhere in the totality of reality. They have no separate existence. How then can they be studied?

Simmel not only admits that the content often or always

modifies the forms of sociation,[50] he explicitly postulates that "the historical facts which guarantee the actuality of the defined societal forms must be cited in their totality."[51] Forms can be demonstrated only in an arrangement of contents, the "synopsis" of which makes them perceptible. Abstraction for Simmel is not—it could not be—abstraction from content-*phenomena,* in which the forms inhere and through which alone they can be set forth, but abstraction from a content-*perspective.* He is anxious to warn us against the formalistic misunderstanding when he points out that forms of sociation must be considered in their concrete realizations, rather than on the basis of the "general" characteristics which their contents manifest.[52] The forms are by no means generalizations which retain only the most common characteristics of all contents. Science has long since developed teachable methods of studying them in this sense. In abstracting forms, one does not simply disregard the non-common elements in the contents in order to arrive at the most general, but rather empty and "formal," characteristics. Forms are not general concepts arrived at by generalization and abstraction, and formal sociology is not the analysis of such general concepts. "Abstracting" must be understood in the radical sense of extracting or extricating from reality something which is not a directly observable and common element in it. In abstracting the forms of sociation, the wealth of phenomena is no more disregarded or repressed than in any other science.

Simmel's program does not rule out content. All it asks is that reality be viewed, not with regard to inherent content, but with regard to its forms. Sociology is offered as the study of the entire realm of sociocultural phenomena; but it must relate them to its proper object, that is, the forms of sociation. The scope of sociology, as a special social science, is in no way limited. It gets its name, not from a restriction of its material, but from the perspective applied to it. It may draw on all facts, not adding them up for what they are worth within the frames of other fields (psychology and economics, for example), but extracting from them their social forms. "Not its object but its manner of contemplation, the peculiar abstraction which it performs, differentiates it from the other historico-social sciences."[53]

In his concrete investigations, Simmel does practice the method he designed in his program, and he does not overstep any of the fictitious limitations which the formalistic misunderstanding has read into this program.

There is another aspect which must be mentioned. For Simmel, no true theory of form seemed feasible. "There is never in existence 'society' in an absolute sense . . . but merely particular species of the same."[54] Sociology is the study of the forms, but it cannot study form per se. Later we shall touch on the broader significance of this statement. It suffices here to say that the lack of rigor in Simmel's sociology is partly a consequence of his dismissal of a theory of form. Lacking such a theory, he could set forth the general meaning of form only by analogy.

In spite of Simmel's fundamental unity of thought and a remotely familiar note struck by some of his arguments, modern readers may find formal sociology something of an archaism. One reason for this may be that the terminology of the social sciences has changed with the advances that have been made since Simmel wrote. Terminologies have a way of absorbing the attention of people to such a degree that even the truly imaginative find it hard to recognize statements for what they are once their apparel has been changed. It is necessary, therefore, to relate Simmel's arguments to modern sociology—not to any particular system or problem, but to the field in general—in such a way as to enable a contemporary reader to realize how extremely modern Simmel's approach is. That quality which makes reading Simmel such a captivating and fascinating experience may then be less puzzling.

The basic problems of formal sociology are still with us. One such problem is to reach an understanding of social action. Simmel pointed out that, sociologically, interaction is more than the sum of actors pursuing their individual goals while being influenced by such favorable or unfavorable moments as the action systems of other actors may represent. Social action contains some unity of the actors. Simmel's argument is fully alive in Florian Znaniecki's approach to social action:

> A real objective social connection between two agents, not merely between two actions, is made only when those agents rise above the one-sidedness of their separate points of view as agents, so as to create together a mutuality of experience and activity which did not exist originally.[55]

The second essential point in formal sociology—the discrimination between form and content as two different aspects of action—is discussed in Talcott Parsons' theory of social action:

> The scheme, that is relative to the units of action and interaction, is a *relational* scheme. It analyzes the structure and processes of the systems built up by the relations of such units to their situations, including other units. It is not as such concerned with the *internal* structure of the units except so far as this directly bears on the relational system.[56]

Even more pointedly, he says:

> In the most general sense the "need-disposition" system of the individual actor seems to have two most primary or elementary aspects which may be called the "gratificational" aspect and the "orientational" aspect. The first concerns the "content" of his interchange with the object world, "what" he gets out of his interaction with it, and what its "costs" to him are. The second concerns the "how" of his relation to the object world, the patterns or ways in which his relations to it are organized.[57]

Whatever differences may exist between formal sociology and Parsons' system otherwise, the distinction he draws here between the two aspects coincides in essence with Simmel's distinction between content and form.

It can, indeed, be maintained "that the problems raised by men like Simmel and Durkheim are still far from settled."[58] But there is a still more fundamental way in which Simmel's approach can be considered as being part of modern sociology. Kurt H. Wolff says of Simmel's system: "It is close to the modern concern with 'social structure.' "[59] Modern sociology has developed an elaborate system of concepts for describing social structure in general; the concepts of status, role, typical expectations, typical actions, and norms are foremost among these. In principle, the forms of sociation are specific roles, statuses, and norms, viewed as reciprocities and as they occur in historical complexes. Conversely, the theory of social structure is merely a theory of form per se.

As explained above, Simmel declared that such a theory was impossible on the ground that only specific forms exist, not form as such. In describing specific forms, he made extensive use of such concepts as "role," "position," and "norm"; but having denied the possibility of a general theory of form, he failed to perceive the significance of these concepts for a general theory of social structure and was forced to introduce his program for a study of the structure of society (in the broadest sense) by analogy, rather than by systematic conceptualization. Modern sociology must not overlook the fact that Simmel was the first to apprehend and point to this peculiar "layer" or "aspect" of social reality. It continues to pay silent tribute to formal sociology by designating social structure as the principle object of sociology. Whether it deals with institutions or processes, the frame of reference is always structure; the study is made in terms of patterns of reciprocal behavior—roles, statuses, and norms. The "limitation" which Simmel placed on sociology has in fact been widely accepted.

Occasionally, Simmel speaks of "pure" forms of sociation. He uses this term—or, more often, various other terms containing the word *pure*—to refer to a complex idea which represents an important element—perhaps even the central element—of Simmel's thought.[60] An inarticulate formulation of his idea of "pure forms" appears in the programmatic essay: "This object, abstracted from reality, may be viewed . . . with reference to such laws, indifferent toward their realization in time and space, as reside purely in the objective structure of its elements."[61] Clarification of this peculiar statement may be found in the essay "Superordination and Subordination." In an attempt to justify an earlier theorem that certain forms of superordination go together with "leveling," he writes:

> It need hardly be mentioned that "leveling" must always be understood here as a wholly relative tendency with very limited possibilities of realization. A basic science of the forms of society must present concepts and concept complexes in a purity and

> abstract completeness which are never shown by the historical realizations of their contents. Yet sociological understanding aims at grasping the fundamental concept of sociation in its particular significances and formations; it aims at analyzing phenomenal complexes into their minute factors to the point of approaching inductive regularities. It can do so only through the auxiliary construction of so-to-speak absolute lines and figures which in actual social life are found only as beginnings and fragments, as partial realizations that are constantly interrupted and modified. In every single social-historical configuration, there operates a number of reciprocities among the elements, which can probably never wholly be enumerated. . . . Sociological cognition so transforms historical phenomena that their unity is decomposed into a number of concepts and syntheses which are defined in a purely one-sided manner and which run, as it were, in a straight line. As a rule, one of these catches the main characteristic of the historical phenomenon under analysis. By bending and limiting each other mutually, all of them together project its image with increasing exactness upon the new plane of abstraction.[62]

Now the idea is clear: the forms, which are found in reality, are not "pure" forms. A multitude of forms are present in every social situation as a historical phenomenon, and each limits the realization of the other. Consequently, only "distorted" forms can be discovered in reality. This situation urgently poses the question of how, this being the case, can sociology ever learn about the "pure" forms. Simmel answers that it must exaggerate certain characteristics of the historical phenomenon to the point where they become "absolute lines and figures," so that they can be defined "in a purely one-sided manner." This method, which was heralded by the programmatic essay, is no longer strictly empirical-inductive. Although it starts with the "social-historical reality," it must finally rely on something else for selecting and exaggerating features of that reality in order to bring out the inherent, structural order of the elements involved. Forms, then, are not merely generalized aspects of "observed" reality and must not be mistaken for general, inductive concepts—notwithstanding their relation to reality. Far from merely mirroring reality, they also render it intelligible to us. The relations among the elements have an "evidence" of their own, and, consequently, their validity does not depend on how often they have found expression in historical reality. In a way, the idea finds a mature expression in the essay that followed "Superordination and Subordination." In "The Persistence of Social Groups," Simmel writes: "It is inevitable that sociology, as an abstract science, can never exhaust the full wealth and complexity of historical reality by the typical relations which it describes."[63] Simmel follows this passage with the reassertion that the typical relations which sociology ascertains are not of the strictly general, inductive kind, and ends by characterizing sociology as a "cognition of typical laws."[64]

There can be little doubt that here is the distinct notion of what has become known as the "ideal-type." Max Weber could not and did not claim to be the first to employ ideal-types, but he is usually given credit for being the first to delineate the true character of the concept and—on the basis of his delineation—to recommend its use in sociology and other branches of the human studies.[65] His methodological treatment of ideal-types is more elaborate, careful, specific, and complete than Simmel's discussions of pure forms. Weber distinguishes between merely heuristic ideal-types and those designed to capture the actual orientations of people, and he warns against the reification of the heuristic concepts. In substance, however, his undertaking is hardly larger than Simmel's, for Simmel asserts that sociology needs concepts which are abstracted from features of historical reality and exaggerated in certain respects so as to bring out configurations and relations which underlie reality but are not fully actualized in it. Such concepts limit one another's actualizations; they carry some intrinsic evidence of their own and are not automatically invalidated by incongruous facts; and they are not simply generalized aspects of reality, although they have an inductive basis. Both Simmel and Weber believe that no strictly logical and teachable method for developing such concepts can be devised.[66]

It appears that the idea of "pure concepts" evolved throughout the course of Simmel's sociological work.[67] It occupies a central position in "The Persistence of Social Groups" and continues to unfold and grow from that point on. In *Philosophie des Geldes,* which Weber read shortly before he wrote his own first programmatic essay,[68] Simmel anticipates the method of the entire book in the Preface and later states it explicitly:

> Innumerable times, we form our concepts of objects in such a manner that experience can show no equivalent of their pure and absolute character; they gain an empirical form only in being weakened and limited by opposing concepts. . . . This peculiar method of exaggerating and reducing concepts yields knowledge of the world which is commensurate with our mode of cognition. . . . Our intellect can grasp reality only by limitations of pure concepts which, no matter how far they deviate from reality, prove their legitimacy by the service they render for the interpretation of it.[69]

When Simmel finally undertook a somewhat methodological treatment of this central idea, he did so in his customarily oblique way, and, moreover, he immersed it in a comprehensive analysis of history.[70] At the time, Weber had just published his own outline of ideal-types in "Die Objektivität sozialwissenschaftlicher und sozialpolitischer Erkenntnis."

It might be argued that Weber would never have considered applying the method of ideal-types to such a topic as money. This is true enough. Weber narrowed the range of application of ideal-types to historically circumscribed phenomena, and in doing so he may have lodged an implicit criticism of Simmel, particularly of his laxity in the use of terminology. But this is, at least partially, a deceptive summary of the situation. By the time he wrote *Philosophie des Geldes,* Simmel had become accustomed to referring to historically circumscribed phenomena by means of pure concepts. When he speaks of "the objective spirit of modern marriage"[71] and of "the metropolitan type of individuality" or "metropolitan man,"[72] he is well aware of using such concepts. Furthermore, Weber never actually restricted the method of ideal-types to the characterization of unique historical complexes, but seems to have planned and used it to ascertain functional laws and relations.[73] Therefore, though there are differences, the range of application of pure concepts is basically and systematically identical in both Simmel's formal and Weber's *verstehende* sociology.

The community of ideas between Simmel and Weber is not

confined to their agreement concerning the pure concepts. In spite of conspicuous differences in style, thought, terminology, and presentation, and differences in degrees of precision, explicitness, and elaboration, the fundamental understandings and frames of reference of formal and *verstehende* sociology are very similar—perhaps, identical. It has been noticed that Weber's types of social action have their counterpart in formal sociology.[74] In addition, Weber's definition of social action[75] exhibits the understanding of function which Simmel had introduced in his idea of interaction. And, like Simmel, Weber sees the regularities of behavior rooted in reciprocal orientations.[76] Like Simmel, he is anxious to exclude all merely identical behavior ("parallel," "statistical" phenomena)[77] from social action. Like Simmel, he frees sociology from psychology.[78] The principal identity of viewpoint can be found in Weber's repeated comments that the same social action may be performed by various actors for entirely different reasons—this is the very argument on which Simmel had based his distinction between form and content.[79]

Aside from his concrete investigations, Weber's contributions to sociology appear to lie in his discriminating systematization and conceptualization, and in the establishment of operational criteria, rather than in the development of new basic understandings. Among other things, the introduction of such concepts as "chances" or "expectations," together with the systematic and controlled use of them, and the investigation of the connections between *verstehen* and causal analysis, mark Weber's achievements in the field of methodology; and from them, sociology, including his own concrete investigations, has profited enormously. What Simmel had deemed impossible, a theory of form in general, emerged in Weber's work.

Whatever the relations between the two men may have been, they should be placed in historical perspective, and should be related, above all, to the issue which Heinrich Rickert, more than anybody else, had forced on German science at the turn of the century. Rickert's rigid belief that only the natural sciences were capable of ascertaining laws was widely shared, and, in consequence of it, the "cultural" sciences were limited to the treatment of unique historical phenomena. This limitation excluded any generalizing sociology from their ranks. In view of this historical context, it seems strange that Weber so openly acknowledged his indebtedness to Rickert, whereas his references to "my friend Simmel"[80] are rather perfunctory or dilatory, often fastening on minor points in Simmel's works.[81] It could be that Weber's sense of meticulous scholarship and his distaste for anything that lacked precision or was reminiscent of intuition led him to underestimate Simmel's value to systematic sociology.[82] Unfortunately, Weber's tribute to Rickert placed him in opposition to Simmel and, moreover, to sociology. There could be no mistaking this at a time when one issue kept all German scholars under its spell. Simmel, in open defiance of the dichotomy which Rickert and others had imposed on the entire realm of German scholarship—the rigorous distinction between natural (generalizing) and "cultural" (individualizing) sciences, a distinction which made sociology a historical discipline—had written: "If the alternative to which nowadays every science is put is whether it aims at finding eternally valid laws or at describing and understanding single historically real processes, . . . then the necessity of a decision does not apply to the problem as here posed."[83] This leads directly to the later characterization of sociology as the cognition of "typical laws."

However, in spite of his recurrent recognition of Rickert's system, Weber assumed the very position taken by Simmel. Sociology was expected to find typical relations. Indeed, Weber's thought has, at best, a thin veneer of Rickert's philosophy; and Rickert himself, in spite of his efforts to show Weber's dependence on his philosophy, was forced to admit it eventually.[84]

As Simmel's sociology emerged in his series of papers, the term "forms" came more and more to stand for an ideal-type of reciprocal orientations. His terminology was changing. The word *Typus,* which he adopted as a synonym for *Form* in the late 1890's, occupies a prominent place in *Philosophie des Geldes;* and in his *Soziologie, Typus* and *Formtypus* have largely replaced *Form.* This conception of forms as ideal-types implies a particular view of their ontological status, which sets them off distinctly from generalized and abstract concepts. Throughout his major sociological works—the two just mentioned and the 1905 edition of *Die Probleme der Geschichtsphilosophie*—Simmel vindicates the "dignity" of the forms of sociation.[85] In recurring statements, he extends their validity beyond the strictly empirical realm.

Simmel speaks of two aspects of the dignity of the forms. In the first, as explained in "The Persistence of Social Groups," it resides in the fact that forms are superior to individual existences and are not subject to individual wills because they persist while individuals come and go. This persistence of the forms and the irrelevance of the individuals involved in them do not result from some supra-individual force, but are accounted for by the nature of group interaction. Since they are operative in all members of a group, the reciprocities cannot be changed by them at will. There are other reasons, but their "dignity" is deceptive: they reflect only the individual's limitations and do not explain the persistence of the forms.[86]

Most of the time, however, when discussing this peculiar status of the forms, Simmel is referring to the second aspect, the authentic dignity, which lies in the "objective structure" of their elements. This structure is independent of its historical realizations.[87] Forms, in this sense, represent typical laws. Certain elements go together. They "fit." These "objective" clusters can refer to simultaneous elements or to sequences of elements. To use an earlier example: In certain types of superordination, there exists a tendency toward "leveling." The absence of this tendency indicates that there is either an obstacle to the full realization of the ideal-type or a lack of other "typical" elements of the constellation, in which case a different type of superordination must be found to reveal the "fit" of the co-existing, essential elements.[88]

Although this may strike a modern reader as a "philosophical"—if not outright "metaphysical" and "speculative"—idea, it is nonetheless not wholly foreign to contemporary sociology. Max Weber, in spite of his insistence on causal analysis as a check on the meaningful relations of elements which are claimed to inhere in an ideal-type, urged sociology to derive the laws of social reality from "type-concepts," that is, from constellations of elements whose "fit" can be demonstrated by their meanings.[89] The same principle, however, can also be found to underlie all functional approaches. If the elements of social structure are not independent of each other, then it must be possible, within limits, to determine from a number of them something about the rest.

Simmel is not unaware of the limitations of this method. In his investigations he points out repeatedly that a given typical constellation of elements, though tending to go with certain other elements, may also be found with different ones, depending on which additional phenomena in the situation may change the "functional" value and meaning of the elements. The "objective structure" of a form of sociation is always provisional; and for this reason he denies the status of natural laws to the "laws" inherent in the typical forms of sociation.[90]

What, then, is the ontological status of the forms of sociation? For the mature Simmel, they have come to mean typical clusters of reciprocal orientations whose "objective structure" rests on the affinity which the orientations possess by virtue of the meanings they have for the actors. They are neither generalized aspects of social reality nor merely heuristic principles but are operative in the actors, as we saw before. As Simmel points out in the second chapter of the second edition of *Die Probleme der Geschichtsphilosophie,* they must not, on the other hand, be considered adequate causes of action. They have an empirical basis; but because of their inherent "objective structure," they must be given a status above that of merely empirical generalizations.

The characteristics of the forms may be presented in a summary statement as follows: Forms represent a specific "layer" of reality. Although they cannot—and are not meant to—account for interaction itself, they are operative in it; they account for its patterns. They exert constraint in the structuring of actions, but they do not do so only in that they are found directly operative in a social situation: if a form of sociation is certain elements-in-relation, then the recurrence of some of these elements must indicate the recurrence of the others, unless it can be demonstrated that some of the relevant conditions have changed and that, consequently, a different form of sociation is in question. In addition, if forms have an inherent tendency in time to result in certain new configurations, then a similar process will be repeated upon each occurrence of the initial form. In that they recurrently bring about typical situations and typical changes, forms provide a basis upon which predictions can be made.[91]

Boskoff is correct in writing that "the forms of sociation cannot be justly characterized as unreal, empty . . . for they are derived from an analysis of empirical phenomena."[92] But this must not lead to the belief that they are merely generalizations or heuristic concepts for the organization of data. Forms are reciprocal orientations which go with typical situations; and typical situations are obviously assumed to transcend, in their radical meaning, any particular culture—that is, no culture is entirely free to "define" typical situations. This constitutes, in the end, the "dignity" of the forms of sociation; it is this that gives them a validity which is independent of their historical frequency.

There is an elusive yet important difference between formal sociology and the predominant contemporary sociology. The latter conceives of itself as the study of society, and society is explained, by and large, in terms of roles, statuses, and norms. Curiously enough, these specific roles, statuses, and norms are in turn explained in terms of society; they are acquired in the process of socialization and are made strong by rewards and punishments. The emphasis of modern sociology lies on this socialization into given roles. In a way, then, modern sociology is predominantly concerned with a description of the structure of society as a going and persisting phenomenon.[93] The individual appears largely as a mere functionary in society, for the structural pattern is conceived as a social system, and society, as such a system, is the object of investigation and the ultimate unit of reference.

By contrast, the prime object of investigation for Simmel is sociation. It is given priority over society in his system. According to Simmel, sociology cannot directly study society as a unit, as a social system, but must investigate the forms of sociation. Society is a composite of these forms of sociation,[94] and they must be understood in and by themselves, and not merely as functional ingredients of an inclusive system. It has been remarked that Simmel does not clearly distinguish between group and society.[95] This is not an oversight on his part. The distinction is incidental to an approach which makes the forms of sociation, rather than society as a social system, the object of analysis. In order to understand social reality, we must not interpret phenomena as functional variables or as elements of a system, but must ascertain those basic possibilities of reciprocal orientation which underlie social reality and structure interaction. The forms of sociation stand in their own right and must be studied in their own right; they have independent force and meaning in and of themselves, even though their observable effect may be obscured by limitations inherent in the composite character of society. Simmel considers it fallacious to assume that

> all these forms—hierarchies and corporations, competitions and forms of marriage, friendships and customs of sociability— . . . merely occur as moments in already existing societies. . . . This idea is prompted by the fact that in every known society a great number of such forms of union, that is, of sociation, are operative. Consequently, if a single one of these disappeared, "society" would still remain. . . . But if we eliminate in thought *all* these particular forms, no society remains.[96]

This approach may tend to minimize the effects which culture or society, as a system, has on all of its parts. On the other hand, it is a safeguard against any reification of society and, moreover, against the temptation to restrict sociological analysis to the description of how a social structure persists. In the delineation of its object of investigation, formal sociology heeds the fundamental problem of how forms originate. It matters little that Simmel provides no definitive answer when he explicitly deals with the question in "How Is Society Possible?" What is of real interest is that the choice of object makes formal sociology, in principle, immune to the predicament that plagues much of modern sociology, that is, the conspicuous cleavage between the theory of social structure and the theory of social change. Alvin Boskoff has recently pointed out the bewildering aspects of this situation.[97] The source of the dilemma does not lie in the fact that the concept of social structure as such eludes the understanding of the dynamics of social life, but in the fact that social structure is, in the main, conceived of as the mechanism for the persistence of groups and the transmission of culture. The theory of social structure has tended to become a theory of social statics, failing to explain social change or even systematically to allow for its possibility. In some textbooks, the cursory treatment of social change is found to relapse into a discourse on naïve common-sense concepts which beg the problem by locating the cause of change in, for example, "social movements," for which there can be no systematic accounting within a theory of social structure that is confined to the static aspect of society.

Formal sociology does not encounter these difficulties. Simmel knows of socialization and cultural learning; he is in no way blind to the fact that many forms of sociation are institutionalized. Fundamentally, however, sociation does not so much refer to those reciprocities which "society," in one way or another, inculcates in its members as to those which originate in interaction. Simmel urges sociology to consider the seemingly negligible forms of sociation, as they occur in everyday life, in addition to the crystallized and organized patterns of interaction. By this recommendation in the programmatic essay, he is not suggesting a merely quantitative extension of the field of investigation, and any interpretation of it as such misses an essential point.[98] For Simmel, these negligible forms have priority inasmuch as they retain what is spontaneous in sociation. His major emphasis lies on the process in which sociation emerges, not on that in which a given form of sociation persists. Forms represent society in its *status nascendi,* as Simmel put it, not in regard to its beginning in time but to the continuous spontaneity through which it is sustained.[99]

Forms develop in interaction. And this means not only that a form originates in the process of interaction and subsequently restrains and structures the actors' behavior, but also that the actors "add" elements to, or "subtract" elements from, established forms. For Simmel, the actors never lose this spontaneity, this influence on forms. The forms thus have a dual character, at once superior to the actors and subject to them. They operate on the actors, and the actors operate on them. This duality is particularly striking in Simmel's analyses of those forms in which the typical relations of the elements, and the typical tendencies inherent in them, are almost invariably based on the spontaneity of the actors, who are shown to adopt or drop practices and institutions for what seem to be reasons of their own. To illustrate by the example used earlier: Leveling, as a tendency inherent in a specific form of sociation, rests on the desire of the superordinate to prevent the rise of groups that would challenge him. A minimum of attention in reading Simmel's analysis reveals that motives, interests, and so on, appear as the true moving forces.[100] However, in following their interests and motives, the individuals actually comply with the forms.

This dual character of the forms of sociation is deceptive. The form "rule-by-one," for example, contains, as a typical ingredient, the tendency towards leveling and can thus be said to compel the ruler to abide by it. But there is, of course, such a form only because, among other things, the ruler can understand that the situation demands it. It is possible for forms to operate on individual actors only because the actors "understand" the situation. Forms are the latent reciprocities of typical situations. And the "understanding" of a situation, that is, the grasping of its essential and typical features, is, for Simmel, not restricted to those situations which culture has revealed to the actors as typical. Formal sociology rests on the assumption that meaningful action can originate in the individuals. It is this assumption which allows for the peculiar understanding of society in which man is at once object and subject, an understanding of society which grasps it in its static and dynamic aspects at the same time.

By the very nature of its approach, formal sociology has an affinity to the dynamic aspect of social reality. Since the component elements, the forms of sociation, are not viewed as variables of a given social system on which they are fundamentally dependent, society is not conceived of as an inert body seeking solely to maintain itself in the status quo. Forms express not only existing reciprocal orientations but also offer fundamental possibilities of social interactions as they originate, develop, and change. In this respect, they provide a basis for making predictions, and formal sociology seems close to being a full-fledged theory of social change.

Actually, however, the predictive value of the forms of sociation is limited. Since society is a composite phenomenon, historical reality is never exhausted by any specific form; a number of forms are always operative in reality and we cannot fully reconstruct reality as a combination of them.[101] Consequently, although the forms are instruments of prediction by virtue of their ontological status, their actual use as such is restricted. They cannot be applied to society as a whole, as a system, but only to specified aspects of it. If only one form were operative in society, we could predict actual social change. But not knowing precisely the relative contribution of any specific form, we can only assert that the presence of that form makes for a certain tendency which is part of the social situation. As Simmel usually puts it, the pure forms underlie social reality without ever being fully realized, since the various forms which make up this reality limit one another's actualizations. In formal sociology, social change means tendencies in specified aspects of society. Formal sociology is incompetent to deal with the problem of a change of society itself, a change of the whole system. It cannot be otherwise, for it refuses to regard society, as conceived of as such a system, as its proper object.

On the other hand, as is well known, Simmel subscribed to broad theories of historical change, that is, to theories of the long-term changes of social systems. In the main, they are a peculiar and interesting variety of Tönnies' thesis with its emphasis on the historical growth of differentiation and the increase of rationality. We are not interested in Simmel's concrete views of historical change, as set forth in his early *Über sociale Differenzierung,* and later, with slight modifications, in *Philosophie des Geldes*. Rather, we ask how this theorizing can be reconciled with the restriction in matters of social change that he places on formal sociology.

The answer is that the problem of historical change, that is, the problem of how to account for the changes of society as a whole, is assigned to a branch of inquiry which borders on formal sociology and into which it blends, namely, philosophical sociology or the philosophy of history.[102] This investigation differs from historical analysis, which is causal analysis. The historian, who wants to explain historical facts with the intention of arriving at a general knowledge of historical processes, must array the phenomena in their causal connections. It is this strictly empirical and generalizing approach which part of modern sociology believes to be the solution to the problem of social change.[103] While Simmel considers this approach legitimate, he sees no hope that it can ever truly replace philosophical sociology. As he sees it—and here I can merely indicate the central principle of his argument—a theory of historical change transcends empirical generalizations since it must engage in operations other than causal analysis. We cannot locate, for example, in a less differentiated and earlier period any general cause of subsequent differentiation. All we find are specific causes of specific events which somehow add up to that differentiation. Modern sociology, aware of the elusive character of concepts by which historical changes can be grasped, has urged abstention from speculation in the hope that empirical generalizations and causal analyses, based on controlled observation and experimentation, will eventually fill the vacuum and furnish a satisfactory theory of historical change. Simmel would have found fault with this attitude. For him, philosophical sociology was not merely speculative (for him, this word had little of the derogatory meaning it has since acquired). He conceded that the "laws" of change which philosophical sociology could formulate did not state causes, but he would have rejected the view that they were entirely without empirical foundation. Rather, he regarded them as a peculiar kind of abstraction, capable of summing up the course of events on the level of general configurations. It is not an approach *faute de mieux,* but stands in its own right.[104] And he would have considered it unreasonable to assume that more observational data and greater rigor in experimentation would lead to a causal theory of social change.

Simmel's position, which hands over the problem of social change in its historical dimensions to an ally and complement of formal sociology—philosophical sociology—may strike modern readers as the metaphysician's evasion of empirical issues. But it might also be considered a sobering view, guarding against the evasiveness of a position which expects the formulation of laws of historical change from continuing, comparatively untheoretical experimentation and the collection of data.

1. Nicholas S. Timasheff, *Sociological Theory, Its Nature and Growth* (New York: Doubleday & Company, Inc., 1955), p. 99. What we object to here is the tendency to regard formal sociology as a collection of scattered, intuitive—even brilliant—insights, which have, however, no foundation in Simmel's theory.

2. "General Sociological Theories of Current Reference," in *Modern Sociological Theory in Continuity and Change,* ed. Howard Becker and Alvin Boskoff (New York: Dryden Press, 1957), p. 82.

3. For an early expression of this criticism, see Pitirim Sorokin, *Contemporary Sociological Theories* (New York and London: Harper & Brothers, 1928), pp. 513 f., *passim.* For another recent version, see Samuel Koenig, *Man and Society* (New York: Barnes & Noble, Inc., 1957), p. 250.

4. *Systematic Sociology in Germany* (New York: Columbia University Press, 1929), p. 44, *passim.*

5. See, for example, Sorokin, *op. cit.,* pp. 495, 499, 503, 513; Raymond Aron, *German Sociology* ([1936] London: William Heinemann, Ltd., 1957), pp. 5-8; and Logan Wilson, "Sociology of Groups," in *Twentieth Century Sociology,* ed. Georges Gurvitch and Wilbert E. Moore (New York: Philosophical Library, 1945), p. 144.

6. Timasheff, *op. cit.,* p. 102.

7. Sorokin, *op. cit.,* p. 513.

8. For a brief account of the evolution of Simmel's thought, see Maria Steinhoff, "Die Form als soziologische Grundkategorie bei Georg Simmel," *Kölner Vierteljahrshefte für Soziologie,* IV (1925), 215-59. Since Simmel's major sociological work, *Soziologie. Untersuchungen über die Formen der Vergesellschaftung* (Leipzig: Duncker und Humblot, 1908), is a republication of earlier works which have been reworked, there is no critical edition of this work, and this makes a definitive interpretation of Simmel's sociology impossible. Cf. Kurt H. Wolff (ed.), *The Sociology of Georg Simmel* (Glencoe, Ill.: Free Press of Glencoe, Illinois, 1950), p. xxxiii.

9. I am not concerned with the question of whether or not von Wiese's system is in substantive accord with formal sociology. My concern is that the dominant interpretation of von Wiese's system has tended to reinforce what I have designated as the formalistic misunderstanding of Simmel's sociology. No attempt will be made to prove this point in the present

paper, however. As to Weber, I shall deal later with one particular aspect of the relation between formal and *verstehende* sociology.

10. The connection between this issue and Simmel's reception has been unfortunate. The difficulty lies in the fact that the term "general social science" has two meanings. Simmel rejected the use of the term to designate an enterprise which was expected to integrate the findings of all "cultural" studies, but he did not intend to confine sociology, as a special social science, to only a portion of social phenomena. What is "general" about sociology for him is that it studies what is *social* in all social phenomena. Sociology is a "special" social science, for Simmel, in that it abstracts from certain material aspects which are studied by the other social sciences. Albion W. Small found it difficult to understand this position, as may be seen from the comments with which he freely accompanied his translation of Simmel's essay, "Das Problem der Soziologie" ("The Problem of Sociology," *American Journal of Sociology,* XV [1909], 289-320; in this volume, see pp. 310-36). The confusion is still with us. Drawing on Sorokin, Robert Bierstedt, on page 15 of his *The Social Order* (New York: McGraw-Hill Book Co., Inc., 1957), makes a point of proving that sociology is a general social science by arguing that it studies those phenomena that are common to all human interaction. This is Simmel's reason, precisely, for declaring sociology a special social science, that is, a science studying some specific aspect of all phenomena of interaction. It can easily be seen that this confusion has presented an important obstacle to an understanding of Simmel's sociology which began with the call for a special social science. Cf. *Soziologie,* p. 8 (in this volume, see p. 311).

Whenever possible I have used available translations; however, when the title is given in German, the translation is mine. Alternate references are placed in parentheses.

11. See Albert Salomon, "German Sociology," in Gurvitch and Moore, *op. cit.;* Rudolf Heberle, "The Sociology of Georg Simmel: The Forms of Interaction," in *An Introduction to the History of Sociology,* ed. Harry Elmer Barnes (Chicago: University of Chicago Press, 1948), pp. 249-73; and Wolff, *op. cit.*

12. Wolff, *op. cit.,* p. xxxix.

13. The term *form* not only figures in Simmel's sociological writings but also pervades his entire work. See Rudolph H. Weingartner's essay "Form and Content in Simmel's Philosophy of Life," pp. 33-60 in this volume.

14. Both Abel and Steinhoff have adopted this approach in the works mentioned above. Their failure to arrive at a correct understanding testifies to the danger of this method. It is strikingly obvious in Abel's book. On the basis of his classification of forms, he reaches the verdict that two kinds of forms exist which cannot be reconciled (pp. 30 ff., 46 ff.) without ever noticing that the discrepancy has been introduced by his own classification.

15. My major source is the programmatic discussion which Simmel offered in "Das Problem der Soziologie," in *Soziologie*.

16. Small, *op. cit.*, p. 295 (*Soziologie,* p. 4).

17. See Sorokin, *op. cit.*, pp. 495 ff. Cf. Wolff, *op. cit.*, p. xlvi, n. 32.

18. See Heberle, *op. cit.*, p. 264.

19. Cf. Steinhoff, *op. cit.*, pp. 218 ff. See also Leopold von Wiese, *Soziologie. Geschichte und Hauptprobleme* (Berlin: de Gruyter, 1950), p. 123. The remark that Simmel failed to develop a system is almost universal in accounts of Simmel's sociology. However, such a broad assertion does not sufficiently distinguish between the systematic idea underlying Simmel's sociology and the execution of this idea in a fully developed system.

20. Quoted in Wolff, *op. cit.*, p. xxvi.

21. *Ibid.*, p. xxxiii (*Soziologie,* p. 14 n.).

22. See Small, *op. cit.*, p. 309 (*Soziologie,* p. 13).

23. That is, "Das Problem der Soziologie," which will be referred to throughout as "Simmel's program" or as "Simmel's programmatic essay."

24. Cf. Wolff, *op. cit.*, pp. xxxii f., xxxv.

25. Cf. n. 19, above.

26. Cf. Simmel's own statements in *Soziologie,* pp. 3, 372, *passim.*

27. Cf. *Soziologie,* p. 422, and "The Problem of Sociology," *passim.*

28. The term "action system" has been adopted merely as a convenient conceptual tool with no intent to link it to, or identify it with, any of the modern approaches to a theory of action, such as that of Talcott Parsons.

29. *Soziologie,* pp. 18, 19 (Small, *op. cit.*, pp. 315 ff.).

30. Wolff, *op. cit.*, p. 182.

31. See *Soziologie,* pp. 5 f., 424 f. See also Georg Simmel, *Die Probleme der Geschichtsphilosophie. Eine erkenntnistheoretische Studie* (2nd rev. ed.; Leipzig: Duncker und Humblot, 1905), pp. 103 ff.

32. *Soziologie,* p. 22.

33. "[Sociation] is thus the form, actualizing itself in countless various types, in which individuals . . . grow together into a unity." Quoted from Small, *op. cit.*, p. 297 (*Soziologie,* p. 5). Cf. Albion W. Small (trans.), Georg Simmel's "How Is Society Possible?" *American Journal of Sociology,* XVI (1910), 372-91 (*Soziologie,* pp. 21-31; in this volume, see pp. 337-56).

34. *Soziologie,* p. 422.

35. *Ibid.*, p. 22 ("How Is Society Possible?" p. 373).

36. Sometimes Simmel speaks of the "spontaneity" of an "agreement"; at other times, of the fact that the actors are "conscious" of one another; and, at still others, of "synthesis." The uncertainty of his characterization of sociation derives from his belief that no basic theory of this form per se is possible.

37. Wolff, *op. cit.,* pp. 40 f. See also *Soziologie,* p. 5.

38. See Small, "The Problem of Sociology," pp. 297-99 (*Soziologie,* pp. 5-7). See also Heberle, *op. cit.,* p. 251. Heberle misses the point of Simmel's argument (which will be presently taken up in the text). As Heberle sees it, Simmel is concerned with what permits the isolation (by abstraction) of the forms of sociation. For Heberle, it is the fact that the same forms contain different contents, and vice versa, which makes such an isolation possible. For Simmel, however, the major problem is whether or not the distinction between form and content can be justified. The methodological question of "abstracting" the forms is discussed in *Soziologie,* pp. 11-13.

39. *Soziologie,* p. 5 (Small, "The Problem of Sociology," p. 297).

40. See Small, "The Problem of Sociology," *passim,* and "How Is Society Possible?" *passim.* See also *Soziologie,* pp. 402, 421 f., 461, 566 f.

41. *Soziologie,* p. 22.

42. *Ibid.,* p. 23.

43. *Ibid.,* p. 5 (Small, "The Problem of Sociology," p. 297).

44. *Soziologie,* p. 18 (Small, "The Problem of Sociology," p. 315).

45. *Soziologie,* pp. 11-13 (Small, "The Problem of Sociology," p. 306 ff.). Cf. n. 38, above.

46. Sorokin, *op. cit.,* p. 495. Cf. Aron, *op. cit.,* pp. 6, 8.

47. Sorokin, *op. cit.,* p. 501.

48. Abel, *op. cit.,* p. 27; cf. p. 30.

49. Sorokin, *op. cit.,* p. 313.

50. See *Soziologie,* pp. 8, 10, 451.

51. *Ibid.,* p. 12 (Small, "The Problem of Sociology," p. 307; cf. the statement on p. 304 that the form is "actualized through its contents.")

52. *Soziologie,* p. 10 (Small, "The Problem of Sociology," p. 304).

53. Small, "The Problem of Sociology," p. 301 (*Soziologie,* p. 8).

54. Small, "The Problem of Sociology," p. 303 (*Soziologie,* p. 10).

55. *Social Actions* (New York: Farrar & Rinehart, Inc., 1936), p. 121.

56. *The Social System* (Glencoe, Ill.: Free Press of Glencoe, Illinois, 1951), p. 4.

57. *Ibid.,* p. 7.

58. Reinhard Bendix, "Max Weber's Interpretation of Conduct and History," *American Journal of Sociology,* LI (1946), 518.

59. Wolff, *op. cit.,* p. xxxvi. Cf. Heberle, *op. cit.,* p. 258.

60. In "Fundamental Problems of Sociology" (contained in Wolff, *op. cit.,* pp. 1-84), the term "pure forms" has been divested of most of this earlier meaning and serves a different purpose. Simmel's silence on the problem of "pure concepts" may be interpreted as a reluctance to pursue his theory of pure concepts after Max Weber had become identified with the method of "ideal-types." In any case, his work of later years shows that he had not changed his fundamental position on the matter.

61. *Soziologie,* p. 10 (Small, "The Problem of Sociology," p. 305).

62. Wolff, *op. cit.,* p. 200 (*Soziologie,* pp. 113 f.).

63. *Soziologie,* p. 418 n. Cf. n. 67, below.

64. *Soziologie,* p. 418.

65. In his first programmatic essay, "Die Objektivität sozialwissenschaftlicher und sozialpolitischer Erkenntnis," *Archiv für Sozialwissenschaft und Sozialpolitik,* XIX (1904), 22-87. For a translation, see Edward A. Shils and Henry A. Finch (eds.), *Max Weber on the Methodology of the Social Sciences* (Glencoe, Ill.: Free Press of Glencoe, Illinois, 1949), pp. 50-112. Cf. Talcott Parsons, "The Contribution of Max Weber," in Barnes, *op. cit.,* p. 291.

66. Weber's positions on these matters can be seen in the essays "Die Objektivität sozialwissenschaftlicher und sozialpolitischer Erkenntnis" and "Über einige Kategorien der verstehenden Soziologie," *Logos,* IV (1913). For his discussion of the idea that the forms limit one another's actualizations, see Max Weber, *Gesammelte Aufsätze zur Religionssoziologie* (Tübingen: J. C. B. Mohr [Paul Siebeck], 1920), I, 273, 424 ff. See also Max Weber, *Gesammelte Aufsätze zur Wissenschaftslehre* (Tübingen: J. C. B. Mohr [Paul Siebeck], 1922), p. 521.

67. Simmel's *Soziologie* (1908) is, in substance, a collection of articles previously published during the period from 1890 to 1907. Not having access to all of his essays in their original versions, I cannot go beyond establishing the fact that Simmel had developed the nucleus of a theory of pure concepts prior to Weber's first outline of ideal-types. As far as I can ascertain now, the idea of pure concepts is entirely missing in Simmel's writings before 1896-97. At least, the translations of the early drafts of his essays which appeared in American journals show no clear understanding of the character of sociology as described by ideal-types, even though his insistence on "the abstract character of sociology" may have to be interpreted in light of a later passage from "The Persistence of Social Groups," *American Journal of Sociology,* III (1898), 691 n., where the nucleus of the idea of pure concepts is clearly and definitely recognizable.

68. H. H. Gerth and C. Wright Mills (eds.), *From Max Weber: Essays in Sociology* (New York: Oxford University Press, 1946), p. 14.

69. *Philosophie des Geldes* (Leipzig: Duncker and Humblot, 1900), p. 135. See also p. 552 and *passim.*

70. *Geschichtsphilosophie.*

71. *Philosophie des Geldes,* p. 497. Cf. *Soziologie,* p. 270.

72. Wolff, *op. cit.,* pp. 409, 411.

73. See Max Weber, *Gesammelte Aufsätze zur Wissenschaftslehre,* p. 520, and Alexander von Schelting, *Max Webers Wissenschaftslehre* (Tübingen: J. C. B. Mohr [Paul Siebeck], 1934).

74. Salomon, *op. cit.,* p. 600.

75. Weber, *Gesammelte Aufsätze zur Wissenschaftslehre,* pp. 405 ff.

76. *Ibid.,* pp. 408, 428.

77. *Ibid.,* p. 430.

78. *Ibid.,* pp. 408, 428, 430, 436. Simmel's and Weber's attempts to exclude psychology (including social psychology) from sociological analysis must be read in light of what they understood psychology to be and what psychology was at the time. This opposition to psychology on the part of Simmel does not necessarily conflict with the views of some interpreters who regard his sociology as a variety of social psychology.

79. *Ibid.,* pp. 404, 436, *passim.* As a matter of fact, the similarities between Simmel and Weber go much further than this; and I am not referring to those parts of Simmel's sociology—his view of differentiation, for example—which reflect, directly or indirectly, trends and assumptions common among German scholars at the time. Although we find this very same idea of differentiation in Weber, both men were here only participants in a broad stream of current thought. However, it is quite obvious that Weber's "Über einige Kategorien der verstehenden Soziolgie" is strongly influenced by Simmel. In fact, Sections V and VI of this paper are hardly more than a systematization of Simmel's basic understandings and terminology; they freely borrow some of Simmel's characteristic teachings, such as that concerning conflict.

80. Gerth and Mills, *op. cit.,* p. 115.

81. See the many references to Simmel, mostly in footnotes, throughout *Gesammelte Aufsätze zur Wissenschaftslehre.* For an instance of the dilatory character of these references, see p. 97. For an example of Weber's criticism of irrelevant points, see p. 76, where he attacks a statement of Simmel's, the true significance of which he is unaware because he has disregarded the context in which it is made.

82. See *Gesammelte Aufsätze zur Wissenschaftslehre,* p. 403, n. 1. See also Max Weber, *Grundriss der Sozialökonomik,* III. *Abteilung: Wirtschaft und Gesellschaft* (Tübingen: J. C. B. Mohr [Paul Siebeck], 1925), p. 1.

83. *Soziologie,* p. 10 (Small, "The Problem of Sociology," p. 305).

84. Heinrich Rickert, *Die Grenzen der naturwissenschaftlichen Begriffsbildung* (Tübingen: J. C. B. Mohr [Paul Siebeck], 1929), pp. xxiii f., and Rickert, "Max Weber und seine Stellung zur Wissenschaft," *Logos,* XV (1926), 222-37.

85. *Soziologie,* pp. 10, 422 f., 418 n., *passim.* Cf. *Geschichtsphilosophie,* p. 107 f.

86. *Soziologie,* pp. 376 ff.

87. See n. 85, above.

88. Simmel sets forth this idea in terms of such concepts as "dualism" or "polarity." Cf. *Soziologie,* pp. 536 f., 134, 188, 569, *passim.*

89. Weber, *Gesammelte Aufsätze zur Wissenschaftslehre,* p. 520.

90. *Soziologie,* p. 152, *passim.*

91. The use of the forms for making predictions is limited. Historical laws cannot be derived from them; these must be treated on a different level, as we shall show below.

92. Boskoff, "From Social Thought to Sociological Theory," in Becker and Boskoff, *op. cit.,* p. 26.

93. Although there is no intention of overlooking the many pioneering ventures which seek a comprehensive theory of society, capable of accounting for both its static and dynamic aspects, the reference here is specifically to the textbook literature.

94. "There is never in existence 'society' in an absolute sense, i.e., of such a sort that all these particular phenomena would occur in accordance with 'society' as a presupposition; for there is no such thing as reciprocal influencing in an absolute sense but merely particular species of the same. With the occurrence of these species society also puts in an appearance. They are, however, neither the cause nor the consequence of society. They are themselves immediately society." Quoted from Small, "The Problem of Sociology," p. 303 (*Soziologie,* p. 9). Cf. *Soziologie,* p. 5.

95. Timasheff, *op. cit.,* pp. 99 f.

96. *Soziologie,* p. 8 (Small, "The Problem of Sociology," p. 302).

97. Boskoff, "Social Change: Major Problems in the Emergence of Theoretical and Research Foci," in Becker and Boskoff, *op. cit.,* pp. 260-302.

98. See Floyd N. House, *The Development of Sociology* (New York and London: McGraw-Hill Book Co., Inc., 1936), p. 389. See also Heberle, *op. cit.,* p. 252.

99. *Soziologie,* p. 15 (Small, "The Problem of Sociology," p. 311).

100. As far as I can see, no serious attempt has ever been made to follow the advice which Simmel offers on p. 13 of *Soziologie.* Here he says

that an understanding of his idea of formal sociology should be sought in his concrete investigations. What, actually, is the method he practices in them? What answer do they give to the inquiry concerning the "forces, relations, and forms" of sociation that he proposes on p. 8 of *Soziologie*? This article suggests an approach to a fuller understanding of formal sociology by drawing attention to the fact that, throughout his essays, Simmel presents the forms and their inherent tendencies as consequences of motives, or as modes of expression which are appropriate for certain ends. In the frame of reference of formal sociology, these motives must obviously be understood not as belonging to the individual action systems but as derived from typical situations. It is assumed that the actors possess certain reciprocal orientations, including motivations, which, regardless of the contents of their individual action systems, are among the inherent necessities of typical situations.

101. See *Soziologie,* p. 418; *Geschichtsphilosophie,* pp. 100, 102 ff.; and *Philosophie des Geldes,* p. 552.

102. See *Soziologie,* pp. 20 ff., and Wolff, *op. cit.,* pp. 23 ff. For a complete discussion see *Geschichtsphilosophie,* Chap. ii.

103. For an example, see Richard T. LaPiere, *Sociology* (New York and London: McGraw-Hill Book Co., Inc., 1946), pp. 180 ff.

104. *Geschichtsphilosophie,* p. 107.

SIMMEL'S IMAGE OF SOCIETY

HUGH DALZIEL DUNCAN

Our image of society determines how we think about society. If we use mechanical models for thinking about society, we can say nothing very rigorous about communication as symbolic interaction or role-playing unless we reduce communication to "signaling," "feed-back," "built-in purposes," and so on. The same holds true, of course, for models derived from aesthetic or religious experience. When we say society is a "configuration," like that of a great painting, there is little we can say about verbal communication because paintings do not talk.

We do not avoid the necessity of rigorous thinking about society when we construct hypotheses which, we assert, will be validated by "operations" of how we use our hypothesis in reference to data. Our selection of hypotheses determines our selection of data. However rigorous our techniques of investigation, the question of whether we are finding out what we need to know still remains. When we take over images or models from fields outside of sociology proper, we must make clear the relevance of such images to the solution of sociological problems. We know that sacred beliefs are acted out in ritual, but we know too that men act out their beliefs in non-religious ways. I may believe in critical intelligence as the ultimate social good. To apply ritual concepts taken from religion (and only the tragic sacrificial moment of religion) to the social expression of critical intelligence may tell us something about ritual but not much about intelligence.

Few sociologists were more aware of the need for careful consideration of models of sociation than Simmel.[1] In every turn and twist of his thought, as in his moments of sheer illumination when sociology suddenly becomes a great path into the hearts and minds of men, Simmel's concern over the meaning of the concept "society" is manifest. From his early days as a lecturer at the University of Berlin[2] to his last years at Strasbourg he asks, How are we to think about the forms of sociation if we assume that the primary fact of sociation is interaction?[3]

"Pure sociology," as Simmel calls it (to distinguish it from "general" and "philosophical" sociology) investigates "the societal forms themselves, in hope of creating a grammar of the forms of sociation." Pure sociology must abstract the element of sociation. "It isolates it inductively and psychologically from the heterogeneity of its contents and purposes, which, in themselves, are not societal. It thus proceeds like grammar, which isolates the pure forms of language from their contents through which these forms, nevertheless, come to life."[4] For whatever the content of social experience, forms of sociation, such as "superiority and subordination, competition, division of labor, formation of parties, representation, inner solidarity coupled with exclusiveness toward the outside,"[5] are common to all. The identification, systematic ordering, psychological explanation, and historical development of pure forms of sociation become the central task of sociology.[6]

Simmel's image of sociation, then, is *interaction* which has both *form* and *content*. While the form cannot be abstracted completely out of contents, the materials with which social life is filled, and the motivations "by which it is propelled," are not social. Hunger, love, work, religion, technology, or reason are factors in sociation only when "they transform the mere aggregation of isolated individuals into specific forms of being with and for one another—forms that are subsumed under the general concept of interaction."[7] Simmel then argues that forms, originally developed to satisfy our needs, "remove themselves from the service of life that originally produced and employed them" to develop *in terms of their own resources as forms.* Thus cognition is no longer bound to practical ends but chooses its own objects, shapes them according to its own needs, and is interested in nothing beyond its own perfection. So, too, with law. Law may be defined simply by the relationships established among legal forms which determine in their "own right and not by legitimation through any higher, extrinsic agency, how the contents of life should be shaped."[8]

"This complete turnover, from the determination of the forms by the materials of life to the determination of its materials by forms that have become supreme values, is perhaps most extensively at work in the numerous phenomena that we lump together under the category of *play*"—as seen in the "hunt; the gain by ruse; the proving of physical and intellectual strength; competition."[9] Sociability itself is the most characteristic autonomous form, or play-form, of sociation. Men band together in economic associations, blood brotherhoods, religious societies, and the like, yet in addition to the satisfaction of these specific interests, all such sociations are characterized by a feeling among the members of being sociated and by the satisfaction derived from this. Like art, sociability abstracts sociation out of our relationships and makes it into pure forms. Thus even the most primitive societies speak of "good form" as a value in itself. And although the actual, life-conditioned motivations of sociation are of no significance to sociability, the forms of sociation may by their formal excellence enhance life when they are returned to it.

Sociability has no objective purpose, no content, no extrinsic results; it depends entirely on the actors in the moment of sociation. Its aim is nothing but the success of the sociable moment and, at most, a memory of it. Here "society" is "that being with one another, for one another, against one another which, through the vehicle of drives or purposes, forms and develops material or individual contents and interests."[10] At any social gathering, the moment of warmth, of deep enjoyment of solidarity, occurs precisely at the moment when sociability frees itself from all ties with contents. We are no longer rich, poor, old, young, learned, ignorant, beautiful, ugly, genteel, or vulgar, for now we are transformed into actors in a drama of sociation. As we greet, chat, move from one to another, bow, sip drinks, a new relationship, the relationship of sociability, is born. We are now in the realm of manners which exist for the sake of the fascination that the freedom from all ties with contents diffuses throughout the group.

While Simmel offers many illustrations of what he means by forms of sociation, he selects the kind of sociability we experience at a social gathering as his representative illustration. At three decisive moments in his career he turned back to such moments of pure sociability for the image of man in society which was to dominate all his sociological writings. He knew that he must clarify his ideal form of sociation before he could establish a firm foundation for a science of sociology. Thus in an early footnote to his *Soziologie* of 1908, he says: " . . . I have not been able to clarify the fundamental idea of the present volume . . . the pretension of any systematic and definitive completeness would be . . . a self-illusion."[11] But in his "Soziologie der Geselligkeit,"[12] which he used as an opening address at the first meeting of the German Sociological Society in 1910, Simmel returns to his image of sociability: "Associations are accompanied by a feeling for, by a satisfaction in, the very fact that one is associated with others and that the solitariness of the individual is resolved into togetherness, a union with others."[13] In his final summation of his sociological views, the *Grundfragen der Soziologie* of 1917, he entitles his third chapter "Sociability (An Example of Pure, or Formal, Sociology)."

Now, by "pure form" Simmel does not mean an imaginary fiction like Goethe's schematic idea of an animal archetype, but a form which is pure because its content is wholly societal, or, as he states it, wholly determined by sociability. In his discussion of the problems of sociology in the first chapter of his *Soziologie,* Simmel makes this clear.

> Men regard one another, and men are jealous one of another; they write one another letters or dine together; they meet in sympathy or antipathy quite apart from all tangible interests; their gratitude for altruistic service weaves a chain of consequences never to be sundered; they ask the way of one another, and they dress and adorn themselves for one another;—these are instances chosen quite at random from the thousand relations, momentary or lasting, conscious or unconscious, transitory or fraught with consequences, which, playing from person to person, knit us incessantly together. Every moment such threads are spun, are dropped and again caught up, replaced by others, woven up with others. These . . . determine all the tenacity and elasticity, all the variegation and unity of this so intelligible and yet so mysterious life of society.[14]

In the *Grundfragen,* he gives sociability a specific psychological content: " 'Society,' " properly speaking, "is . . . being with one another, for one another, against one another . . . ."; and it is these forms themselves, *not* "drives or purposes," which develop material or individual contents and interests.

When specific interests determine social form, they prevent the individual from presenting his peculiarity and uniqueness in too unlimited a fashion. When there are no such interests, the subordination of the individual to the group (and his realization through the group) is accomplished simply by the power of the forms of sociation as such. Indeed, without the reduction of personal intimacy and autonomy brought about by this form, no purely social gathering could exist. It is enabled to do so through *tact,* whose most essential task is to set the limits of the individual's impulses, ego stresses, and intellectual and material desires. Purely intimate traits, individual character, mood, and fate—like wealth, social position, erudition, fame, skill, and merits—must not intrude in moments of sociability. To allow them to do so is tactless because it militates against interaction. But this surrender of subjective inward spheres of personality does not (in moments of pure sociability) demand complete acceptance of objective, group-determined elements. So long as subjective or objective elements dominate relationships, sociability cannot become a value in itself but only a bridge or mediation between the two.

The positive formal motive of sociability is thoroughly democratic. The end of sociability is expressed in "the axiom that each individual should *offer* the maximum of sociable values (of joy, relief, liveliness, etc.) that is compatible with the maximum of values he himself *receives.*"[15] This democratic character of sociability can be realized only within a given social stratum, for sociability among members of very different social strata is inconsistent and painful. Sociability creates an ideal sociological world in which the pleasure of the individual is closely tied up with the pleasure of others. In principle, nobody can find satisfaction if it has to be at the cost of diametrically opposed feelings in others. Social forms other than sociability exclude such opposition, but in all of these some superimposed ethical imperative operates. In sociability it is excluded by the intrinsic principle of the social form itself.

Yet this world of sociability which reaches its most characteristic expression among equals, and which is the only world wherein a democracy of the equally privileged exists without friction, is an *artificial* world. It is composed of individuals who strive to create an interaction so pure that it cannot be spoiled by material or individual wants.

> If sociation itself is interaction, its purest and most stylized expression occurs among equals—as symmetry and balance are the most plausible forms of artistic stylization. Inasmuch as it is abstracted from sociation through art or play, sociability thus calls for the purest, most transparent, and most casually appealing kind of interaction, *that among equals.*[16]

There are many wonderful examples of such pure moments of sociability scattered throughout Simmel's writings.[17] Even in his most abstract analysis there is a kind of radiance and wonder over the mystery and power of the social bond itself.

"Style is always something general. It brings the contents of personal life and activity into a form shared by many and accessible to many."[18] "One adorns oneself for oneself, but can do so only by adornment for others."[19] Thus it is a great mistake to think that because it always functions in the case of an individual, adornment must be an individual work of art. On the contrary, *because* it is to serve the individual, it may not be of an individual nature—any more than the piece of furniture on which he sits, or the fork he uses to bring food to his mouth, may be individual works of art. The work of art cannot be incorporated into another life for it is a self-sufficient world. Adornment, on the other hand,

> intensifies or enlarges the impression of the personality by operating as a sort of radiation emanating from it. . . . One may speak of human radioactivity in the sense that every individual is surrounded by a larger or smaller sphere of significance radiating from him; and everybody else, who deals with him, is immersed in this sphere. It is [a] . . . mixture of physiological and psychic elements; the sensuously observable influences which issue from an individual in the direction of his environment also are, in some fashion, the vehicles of a spiritual fulguration. . . . The radiations of adornment, the sensuous attention it provokes, supply the personality with . . . an enlargement or intensification of its sphere.[20]

The personality is enhanced because the body is adorned.

The world from which Simmel drew his examples of sociability has been well described in one of the most moving passages in *Amiel's Journal.*

> In society, one must have an air of living on ambrosia and having only noble preoccupations. Care, want, passion do not exist. All realism, being brutal, is suppressed. It is taken for granted that these goddesses have come down from Olympus and are not subject to any of the earthly infirmities. They have no vital organs, no weight; they retain, of their human nature, only that which is needed for grace and pleasure. In a word, what is called the great world grants itself for the moment a flattering illusion, that of being in the ethereal state and breathing the life of mythology. For this reason, any vehemence, any cry of nature, any real suffering, any unreflecting familiarity, any frank token of passion shocks and reverberates in this delicate atmosphere; any crudity at once destroys the collective work, the palace of clouds, the magic architecture that has been erected by the common consent. It is rather like the harsh cock-crow that dissolves all the enchantments and puts the fairies to flight. Gatherings of the elite unconsciously try to produce a sort of concert of the eyes and ears, an extempore work of art. This instinctive collaboration has a real charm, for it is a festival of wit and taste and transports the actors into the sphere of the imagination; it is a form of poetry and the way in which cultivated society recompenses, by reflection, the vanished idyll and the engulfed world of Astrea.[21]

The artificiality and playfulness of sociability should not blind us to the great power of such forms. Only a highly superficial rationalism looks for social power among concrete contents in social experience and brands sociability as shallow foolishness. The power of forms of sociation becomes obvious once we observe how the sexual drive is subordinated to the demands of sociability. In the sociology of sex we find a play-form: coquetry. "The coquettish woman enormously enhances her attractiveness if she" makes a man think she is about to surrender but at the decisive moment indicates she is not really serious after all. "Her behavior swings back and forth between 'yes' and 'no' without stopping at either."[22] The male partner of the coquette enters the game when his conduct is no longer dominated by hope for satisfaction of his lust. For coquetry unfolds its charms precisely at the moment when it transcends the reality of erotic desire as consent or refusal. So long as erotic desire dominates, the man and woman are but two individuals trying to satisfy a bodily need (even though there will be other satisfactions). But "under the sociological sign of sociability from which the center of the personality's concrete and complete life is barred, coquetry is the flirtatious, perhaps ironical play, in which eroticism has freed the bare outline of its interactions from their materials and contents and personal features."[23]

And when we turn to conversation, "the most general vehicle for all that men have in common," we find that sociable talk has no immediate purpose. We talk for the sake of talking, but no one confuses such talk with idle chatter or nonsense. "In purely sociable conversation, the topic is merely the . . . medium through which the lively exchange of speech unfolds its" charm, the charm of the art of conversation, which has its own laws. In such moments the same forms of relationship exist that we find in many contents of social experience. We quarrel, appeal to norms recognized by both parties; we pacify our quarrel by compromise and common discovery of shared convictions; we accept new ideas hopefully; and we agree to disregard what we cannot agree on. In talk, however, these forms "derive their significance from themselves, from the fascinating play of relations which they create among the participants, joining and loosening, winning and succumbing, giving and taking."[24] We are not indifferent to content. Good talk must be interesting, fascinating, even important. But it is the "relatedness" and the forms of this relatedness we prize in such moments of sociability.

There are, of course, numerous ways of thinking about society. Simmel wrote significantly in many fields. Philosophers, historians, psychologists, and sociologists who neglect his work risk going over ground which he has already covered. Dilthey and Collingwood in philosophy, and Park,[25] von Wiese, Becker, Burgess, and many other sociologists, offer eloquent witness to Simmel's greatness. Wolff indicates this in his notes on Simmel.[26]

The value of Simmel's model of sociation may be summed up by saying that *he keeps our attention focused on the specifically sociological aspects of social experience.* He forces us to ask always: What, really, are we talking about when we talk about a sociology of society? His search for a model of sociation, "that being with one another, for one another, against one another which, through the vehicle of drives and purposes, forms and develops material or individual contents and interests,"[27] never ends. In the *Grundfragen der Soziologie* of 1917, as in his last work, *Lebensanschauung,* published in 1918, he struggles with all the force and virtuosity of a subtle mind versed in philosophy, history, ethics, religion, art, and psychology to reach a clear definition of "society." This struggle has become one of the great legacies of sociology. Those who attempt creation of sociological models without reading Simmel delude themselves. As many of us have discovered in our excursions into sociological theory, the figure of Simmel often appears toward the end of the journey. We greet him with dismay as well as respect, for he is coming back from a point we are still struggling to reach.

Our present concern with interaction is but one example of this. When we talk about interaction, what exactly are we talking about? How do we study it? *What are the data of interaction?* Over a half-century has passed since Simmel began his description of interaction; yet we still go on talking about social structure with little reference to function. Common sense teaches us that we "function" in role enactment through *symbolic* interaction whose societal meanings arise *in* communication. We do not "have" meanings and then share them. On the contrary, as we communicate we create meanings. What we know about motivation is derived from what is said about it. We can argue that symbols are but a terministic screen beyond which lies the reality of motivation, and then go on describing our reality in terms of physical or human nature, family roles, supernatural or sociopolitical "laws." But wherever we assign our causes, when we return to specifically *human* experience we must deal with *expressions* of these causes in *symbols.*[28]

In his discussion of knowledge, truth, and falsehood in human relations, Simmel says: "Human interaction is normally based on the fact that the ideational worlds of men have certain elements in common, that objective intellectual contents constitute the material which is transformed into subjective life by means of men's social relations. The type, as well as the essential instrument, of these common elements is shared language."[29] He held that sociability reaches its forms of interaction through "*conversation,* the most general vehicle for all that men have in common."[30] Thus while he argued that the science of sociology must concern itself with structure, he did *not* mean mechanical or biological but *symbolic* structure as we know it in art and play. "Freed of substance . . . play gets its cheerfulness but also that symbolic significance which distinguishes it from pure pastime . . . . Sociability (. . . and the more so as it approaches pure sociability) takes on a symbolically playing fullness of life and a significance which a superficial rationalism seeks only in content." "Sociability is, then, the play-form of association and is related to the content-determined concreteness of association as art is related to reality."[31]

To elaborate fully what Simmel meant by art lies beyond the scope of this paper. He was not, in his role as sociologist, interested in creating a sociology of art,[32] but he thought that the sociologist could learn much from the relationship between art and reality.

> In all art, in all the symbolism of religious life, in great measure even in the complex formulations of science, we are thrown back upon this belief, upon this feeling, that autonomies of mere parts of observed reality, that the combinations of certain superficial elements possess a relation to the depth and wholeness of life, which, although often not easy to formulate, makes such a part the bearer and the representative of the fundamental reality. From this we may understand the saving grace and blessing effect of these realms built out of the pure forms of existence, for in them we are released from life but have it still. . . . [Art] perhaps reveals the secret of life; that we save ourselves not by simply looking away from it but precisely in that in the apparently self-governing play of its forms we construct and experience the meaning and the forces of its deepest reality but without the reality itself. Sociability would not hold for so many thoughtful men who feel in every moment the pressure of life, this emancipating and saving exhilaration if it were only a flight from life, the mere momentary lifting of its seriousness. . . . The freeing and lightening, however, that precisely the more thoughtful man finds in sociability is this: that association and exchange of stimulus, in which all the tasks and the whole weight of life are realized, here

is consumed in an artistic play, in that simultaneous sublimation and dilution, in which the heavily freighted forces of reality are felt only from a distance, their weight fleeting in a charm.[33]

As Wolff points out in his note on "form," there are ambiguities in Simmel's forms of sociation.[34] Even if we put aside ontological considerations to construct heuristic methodological tools, Simmel's forms offer many difficulties. For despite his reference to art, play, and communication, it is very difficult to distinguish the empirical referents of his forms. This is not because he offers few illustrations. On the contrary, his work, unlike that of modern theoreticians such as Parsons, is studded with illustrations so brilliant and dazzling that sheer admiration and delight still criticism. But when we return from the heights to ask ourselves how we can fashion methodological tools out of a profound conviction that we know something of societal reality, Simmel's forms become singularly elusive.

Simmel's worst ambiguity lies in his mixture of images. He has not one but several representative illustrations of what he means by society. We are never sure, when he uses an image of play, whether he means *play* as in drama or in games or as in the *play* of forces over a physical field—in magnetic currents, among atoms, and so on. Thus in his speech on the "Soziologie der Geselligkeit" we are told that in his familiar image of the forms of social life, "all the with-one-another, for-one-another, in-one-another, against-one-another, and through-one-another, in state and commune, in church and economic associations, in family and clubs," are like atoms. "The energy effects of atoms upon each other bring matter into the innumerable forms which we see as 'things.' Just so the impulses and interests, which a man experiences in himself and which push him out toward other men, bring about all the forms of association by which a mere sum of separate individuals are made into a 'society.' " But then, we are told, this physical "constellation" really must be thought of as "art or play."[35]

Like Freud, Simmel is uneasy at times over mixing quantitative and qualitative images. "It may be an open question whether the concept of play impulse or an artistic impulse possesses explanatory value." But "at least it directs attention to the fact that in every play or artistic activity there is contained a common element not affected by their differences of content." That is, the *content* of sociation is like the "energy affects of atoms," but the *form* is like art or play. But how can an art form be derived from a material content? What is the relevance of a conception of art to a conception of energy? And, finally, what *kind* of art is Simmel talking about? Only an exhaustive study of Simmel's imagery could answer this; but even a hasty view indicates that when he uses the term "art," he is thinking of visual art. "If association is interaction at all, it appears in its purest and most stylized form when it goes on among equals, just as symmetry and balance are the most outstanding forms of artistic stylizing of visible elements."[36]

A further ambiguity in the imagery Simmel uses is in the relationships between the individual and society. He discusses these as, among other things, "sociability thresholds." The personality has "outside" referents such as political and economic contents of experience; and it has "inside," subjective and personal, "purely [inward] spheres." Sociability makes passage from one to another possible; but this, Simmel argues, is not "true" sociability. For objective and subjective experience are nourished from a "common but somewhat undefinable source of energy, the ego."[37] The ego is a system of its own. It is not to be confused with inner, subjective "thresholds," with their "zigzag motions, the chaotic whirling of images and ideas which objectively are entirely unrelated to one another, and their logically unjustifiable, only so-to-speak probative, connections." For the ego must select from "that psychological real whole whose absolutely exact report (absolutely exact in terms of content and sequence) would drive everybody into the insane asylum."[38]

The ego functions by choosing the audience to whom one communicates. Only "fragments" of our inner life can be revealed, even to our closest fellow men; and "what is more, these fragments are not a representative selection, but one made from the standpoint of reason, value, and relation to the listener and his understanding. Whatever we say . . . is never an immediate and faithful presentation of what really occurs in us during that particular time of communication, but is a transformation of this inner reality, teleologically directed, reduced, and recomposed."[39] How does this transformation take place in the ego, and by what means do we "select" our audience?

The answer to both these questions is communication. But then we should expect Simmel to show *how* forms of sociability are determined by communication and how they in turn determine communication. And if by communication Simmel means not only gesture but also the forms of expression created by art,[40] then we should expect Simmel to turn to art for analysis of how forms of sociation are created and sustained. It can be argued, of course, that Simmel had no interest in creating hypotheses. Yet even if we admit this, there is still the problem of inner consistency, or logical model-construction, which must be solved according to canons of good theoretical construction. But Simmel never makes clear whether the acting individual is a bearer or a creator of psychic social energy. That is, although he discusses the acting individual in terms of role enactment, we are never sure of the existence of the individual except as a bearer of psychic social energy which the individual does not determine, yet which cannot exist without him.

Lotze[41] pointed out that *even* in a physical field, interaction cannot be conceived of without reference to points or agents which are internally modified by, and in turn modifiers of, the process which affects them. We say that the impact of one element on another communicates motion, so that the element struck passes from a state of rest (or from one phase) to one of motion (or to another), while the striking element has experienced a change of an opposite character. Even as description of a physical field, however, this explains nothing, for if all that happens is the communication of motion, why does it not pass through the stricken element and leave its state unchanged?

This is *not* simply a "metaphysical problem" which we can thrust aside "to get down to business" as rugged empiricists. The same dilemma haunts Parsons' work. If statuses and roles are "analogous to the particle of mechanics, not to mass or velocity,"[42] but are "not in general attributes of the actor,"[43] how can we form hypotheses for dealing with the data of sociation? And if our model is mechanical, how are we to deal with change and communication? We can reduce communication to signals, or interaction to game-theory, in which actors do not motivate through symbols but indicate through signals, but we must make clear why we do so. And if we say that our analogies hold true for society because they hold true in biology, physics, and so on, what are we to do when biologists and physicists themselves tell us that we have *not* described their models accurately?

Park and Burgess were aware of Simmel's ambiguity. They turned to communication as "the medium of interaction,"[44] but their model of communication was only another variant of mechanism. Now interaction became process, and processes such as imitation and suggestion were but "mechanisms of interaction." Simmel's "being for, with, and against one another" was transformed into "social forces," such as competition, conflict, accommodation, and assimilation. New terms, however, do not change the problem, which still is, What are the *data* of social process? How can we create hypotheses which will allow us to deal with social process as *facts*? We know men compete, but how can we study this? And if we study it as sociologists, how does sociology differ from any other approach?

We can learn much from Simmel's failure to reduce theory to hypotheses through confusion of mechanical and human images. While there is little evidence that Freud knew much about Simmel, there can hardly be any question that he too suffered from the dilemma of how to use the mechanical concepts of science for the study of psychic experience. But Freud, unlike Simmel, rejected his early mechanical models.[45] He turned to art because only in art could he find the kind of *structure* he needed to deal with the *symbolic data* offered him by patients. This was not an easy choice for Freud. As Jones tells us in his biography of Freud, hopes for a mechanical model of human mentation were never abandoned. But the hard facts of therapy, of patients whose suffering continued or lightened, drove Freud to create methods and techniques derived from symbolic expression in drama, jokes, fairy tales, and myths.

Briefly stated, the question Simmel leaves unanswered is this: *How can forms of sociation which are "like" art or play be thought of as mechanical*? For if they are like art, they are not mechanical; and if they are mechanical, they are not art. This question has not yet been answered, but we ought to realize that it does not disappear simply because we do not face it. It plagued Freud,[46] as it did Mead and Dewey, who insisted that if mind is social, it must arise in and through communication. But communication cannot be a process which somehow passes through one individual to another, for in such passage the individual becomes meaningless. Nor do we solve anything by saying that roles, not individuals, are the proper concern of sociologists. Roles, like forms of sociation, must be internalized before they can be enacted. Theories of role cathexis couched in physical or mechanical terminology are merely another return to mechanistic models of sociation.

Descriptions of structure which do not derive from a function to which the structure is related can never become theories but must remain fictions. So long as we go on spinning out structural descriptions, we are like the workman who elaborates endlessly a scaffold whose meaning exists only when the building within gets under way. What is our building? What specifically is the structure and function, or as Simmel put it, the form and content, of sociation? It is to Simmel's great credit that he forces us to ask this question, as he himself asked and answered it in so many wonderful ways. The past generations of American sociologists abandoned theory in the hope that method could evolve from ever more refined technique. Our generation knows that there is no road back from technique to theory, but that many roads open from theory to method, and from method, in turn, to technique.

We have not yet had our Marx, Darwin, Einstein, or Freud, and until we do, there is little use in closing our minds to theory. Neither is there any virtue in going over the same ground and changing signposts on terrain already well traveled. Surely there is no need for any more mechanistic theories of society. However we dress them up, they still do not tell us what we want to know about specifically *human* forms of interaction. These, as we all know, are symbolic interactions which take place in acts through roles.

The problem for our generation of sociologists is not to explain away the symbolic or to treat it as residual to non-symbolic elements. For if society exists in and through symbolic expression, the fate of sociology as a science will be determined by our ability to deal with symbols. Structural theory must be derived from symbolic function. Hypotheses must be created which relate to the symbolic facts of sociation. It is easy enough to say this now, because we inherit the thought of men like Simmel, who struggled to free the science of sociology from the science of matter. The question for Simmel's generation was, How is *any* science possible if we do not follow the canons of physical science? The question for ours is, How can we construct hypotheses to deal with the observable facts of human sociation? Mead has shown how communication determines consciousness. Kenneth Burke has created a dramatistic model of communication in which symbolic interaction can be thought of as *both* form and content. The great task of theoretical construction has been done for us. We can now enter the analysis of symbolic experience along clearly marked paths.

1. Only those who inherited and carried on the great tradition of German sociology can speak with much authority on Simmel. To understand a man's image of society, we must know well not only the form and content of his thought but the language in which these are expressed. Americans who seek to carry on in this tradition owe much to Kurt H. Wolff for his work *The Sociology of Georg Simmel* (Glencoe, Ill.: Free Press of Glencoe, Illinois, 1950). The quotations from this work which follow are used by permission of the Free Press of Glencoe, Illinois.

2. See *Soziologische Vorlesungen von Georg Simmel, gehalten an der Universität Berlin im Wintersemester 1899,* published by the Society for Social Research of the University of Chicago, 1931. Ser. 1, No. 1.

3. ". . . If society is conceived as interaction among individuals, the description of the forms of this interaction is the task of the science of society in its strictest and most essential sense." Wolff, *op. cit.*, pp. 21-22.

4. *Ibid.*, p. 22.

5. *Ibid.*

6. *Ibid.*, p. 23.

7. *Ibid.*, p. 41.

8. *Ibid.*, p. 42.

9. *Ibid.*

10. *Ibid.*, p. 43.

11. *Soziologie. Untersuchungen über die Formen der Vergesellschaftung* (Leipzig: Duncker und Humblot, 1908), p. 17, as translated by Wolff, *op. cit,* p. xxxiii.

12. This is translated as "The Sociology of Sociability" by Everett C. Hughes, and appears in the *American Journal of Sociology,* LV (November, 1949), 254-61. The quotations from this translation which follow are used by permission of the *American Journal of Sociology.*

13. *Ibid.,* p. 255.

14. *Soziologie,* p. 19. I have used R. M. MacIver's translation of this passage as quoted in Howard Becker, *Systematic Sociology on the Basis of the* Beziehungslehre *and* Gebildelehre *of Leopold von Wiese* (Wisconsin ed.; Gary, Ind.: Norman Paul Press, 1950), p. 25.

15. Wolff, *op. cit.,* p. 47.

16. *Ibid.,* p. 49. The italics are Simmel's.

17. One of these is the "Exkurs über den Schmuck," translated as "Adornment" by Wolff, *ibid.,* pp. 338-44.

18. *Ibid.,* p. 341.

19. *Ibid.,* p. 339.

20. *Ibid.,* pp. 339-40.

21. *The Private Journal of Henri Frederic Amiel,* trans. Van Wyck Brooks and Charles Van Wyck Brooks, and with an Introduction by Bernard Bouvier (New York: Macmillan Co., 1935), pp. 337-38. Elite sociability is used as a representative example of the power of society by many writers, notably, Tolstoy, Proust, and Henry James, but the general character of sociability can be described in any context. Thus in Mark Twain we find wonderful descriptions of it among boys.

22. Wolff, *op. cit.,* p. 50.

23. *Ibid.,* p. 51.

24. *Ibid.,* p. 52.

25. "Simmel's most important contribution to sociology has never been understood in this country. . . . He has written the most profound and stimulating book in sociology, in my opinion, that has ever been written." See Park's comment on the advertisement for *The Social Theory of Georg Simmel,* by Nicholas J. Spykman, in the back of Robert E. Park and Ernest W. Burgess' *Introduction to the Science of Sociology* ([1921] Chicago: University of Chicago Press, 1926). In an autobiographical note published in a collection of Park's papers, *Race and Culture* (Glencoe, Ill.: Free Press of Glencoe, Illinois, 1950), p. vi, Park says, "I spent a year at Harvard and then went abroad. I intended to stay abroad for a year, but I remained for four years. There, listening to the lectures of Georg Simmel, at Berlin, I received my only formal instruction in sociology."

26. Wolff, *op. cit.*, pp. li-liv, lix-lxi.

27. *Ibid.*, p. 43. This is to be found in the *Grundfragen der Soziologie,* Simmel's last explicit sociological statement on the nature of socialization.

28. This is Dilthey's point, of course. It is also the basis of Charles Horton Cooley, George Herbert Mead, and John Dewey's conception of societal interaction. Kenneth Burke deals explicitly with this subject in his paper, "Fact, Inference, and Proof in the Analysis of Literary Symbolism" (Chap. xix), in *Symbols and Values: Thirteenth Symposium of the Conference on Science, Philosophy and Religion,* ed. Lyman Bryson, Louis Finkelstein, R. M. MacIver, and Richard McKeon (New York and London: Conference on Science, Philosophy and Religion in Their Relation to the Democratic Way of Life, Inc. [Distributed by Harper & Brothers], 1954). I have discussed this point in my *Language and Literature in Society* (Chicago: University of Chicago Press, 1953).

29. Wolff, *op. cit.*, p. 315.

30. *Ibid.*, p. 51.

31. Hughes, *op. cit.*, p. 255.

32. Nevertheless, his descriptions of forms of sociation are of inestimable value when applied to the social content of art. For if by "social" we mean "social order," the *forms* social order assumes must be described.

33. Hughes, *op. cit.*, p. 261.

34. Wolff, *op. cit.*, p. li, n. 60.

35. Hughes, *op. cit.*, p. 254.

36. *Ibid.*, p. 257.

37. *Ibid.*, p. 256.

38. Wolff, *op. cit.*, "The Nature of the Psychic Process and of Communication," a section of Simmel's discussion of knowledge, truth, and falsehood in human relations, pp. 311-12.

39. *Ibid.*, p. 312.

40. Art is not the only form of expression, of course. There are play, rhetoric of various kinds, and so on. But since Simmel refers to art forms so frequently, it is reasonable to discuss expression as art here. Freud, on the other hand, is much more rhetorical in his imagery, although he, too, falls back on mechanistic images when discussing mentation as function. Thus we hear of "displacement."

41. Alexander Thomas Ormond discusses Lotze's contribution in his *Foundations of Knowledge* (London and New York: Macmillan Co., 1900).

42. Talcott Parsons, *The Social System* (Glencoe, Ill.: Free Press of Glencoe, Illinois, 1951), p. 25.

43. *Ibid.* The components of interaction are discussed on pp. 3-22, 24-26.

44. See "Social Interaction," in Park and Burgess, *op. cit.*

45. For a discussion of this, see Ernest Jones, "Freud's Theory of the Mind" (Chap. vii), *Sigmund Freud: Life and Work* (London: Hogarth Press, 1953), Vol. I. See also the editor's introduction to Vol. IV of the standard English edition of Freud's works, edited by James Strachey (London: Hogarth Press, 1953).

46. As Jones points out, recent electronic theories of cerebral functioning are going over ground already covered by Freud some sixty-five years earlier (Jones, *op. cit.,* pp. 430, 431). Freud abandoned his ingenious mechanical model of neurological function for the very simple reason that it did not help him to deal with the *observable data* of mentation, namely symbols. As he wrote in his introduction to the case history of Fräulein Elizabeth von R., "I have not always been a psychotherapist. Like other neuro-pathologists, I was trained to employ local diagnoses and electro-prognosis, and it still strikes me myself as strange that the case histories I write should read like short stories and that, as one might say, they lack the serious stamp of science. I must console myself with the reflection that the nature of the subject is evidently responsible for this, rather than any preference of my own. The fact is that local diagnosis and electrical reactions lead nowhere in the study of hysteria, whereas a detailed description of mental processes such as we are accustomed to find in the works of imaginative writers enables me, with the use of a few psychological formulas, to obtain at least some kind of insight into the course of that affection. Case histories of this kind are intended to be judged like psychiatric ones; they have, however, one advantage over the latter, namely an intimate connection between the story of the patient's sufferings and the symptoms of his illness—a connection for which we still search in vain in the biographies of other psychoses" (pp. 160-61 of Vol. II of the standard English edition of Freud's works). Jones also quotes the minutes of the meeting of November 10, 1909, at which Freud told his group: "Dream symbols that do not find any support in myths, fairy tales, popular uses, etc., should be regarded as doubtful" (Jones, *op. cit.,* II [1955], 493). Sociological theory which treats symbols as epiphenomenal or residual *cannot* deal with communication.

SOME ASPECTS OF SIMMEL'S CONCEPTION OF THE INDIVIDUAL

MATTHEW LIPMAN

To sociologists and social philosophers alike, few problems have been as haunting, as challenging, as persistently intriguing as the problem of individuality. For in what, precisely, does individuality consist? In our difference from others, or in some intrinsic and essential quality or structure of the self? Even should we agree that individuality is bound up with social differences, we find ourselves enmeshed in new perplexities. And if we attempt to resolve these perplexities by appealing to history, we find that, with the passage of time, the dominant formulations of the problem have radically altered. Individuality in primitive society tends to be defined by the extent to which one approximates a social type. Social types are established by the cultural traditions of the community, and the more one realizes the type, the more individualized he is considered to be. It is not far from this point of view to that of the Greeks, who discard the notion that social types must be accepted uncritically as norms. Instead, they examine social relationships, isolate those which appear to be values, idealize them, and then consider that to be individual which most perfectly participates in the ideal. It is only with Aristotle that this approach is systematically transformed: attention is directed away from form as the agency of individual determination and is focused instead upon the individuating function of material content. This statement of the problem in turn foreshadowed the more modern view that conformity to type is a denial of individuality. We have been inclined to think that individuality is constituted by deviation from type, by nonconformity. The more we depart from established norms, the more we appear to stand out as distinctive. In time, however, such departures become stylized and conventional. Consequently, the demand for individuality is renewed and intensified.

Since the ideology of Western society is largely composed of notions stemming from Christianity, romanticism, and liberalism (with their respective versions of religious, aesthetic, and political individualism), it has steadily insisted upon the incomparability, induplicability, and uniqueness of the individual human being. This insistence is frequently hortative rather than descriptive; it is not necessarily rooted in empirical observation of individual differences. In democratic societies, where pluralistic values are predominant, uniqueness is as readily imputed to the individual as is diversity to the group.

The individual can also be regarded as simply a chance intersection of social relationships, expendable as a means to some overriding social end, and duplicable if liquidated. Clearly, the affirmation or denial of essential personal differences is at the heart of many contemporary ideological controversies.

For the philosophically oriented social scientist, the problem of individuality is thus complicated by traditional disputes among theologians, metaphysicians, and political ideologists. All sorts of strands are here knotted up, and each seems to involve some exasperating dualism: universal vs. particular, general vs. specific, type vs. instance, law vs. case, norm vs. deviation, and so forth. In Simmel's philosophical sociology, some parts of the knot are unraveled; some are cut; and some remain as entangled as ever.

The construction of a theory of individuality might well begin with a metaphysical formulation of the problem, but in approaching Simmel's writings on the subject it may be more useful to turn first to the epistemological problem of how *individuals* come to be observed, and how the distinctive trait of *individuality* is discerned and identified. For as we originally understand these terms, an individual is a specific and concrete entity, while individuality is the characteristic attribute of all individuals.

There are many points of similarity between Simmel's approach to the problem of knowledge—especially knowledge of individuals—and the general theory of *Verstehen* as outlined by Dilthey. There are also significant similarities between Simmel and Bergson, although Simmel does not appear to be particularly perturbed by the seeming contradiction between "intuition" and "understanding." Most interesting, however, is the contrast between the epistemological frameworks which Simmel and Bergson choose to emphasize. For if Bergson repeatedly asks that we admit the importance of time, Simmel is just as insistent in stressing the significance of space. If Bergson is concerned with passage and duration, with the movement and change of the object observed, Simmel is preoccupied with the object's stability. Bergson contemplates duration as an observer, standing idly on a bank, might watch a river sweep by: the observer is more or less fixed, the object flows on. Simmel views it as one might examine a cathedral: while one walks outside it, around it, within it, or looks down upon it; it endures.

Bergson relies upon an illustration drawn from motion-picture photography: Movement is fundamentally unanalyzable; it can be reduced only to specious units, each without motion; and these units, when viewed sequentially and properly phased, re-create merely the illusion of movement. Bergson's cameraman is stable, whereas Simmel's, mounted on a mobile crane, is in constant movement, for Simmel is more concerned with the spatiality of the observed object than with its temporally phased fluctuations. The process of observation itself becomes dynamic, entailing as it does a constant search for new viewpoints: now pressing forward for a close-up, now bearing down still more for a microscopic scrutiny of some intimate detail, now pulling suddenly back for a broader perspective or an aerial view.

This restless movement of the observer causes a continual shifting of focus. For a moment, all is blurred; he adjusts himself to the changed conditions of observation; all becomes clear again. From each moment of clarified vision, where an organized field can be envisaged, individuality emerges. It is not that the object is completely individualized and that we simply learn more about it from each new vantage point. Rather, the object exists as a permanent condition of infinitely individualized, infinitely varied experiences. Individuality is a characteristic of the experiential transaction involving subject and object, although usually, in our confusion, we attribute it now to the one component, now to the other.

The house seen from a distance of three yards is the same object when seen from a distance of thirty yards, but in each case the optical representation is singularly different. Each ordered experience is an individual. The relationships of which it is composed are unique to it and cannot be transposed with those of another individual since every change in distance involves a change in proportion. Simmel's epistemology does not deny the existence of the object itself, either as the condition for the emergence of individualized experiences or as a limit of scientific abstraction. Nevertheless, there is a tendency in Simmel to permit the object to become remote, a kind of Kantian *Ding an sich,* whereas the real objects of knowledge become the structured relationships of our experience.

Every standpoint is privileged to disclose relationships visible from no other standpoint:

> If A and B have different conceptions of M, this by no means necessarily implies incompleteness or deception. Rather, in view of the relation in which A stands to M, A's nature and the total circumstances being what they are, A's picture of M is true for him in the same manner in which, for B, a different picture is true. It would be quite erroneous to say that, above these two pictures, there is the objectively correct knowledge about M, and that A's and B's images are legitimated to the extent to which they coincide with this objective knowledge. Rather, the ideal truth which the picture of M in the conception of A approaches—to be sure, only asymptotically—is something different, even as an ideal, from that of B. It contains as an integrating, form-giving precondition the psychological peculiarity of A and the particular relation into which A and M are brought by their specific characters and destinies.[1]

Simmel maintains that what is involved here is a "structural principle" of the relativity and equivalent correctness of all perspectives in so far as they are able to bring the field of visualization into focus. Given a constant, stable object, there are innumerable variables—for example, the psychology of the observer, his relative distance—which contribute to and compose the individual that emerges in experience.

Yet, paradoxically, if the object is to be viewed "in perspective," it must be seen from more than a single point of view. We need both distance and nearness. Also, we need "inside knowledge" as well as an understanding of the external factors (pp. 7, 97 n.). Gradually, a curious reversal occurs. In the initial observation, the object is subordinated to the individuality of the experience. But every additional observation contributes to the construction of the individuality of the object. This abstracted individuality is a composite pattern of relationships as discerned from a variety of perspectives. It is not necessarily more "correct" than the individuality of any direct observation from a single standpoint. It may, however, have a depth or fullness which single observations often lack.

Thus far, little has been said about the sensitivity of the observer. Yet what we call individuality is partially determined by our sensitivity to individual differences. When these differences are relatively great, an acute observer is not needed to discern them; but when they are slight, we often become sensitized to them, as inhabitants of a jungle become accustomed to noting innumerable minor variations of greenness. It follows, then, that if our threshhold of sensitivity increases as the differences among perceived individuals diminish, the experienced differentiation appears to be negligible. The smaller the differences, the more they are magnified. In this sense, a shrinking universe might not necessarily appear to be shrinking to its inhabitants, and a society of individuals who were becoming increasingly uniform might appear to them absolutely unchanged in its variety.

An individual is a unified set of relationships in the field of visualization. A society, a style, an epoch, a person, a physical thing, an experience—these can all be individuals. It is not that they are wholly subjective or wholly objective. Independent of observation, the relationships of which such individuals are composed may already be patterned to a pronounced degree. But the individualized structure or form is rounded out in the act of intellectual understanding. Another way of putting this might be to say that, for Simmel, individuality is neither wholly discovered nor wholly invented. It is *produced,* although it is not so much a product as a natural production. Yet it cannot be denied that Simmel wavers in his formulation of individuality. Now he views the individual as an intellectual synthesis, now as a category of the understanding, now as a structure at least partially objective. His intent, apparently, is to suggest that individualization is both a basic mental habit and a tendency to distinctiveness and discreteness in events. What becomes individuated in experience we call an individual, but our concept only makes more pronounced a structure that was already immanent. Simmel believes that scientific understanding requires the disclosure of individuals, for it is essentially an abstractive process concerned with the discovery of structural unities. This is why he is able to remark that individuals are "the immediate, concrete data of all historical reality" (p. 40): apparently we have no better way of organizing our experience so as to make it comprehensible.

We must understand, however, that our emphasis upon individuals cannot deny reality to that which is not individualized. This is true whether the non-individual is content (as compared to form) or background (as compared to pattern). Simmel does not preoccupy himself too greatly, however, with the futile problem of whether individuals are ultimately more real than that of which they are composed or that against which they stand out.

Certainly, the figure-ground opposition is an important conceptual instrument for Simmel, for he often speaks of individuality as a pattern whose pronouncedness must be seen against the background of what it is not—of what contrasts with, or even contradicts, it. (This chiaroscuro technique makes quite plausible his interest in Rembrandt—especially since Rembrandt used that technique for the purpose of intense individualization.) The individual stands over against the common or the general; the individualized experience contrasts with the ordinary, commonplace experience. We prize the individual in this sense, not because of its intrinsic value, but because it occurs in a context of triviality, monotony, mediocrity. We value the rare, fresh, spontaneous relationships which stand in such contrast to the insipid dreariness of ordinary relationships. The greater the routinization of the world, the more the genuine individual stands boldly in relief against it. The commonplace modestly withdraws to the background, but without it the pattern of individuality could not emerge.

Of equal or perhaps greater importance for Simmel is the form-content distinction. Contents are common, indiscriminate, undifferentiated; forms alone are individualized. A form may be taken to be a pattern or *Gestalt* in terms of which contents have been ordered. But individuality may also consist in the quality—the *Gestaltqualität*—of that pattern.

Change, activity, flux—these exist in the passage or flow of contents, although each content is what it is: unchanging, yet passing on. Forms themselves remain the same, forever independent of alteration. Bureaucracies differ, marriages differ, secrets differ, but not the forms of bureaucracy, marriage, or secrecy. The more things change, the more they remain *formally* the same.

This is still an oversimplification. First, because contents—the *material*, Simmel calls it (pp. 40-42), of individuality—already have a tendency to form. We might call it a *matrix*. Second, because to the extent that matrices exist, contents become unchanging. Digestion is a process that has gradually developed with life. To the extent that it distinguishes itself from non-digestive processes, it attains the matrix of form. But only with the full-fledged emergence of form can we speak of the emergence of individuality. One becomes an individual when one functions as an autonomous and integrated whole, which can if necessary become subordinate to a segment of itself.

For example, there are innumerable impulses, drives, movements, and interests in biological existence. Some of these may develop into a "mating tendency." As yet, this is only the matrix of form. There is a further development into what we call marriage, and marriage has thus far persevered as an institution because it has transcended its instrumental function and become an end in itself. People avoid divorce "so as to preserve the marriage." Similarly, random pleasurable movements become play, and playfulness is an ingredient in the development of art, but art is a form which has value in itself: one may devote oneself to art, live for art. It becomes autonomous.

It is in this manner that one develops the form of individuality. Each person may have differently organized the raw materials of life—impulses, drives, tendencies. But until that organization persists for its own sake, mastering the separate activities so that they can contribute to the perseveration of the whole, and the whole can subserve the part, one has not yet achieved individuality. Differentiation may have been a natural result of the struggle for survival, but the appearance of individuality means that one now survives *in order to be* differentiated, unified, and autonomous. Contents may be individuated, but only forms are individualized, having transcended the conditions of their origin.

It is usually believed that individuality is reduced when the individual participates in a group. Simmel does not contradict this impression—he even accentuates it. In the group, individuality tends to be reduced not merely to the average but to the lowest, moral feelings, the most primitive or superficial thoughts. The larger the group, the lower the moral and intellectual level of those who compose it is likely to be (pp. 36-39). Yet this is only one consequence of group membership; there are compensatory consequences. To affiliate oneself with a group is to determine and define oneself more precisely in respect to it. One becomes, or is seen as, similar to others in the group but dissimilar to the totality of individuals outside it. To belong to a second group further limits one's similarity to others and increases one's dissimilarity. Thus the greater the number of groups to which one belongs, the less likely it is that the totality of one's affiliations will be identical with anyone else's totality. The cumulative effect of group affiliation turns out to be increasing differentiation and individualization. Simmel asserts that "the larger the number of groups to which an individual belongs, the more improbable is it that other persons will exhibit the same combination of group-affiliations, that these particular groups will 'intersect' once again (in a second individual)."[2]

There is a certain hazard in such a statement. In a society that is highly conventional, group affiliations may be so rigorously prescribed that one may belong to a large number of groups without perceptibly increasing one's differences from others. Yet Simmel reminds us that it is not, after all, the mere sum of one's affiliations which helps to constitute one's singularity: it is the unique *pattern* of those affiliations. Quantitative changes in a sociological structure do result in distinct qualitative differences (pp. 115-17). The addition or subtraction of a single, apparently insignificant element may utterly transform the quality of the whole. An individual's uniqueness may therefore result from an uncharacteristic affiliation which nevertheless radically alters the whole of his character.

Just as group membership can both diminish and enhance individuality, so the establishment of universals in the social order has a double-edged effect. Thus Simmel asserts that the rise of a money economy in which a universal means of exchange was substituted for diversified particular means was to a considerable degree responsible for the rise of individualism. Yet the individualizing power which money confers has its other side: such power is achieved at the cost of de-individualizing other beings, whom one tends to evaluate in monetary terms. Here we confront the Nietzschean belief that there is a world economy of individuality, with the result that its increase in the few takes place at the expense of the depersonalized many.

The positive side, however, is also inescapable. Universals can function subserviently to all individuals, heightening their uniqueness. When, for example, we assert that all men have equal and identical rights, the universality we stipulate does not constrain men's individuality but liberates it, especially if we insist that all men have the identical right to be treated as individuals. In Simmel's writings, universality represents a necessary condition for humanity, while individuality represents a sufficient condition.

The secret of individuality, therefore, lies in the transmutation of the impersonal, general, necessary conditions of life into the personalized, differentiated, sufficient conditions of being alive as a human individual. For example, while sexual relationships form the general condition of all marriages, genuine marriage involves more than sexuality.

It follows that the general conditions of social life require the establishment of norms. In a large society, obedience to a norm is not an individualizing form of conduct, whereas we do become distinctive once we violate the norm. "Greeting somebody in the street proves no esteem whatever, but failure to do so conclusively proves the opposite" (p. 400). In a smaller society, however, where there is a large number of particular norms, conformity to norms is taken as a sign of individuality and distinction. In a complex mass society, made up of highly differentiated individuals, norms must be general rather than specific, few rather than many. If in seeking to allow greater freedom to its members, a smaller society crystallizes norms in a wide variety of specific forms that seem to be appropriate to individual needs, it is, on the other hand, likely to permit less differentiation than it would if the lack of freedom were confined to only very general and pervasive features. Simmel remarks that democratic societies initiate relatively simple, general measures, whereas aristocracies try to do justice to the peculiarities of individual elements (p. 143). If modern individuality arose under the despotisms of the Italian Renaissance, it was because the political character of the individual could be factored out and repressed, while the development of all other aspects of his individuality could be encouraged and stimulated (p. 204). Simmel here touches upon the antinomy between freedom and individuality which is entailed in the contrast between democracy and aristocracy.

Central to Simmel's presentation of the problem of individuality is his analysis of the contrast between the philosophical outlook of the eighteenth century and that of the nineteenth.

The Enlightenment sought to emancipate man from the historical bonds of traditional institutions. In liberating men from servitude to the past, it believed it was liberating a human nature that was common to all, identical in each human being. Human freedom could be achieved simply by releasing men from the conditions which caused inequality. In this sense, the eighteenth century stood for a break with one's predecessors.

Individualism in the nineteenth century, on the other hand, meant a break with one's contemporaries. Especially under the impetus of the romantic movement, men were stimulated to differentiate themselves. Individuals had to be liberated from custom and convention so as to be most truly themselves. Freedom was thought to be the consequence of encouraging men to be infinitely differentiated and diversified, even if this entailed drastic inequalities. In short, Simmel remarks, "Eighteenth-century liberalism put the individual on his own feet: in the nineteenth, he was allowed to go as far as they would carry him" (p. 83).

What the eighteenth century failed to understand was that the emancipation of men from an oppressive social system, in the name of equality, would lead directly to the oppression of men by one another, also in the name of equality. Unless the freedom of the strong is restricted (through law or the ethics of fraternalism), the strong restrict the freedom of the weak. An equal measure of freedom for all, therefore, leads to inequality, to the concentration of power and the monopolization of opportunities.

The eighteenth century may have had some fleeting faith that the spirit of fraternity would resolve this antinomy between equality and freedom. But it pinned its hopes on the notion of law. The individual is to be conceived of as an instance of a general rule. That which differentiates the particular case is merely accidental, external, trivial. The essence of man, his humanity, lives in each individual, is an atomic unit, everywhere alike, and absolutely amenable to universal law. Because this unconditionally identical core in all men finds its freedom in submitting to the requirements of universality, in lawful rather than lawless behavior, men themselves achieve freedom by liberating the humanity within them. To be moral is to deny yourself privileges which you might ordinarily take on the grounds that you are different from others. In this view, articulated most clearly in Kant, to be moral is to submit oneself to universal law, and to be lawful is to be free.

In brief, the attitude of the eighteenth century was that individuals are homogeneous and basically undifferentiated. The atomic individuals who constitute society are bound together solely by means of law, which applies indiscriminately to one and all since one and all are essentially alike. This is a quantitative individualism that treats the individual as a unit, as a separate entity. Simmel calls it the individualism of singleness (*Einzelheit*).

In contrast, the following century developed a qualitative emphasis which may be called the individualism of uniqueness (*Einzigkeit*). As single, one attains the freedom that is permitted to whatever falls *within* the law. As unique, one is free by falling *outside* the law. As single, one is an instance, an exemplification, of mankind. As unique, one's context is society, which exists as the background against which one stands out: one's fellow men conveniently provide one with innumerable points of unlikeness.

The romantic feels that his self is absolutely specific and irreplaceable. Individuality becomes precious because it is incomparable; priceless, because matchless. Yet one's uniqueness escapes possession. It remains an ideal to be longed for: the individual seeks his self "as if he did not yet have it" (p. 79).

This, then, is the qualitative individuality of the romantic period, originating in Herder and Rousseau. It will be recalled that Rousseau, at the very beginning of his *Confessions,* asserts that he may not be better than other men but at least he is different. This voices precisely the essence of the interpretation of individuality as uniqueness. The doctrine was elaborated by Schlegel and Schleiermacher. In the latter (as afterward in Royce), the realization of one's uniqueness becomes a moral duty, that which one is called to do because the absolute can live only in the individual—hence one's responsibility to become a unique monad mirroring the universe.

The radical shift in the interpretation of individuality which was introduced with romanticism was also reflected in social and economic developments. The rigid class structure of the *ancien régime* had enforced social distinctions regardless of merit. Such injustice seemed to liberals of the time a denial, not of legitimate individual differences, but of the fundamental similarity and equality of all human beings. However, their nineteenth-century successors attempted to construct a social order which would take individual differences into account. The institutions entrusted with the legitimation and enforcement of differences were *competition* and the *division of labor.* Although free competition would seem to be associated with the individualism of difference, Simmel suggests that it is really a product of eighteenth-century liberalism, according to which such competition naturally promoted the welfare of all social interests. The doctrine more closely aligned with the individualism of difference was the theory of the division of labor. By this means, the nineteenth century (culminating in Durkheim) sought to maintain and guarantee the existence of precise differences among individuals.

Simmel recognized that unlimited competition and occupational specialization have not been outstandingly successful in promoting individuality. How individuality might be more suitably enhanced, he does not specifically indicate, and his skeptical attitude toward socialism suggests that he did not expect a solution to come from this quarter. Yet he hoped for a higher synthesis, a form which would transcend both the individual and society, blending greater diversities with new unities, thereby realizing and celebrating the idealized possibilities of humanity itself (p. 84). He looked ahead to those "highest types of development" in which there are

> social structures which precisely when they have attained a very large size and a perfect organization, can grant the individual the greatest freedom to live his life according to his own particular norms and in the most individualized form. And on the other hand, there are groups which reach their greatest strength only when their members have attained the most intense and differentiated individualism (p. 110).

Simmel's profound commitment to the nineteenth-century conception of differentiated individuality is here very much in evidence.

If Simmel admired the nineteenth century for its understanding of the *substance* of individuality, he admired the eighteenth century for its grasp of its *structure*. He found that two quite different frames of reference were involved. For the quantitative, universalistic view, the framework is mankind, *humanity*. For the qualitative, particularistic view, the framework is *society*.

That mankind and society are extremely different contexts is a concept which Simmel finds most clearly worked out in Kant and Nietzsche. The values of the individual as a human being are not the same as his values as a social being. One's values as a human being are purely personal qualities, independent of social relationships. Human values are autonomous, intrinsic, and immediate. One's personal worth lies in his "good will," as Kant would say. Society, on the other hand, is chiefly interested in our actions and in the consequences of what we do. It judges us pragmatically, on the grounds of our social utility, whereas humanity judges us by our contributions to the development of mankind, by the extent to which humanity is enriched by our existence.

The stipulation of humanity that we should act to realize human ideals is often in sharp contrast to society's frequent demand that we conform to the average and mediocre. Of course, we should not too hastily assent to Simmel's contention (which links him with the liberalism of de Tocqueville and Mill) that society generally cultivates mediocrity (p. 37). For society may wish to encourage a situation in which diversity and variety are prevalent. After all, mere variety is no threat to it, and perhaps social controls are most effective when the constituents of society are effectively divided among themselves. On such a dead level of diversity, all persons can be equally insignificant and impotent. In fact, it might even be maintained that what is distinctive about twentieth-century society is that it simultaneously encourages the contradictory ideals of social conformity and individual differentiation, so that individuality becomes more than ever an insoluble dilemma.

Empirically, we note that men are similar to one another in some respects, different in other respects. As fact or as tendency, says Simmel, difference is of neither greater nor lesser importance than likeness. But this is not the case with our psychological and sociological interpretations of individuality. "If something is objectively of equal importance in terms of both similarity with a type and differentiation from it, we will be more conscious of the differentiation" (p. 31). We are more interested (at present, at any rate) in the way we differ from others than in the way we resemble them. One comes to think that he is significant only to the extent that he can contrast himself with others. As a matter of fact, Simmel observes that "where such a contrast does not exist, he may even artificially create it" (p. 31). Simmel here moves from the consideration of individuality as such to the analysis of the ways in which we are fascinated by it.

It is tempting to assume that different interpretations of individuality have their appeal for us because they represent alternative modes of achieving ultimate values, such as freedom or happiness. Simmel cautions us, however, against assuming that the choice of interpretation is a purely instrumental choice, seeking merely to adjust means to ends. Instead, the decision of each man as to whether he is, or wants, or ought to be, like or unlike his fellow man is bound to come from the depths of his being. This decision is of the utmost gravity to each individual: "It expresses the existence of man, the substance of his essence" (p. 74). It is not the result of an appraisal of means and ends but the ultimate ground on which all one's other decisions are built. Either we feel, in some ultimate, foundational sense, that we are the same as all other men, or we feel, with equal conviction, that we are basically unique. This choice is at the heart of our civilization. For, as the existentialists would say, the sort of societies we create and the manner of men we are to be will depend on the choice we make.

Again, interpretations of individuality vacillate between the notion that an individual is an elementary unit of some larger complex and the notion that an individual is a single composite organization of parts. If we examine the consequences of the latter assumption, we note that an almost magical transposition can take place. Man has the capacity to decompose himself into parts and to feel any one of these as his proper self, Simmel remarks. The part can stand for, or be interpreted as, the whole. A person can come to believe that his true self consists in some portion of his self. It is this psychological alchemy that enables men to devote themselves so whole-heartedly to separate segments of their lives.

Similarly, the individual may rebel against the feeling that he is merely an atomic member of society. If we take the point of view of the part (either the fragmentary motif of personality or the individual member of society), we insist upon the equivalence of part to whole, or we insist that only in the part is reality to be found. If we take the point of view of the whole (either the whole individual or the whole society), we maintain that the whole is greater than any of its parts, and greater than the sum of its parts.

Although this antinomy cannot be resolved on its own terms, it does not preclude a third interpretation—one that Simmel finds in Goethe and Nietzsche—which is that the individual can best perfect and fulfill himself when he devotes himself to the service of some objective ideal, when he dedicates himself to be the instrument of a cause greater than himself. This ideal cause need not be identical with society or with the aims of society. One becomes the agent of an ultimate value: for the artist, beauty; for the scientist, truth; and so on. The conflict between society and the individual is resolved only by transcending both, by surmounting the vacillations of egoism and altruism and rising to the objectivity of idealized endeavor.

Yet Simmel warns us that the cultivated individual is something more than a specialist, for specialization is usually the result of devoting oneself to a single ideal. Of course, when an individual places himself in the service of an ideal cause, his individuality is not reduced as much as when he becomes a member of a group. But just as he gains individuality by an increasing variety of group participations, so his individuality increases if he dedicates himself to a plurality of ideals.

Since the model of individuality which Simmel constructs relies so frequently upon spatial or geometrical imagery, it is not surprising that he should note two conflicting interpretations of the *boundaries* of the individual. These interpretations correspond to two contrasting modes of vision, as suggested by Wölfflin. In one case, we see things as having sharply defined outlines; in the other, the outlines are blurred and indistinct. Illustrations of this contrast are to be found in the paintings of the classic Renaissance artists as opposed to works done in the baroque style. For Simmel, the individual takes shape as a tangible entity, but one's sharp raw edges (if one is too peculiar, too eccentric) can be abrasive or destructive in social intercourse. One needs to be in touch with one's neighbors in a more sociable, more harmonious manner; hence one develops tact, which is a self-regulatory function aimed at maintaining the smooth flow of interpersonal conduct. To be tactful is thus to suppress one's most personal, most intimate, most unique characteristics for the sake of integrating and blending easily with the group. Tact therefore blurs the edges of the individual. It softens his contours and surrounds him with an aura of approachability and permeability so as to make him less formidable than the tactless individualist.

Every individual is surrounded by an ideal sphere, a zone of personal "honor" which it is considered indiscreet to trespass upon. Discretion is, thus, a recognition of social distance. It is also a recognition of the private, unbreachable innerness of the individual. If to be tactful means the courteous inhibition of one's own unique eccentricities, to be discreet means the awareness of another individual's privacy and distinctiveness.

Simmel's treatment of such topics as tact, discretion, confidence, reserve, and secrecy are at the core of his sociology of intimate relations. It can be seen that in this "internal sociology" he tends to accept the nineteenth-century interpretation of individuality as definitive. Repeatedly, he emphasizes the uniqueness that springs from internal complexity and external incomparability rather than the individuality that is associated with atomic discreteness and subservience to universal law.

Whereas the atomic individual is united to his fellow men by *identity* of interests, the unique individual is bound to them by a *harmony* of interests. When interests are taken for granted as being largely identical, individuals can confront one another totally. The subtleties of intimate rapports do not have to be utilized. The preservation of one's individuality does not require the use of devious, ambiguous stratagems of conduct, such as simultaneous disclosure and secrecy.

On the other hand, unique individuals can engage one another only at odd points or at rare intervals. Like meshed gears, they can touch only at limited segments of their perimeters. Thus, as differentiation among individuals increases, intimacy becomes increasingly difficult to achieve and increasingly precarious once accomplished. Modern man, Simmel observes, "has too much to hide to sustain a friendship in the ancient sense" (p. 326). Once again, we see in Simmel the figure-ground mode of analysis: what the individual discloses of himself must always be seen against the dark background of what he conceals. There is a strong analogy here with G. H. Mead's notion that our understanding of an action must be in terms of its contrast with the actions which might have taken place but were inhibited. For Simmel, that which the individual conceals remains his private psychological property, which the intimate acquaintance honors and respects, acknowledging "the right to question to be limited by the right to secrecy" (p. 329).

However, although modern friendships between unique individuals entail connection in only one or only several respects, it is nevertheless possible that each connection entails the total individual. For as we have already seen, a person may treat a portion of his self as though it were the whole. The inner complexity of the highly developed, highly differentiated individual reveals itself in a multiplicity of specialized facets, through each of which he can express the unity of his inner nature, even though he conceals from each friend other segments of his personality.[3] One can speak here of a division of intimacy as one speaks of a division of labor. In modern man there has developed a type of specialization which permits the *absolute* sharing of oneself with another in a single, limited respect, instead of the restricted sharing of experience in a variety of respects.

We see, then, that what the individual fails to disclose to others is a primary element of individualization (p. 334). With the growth of the metropolis, there has also developed a greater need for reserve and discretion so as to guard one's inner traits from others. Also, one becomes blasé, channeling one's perception of others so as to become unaware of, or anesthetized to, their personal distinctiveness.

The growth of democracy has led to increasing publicity in public affairs, but there has also developed a trend toward even greater secrecy in individual matters.[4] As political authority becomes demystified and rationalized, as secularization increases, the remaining zone of mystery is the individual. What is not apparent in his behavior, we take to be concealed. This may lead to the endowment of the individual with a mystical charisma (especially in liberal democracies) which is referred to as his uniqueness.

On the other hand, if a secret society is created, the whole of it becomes charismatically endowed with uniqueness, while in each member there occurs a loss of self, a de-individualizing, and a heightened emphasis upon similarity (p. 373). The advantage of this de-individualization is that it replaces personal responsibility with collective irresponsibility (p. 374). In such a society, one is held personally responsible only when one's actions are contrary to the explicitly permitted behavior within the group.

A discussion of Simmel's conception of individuality cannot conclude without some reference to the aesthetic dimension of individuality. Individuality may be enhanced by the ornaments with which one chooses to adorn oneself, but such enhancement requires the stylization of ornament, its lack of individual distinctiveness, and its stress, instead, upon a style that is broadly historical or socially oriented. In contrast, we appreciate the work of art precisely because of its incomparability, its transcendence of style, and the manner in which it suggests both the uniqueness of its creator and that of the individual to whom it appeals. Through this deeper realization of the meaning of the non-personal individuality of the work of art, we come to a more profound understanding of the significance of personal individuality in the human being.

How can Simmel's contribution to our understanding of individuality be evaluated? Probably we must acknowledge that he sheds on the problem only a fitful light. His reliance upon a spatial (or pseudospatial) frame of interpretation tends to emphasize the static and extended aspect of the self but neglects those more dynamic aspects, less readily visualized, which are also essential to a just conception of individuality: only cursorily or obliquely does Simmel confront such problems as power, integrity, productivity, and growth.

What is undeniable, certainly, is the sensitivity Simmel shows to the delicate nuances and intricate complexities of the concept of individuality. This sensitivity is particularly fruitful in his explorations of the epistemological, historical, and sociological contexts of the problem. True, the epistemology contains intimations of a metaphysic; the historical account is chiefly a historical application of the sociology of knowledge; and the sociology is tightly interwoven with psychology and aesthetics. But this is because Simmel prefers to follow his insights rather than limit himself to any single discipline or perspective.

Perhaps it is unjust to demand of Simmel a solution to the contradiction between the eighteenth- and nineteenth-century views of individuality. It is a relatively simple matter to say that the conflict is merely between two modes of interpretation. In the one case, individuality refers to whatever is separable, quantitatively isolable. Individuality here is determined by the act of segregation. However, it can also be determined by the act of distinguishing between qualities. Hence the antinomy appears: individuality defined as separateness or as distinctiveness.

Did Simmel wish to formulate a paradox? Or was he seeking to demonstrate that individuality entails a fundamental ambivalence, an equivocality which makes it susceptible of several modes of interpretation? Or did he really believe in the possibility of some higher synthesis? These three theories appear equally plausible as interpretations of Simmel's intent. But the second, with its suggestion of the subtle, ambiguous depths of the self, may be the most fruitful for future inquiry.

1. Kurt H. Wolff (ed.), *The Sociology of Georg Simmel* (Glencoe, Ill.: Free Press of Glencoe, Illinois, 1950), p. 309. Page numbers in parentheses refer to this work.

2. Reinhard Bendix (trans.), "The Web of Group-Affiliations," in Georg Simmel's *Conflict* and *The Web of Group-Affiliations* (Glencoe, Ill.: Free Press of Glencoe, Illinois, 1955), p. 140.

3. Apparently, for Simmel, the most fundamental level of individuality is reached when one observes oneself as a whole by means of a facet of oneself acting as the whole.

4. Although modern life has in some ways decreased in privacy, we have simply invented new modes of reserve and discretion, new techniques of secretiveness. The growth of mass societies does not destroy arcana but causes them to flourish. We can recognize this in the insatiable curiosity that is stimulated in democratic societies concerning the private affairs of individuals. Yet we should not be too sure that the balance between the public and the private has been upset, for as we reveal an increasing amount of what was traditionally secret to the eyes and ears of the profane, more and more of what in the past was public knowledge becomes problematical. The outward signs of wealth and power become increasingly inconspicuous. The locus of power is getting to be an enigma. Even work becomes more private as it becomes more specialized; hence one thinks it of little interest to others and is reticent about it. Gossip, on the other hand, deals with those features of human behavior or motivation which are common to all; consequently, it becomes more and more prominent as a major cultural form.

SIMMEL'S SOCIOLOGY OF POWER: THE ARCHITECTURE OF POLITICS

E. V. WALTER

Political theorists are amphibious by vocation and live in two elements—the ethical and the empirical. Their attention to political power is not limited to the sociological work of empirical description and analysis but inveterately extends to the search for conditions that make the exercise of power legitimate and for the principles that distinguish good from evil forms. One tradition has covered the established order with the halo of legitimacy, providing ideological defenses. The other, or critical, tradition in political theory has penetrated ideological defense and judged power relations by the touchstone of freedom.[1] In both traditions, political theory carries the burden of judgment, applying rational criteria and standards of value, a process which is possible only through a synthesis of ethical and empirical perspectives.

For the critical tradition in political theory, the ethical standard has been seriously weakened by the realities of power in our time. The rise of totalitarianism and the growth of oppression in the liberal states have generated a climate of pessimism in which the criticism of power appears irrelevant and unreal. Power has taken on a demonic quality beyond the reach of immemorial restraints. The old writers lived in another world. With now archaic optimism they numbered the extrinsic limitations on power—the reason and conscience of mankind, the plural countervailing pressures of rival social formations, human dignity, and the spontaneous impulse to freedom—which have faded like lost saints, cherished but invoked in vain. For reason and conscience deteriorate when the mind itself becomes a captive or even an artifact of the state's propaganda apparatus; potential rivals of the state—family, church, economic units—may be rendered inert by irresistible centralization and the politicization of technology; dignity and freedom are figments when entire populations are paralyzed and rendered inanimate by a highly refined apparatus of terror. Even in the liberal-democratic states, one fears that restraint on power has become a luxury to be easily discarded in the next period of intense crisis.

The old way of stating the problem (power *and* society; politics *and* law, *and* custom, *and* morals) is unreal, for power will no longer enter into partnerships. We must turn from judgment by external standards to seek inner mechanisms, and in this search devote ourselves to the refinement of a sociology of power, inspired by the ethical commitment to find ways of bringing power under rational control and to oppose all forms of dehumanization. I would argue, then, that though the traditional ethical-empirical synthesis of political theory has been destroyed by the realities of power in our time, this destruction is the very condition of reconstruction in political theory, and that through the sociology of power the political theorist may find the ground for a new synthesis.

The significance of Simmel's sociology for political theory is more implicit than obvious. In his writing, the space given to the direct examination of power is not extensive: merely a sixth of the *Soziologie* takes up an analysis of domination, subordination, and related matters.[2] Moreover, his writing is profoundly apolitical[3] and even ahistorical;[4] yet his way of seeing society suggests an illuminating way of seeing and understanding power. When power has burst its traditional "political" categories, only certain kinds of apolitical perspectives can apprehend its nature. The demonism of power is like the demonism of society which, Simmel observes, "claims the individual for itself. It wants to make of him a form that it can incorporate into its own structure."[5]

Society, Simmel explains, "develops its own vehicles and organs by whose claims and commands the individual is confronted as by an alien party."[6] Since these forces are set in motion by the needs of individuals but transform themselves, contrary to the original intention, into powers that control these individuals, Simmel's idea of alienation is a tragic concept. In the face of overwhelming social forces, "the deepest problems of modern life derive from the claim of the individual to preserve the autonomy and individuality of his existence. . . ."[7] The individual is a reality and a moral value, and so is society;

but each has separate claims to coherence and wholeness, for the life principle of the individual is different and often in conflict with the life principle of the collectivity. Simmel explicates what we have experienced so deeply—the tragic element in collective life:

> Society strives to be a whole, an organic unit of which the individuals must be mere members. Society asks of the individual that he employ all his strength in the service of the special function which he has to exercise as a member of it; that he so modify himself as to become the most suitable vehicle for this function. Yet the drive toward unity and wholeness that is characteristic of the individual himself rebels against this role. The individual strives to be rounded out in himself, not merely to help to round out society. He strives to develop his full capacities, irrespective of the shifts among them that the interest of society may ask of him. This conflict between the whole, which imposes the one-sidedness of partial function upon its elements, and the part, which itself strives to be a whole, is insoluble.[8]

Individuality and society make rival claims on man, Simmel observes, and in response to these claims,

> man has the capacity to decompose himself into parts and to feel any one of these as his proper self. Yet each part may collide with any other and may struggle for the dominion over the individual's actions. This capacity places man, insofar as he feels himself to be a social being, into an often contradictory relation with those among his impulses and interests that are *not* pre-empted by his social character. In other words, the conflict between society and individual is continued in the individual himself as the conflict among his component parts. Thus, it seems to me, the basic struggle between society and individual inheres in the general form of individual life.[9]

The conflict between the claims of the individual and the claims of society produces

> the deep and tragic ambiguity which pervades the very roots of every societal formation, of every formation of a unit out of units. The individual who lives from his inner resources, who can answer for his actions only if they are directed by his own conviction, is

> supposed to orient his will toward the purposes of others. As something ethical, this remains always a matter of his own will; it flows from the innermost core of his personality. But what is more, he is also supposed to become, in his self-based existence, a member of a collectivity which has its center outside of him. . . . Man *internally* stands under two, mutually alien norms . . . our movement revolving around our own center (something totally different from egoism) claims to be as definitive as the movement around the social center; in fact, it claims to be the decisive meaning of life.[10]

From the conflict, individuals suffer, and the antinomies of collective life pass into the spiritual realm of tragedy—especially, I would argue, tragedy in the Hegelian sense, for the collision between individual and social claims is a conflict

> between powers that rule the world of man's will and action—his "ethical substance." . . . The essentially tragic fact is the self-division and intestinal warfare of the ethical substance, not so much the war of good with evil as the war of good with good. Two of these isolated powers face each other, making incompatible demands. . . . The competing forces are both in themselves rightful, and so far the claim of each is equally justified; but the right of each is pushed into a wrong, because it ignores the right of the other, and demands that absolute sway which belongs to neither alone, but to the whole of which each is but a part.[11]

The power which works through individuals makes them the instrument of a design which is not their own. "They act freely, and yet their action binds them hand and foot." Simmel's social universe is like the tragic universe with its inexorable drive for coherence:

> The whole or order against which the individual part shows itself powerless seems to be animated by a passion for perfection: we cannot otherwise explain its behavior towards evil. Yet it appears to engender this evil within itself, and in its effort to overcome and expel it it is agonized with pain, and driven to mutilate its own substance and to lose not only evil but priceless good.[12]

Sometimes the order presses its claims with such inexorable force that the end is catastrophe, "the violent self-restitution of the divided spiritual unity":

> it is the act of a power immeasurably superior to that of the conflicting agents, a power which is irresistible and unescapable, and which overbears and negates whatever is incompatible with it. . . . The ultimate power thus appears as a destructive force.[13]

Sometimes, however, the tragic conflict may end in peace; the conflicting claims may be softened and an adjustment made between them. Simmel's response to the tragic element, as I shall try to show, is the way of resignation. The conflict proceeds in rhythms and cycles, finding a temporarily fixed form of engagement, bursting that frame, and moving on to new forms. As he expresses it,

> I should like to think that the efforts of mankind will produce ever more numerous and varied forms for the human personality to affirm itself and to demonstrate the value of its existence. In fortunate periods, these varied forms may order themselves into harmonious wholes. In doing so, their contradictions and conflicts will cease to be mere obstacles to mankind's efforts: they will also stimulate new demonstrations of the strength of these efforts and lead them to new creations.[14]

Strife and conflict, if they do not end in catastrophe, are creative and constructive forces in social life, and Simmel recognizes that the coherence of society depends on the antagonisms within it. The idea must have been taken directly from Kant who, perhaps, founded it on an analogy to the Newtonian forces of attraction and repulsion in nature. As Kant observes in his Fourth Proposition:

> The means which Nature employs to bring about the development of all the capacities implanted in men, is their mutual Antagonism in society, but only so far as this antagonism becomes at length the cause of an Order among them that is regulated by Law.
>
> By this Antagonism, I mean the *unsocial sociability* of men; that is, their tendency to enter into society, conjoined, however, with an accompanying resistance which continually threatens to dissolve this society. The disposition for this lies manifestly in human nature. Man has an inclination to *socialise* himself by associating with others, because in such a state he feels himself more than a natural man, in the development of his natural capacities. He has, moreover, a great tendency to *individualise* himself by isolation from others, because he likewise finds in himself the

> unsocial disposition of wishing to direct everything merely according to his own mind.[15]

The antagonism produces evil, but at the same time it impels men to new exertions of their powers and, consequently, to development of their natural capacities. Without antagonism and discord

> men might have led an Arcadian shepherd life in complete harmony, contentment and mutual love, but in that case all their talents would have for ever remained hidden in their germ. . . . Man wishes concord; but Nature knows better what is good for his species, and she will have discord.[16]

Kant considered conflict to be a historical force, an instrument of civilization and progress; but Simmel, who turns aside from Kant's idea of progress, sees it rather as a morphological force, creating pattern and structure within society. A group, he writes, "in order to attain a determinate shape, needs some quantitative ratio of harmony and disharmony, of association and competition, of favorable and unfavorable tendencies."[17] Therefore:

> Concord, harmony, co-efficacy, which are unquestionably held to be socializing forces, must nevertheless be interspersed with distance, competition, repulsion, in order to yield the actual configuration of society. The solid, organizational forms which seem to constitute or create society, must constantly be disturbed, disbalanced, gnawed-at by individualistic, irregular forces, in order to gain their vital reaction and development through submission and resistance.[18]

Society is continually molded by the forces of division and cohesion, working through a variety of principles. In structures based on rational principles, mass emotion may unite the individuals within them; in groups divided by passion, reason and objectivity in the form of law may unite them. Moreover, the body politic may devise techniques to objectify and resolve conflict, as in voting. When a vote is taken,

> two parties confront one another like two independent groups, between which the decision is made by power relations, represented by votes. Voting has the same methodological function

here as have, between parties, diplomatic or other negotiations designed to avoid the *ultima ratio* of fight. Aside from exceptions, here too, the individual after all gives in only if the adversary can make it clear to him that, in case of a serious contest, he would have to pay an (at least) equally severe penalty. Like those inter-group negotiations, voting, too, is a projection of real forces and of their proportions upon the plane of intellectuality; it anticipates, in an abstract symbol, the result of concrete battle and coercion.[19]

The significance of voting is the attainment of a single decision from the many conflicting wills in society. That the minority yields to the decision determined by voting indicates that

> the unity of the whole must, under all circumstances, remain master over the antagonism of convictions and interests. In its seeming simplicity, voting is one of the most outstanding means by which the conflict among individuals is eventually transformed into a uniform result.[20]

Voting illustrates further the tragic nature of social existence, for the minority must not only yield but must positively participate in the action which was decided on against its will and conviction. The uniform character of the decision contains no trace of the minority's dissent and even makes it responsible for the decision, which thus becomes "the most poignant expression of the dualism between the autonomous life of the individual and the life of society, a dualism which is often harmonized in experience, but which, in principle, is irreconcilable."[21]

Union and fission operate rhythmically in social life, and in certain cases conflict and the common hostility of a group to something outside it are the only conditions that permit its unification. Political power is one of the forces that has a double function in society: it unites by domination; then it creates opposition in the subordinated group, causing further coherence by forcing the group to hold together in opposition to the power that dominates it. In a penetrating analysis, Simmel observes:

> Discord, . . . perhaps even more stringently than harmony, forces the group to "pull itself together." In general, common enmity is one of the most powerful means for motivating a number of

individuals or groups to cling together. This common enmity is intensified if the common adversary is at the same time the common ruler. In a latent, certainly not in an overt and effective, form, this combination probably occurs everywhere: in some measure, in some respect, the ruler is almost always an adversary. Man has an intimate dual relation to the principle of subordination. On the one hand, he wants to be dominated. The majority of men not only *cannot* exist without leadership; they also *feel* that they cannot: they *seek* the higher power which relieves them of responsibility; they seek a restrictive, regulatory rigor which protects them not only against the outside world but also against themselves. But no less do they need opposition to the leading power, which only through this opposition, through move and countermove, as it were, attains the right place in the life pattern of those who obey it.[22]

The larger the group, the less intelligent and competent is its behavior. The mass is no mere sum of individuals, but "a new phenomenon made up, not of the total individualities of its members, but only of those fragments of each of them in which he coincides with all others. These fragments, therefore, can be nothing but the lowest and most primitive."[23]

When Simmel describes mass behavior, he falls precisely in the tradition of "crowd sociology"—the genre of Taine, Sighele, Le Bon, and Tarde.[24] This mass is much more volatile than an individual; motivated only by appeals to feelings, emotionally irritable, and moved by a collective nervousness, it is extremist in everything, dominated by simple ideas, less inclined to sympathy, always abusive of power, and in a state of inebriation that suspends moral inhibitions—a condition which, together with the anonymity of the participant, encourages mass crimes. Mass excitement may also inspire a noble enthusiasm and unlimited readiness to sacrifice: "Yet this does not eliminate its distorted character and its irresponsibility," but merely accentuates the difference between mass behavior and the standards of the individual. The mass cannot know the ethical dilemmas that torment the individual; and if the individual lived only according to the norms of the group without observing other standards, "he would be an ethical abnormality, an utterly impossible being."[25]

Simmel's explanation of mass behavior, however, differs from that of nineteenth-century, crowd sociologists: where they explained it by the idea of regression to primitive mentality in a *historical* sense, Simmel prefers the idea of decomposition or the "factoring" of segments out of personality in a *mathematical* sense. In the individual himself, it is possible to separate the elements which form the mass and contribute to the collective whole from the different elements

> which constitute his private property, as it were, and which lift him out of everything he may have in common with others. The first part of his nature can evidently consist only in more primitive elements, that are inferior in terms of finesse and intellectuality. This is so, above all, because it is the existence of these elements alone that we can be relatively sure of in *all* individuals. . . . [They] are coarser and closer to the immediate manifestations and necessities of life.[26]

These primitive factors are organized in a whole, and the group then functions according to the laws of its own being. Because no individual identifies himself with that portion of his personality which is organized in the mass, "no individual feels slighted when the mass is spoken of with contempt."

Thus Simmel's theory of "factoring" explains alienation as well as mass behavior: fragments of individuality are synthesized in a unit which operates according to its own logic and confronts the individual as an alien, superindividual structure. Similarly, it explains how a mass may be easily dominated by an individual or by a small group:

> The structure of a society in which a single person rules and the great mass obeys is to be understood only through the consideration that the mass, that is the ruled, includes only a portion of the personality belonging to the individuals concerned, while the ruler invests his whole personality in the relationship. Lordship over a developed society does not consequently differ so very much from rule over a horde, since the individuals build into the structure of the mass only fragments of their personality and reserve the remainder. There are wanting, therefore, in the mass, as the ruled subject, the resources, adaptabilities, the accommodations, the developments of power, which the whole individual

> possesses through the unity and presence of his total psychical energy. Apart from consideration of this difference, this devotion of a mere fraction of individuality to the mass, the frequent facility of its subserviency is not to be understood.[27]

The whole rulership relation between the one and the many is based on the decomposition of personality; the ruler and the individual within the subject mass do not enter into the relation "with an equal *quantum* of their personality," for, as the ruler invests his entire personality, the ruled invest only fragments. The more individuals there are to rule, the slighter the portion of each which is dominated.

Domination of some form is a logical and structural necessity because the fragments which make up the group are coarse and primitive; "hence, whenever men associate in groups, it serves the purpose of the group to organize in the form of subordination to a few."[28]

Power in the form of subordination and superordination is a constitutive force without which society would lose its coherence. Superiority and subordination are found in every human association and they are by no means necessarily subsequent to the formation of society. "It is rather one of the forms in which 'society' comes into being."[29] Social solidarity is not a necessary condition on which power must depend; on the contrary, a power relation may be "the *cause* of a commonness which in the absence of it could not be attained and which is not predetermined by any other relation among its members."[30] Consequently,

> the form of domination itself means or creates a social tie. More awkward periods, which did not have a variety of interactional forms at their disposal, often had no other means for effecting formal membership in the collectivity than that of subordinating the individuals, who were not immediately associated, to those who were members *a priori*.[31]

Forms of domination and subordination help constitute society, but they are only one type of interaction or "sociation," for the individual ties other men and in turn is bound by others in countless relationships, such as love, division of labor, marriage, friendship, party affiliation, conflict. "Human nature does not allow the individual to be tied to another by one thread alone."[32] Everything that moves individuals to sociate—drives, interests, and so on—is the material or content of sociation:

> In themselves, these materials with which life is filled, the motivations by which it is propelled, are not social. Strictly speaking, neither hunger nor love, neither work nor religiosity, neither technology nor the functions and results of intelligence, are social. They are factors in sociation only when they transform the mere aggregation of isolated individuals into specific forms of being with and for one another—forms that are subsumed under the general concept of interaction. Sociation thus is the form (realized in innumerable, different ways) in which individuals grow together into units that satisfy their interests. These interests, whether they are sensuous or ideal, momentary or lasting, conscious or unconscious, causal or teleological, form the basis of human societies.[33]

Arising from these individual drives, instincts, and interests, interaction forms a system in which men may influence and control others to satisfy their own needs. This system of mutual influence and control for the satisfaction of individual needs makes possible the forms in which power is regularly exercised. Thus two forms of power—the constitutive power of society constructing a whole out of heterogeneous parts, and the power of individual men controlling and influencing each other—are inherent in the very foundation of society, elements in the fundamental act of sociation.

Examining the forms of power, Simmel is interested in their sociological function, especially their effect in producing solidarity or tension within the social unit; but the forms he sees are not essentially different from the categories of classical political theory.

The distinction between, on the one hand, the power that is a constitutive element in society, and, on the other, the specific forms of domination, is a classical distinction. St. Thomas, for instance, in *De Regimine Principum,* draws the distinction between the *principium* and the *modus* of authority. The former, ordained by God, is the very substance of authority and a necessity for social existence. The latter, the constitutional form in which legitimate power or authority is exercised—monarchy, aristocracy, democracy, for example—depends on the decision of the people. Simmel adds the form of domination by an impersonal principle or law, but his types of personal domination are essentially the same as the old Platonic-Aristotelian categories. Domination by one person, including the case of monarchy, is the "primary type and form of the relationship of subordination in general." The form of domination by a group leads him to examine the social conditions of aristocracy and democracy. To these old categories he brings a dazzling sociological virtuosity, tracing out with subtlety and precision the logic of the forms under varying conditions of leveling, gradation, mutual opposition of superordinates, and conflict among subordinates.

That the classical formulations of political theory persist in Simmel's sociology is not so remarkable; he borrows much from Kant, who innovated little in his political theory. One may surmise a direct line of specific political conceptions from Aristotle to St. Thomas, to Hooker and Locke, to Rousseau and the Scottish moralists, and ultimately to Kant. Simmel's conception of power, his ethical distinction between men and things, his concern with the dialectic of freedom and power, and his political conceptions in general are cast in the Kantian mold; but, as I shall try to show, his sociology of power discards the Kantian synthesis of power and freedom and brings forth conclusions quite different from those of Kant.

According to Kant, the historic development of humanity continues the cosmic evolution of nature and culminates in the moral perfection of the individual. Kant believed with Rousseau and other writers of the Enlightenment that politically organized society was a civilizing force, designed to restrain the baser elements in human nature and to perfect the moral character of humanity. From a political perspective,

> the history of the human race, viewed as a whole, may be regarded as the realisation of a hidden plan of Nature to bring about a political Constitution, internally and . . . externally

perfect, as the only state in which all the capacities implanted by her in Mankind can be fully developed.[34]

Today the idea of progress may seem to be an archaic illusion, but to the writers of the Enlightenment it supported the ethical element in political theory and provided a critical touchstone by which existing power relations might be judged. Simmel turns away from the idea of progress, however, and his interest in history is detached and focused on epistemological problems; he is not an "involved" critic. He prefers to attend to "historical development"—not a critical concept but an epistemological problem.

The idea of historical development, Simmel argues, implies that history is a sort of substance, for historical development would have no logical meaning unless there were as an a priori condition something permanent which endures and develops throughout the individual moments of time. If there are only isolated moments of time, he observes, without something that endures throughout them, the idea of development is meaningless.[35] Though history is the science of individual and unique events, these events contain an essence that is outside of time, an element of human universality that transcends time.[36] The mind understands the universal by abstracting from the concrete, and Simmel's sociological system is a logic of society which abstracts in a geometric fashion the pure forms of human interaction from the concrete realities—the "matter" provided by history. History may be regarded as the empirical science of society, sociology as the pure science of society. As Simmel puts it, "A basic science of the forms of society must present concepts and concept complexes in a purity and abstract completeness which are never shown by the historical realizations of their contents."[37] To understand with precision and accuracy the complicated structure of society, "the countless bonds and endless relations," Simmel argues, we must begin

> by leaving out of consideration the differences in the material content of these relations, and by making only the forms of the relations, in all their modifications, crossings and complications the object of our investigations, just as logic becomes a science when we disregard all defined and specific contents of thought

and consider only the forms in which single representations are so combined as to form truths.[38]

The fundamental concept of sociological understanding is the act of "sociation—"interaction" among individuals—and the sociologist uses the data of history as the geometrician uses the shapes of nature. "Sociological cognition so transforms historical phenomena that their unity is decomposed into a number of concepts and syntheses. . . ."[39] Their "relation to actual social life is like that of the approximately exact space forms, that are used to illustrate geometrical propositions, to the immeasurable complexity of the actual formations of matter."[40] Even though Simmel is aware that "social phenomena are too immeasurably complicated, and the methods of analysis are too incomplete" to achieve geometric precision and reduce the concrete historical forms of sociation to "a few simple fundamental forms of human association," he insists on geometric analogies, claiming that

> the significance of geometry appears in the fact that the formal relations which it determines hold good for all possible objects formed in space. In like manner it is the purpose of sociology to determine the forms and modes of the relations between men which, although constituted of entirely different contents, material, and interests, nevertheless take shape in formally similar social structures.[41]

Simmel's writing is full of mathematical and geometric analogies. The latter are usually terms borrowed from solid geometry, and if one attends to his use of them it is not difficult to perceive their function. In his system, the organization of society resembles the structural logic of architecture.

The pages of *Soziologie* are full of architectural metaphors and analogies: pyramid, circle, sphere, level, apex, gradation, "continuous downward gliding of the pressure," distance, proportion, slope, inclined plane, "solidity of the total structure," "forces which support . . . weight," and so on. He rarely uses an organic metaphor, and when he does it usually applies to "historical material" rather than to abstract social forms. The word "web," for instance, a favorite of sociologists with organismic inclinations, is hardly ever used. In one illuminating passage, Simmel compares "the real web of human society" with the "approximately exact space forms" of sociology.[42] In an unfortunate translation, Simmel's chapter, "Die Kreuzung sozialer Kreise" is rendered "The Web of Group-Affiliations." The translator defends his choice of words by asserting that "a literal translation of this phrase, 'intersection of social circles,' is almost meaningless." Thus the translator has missed a great deal of Simmel's meaning, which is conveyed indirectly by analogy and metaphor as well as by direct language. He also declares that

> in using the word "circle" as a synonym for "group," Simmel often plays with geometric analogies; it has seemed advisable to me to minimize this play with words in so far as this seemed compatible with an accurate rendering of Simmel's thought.[43]

On the contrary, an accurate rendering of Simmel's thought would convey that a "web" stretches out and connects, whereas a "circle" closes off and excludes. Simmel's sociological constructs are not clusters of organismic tissues but architectonic structures, and his "circles" are closed perimeters which separate one area from another. His social forms are not expressions of organismic vitality but mechanical structural devices which place limits on life to keep its fluctuating elements under control, and there is no point in imposing organismic prejudices on an architectonic system.

Hidden meaning drives us to analogies for explanation. But there are two kinds of analogy: one is the result of the conscious search for significant resemblances and relationships that is associated with scientific model-building. The other is closer to myth and parable, a fundamental image or a priori intuition which organizes the world and determines the nature of reality. As Simmel put it, "the world surely determines what the content of our cognition shall be, but only because cognition determined beforehand what can be world to us. . . ."[44] Simmel sees society as a "structure," but it may be perceived by other minds as an organism, a machine, a system of energy, a battleground, and so on. Why a social theorist chooses one analogy and rejects others is an important epistemological question; and before one considers seriously what he says, one should determine how he sees.

A number of influences make the structural logic of architecture the dominant analogy in Simmel's mind. Though he departs from Kant in some important respects, he retains the Newtonian perspective of order and symmetry and of logic and mechanics to such an extent that one detects in his writings those "symmetrical architectonic amusements" that made Schopenhauer impatient with Kant. Moreover,. he remains faithful to Kant in his conception that seeing and thinking depend on the faculties of sensibility (space and time) and the categories of the understanding, which leads him to apply a *visual* logic—the logic of spatial forms—to social phenomena. In addition, there is his own Pythagorean fascination with space and number. Number, he believes, is the purest abstraction of form, stripped of all historical concreteness, "completely indifferent to all quality."

In architecture the "relation of number to shape gives us a glimpse of a certain science of space, which, founded perhaps upon geometry, is still not pure geometry. . . ." Furthermore, "architectural masses are rigorously determined by the relationship of the parts to each other, and of the parts to the whole."[45] The architectonic relation between wholes and parts and the harmony of lesser within greater wholes are the foundation of Simmel's sociology. As he stated it:

> The essence of societal formation . . . is this: that out of closed units—such as human personalities more or less are—a new unit emerges. . . . Only society makes that which is whole and centered in itself into a mere member of a more comprehensive whole.[46]
>
> Society claims the individual for itself. It wants to make of him a form that it can incorporate into its own structure.[47]

"According to its cosmic order, the hierarchy of nature and spirit," both in society and in architecture, "usually shows nature as the substructure, so to speak, the raw material, or semifinished product; the spirit, as the definitely formative and crowning element."[48] Each creates its own universe in which spirit and nature find a balance:

> Architecture is the only art in which the great struggle between the will of the spirit and the necessity of nature issues into real peace, in which the soul in its upward striving and nature in its gravity are held in balance. . . . Although architecture, too, uses and distributes the weight and carrying power of matter according to a plan conceivable only in the human soul, within this plan the matter works by means of its own nature, carrying out the plan, as it were, with its own forces.[49]

In the same essay, Simmel suggests a comparison between architecture and politics by pointing out the relation between human design and natural forces in architecture:

> This is the most sublime victory of the spirit over nature—a situation like that which obtains when we know how to guide a person so that he realizes our will through his own. His will has not been overpowered; rather, the very tendency of his own nature is made to execute our plan.[50]

Thus, power relationships, expressed in the forms of superordination and subordination, are reciprocal relationships; and domination is not the exercise of will upon an inanimate object but a form of interaction.

> Nobody, in general, wishes that his influence completely determine the other individual. He rather wants this influence, this determination of the other, to act back upon *him*. Even the abstract will-to-dominate, therefore, is a case of interaction.[51]
>
> The decisive characteristic of the relation . . . is this, that the effect which the inferior actually exerts upon the superior is determined by the latter.[52]

This way of expressing the relationship indicates its resemblance to Kant's idea that politics is the art of using the mechanism of nature for ruling men.[53] Yet it reveals only one side of Kant's theory of politics. Kant recognizes that the consequences of human action are subject to the laws of nature, and operate as phenomena to be examined by the senses and the understanding; nevertheless, freedom and autonomy—not perceptible to the senses and the understanding—are a priori conditions of action. Thus society is a moral world as well as a phenomenal world. Though Simmel retains Kant's ideas of autonomy and freedom as important human values, his approach to society is that of the observer rather than that of the participant; and his perspective is dominated by the first *Critique*[54] in which Kant's conception of society and politics is not fully developed. In the later moral and political essays, as well as in the second *Critique*[55] and the third *Critique,*[56] society for Kant is not merely an object to be studied, as "phenomena" are examined by the methods of the first *Critique;* for the mind also works in society by the faculties of the judgment and the practical reason, not merely by the senses and the understanding. Simmel, however, limits his social epistemology to the senses and the understanding, examining the social world as Kant examined nature.[57]

Simmel takes the idea a step further and suggests that society organizes human life as the mind organizes cognitions. Sociological patterns correspond to the functions of the intellect, which Simmel describes in terms of the Kantian categories.[58] He argues:

> The development which takes place among ideas finds an analogue in the relationship of individuals to each other. . . . Just as a higher concept binds together the elements which a great number of very different perceptual complexes have in common, so do practical considerations bind together like individuals.[59]

Social reality in its historical fullness, together with the inner feelings, moods, needs, and motivations of men, takes on the character of the noumenal, the Kantian *Ding an sich* or "thing-in-itself." This existential, inner historical reality, which is lived but not known in its fullness, emerges into the light of cognition only when it is abstracted in formal definition:

> Man in his totality is a dynamic complex of ideas, forces, and possibilities. According to the motivations and relations of life and its changes, he makes of himself a differentiated and clearly defined phenomenon. As an economic and political man, as a family member, and as the representative of an occupation he is,

as it were, an elaboration constructed *ad hoc.* In each of these capacities, the material of his life is determined by a particular idea and is cast into a particular form. Yet, the relative autonomy of his roles feeds on a common source of his energy, which is difficult to label.[60]

Moreover, men are tied to one another by many bonds and forms of relationships: love, friendship, division of labor, and so on. The real ties are probably homogeneous and inseparable, but we cannot follow this homogeneity "with our mind even though we would"; and the mind must separate the elements in order to understand them.[61] Besides being analytic, the mind's function is synthetic, creating wholes out of fragments:

> One can never know another person *absolutely,* which would involve knowledge of every single thought and mood. Nevertheless, one forms some personal unity out of those of his fragments in which alone he is accessible to us. . . . No psychological knowledge is a mere stereotype of its object but depends, as does the knowledge of external nature, upon the forms which the cognizing mind brings to it and in which it receives the given.[62]

As the mind creates the image of a whole out of fragments of knowledge of a person, society creates a whole out of the fragments of decomposed personalities. No one invests his total personality in any one social relationship; the elements that go into a social relationship, whether it be an intimate relation, such as marriage, or a power relation, such as domination-subordination, are "factored" out of the total personality. But

> personality itself is completely outside any arithmetic concept. Therefore, when we speak of the "whole" personality, of its "unity," of a "part" of it, we intend to convey something qualitative and intimate, something which can be experienced only through intuition.[63]

Each social group and society itself perform the architectonic function of constituting a whole from the fragments factored out of human personalities; and the constituted whole acts according to the laws of its own being. Thus mind and society have in common an architectonic nature, constituting wholes out of "factors." This conception of mind Simmel derives from Kant, who explains:

> By the term *Architectonic* I mean the art of constructing a system.[64]
>
> Human reason is by nature architectonic. That is to say, it regards all cognitions as parts of a possible system, and hence accepts only such principles as at least do not incapacitate a cognition to which we may have attained from being placed along with others in a general system.[65]
>
> Reason cannot permit our knowledge to remain in an unconnected and rhapsodistic state, but requires that the sum of our cognitions should constitute a system. It is thus alone that they can advance the ends of reason. By a system I mean the unity of various cognitions under one idea. This idea is the conception—given by reason—of the form of a whole, in so far as the conception determines *a priori* not only the limits of its content, but the place which each of its parts is to occupy.[66]

Society does the same: it constructs a system, uniting the parts—individuals and groups—under a single social form, and determining the limits of the parts, the place each is to occupy, and their relation to each other. The mind constructs systematically according to the internal requirements of the pure reason; but when it works with external materials the creation of a system is an exercise of power. As Simmel observes, "All system-building, whether of science, conduct, or society, involves the assertion of power: it subjects material outside of thought to a form which thought has cast."[67]

The methodological disjunction between the material elements of society, including emotions, needs, and motivations, and the formal elements constructed from this material, has the effect of dehumanizing the social structure and of causing the loss of the human person, reducing him to a suffering fragment in the social whole. Simmel declares that the loss of the individual to the structure is tragic; but this loss does not become the basis for criticism of the structure or of the process that builds it. The forms are not judged by how they serve or deny the needs of individuals, but merely by the criteria of logic and coherence. Domination and subordination, whether benign or malevolent, are technical requirements of society and are to be accepted with resignation. Indeed,

> for the majority of men, coercion probably is an irreplaceable support and cohesion of the inner and outer life. . . .
>
> In comparison with this functional significance of coercion as such, its particular content is of only secondary importance. Senseless coercion may be replaced by sensible coercion, but even the latter has its significance, which is relevant here, only in that which it shares with the former.[68]

Forms survive the conditions that produce them—a process Simmel calls "autonomization."

> It is a fact of the greatest sociological importance that innumerable relationships preserve their sociological structure unchanged, even after the feeling or practical occasion, which originally gave rise to them, has ended.[69]
>
> Sociological connectedness, no matter what its origin, develops a self-preservation and autonomous existence of its form that are independent of its initially connecting motives. Without this inertia of existing sociations, society as a whole would constantly collapse, or change in an unimaginable fashion.[70]

Forms are produced by specific material conditions, then determine by their own logic and in their own right—not in obedience to some higher agency—"how the contents of life should be shaped." This autonomy permits them to endure even after the conditions have changed.

Simmel demonstrates that certain forms of interaction, such as "sociability" and the court etiquette of the *ancien régime,* have existed as play forms, void of content, and enduring for their own sake. This insight suggests that power, too, has its own "freely suspended forms," in which domination exists for its own sake apart from any gain to the superordinate. Recent cases of terrorism come to mind in which no gain to the terrorist is apparent except the total domination of the victims. Never before has it been so important to investigate the limits of autonomization and the processes by which autonomous forms change and take new shapes.

However, Simmel's perspective is not historical; it is aesthetic and cyclical. He brings to society a classic sensibility, seeing "a brief, perfectly balanced instant of complete possession of forms."[71] The purpose of form is to hold in check the flux of inner life. A fundamental dualism pervading social interaction "consists in the fact that a relation, which is a fluctuating, constantly developing life-process, nevertheless receives a relatively stable external form"; and there is always a "fundamental, formal contrast between the essential flux and movement of the subjective psychic life and the limitations of its forms."[72] The formal relations tend to solidify, inhibiting further development, for the external form "is incapable of adapting to the vibrating life and the more or less profound changes" of the inner realm. After a time, the forms cannot restrain the inner flux and

> when the life, which pulsates beneath outlived forms, breaks these forms, it swings into the opposite extreme, so to speak, and creates forms ahead of itself, forms which are not yet completely filled out by it. . . . Another example is the change of a political constitution, by which obsolete forms that have become unbearably oppressive are replaced by freer and larger ones, while the reality of the political and economic forces is not always ripe for them: an overly narrow frame is replaced by one which, for the time being, is still too wide.[73]

But this formulation does little more than state the problem —that forms do change. To come to grips with the realities of power and their relation to social change, one must go beyond the logic of their forms. If the material conditions do change, then they will produce new forms. When do the old forms prevent new ones from emerging? Under what conditions do new forms conflict with the old? When do they supersede the old? If both exist simultaneously, which will "shape the contents of life"? Simmel gives no clue to the answer.

The sociological problem of power requires an explanation of the technical means by which homogeneous and coherent forms are composed from the actions of diverse individuals. Simmel is more concerned with a taxonomic analysis of these forms than with a search for the causes that permit specific men to mobilize and to direct the energies of others. His formalism diverts him from the causal questions: he prefers to examine the logic of construction rather than to inquire into the forces that move specific men to create specific social forms.

Moreover, he avoids seeking the precise relation between "content" and "form." Are the forms abstracted from "life," factors that produce real effects; or are they merely common denominators that the mind perceives? In other words, one must have a principle to distinguish an abstraction that is *essential* from one that is *accidental.* "Whiteness" is an abstraction common to lead and snow; but it does not indicate that lead is related to snow in any significant way, nor does it suggest what lead and snow actually *do* in the world.

On Simmel's own Kantian premises, the analogy of geometry with sociology is far from adequate. The geometrician "suspends" time and sees only space; but before the sociologist can abstract any pseudogeometric forms from history, his material has already traversed the dimension of time. One may question whether "history" does indeed give the sociologist "raw" material from which he may abstract as the geometrician abstracts from the concrete forms of nature. Before they become "history," events are transformed by the mind and the imagination of the historian, and history is anything but raw phenomena.[74]

Since Simmel limits rational process to the intelligible realm of suprahistorical forms and considers history an inscrutable realm of movement and flux, he departs from Kant's idea that history is justified by "its progressive elaboration of right" and that only through the objective principle of development can the autonomy of the subjective will be brought into harmony with order.[75] Kant's idea is closer to the classical conception of politics—that the state is founded on justice.

For Simmel, societies move willy-nilly from one political form to another, according to the requirements of structure. He is skeptical, of course, of all political struggles for freedom. Revolutions merely permit the liberated subordinates to rise into the ruling stratum and continue the old forms of domination.[76]

Simmel can only hope for a political structure that limits its constraint to "external matters" and does not penetrate "into the layers that are decisive for life-feeling and personality-value." In such a structure it would not matter even if the external form were despotic. Indeed, in the despotisms of the Italian Renaissance (where "modern individuality" actually had its beginning) and in the regimes of Napoleon I and Napoleon III,

> it was for the direct interest of the despots to allow the largest freedom to all those aspects of personality which were not identified with the regulated mass, *i.e.*, to those aspects most apart from politics. Thus subordination was more tolerable. It is one of the highest tasks of administrative art to distinguish properly between those characteristics of men with respect to which they may be included in a leveled mass, and those other characteristics which may be left to free individual development.[77]

Simmel did not foresee, of course, that modern political power would develop forms which tend to deny all private "living space," and produce a mass designed to absorb the entire personality.[78]

Simmel internalizes and psychologizes freedom, moving it from the realm of external relations to the inner life. Power is inevitable as a structural necessity; and one cannot hope to modify the external forms of subordination and domination but can merely try to remove the degradation and bad psychological consequences which result. The ethical perspective is divorced from social relationships:

> Ethics conceived of as a kind of sociology is robbed of its deepest and finest content. This is the behavior of the individual soul in and to itself, which does not enter at all into its external relations: its religious movements, which exclusively serve its own salvation or damnation; its devotion to the objective values of knowledge, beauty, significance, which transcend all connections with other people.[79]

Thus Simmel arrives at a secularized form of the Lutheran theory of power. There are two worlds—the inner world of love and the external world of power; the latter is moved by coercion and the necessity for order, the former by the heart.

Simmel's approach to power ends in an attitude of tragic resignation. His sociology illuminates the role of power in the inexorable system-building work of society; but as a political or social philosophy, his work does not offer a satisfactory theory of power, especially for the critical tradition. It isolates the ethical realm from external relations, relinquishes freedom to the necessities of power, and ultimately dehumanizes politics.

In our time, the tragic element in power stands out stark and unrelieved. We understand that without the state, as Aristotle put it, man is either a beast or a god—only in society is it possible for men to be truly human. Yet we also know that the political organization of society has committed, and will continue to commit, the highest crimes of dehumanization. Despite our alienation from political power, we have a certain intimacy with it—the intimacy of a captive with his keeper. We may declare with Vico that "the social world is certainly the work of men," yet we know that in this world, suprahuman forces work in hidden ways and employ the energies of men with cunning to forge the bonds that hold them. The fading of traditional extrinsic limits on power moves us to look for ways to reconstruct the lost synthesis of political theory. The sociology of power may be helpful in this reconstruction, even though it does not offer in itself an adequate theory of power. We may hope that precise scientific analysis of the techniques of power will reveal inherent in its secret processes and inner mechanisms some intrinsic limitations that are hidden and not now apparent. Perhaps the sociology of power will disclose some of the secrets of its nature and teach us techniques of evasion and of control. Only by understanding the nature and habits of the Cyclops did the wily Ulysses escape from the cave.

1. Cf. Franz Neumann, *The Democratic and the Authoritarian State* (Glencoe, Ill.: Free Press of Glencoe, Illinois, 1957), pp. 3-5, 160-62.

2. *Soziologie. Untersuchungen über die Formen der Vergesellschaftung, 1900* (3rd ed.; Leipzig: Duncker und Humblot, 1923).

3. Cf. Kaspar D. Naegele, "Attachment and Alienation: Complementary Aspects of the Work of Durkheim and Simmel," *American Journal of Sociology,* LXIII (1958), 588-89.

4. Kurt H. Wolff, "The Challenge of Durkheim and Simmel," *American Journal of Sociology,* LXIII (1958), 596.

5. Kurt H. Wolff (ed.), *The Sociology of Georg Simmel* (Glencoe, Ill.: Free Press of Glencoe, Illinois, 1950), p. 61.

6. *Ibid.,* p. 58.

7. *Ibid.,* p. 409.

8. *Ibid.*, p. 59. Certain writers in the Neo-Kantian and Neo-Hegelian tradition continue to explore the tragic element in power and the insoluble antinomies of collective life. Cf. Gustav Radbruch, "Rechtsphilosophie," trans. K. Wilk, in *Legal Philosophies of Lask, Radbruch and Dabin* (Cambridge, Mass.: Harvard University Press, 1950); and Hans Fehr, *Die Tragik im Recht* (Zurich: Schulthess and Co., 1945).

9. *Ibid.*, pp. 58-59.

10. *Ibid.*, p. 248.

11. A. C. Bradley, "Hegel's Theory of Tragedy," in *Oxford Lectures on Poetry* (London: Macmillan Co., 1909), pp. 70-72.

12. A. C. Bradley, *Shakespearean Tragedy* (New York: Macmillan Co., 1949), p. 38.

13. A. C. Bradley, "Hegel's Theory of Tragedy," pp. 90-91, 73.

14. Wolff, *The Sociology of Georg Simmel*, p. 84.

15. W. Hastie (trans.), "The Natural Principle of the Political Order," in *Kant's Principles of Politics* (Edinburgh: Clark, 1891), pp. 9-10.

16. *Ibid.*, p. 11.

17. Kurt H. Wolff (trans.), "Conflict," in Georg Simmel's *Conflict* and *The Web of Group-Affiliations* (Glencoe, Ill.: Free Press of Glencoe, Illinois, 1955), p. 15.

18. Wolff, *The Sociology of Georg Simmel*, p. 315.

19. *Ibid.*, p. 242.

20. *Ibid.*, p. 240.

21. *Ibid.*, p. 249.

22. *Ibid.*, p. 193.

23. *Ibid.*, p. 33.

24. Cf. Philip Rieff, "The Origins of Freud's Political Psychology," *Journal of the History of Ideas*, XVII (1956), 235-49; Franz Neumann, "Anxiety and Politics," *ibid.*, pp. 270-300. Kant was ambivalent toward mass behavior: he claimed that Rousseau taught him "to honor men" and not to despise "the rabble who know nothing," but he also wrote that "new prejudices will serve as well as old ones to harness the great unthinking masses." See L. W. Beck (trans.), "What is Enlightenment?" in Kant's *Critique of Practical Reason and Other Writings in Moral Philosophy* (Chicago: University of Chicago Press, 1949), p. 287.

25. Wolff, *The Sociology of Georg Simmel*, pp. 28, 36.

26. *Ibid.*, pp. 28, 29.

27. Albion W. Small (trans.), "Superiority and Subordination as Subject Matter of Sociology," *American Journal of Sociology*, II (1896), p. 174.

SOCIOLOGY OF POWER

This is an earlier draft of *Soziologie,* Chap. iii, translated as Part III, "Superordination and Subordination," in Wolff, *The Sociology of Georg Simmel.*

28. Wolff, *The Sociology of Georg Simmel,* pp. 76-77.

29. Small, *op. cit.,* p. 169.

30. Wolff, *The Sociology of Georg Simmel,* p. 192.

31. *Ibid.,* p. 297.

32. Wolff, "Conflict," p. 21.

33. Wolff, *The Sociology of Georg Simmel,* p. 41.

34. Hastie, *op. cit.,* p. 21.

35. Georg Simmel, *Die Probleme der Geschichtsphilosopie. Eine erkenntnistheoretische Studie.* ([1892] 2nd ed.; Leipzig: Duncker und Humblot, 1905), p. 150.

36. *Ibid.,* pp. 4, 20, 31.

37. Wolff, *The Sociology of Georg Simmel,* p. 200.

38. Small, *op. cit.,* p. 189.

39. Wolff, *The Sociology of Georg Simmel,* p. 200.

40. *Ibid.,* p. 152.

41. Small, *op. cit.,* p. 168.

42. Wolff, *The Sociology of Georg Simmel,* p. 152.

43. Reinhard Bendix (trans.), "The Web of Group-Affiliations," in Georg Simmel's *Conflict* and *The Web of Group-Affiliations* (Glencoe, Ill.: Free Press of Glencoe, Illinois, 1955), p. 125.

44. Quoted in Wolff, "The Challenge of Durkeim and Simmel," p. 594.

45. Henri Focillon, *The Life of Forms in Art,* trans. C. B. Hogan and G. Kubler (2nd ed.; New York: Wittenborn, Schultz, 1948), p. 20.

46. Wolff, *The Sociology of Georg Simmel,* p. 239.

47. *Ibid.,* p. 61.

48. From Simmel's charming essay, "The Ruin," as translated in this volume by David Kettler, p. 262.

49. *Ibid.,* p. 259.

50. *Ibid.*

51. Wolff, *The Sociology of Georg Simmel,* p. 181.

52. Small, *op. cit.,* p. 170.

53. L. W. Beck, "Perpetual Peace," *op. cit.,* p. 332.

54. J. M. D. Meiklejohn (trans.), *Kant's Critique of Pure Reason* ("Everyman's Library" [London: Dent, 1934]).

55. L. W. Beck, *Critique of Practical Reason.*

56. J. H. Bernard (trans.), *Critique of Judgment* (New York: Hafner Publishing Company, Inc., 1951).

57. In the first *Critique,* Kant shows that knowledge of phenomena is based on the process of cognition, which organizes sense data in concepts by uniting the faculties of intuition with the categories of the understanding. The data of sense are constituted through the aesthetic faculties of intuition (space and time), organized into a synthesis by the imagination, and transformed into concepts by the categories of the understanding (quantity, quality, relation, modality). "Thoughts without content are void; intuitions without conceptions, blind."

58. Bendix, "The Web of Group-Affiliations," p. 172. Cf. Kant, *Critique of Pure Reason,* Second Part ("Transcendental Logic"), First Division.

59. *Ibid.,* pp. 127, 128.

60. Wolff, *The Sociology of Georg Simmel,* p. 46.

61. Wolff, "Conflict," p. 21.

62. Wolff, *The Sociology of Georg Simmel,* p. 308.

63. *Ibid.,* p. 202.

64. Meiklejohn, *op. cit.,* p. 471.

65. *Ibid.,* p. 287.

66. *Ibid.,* p. 471.

67. Wolff, *The Sociology of Georg Simmel,* p. 357.

68. *Ibid.,* pp. 299, 300.

69. *Ibid.,* p. 380.

70. *Ibid.,* pp. 380-81.

71. Focillon, *op. cit.,* p. 12.

72. Wolff, *The Sociology of Georg Simmel,* pp. 385, 386.

73. *Ibid.,* p. 386.

74. R. G. Collingwood, *The Idea of History* (New York: Oxford University Press, 1946).

75. Hastie, *op. cit.,* pp. xxi, xxiv.

76. Wolff, *The Sociology of Georg Simmel,* pp. 274, 281-82.

77. Small, *op. cit.,* p. 175; cf. Wolff, *The Sociology of Georg Simmel,* p. 203.

78. Cf. Hannah Arendt, "Ideology and Power: A Novel Form of Government," *Review of Politics,* XV (1953), 303 ff.

79. Wolff, "Conflict," p. 25.

THE TIME AND THOUGHT OF THI YOUNG SIMMEL

PAUL HONIGSHEIM

The Berlin in which Simmel started his teaching and writing consisted of many heterogeneous social and cultural groups, institutions, and movements. Those which were of importance in his life will be enumerated and briefly commented upon.

The old Prussia was represented by feudal estate owners, their relatives who dominated army and high administration, and the Protestant State Church officials. All of these groups were connected with the conservative party, which made concessions to anti-Semitism.

Conservative Protestant artisans and storekeepers desired a precapitalistic society organized by guilds. They disliked capitalism, a money economy, and the Jews, the alleged representatives of the money economy. They voted an anti-Semitic, or the so-called Christian-Social, ticket.

The new industrialists and merchants tried to imitate the feudal landlords and to have their sons become cavalry officers or members of fashionable dueling student organizations. Religion to this group was a means of domesticating the masses. Politically, they favored the national-liberal deputies who had supported Bismarck, had been set aside by him, but continued to admire the "Iron Chancellor."

The left-wing liberals had influence, not in national, but in municipal, politics. If they had an interest in religion at all, they were connected with "liberal," that is, Biblio-critical, Protestantism. More than in religion, however, they were interested in naturalistic and realistic philosophy, literature, painting, and theatre. Through such interests, they involuntarily became ever more closely allied with the socialists.

The socialists, because of the increasing number of union members and the power of bureaucratically functioning leaders of unions and co-operatives, abandoned their Marxian, revolutionary background and turned social reformers. Their *Weltan-*

schauung was largly an imitation of left-wing liberal naturalism and realism.

The University of Berlin. The traditional German professor, who did his own scholarly writing in his own simple home without compensation because he felt it his religiously enforced duty to do so, was beginning to disappear. A university post, even that of an unsalaried *Privatdozent,* had become a fashionable and distinguished position for the son of a successful tradesman; within the university, however, the *Privatdozent's* power and influence were still less than the full professor's.

In history, the important men were adherents of Ranke or Treitschke, concentrating on foreign policy and great statesmen and generals. In economics, Schmoller, one of the founders of state-supported social policy, was the dominant figure, and the leader, as well, of a large school of social and economic historians. Statistics had a long history in Germany, going back to Gottfried Achenwall and August Ludwig von Schlözer in Göttingen. It was taught, however, not by professors but by practitioners whose main occupation was the directorship of statistical offices outside the university. At the time of the young Simmel, interest in statistics was on the increase. Sociology was not taught at all. Psychology, by contrast, had a considerable tradition. Since the days of Herbart and Moritz Wilhelm Drobisch, there had been a tendency toward quantitative or mathematical psychology; its major representatives, professors of philosophy, considered psychology a branch of their main field of competence. Mathematical psychology, however, came to be replaced by experimental psychology, which for some time even enjoyed protection from the governments of certain German states. Some of these liked to give full professorships in philosophy to experimental psychologists, who usually were neither affiliated nor in conflict with religious and political groups. Max Weber and others protested against such appointments, but schools like those of Wundt and Carl Stumpf flourished nevertheless. In philosophy, Dilthey, who stood in the tradition of German idealism, was considered above all a philosopher of history and culture. The Neo-Kantianism of Friedrich Albert Lange and his followers had hardly reached Berlin.

The unofficial Berlin culture. Materialism, mechanism, and similar conceptions of primarily English origin became popular among scientists and physicians such as Virchow. Like many other adherents of these views, Virchow was also an enemy of Bismarck. Along with countless other left-wing liberals and socialists, he considered natural science "the religion of our epoch" and propagated realistic novels and dramas by such writers as Zola, Ibsen, Bjornson, and Sudermann. These promotional activities were carried on mainly within and through private associations and theatres, socialist theatre-consumer organizations, and associations for adult education, prominent among which was one largely guided by Julius Lippert, a well-known popularizer of social Darwinism.

The antirationalistic protest against urbanization, rationalism, and materialism was to some extent linked, through Schopenhauer, Nietzsche, and others, with original German romanticism. This protest started slowly, and in the beginning went almost unnoticed. Two very different figures among its representatives were, first, Julius Langbehn, the so-called *Rembrandtdeutsche,* who glorified German peasants and craftsmen of the past and disdained his own time and surroundings to the point of living a completely secluded life, and who was not rediscovered until later years; and second, Stefan George, the poet who glorified the elite, hierarchy, and discipline, and who likewise lived in seclusion except for the presence of his wholly devoted disciples.

Simmel started in the "unofficial Berlin culture" and ended close to the antirationalistic movements and in friendship with Stefan George, to whom he dedicated one of his last books. His best-known sociological work, *Soziologie,* published in 1908, stands midway between the two epochs, which followed each other without any break. In the first of these periods, Simmel anticipated some of the positions which he elaborated in the second.

Simmel began his career as a Jew in a Berlin and a university both of which were becoming increasingly anti-Semitic.[1] This fact proved a handicap to his career throughout almost his entire life. He was a teacher at Berlin University, where he received little or no salary, until the age of fifty-six, and his Jewish background was one of the causes of his partial isolation. Another was his failure to identify himself with any of the political and social groups that characterized his time and place. None of them, he feared, granted the individual independence.[2] He could fully espouse neither the Empire with its centralization nor liberalism with its abstract laissez-faire program, which, he thought, actually led to dominance by big business, a prospect hardly favored by many of his liberal contemporaries. Nor, finally, could he embrace socialism, with its glorification of the masses, although he was never antagonistic to the workers.[3]

Like many Western Jews, Simmel did not adopt the Jewish faith, but unlike some of them, he did not consider Protestantism, orthodox or liberal, as a possible alternative (Catholicism, generally speaking, had not yet re-entered the picture). The groups nearest to him were the independent liberal thinkers, Darwinists and progressivists, outside the university. Simmel embraced their views, but only to some extent and for a short time, as two of his earliest publications show: the brief *Über sociale Differenzierung* of 1890 and the two-volume *Einleitung in die Moralwissenschaft* of 1892-93. As further editions of the latter work were required, Simmel left it completely unchanged —not because he felt changes were unnecessary, but because, as he wrote, he would have to change too much. This suggests that, though he had repudiated some of the positions taken, he considered them important enough to let them stand on the record. Both books, indeed, contain more than one passage which anticipates the second epoch—especially the ideas on sociology—and even the third, that of the "philosophy of life." Accordingly, it is useful to examine the major points advanced in these two publications. We shall first present them, and then, in a brief concluding section, scrutinize them in the light of Simmel's later phases.

A superficial glance at these books may make the reader feel that he is perusing a work by Spencer, Lippert, or Sumner. There is insistence on the hereditary character of criminal inclination, even a protest against the preservation of the weak, who will transmit their inferiority to future generations.[4] On the other hand, even in these early writings, Simmel asserts that the basic assumption of social Darwinism is an unproved hypothesis: the overcoming of enemies is not the decisive cause of the origin of new species, and the effect of the struggle for existence is favorable to the whole only because of periods of intermittent truce.[5] Moreover, Simmel insists that it is impossible to base political claims on Darwinistic theories—or on any biological theories.[6] Such criticisms of social Darwinism will reappear in much stronger form in the writings of the later, Neo-Kantian Simmel.[7] In his first period, his theories seek support in ethnological observations.[8] This interest in ethnology will also play a role in Simmel's second stage,[9] a matter which is taken up elsewhere in this volume.[10]

The young Simmel stands between two epochs in regard not only to Darwinian biology but also to the optimistic, progressivistic mood characteristic of Darwinism.[11] While he sees some goodness in primitive man, he believes in the possibility of progress, particularly—in accord with his previously mentioned theory concerning inherited attributes—as marking a decrease in the time required to pass through or overcome inherited evil. On the other hand, he sharply diverges from the unrestricted optimistic eudaemonism and progressivism of so many of his contemporaries.[12] He does not think that the machine has liberated man from work so much as that it has made him one-sided. Here, clearly, are anticipations of the *Philosophie des Geldes*[13] and other later works.

Two methods of obtaining knowledge, closely connected with the belief that the methods of the natural sciences are the model for other sciences and that quantification is possible in the cultural sciences, too, are statistics and psychology.[14] These methods, which began to play an essential role at the time under discussion, appear in Simmel's work. Simmel emphasizes the importance of statistics as a means of making factual statements, especially in applied science (for example, in the study of child labor), but he warns against drawing unwarranted conclusions from statistics. This interest is short-lived, and vanishes rather completely from Simmel's subsequent work.

Thus, in respect to statistics the young Simmel, at least for a short time, conformed to his environment; not so, however, as regards experimentation and quantification in psychology.

Simmel did lecture on psychology, but like Hans Adolph Driesch, and unlike Wundt, Stumpf, and their followers, he taught its non-experimental variant. He insisted that psychology is unable to formulate laws of the kind found in the natural sciences because every effect of every psychic activity is interrelated with countless other phenomena, a fact which makes definitive cause-effect statements impossible. Moreover, many psychological concepts can be attained only through introspection, and thus contain subjective elements. The aim of psychological observation, therefore, can only be that of helping the individual, who has a disposition similar to the psychological observer's, to become conscious of this disposition.

This interpretation suggests the later idea of the unique individual who cannot be expressed rationally and can be understood only through intuition by another adequately structured for the task. Contrary to the belief of some social Darwinists, this individual is not an egotist; greatness is not identical with selfishness. The logically unexplainable individual, whose appearance in history cannot be predicted,[15] is to become one of the cornerstones of Simmel's thinking and feeling in his middle and, especially, his last period.[16]

Such anticipation is even more pronounced so far as the individual's ethical attitude and valuation are concerned. According to the young Simmel, the correctness of an ethical norm can never be proved by logic, which is not the ultimate criterion by which the ethical dignity of an action is guaranteed. Instead, this criterion is a subjective one. Moreover, duties have their origin in the relations between men that are directed by antagonistic, subjective criteria; and thus, inevitably, there will be collisions between them.[17] In this autonomistic, antirationalistic conception of ethics, we have an anticipation of Simmel's late, vitalist period, in which he claimed that since all activity is a manifestation of life, ethics, too, takes its direction from life itself.[18]

This vitalism is a far cry from the early Simmel, with his acceptance of some Darwinistic notions. Nevertheless, certain characteristic traits of his work are constant from beginning to end. If we classify the topics Simmel dealt with in his first phase, we shall see which of them differ from his later ideas, and which anticipate them. Interest in statistics corresponded to the Berlin environment of Simmel's youth, but it later disappeared. Ideas, similarly taken from his milieu but subsequently abandoned, were those concerning the importance of heredity, opposition to protecting the weak, belief in the goodness of primitive man, and the conception of progress previously described.

The young Simmel responded to other problems of his epoch with reactions basically different from those of most of his contemporaries—reactions which anticipated Simmel's later development. They included his modification of current notions concerning the origin of new species; his ideas on the effects of the struggle for existence; his rejection of biological theories as bases of political claims; his refusal to consider the rise of the machine and the specialization of labor per se as constituting progress; his insistence on the limited capacity of psychology to formulate laws modeled on those of the natural sciences; and his argument against the logical justifiability of ethical criteria which guarantee the dignity of the individual and of the choices which direct the individual's activities.

1. Simmel's main writings during the first epoch are *Über sociale Differenzierung. Sociologische und psychologische Untersuchungen* (Leipzig: Duncker und Humblot, 1890), and *Einleitung in die Moralwissenschaft. Eine Kritik der ethischen Grundbegriffe* (Berlin: Hertz [Besser]), Vol. I, 1892, Vol. II, 1893. Among Simmel's later publications these are cited for comparison: *Philosophie des Geldes* ([1900] 2nd ed.; Leipzig: Duncker und Humblot, 1907), *Kant. Sechzehn Vorlesungen gehalten an der Berliner Universität* (Leipzig: Duncker und Humblot, 1904), *Die Religion* (Frankfurt am Main: Rütten und Loening, 1906), *Philosophische Kultur. Gesammelte Essays* ([1911] 2nd ed.; Leipzig: Kröner, 1919), and *Lebensanschauung. Vier metaphysische Kapitel* ([1918] 2nd ed.; Munich and Leipzig: Duncker und Humblot, 1922).

2. *Moralwissenschaft,* I, 18, 121, 192.

3. *Philosophie des Geldes,* p. 466; *Philosophische Kultur,* pp. 168, 252 ff.

4. *Moralwissenschaft,* I, 117; *Differenzierung,* p. 37.

5. *Moralwissenschaft,* I, 108 ff.

6. *Ibid.,* p. 118.

7. *Kant,* pp. 108 f.; *Religion,* p. 79.

8. *Moralwissenschaft,* I, 23, 76, 92, 380; *Differenzierung,* p. 61.

9. *Religion,* pp. 19, 24 ff., 50, 70.

10. See Paul Honigsheim, "A Note on Simmel's Anthropological Interests," the next paper in this volume.

11. *Moralwissenschaft,* I, 76, 92, 380.

12. *Ibid.,* pp. 328, 376, 391.

13. *Philosophie des Geldes,* pp. 311 ff., 318, 329, 363, 369 f., 496, 521, 531.

14. *Moralwissenschaft,* II, 11, 191 f,. 424 ff.; *Differenzierung,* p. 7.

15. *Moralwissenschaft,* I, 90 ff., 105, 126; II, 64; *Differenzierung,* p. 58.

16. *Kant,* pp. 2 ff., 125, 133 ff., 157, 260-65; *Lebensanschauung,* pp. 226-32.

17. *Moralwissenschaft,* I, 40; II, 50, 64, 130, 385.

18. *Lebensanschauung,* p. 235.

A NOTE ON SIMMEL'S ANTHROPOLOGICAL INTERESTS

PAUL HONIGSHEIM

German ethnology did not have its beginning in academic circles—probably, for three major reasons. First, in the nineteenth century, Germany had no colonies and therefore lacked the essential interest in native peoples. Second, the predominant religious group, the Lutheran State Church, had not been able to do much missionary work. Third, the German historians, one of the most influential academic groups, considered the modern state the most important social institution and the true object of investigation. Accordingly, they neglected the study of prehistory and of societies that existed prior to the development of the state.

Rather, ethnology had its beginning in two other movements, neither of which were academic in the orthodox sense of the term.[1] The first was German romanticism with its interest in the culture of the "folk," which, it believed, exhibited the authentic or true existence of man. The main representatives of romanticist ethnology were Karl Friedrich Vollgraf and Johann Jacob Bachofen. Vollgraf considered the disappearance of primitive life an irreparable damage to mankind. He remained unnoticed, however, and was rediscovered only after the First World War, when his importance as a forerunner of Spengler was realized. Bachofen emphasized the importance of the ancient matrilineal form of society and the faculty of mystical intuition, and believed the two to be closely related. His theory was ridiculed by the rationalist Mommsen, the dominant historian of antiquity of the time, and his followers.

The second avenue for the emergence of the German interest in ethnology was the philosophy and the psychology of Herbart. Herbart had been influenced by romanticism less than other philosophers. He asserted that every individual passes by necessity through a number of stages of consciousness, and he published this view at the time when German romanticists, pre-Marxian and Marxian Socialists, and English social Darwinists were emphasizing the function of the group as opposed to that of the individual.

The application of Herbart's stages of consciousness to human group life in general, and to preliterate society in particular, resulted in the basic ethnological theory of Adolf Bastian.[2] According to Bastian, all preliterate groups independently and automatically pass through the same sequence of stages of group consciousness. These stages manifest themselves in similar cultural traits, social institutions, and forms of economic production in all groups. This "evolutionism" or "parallelism" became the dominant ethnological theory in Germany from 1850 to 1900. Many social theorists were influenced by it—Felix von Luschan, the Africanist; Heinrich Preuss, the archaeologist; Heinrich Schurtz, the exponent of the sociological importance of young men's associations in preliterate societies; Eduard Georg Seler, one of the analysts of pre-Columbian mathematics; Karl von den Steinen, a student of tribes in Brazil; and the popularizers Ernst Heilborn, Friedrich von Hellwald, and Julius Lippert.

Protest against this parallelism appeared in the ideas of thinkers who emphasized the historical diffusion of human cultural traits. It began with Ratzel, but his pioneering investigations into the diffusion of the forms of the bow and arrow attracted no attention. The diffusionist position was actually established by the later and more extensive publications of Bernhard Ankermann, Graebner, and Father Schmidt and his school.

When Georg Simmel began his career, he was to some extent influenced by optimistic positivism, as popularized by Lippert, and, therefore, also by evolutionistic parallelism. This influence manifests itself in his references to Lippert and in some assertions regarding physical anthropology and ethnology that he makes in his early books, *Einleitung in die Moralwissenschaft* and *Über sociale Differenzierung*. His study of physical anthropology led him to adopt two concepts strongly supported by positivists of the time: the notion that "evil predispositions" are to some extent hereditary, and the idea that the stages of a child's life correspond to the stages through which preliterate peoples pass.[3] However, his interest in the function of the naturalistic factor in human social life soon diminished and reappeared only occasionally in the work of his later period. An example of this reappearance is the assertion that marriage for money means a deterioration of the species.[4]

Ethnology played a much more important role in Simmel's early thinking. Along with some of his contemporaries—those who were not pure social Darwinists—he shared to some extent the conviction that man's innate goodness is proved by the nature of primitive life. His first proof was primitive communism, which shows that man is not exclusively selfish. As his second proof, he pointed out that preliterate peoples do not talk about ethics, but they are able to know and punish as unethical, behavior which they consider a deviation from the normal, that is, the ethically right; the feeling that what is right can and must be done, is basic to preliterate cultures.[5] In addition, both of these arguments furnished Simmel with proof that in preliterate society the possibility of an individual's making autonomous decisions is almost non-existent—that, in fact, the individual does not exist.[6]

Discussions of economic groups played an important role in the thinking of Simmel and many of his contemporaries. For the late nineteenth century was the time when the concept of original collectivism was accepted by such heterogeneous personalities as the conservative Bachofen, the American evolutionist Lewis Henry Morgan, the economic determinist Friedrich Engels (who was influenced by both of the former), Marx, and Simmel.[7] Later, especially in his *Philosophie des Geldes,* Simmel observed that in primitive societies the land belongs collectively to the kin as a whole, the livestock belongs collectively to the special subfamily, but the mobile goods are the property of the individual, for they are supposed to be destroyed after his death.[8] The most mobile of all kinds of properties is money. Consequently, there is a close interrelationship between the development of a money economy and the growth of the role of the individual and the recognition which is given to him.

Next to economic life, the matrilineal family was of most interest to the young Simmel. Bachofen and Morgan had defined this as a stage through which all societies must pass after going through the stage of primitive collectivism, and had asserted that the shift from matrilineal to patrilineal organization involved a change from collective to private property.

Official historians ignored or laughed at this theory; nevertheless, Lothar von Dargun, Lippert, Albert Hermann Post, Schurtz, Westermarck, and other liberal evolutionists, as well as Engels, Bebel, and other Marxians, accepted and popularized it.

In his early years, Simmel, as well as accepting the theory of primitive collectivism, also accepted the theory of matrilineal society as a recurring stage in human development, and he made explicit reference to Bachofen and Lippert in this regard.[9] Other forms of family organization with which nineteenth-century ethnologists were concerned—exogamy, primitive promiscuity, and polyandry, for example—are not discussed in his writings, proving that the whole problem of the sequence of types of organizations did not overly preoccupy him. This is also suggested by the fact that even his concern with the matrilineal problem disappears in his later work, from which he eliminates all naturalistic elements in general and turns instead to such Neo-Kantians as Max Weber—as witness his *Philosophie des Geldes,* his books on Kant, and those on the sociology of religion.

In these books, as in all of his writings, he uses comparative history, including the history of preliterate culture, as a point of departure. His main assertions concerning the latter are as follows:[10] The primitive group is simultaneously a familial, political, economic, and religious group. It defines itself as a superhuman and metaphysical entity and is so considered by its members. At a later stage of development, this self-glorification may lead to a henotheistic belief, that is, one characterized by the exclusive worship of a paternal god who is supposed to stand in a unique relation to the group. In other cases, this self-glorification leads to a self-idolization of the group itself, such as that which was found among the Arabs before Mohammed; in this case, little impetus remains for the worship of an extramundane divinity. In either event, the group, rather than the individual, is emphasized. Consequently, as Simmel's concern for the problem of protecting the individual against domination by the group becomes greater, his interest in preliterate cultures, in which individuality is supposedly non-existent, virtually disappears.

Anthropology occupies a very small place in the total body

of Simmel's writings. His attention to certain biologistic notions of the age and his speculations on primitive culture and evolutionary stages are little more than concessions to currently popular trends. Still, they are not irrelevant to an understanding of his career. They date largely from its earlier phase, and as he moves away from naturalism and positivism, he loses his concern with anthropological theories as well. His own influence began after he transcended that early stage.[11]

1. For pertinent ethnological schools and theories, see the following publications by Paul Honigsheim: "Adolf Bastian und die Entwicklung der ethnologischen Soziologie," *Kölner Vierteljahrshefte für Soziologie,* VI (1926), 61-76; "Soziologische Fragestellungen in der gegenwärtigen prähistorischen und ethnologischen Literatur," *ibid.,* VII (1928), 331-43, 427-46; "Ein Wort zu Adolf Bastians 100. Geburtstag," *Jahrbuch für prähistorische und ethnographische Kunst,* I (1927), 82-91; "Die geistesgeschichtliche Stellung der Anthropologie, Ethnologie und Urgeschichte," in *Festschrift, Publication d'Hommage offerte au P. W. Schmidt,* ed. W. Koppers (Vienna: Mechitaristen-Congregations-Buchdruckerei, 1928), pp. 844-64; and "Eduard Hahn und seine Stellung in der Geschichte der Ethnologie und Soziologie," *Anthropos,* XXIV (1929), 587-612.

For a more general discussion, cf. Paul Honigsheim and Gottfried Eisermann, "Geschichte der Soziologie," in *Die Lehre von der Gesellschaft,* ed. Gottfried Eisermann (Stuttgart: Ferdinand Enke, 1958), pp. 1-64.

2. One of Simmel's teachers. See Simmel's vita, which is reprinted in Michael Landmann, "Bausteine zur Biographie," in *Buch des Dankes an Georg Simmel,* ed. Kurt Gassen and Michael Landmann (Berlin: Duncker und Humblot, 1958), p. 15.

3. *Einleitung in die Moralwissenschaft. Eine Kritik der ethischen Grundbegriffe* (Berlin: Hertz [Besser], 1892), pp. 380 f.

4. *Philosophie des Geldes* ([1900] 2nd ed.; Leipzig: Duncker und Humblot, 1907), pp. 420 f.

5. *Moralwissenschaft,* I, 92; II, 23 f.

6. *Ibid.,* II, 23.

7. *Ibid.,* I, 92.

8. *Philosophie des Geldes,* pp. 383 ff.

9. *Über sociale Differenzierung. Soziologische und psychologische Untersuchungen* (Leipzig: Duncker und Humblot, 1890), pp. 61 ff.

10. *Die Religion* (Frankfurt am Main: Rütten und Loening, 1906), pp. 24, 50, 70.

11. On this early stage, see Paul Honigsheim, "The Time and Thought of the Young Simmel," the preceding paper in this volume.

SIMMEL IN GERMAN SOCIOLOGY

HEINZ MAUS

Through much of the nineteenth century, Comte's philosophy of history was considered the embodiment of the new science of sociology. This new science was devoted to progress. At the same time, however, it approved the status quo in that it had thrown off theological remnants and metaphysical scruples which might have had some justification in the past, but now were only obstacles to the triumph of science and technology. Toward the end of the century, Spencer's voluminous work also began to attract attention. Like Comte's, it was esteemed primarily because of the philosophy of history it contained. In Spencer's view, nothing, not even the state, must interfere with natural development, which had led from early barbarism to a peaceful industrial society. His philosophy of history was made scientifically respectable by empirical ethnographic material, by the use of psychological categories, and by the very valuations which they contained.

Thus, when Durkheim and Simmel started to write, sociology was largely identified with Comte's and Spencer's comprehensive programs. These programs found competition, however, in historical materialism. But materialism engendered uneasiness, in part because of its refusal to allow the historical development of society to end with the contemporary stage. And although Comte and Spencer had asserted that the natural law of development demonstrated the scientific character of sociology, this view was called into question when the Marxists—Kautsky and Labriola, for example—appealed to the same kind of natural law to predict the end of the capitalist order. In the face of such a threat, biology, not sociology, seemed to offer a secure foundation by arguing that natural selection, necessitated by the struggle for survival, determines social conditions: instead of pursuing the insane utopias of the world reformers, it was deemed wiser to adapt to the free play of the fittest. Yet this social biology, according to which men are only members of the species, members who are judged by their fertility and usefulness in war, was too crude not to arouse opposition. It spurred to new life what was left of idealistic philosophy.

It did so in Germany. Sociology, which was identified with Comte's system, had had a hard time there. While Comte had become known fairly early,[1] his first publication seems to have aroused little interest. He did write John Stuart Mill in 1842 that he had learned of people in both Berlin and Göttingen who were at work on a translation of his *Cours de philosophie positive.*[2] And in 1859, Rudolf Haym published in the *Preussische Jahrbücher,* the scientific-political organ of the German liberals, an essay by Karl Twesten on the doctrine and writings of Auguste Comte which was "almost a program of the opinions . . . we have of the value and treatment of the historical sciences."[3] This was directed against the conservative-romantic conception of history. Haym's comment suggests that until that time Comte had been regarded by the academic world as a "confused mind,"[4] since only journalists and compilers of cultural histories had resorted to him.

Comte's sociology did not take hold in Germany until the 1880's.[5] It soon met with vigorous opposition, which was extended to sociology in general. Thus in his "Introduction to the *Geisteswissenschaften*" (the term is the German translation of Mill's "moral sciences"), Wilhelm Dilthey denied sociology any scientific character whatever. Not only was the task which it had set itself—to "bring about a scientific guidance of society"[6]—impossible; but the methods it was using for this purpose could not produce any lasting increase in knowledge—they were, in fact, wholly wrong.[7]

The historical antecedents of sociology in Germany ran in two currents.[8] One was formed by the comprehensive philosophies of history, from Herder and Hegel[9] to Marx's dialectic. All of these carried marks of the Enlightenment—belief in the ideal of humanitarian culture, in progress in the consciousness of freedom, or in the organization of a social order in which the rule of a minority would be replaced by the community of free individuals. The other current was the historical school of jurisprudence,[10] which was directed against the philosophies of the French Revolution and the Enlightenment and which fed on romanticism. French Restoration philosophy, that of de Maistre and Bonald, passed on to Comte the conception of a society which transcends individuals, which precedes them logically and in time, and which includes past generations. During the same period, the historical school of jurisprudence also developed the idea of a lasting social totality that has its own history, in which individuals participate but which they cannot simply "make." This history exists without individuals' doing anything about it, as it were; they must accept the "real reality," which manifests itself above all in traditional institutions. In the social totality of the historical school of jurisprudence, the *Volk* ("the folk" or "the people"), everything has grown "from inner necessity" and is thus connected and in interaction with everything else. The appeal is to "life," as against the "construction" of history by reference to the Hegelian *Idee* (that is, freedom). The enemy of this notion is the rational philosophy of history of Hegel, who had fought against the petty notion that whatever existed at any time was, by right, right forever—even though it had long since become wrong.[11] Eventually, this "life" deteriorated to mere philology: it became the given, the tradition which is laid down in the "texts," that is, the historical sources and records. This Alexandrine erudition came to accumulate enormous masses of data; whatever could in any way be documented was accepted as fact. The "meaning" of history was no longer an issue because it was clear: it was the continuity of hallowed tradition.

This tradition was threatened, and eventually dissolved, by industrialization. The bourgeois view, though oriented less toward the Middle Ages than toward traditional rationalism—ascribing reason to the self-interest of the individual and aiming at a new political order—had not managed to re-establish a continuity which would produce new strength. On the contrary, thinkers began to consider bourgeois values mere frills. Nietzsche spoke with contempt of the "cultural philistine" and himself contributed to the dismantling of these values. Through historical and psychological relativization, their transvaluation became a devaluation—the only question became that of their utility.

Another factor disrupting the tradition was the rising proletariat. It, too, could no longer be understood within the historical continuity of master and apprentice. The proletariat insisted that the ideals of the bourgeoisie be taken out of the heaven of ideas and made into concrete realities; in a most disturbing manner, it took history seriously, not merely accepting it, but interfering with it through the Secretariat General of the International Workingmen's Association (First International). A serious crisis developed "in the general philosophical foundations . . . of historical thought, in the conception of historical values by reference to which we must construe the context of history."[12]

This crisis was aggravated by the separation of the methods employed in the historical and natural sciences. In the face of advances in natural science, the historians' protestations that they, too, were trying to give their work a rigorously scientific character sounded obsolete or "poetic"; the attempt at historical interpretation, "metaphysical." This accusation attained full force only toward the end of the century, however. For as a consequence of the historical school of jurisprudence, which had conceived of culture as a totality whose particulars were to be grasped in the context of the larger whole, German historiography had occasionally shifted from political to cultural history, which in turn had split up into economic history, legal history, religious history, and so on. Historiography brought together the materials which, ever since Voltaire and Condorcet—and especially since Comte and Spencer—had also been the materials of early sociology: those of the cultural and social history of human society. (To the degree that sociology was concerned with social organization and social institutions, they were already treated by political science.) "Never, however," the historian Treitschke declared, can "*one* science be imagined which covers all these heterogeneous things," unless the *state* is considered "the consistently ordered society."[13]

Although in 1858, the liberal Robert von Mohl had argued for a science of society which was to deal with communities, churches, and tribes rather than the state, the first German contributions to sociology tended to see everything *sub specie etatis*—tended, at least, to let all history terminate in the extant order. In the 1840's, for instance, Lorenz von Stein had been both fascinated and frightened by the Saint-Simonists and other French socialists, and had suggested that the proletarian-revolutionary forces should be absorbed in a social monarchy. Eventually, he became the "father of administrative science," and sociology lost the sting of its social criticism, being reduced to a scheme of formal concepts which formed part of von Stein's system of political science (*System der Staatswissenschaft,* 1856). W. H. Riehl (who because of his old-fashioned patriarchal love of folklore has occasionally been elevated to the rank of founder of an "autochthonous" German sociology) warmly wished that the "art of domestic administration" would manage, with the help of sociology (which he called the "study of the people" [*Volkskunde*]), to make one believe that the police, even at their nastiest, acted straight from the people's soul. In view of this, Treitschke could argue with superb irony for the primacy of the state as "the consistently ordered society."

The first great work which was expressly based on Comte and Spencer, that is, on "Western" sociology—Schäffle's *Bau und Leben des socialen Körpers* ("Structure and Life of the Social Body," 1875-78)—carried the analogy between an organism and society to such grotesque lengths that only Schäffle's erudition and his merits in other respects protected him from ridicule; his presentation, despite its stimulating qualities, made people shy away from this "newfangled" discipline. The work that is the first that can be called sociological in the modern sense of the term—Tönnies' *Gemeinschaft und Gesellschaft* (1887)—remained almost completely unknown for some time, despite its provocative subtitle, which promised a treatise on communism and socialism, matters that were as much objects of curiosity as they were of theoretical and practical repudiation. Elements of romanticism, the Enlightenment, and positivism—even of historical materialism—converged in Tönnies' book; it is hard to classify it under the proper discipline, particularly in respect to its politics.

What became decisive for the development of sociology was not the influence of Schäffle nor Tönnies but that which the so-called socialists of the chair were gaining toward the end of the century. (This is a misleading term as it was applied by dogmatic liberals to conservatively oriented groups who wanted to prevent a social revolution by means of social-political measures.) The socialists of the chair were economists, economic historians, jurists, statisticians—in short, representatives of the "political sciences" (*Staatswissenschaften*). In 1872, under the leadership of Gustav Schmoller, they formed the *Verein für Sozialpolitik* ("Society for Social Policy"). It was composed of national-minded citizens of conservative leanings. They were remarkably solid scholars, at home in archives but open to modern currents, familiar with ancient history and with the materials of contemporary ethnologists, worried about the excesses of modern capitalism and disquieted by the so-called social question, believers in the Bible and at the same time skeptics, distrustful of grand theories of philosophy of history and insistent on the gathering of facts, tending toward the historical relativization of values but holding on to certain supreme values alleged to transcend history or at least to remain unchanged throughout it—not least among them being the "cultural value of the state" and the value of the individual nature of the cultivated person.

Open to the tendencies of the modern period as they were, the socialists of the chair no longer simply rejected sociology. To be concerned with it had become fashionable for those who wanted to be considered progressive. Schmoller himself spoke of his own field, economics, as a "normative science of society," and the jurist Rudolf von Jhering referred to sociology (in the second volume of his *Zweck im Recht* ["Purpose in Law"], 1883) and called his "social-historical theory" of the rules of social interaction a "branch of the sciences of society." In 1888, Gustav Rümelin declared that "the modern concept of society has really become more exactly definable and scientifically usable through the application and increasing diffusion and elaboration of the statistical method." In saying this, he, too, spoke as a representative of the younger historical school, according to which economics, a part of the "sciences of the state," was a social or cultural science: economic phenomena could really be studied only in connection with social and historical phenomena. For this purpose, statistics was once more given a place of honor as the art of drawing inductive conclusions from exact description.

This is the milieu in which German sociology arose—Max Weber's as much as Georg Simmel's. Simmel's earliest sociological studies were published in the *Jahrbuch für Gesetzgebung,*

Verwaltung und Volkswirtschaft des Deutschen Reiches ("Annual for Legislation, Administration, and Economics of the German Reich"), which was edited by Schmoller.

Die Philosophie der Geschichte als Soziologie ("Philosophy of History as Sociology"), the first dogmatic history of sociology in the German language, was published by Paul Barth in 1897. It took little notice of Simmel. In his review of this fat volume, Tönnies

> cannot help declaring it as simply unjust that as intelligent a work as Simmel's *Über sociale Differenzierung* is disposed of by some ironical remarks in the midst of eleven pages dealing with [of all people] P. von Lilienfeld; and of other contributions of Simmel's there is no mention at all.[14]

Tönnies, however, was convinced that Barth would change his opinion:

> It cannot be Barth's lasting and serious view that a thinker like Simmel has less right to be "heard" in sociological matters than have Messrs. P. v. Lilienfeld, A. Fouilée, R. Worms, L. F. Ward—Barth won't undertake to defend such a view.

Adolph von Wenckster, Schmoller's assistant, expressed himself even more sharply on Barth's disregard of Simmel:

> ...The nature, aim, and achievement of modern sociology come out much more intensively, much more understandably, in a single short essay by Georg Simmel than in the whole big book by Barth.[15]

Finally, in 1909, the *Handwörterbuch der Staatswissenschaften,* the standard reference work in the social sciences, which was marked by the spirit of the younger historical school, called Simmel "the most important German sociologist."[16] It praised him

> for having reduced to a more modest measure those exaggerated claims of sociology by which it declares itself to be the true heir of philosophy of history. . . . All those secret or open desires to supplement imperfect actual experience by speculation; all at-

> tempts to unriddle the meaning and purpose of society and to define its value [may be considered, indeed, as] demonstrations of a metaphysical need

—but science has nothing to do with them. Simmel is acclaimed for "the new perspective in all sciences of culture" which he has introduced, that is, for sociology as a method. But this praise also implies relief over the fact that the established social or political sciences will no longer be disturbed by the "trespasses"[17] of sociology.

In the beginning, it was not easy to define Simmel's position: "His early writings seem at first to be destructive rather than constructive, critically analytical, but not exactly rich in objective insights."[18] His *Einleitung in die Moralwissenschaft* ("Introduction to Moral Science")—which he later disowned but which the Frenchman Célestin Bouglé considered to be especially characteristic of contemporary German philosophy and social science—seemed to show

> that each of the fundamental ethical concepts represents a collection of the most variegated, often contradictory tendencies and motives; and, what is more, that it only seems to have content while actually it is a mere verbal pod covering a content particularly appreciated or abhorred at the time.

If the aim of Simmel's book was

> to incorporate ethics partly in psychology, partly in social science, partly in history, by means of a historical-psychological treatment of the facts put together under its heading,[19]

such an undertaking was felt to constitute a disturbing relativization of values. Again and again, therefore, Simmel's real achievement is said to be his re-establishment of sociology as an "empirical science of society," which, above all, had to remove obstacles, dispel traditional prejudices, and reject claims launched by metaphysics and philosophy of history.[20]

This new "science of reality" (Simmel's own coinage) was, however, a peculiar affair. Frischeisen-Köhler observed

> that Simmel's studies are not tied to the objective facts with which they start. Their aim is not to investigate concrete realities, to

> find and present facts. The communication of factual social material is not to be—as Simmel himself stresses in his great *Soziologie*—even a subordinate purpose of this work.[21]

And the Marxist Georg Lukács wrote that Simmel in his

> sociology is sensitive only to the most immediate and abstract categories of the relations of social life and assiduously avoids all serious substantive problems. . . . Above all, he does not concern himself with concrete historical-social causation. While economics and sociology are broadly treated, they nevertheless emerge as something superficial.[22]

This is an accusation which Durkheim, too, made of Simmel.

In 1900, Durkheim published a critique of Simmel's sociology in the *Rivista italiana di sociologia.* He had published Simmel's "The Problem of Sociology" (which was to be the first chapter of *Soziologie*) in the first volume of his *Année sociologique*—which may give an idea of the renown Simmel enjoyed even outside Germany. In his critique, Durkheim argues that in his essay Simmel keeps sociology "in the atmosphere of metaphysical ideology."[23] Sociology, Durkheim maintains, cannot be denied the right to constitute itself by means of abstract ideas since every science proceeds in this manner; but the steps in the process of abstraction must be worked out methodically and the facts analyzed in this process must be classified according to differences in their nature; otherwise, abstraction is bound to degenerate into speculative construction—if not vague mythology.[24] By what right, Durkheim asks, does Simmel separate—and separate so radically—the form and content of society? Simmel asserts that the form alone has social character while the content has such character only indirectly.[25] And yet, Durkheim argues, it can be seen at first glance that collective traditions—religious, legal, moral, and economic practices—are social facts just as much as the external forms of sociability are. In addition, these phenomena constitute living and acting society itself; consequently, it is strange that we are asked to think of the group as a kind of empty form.[26] If sociology is to deserve the name of science, it must consist in something other than philosophical "variations" on certain aspects of social life, chosen more or less accidentally according to personal taste.[27] Above all, Durkheim contends, Simmel pays no attention to the fact that society also acts. He is too intrigued by the various forms of society which are studied by social morphology to remember this. But sociology must not only describe these forms, it must also explain them; that is, it must connect them with their causes and determine their functions—causes and effects, however, are not given once and for all but are in constant flux.[28] Sociology must be oriented historically; it must go to comparative history which offers it the "only instrument" for ascertaining how, for instance, institutions have been formed, what causes have produced them, and so on.[29] What Simmel calls "form" has only a metaphorical meaning. Sociology must hold on to real social forms;[30] this is the only solid foundation of its method.

Whether or not this critique, published in an Italian learned journal, ever became known in Germany, the German translation of Durkheim's *Règles de la méthode sociologique* in 1904 had little effect; Simmel's formal sociology triumphed. Durkheim's *De la division du travail social* was regarded, above all—by Schmoller, who reviewed it, for example—as a contribution to economics. Tönnies corrected the misunderstanding according to which Durkheim's mechanical and organic solidarity coincided with his own *Gemeinschaft* and *Gesellschaft.* Vierkandt barely mentioned *Les formes élémentaires de la vie religieuse*—and Vierkandt was a trained ethnologist. Only later, particularly through Marica's analysis,[31] did Durkheim's method become somewhat better known; but it displeased and produced uneasiness. The slogan of "sociologism" was quickly seized upon to reject once again sociology's claim to intensive preoccupation with the contents of social forms. It is true that later Leopold von Wiese advised German sociologists to study Durkheim. But his major concern was that they learn that the proper approach to social phenomena is not to start from individual psychology and to proceed introspectively, but to start, as Durkheim had proposed, "from the outside," considering social phenomena as *sui generis.* However, following Simmel's example, von Wiese taught abstraction from the historical, economic, or other contents of social facts, and worked at the elaboration of a "theory of the categories of society," which Gothein had identified as characteristic of Simmel's sociology.[32]

Durkeim has remained practically unknown in Germany,[33] but the magnificent "torso"[34] of Simmel's sociology has had its effect, above all on methodology. A partial explanation of this lies in the fact that German intellectuals, who are characterized by pious loyalty to the state, have been united in their resistance to a science that, because of the wavering tendency of its philosophy of history, seems to border on socialism. If necessary, sociology could be made part of the existing apparatus of science; and historians had enough points of contact with it to consider themselves sociologists. However, that philosophical-historical tendency of sociology—no matter that it might have looked so abstruse in this or that case that it did not have to be taken seriously from the start—nevertheless had a sting. This was that the historical foundation of the state, along with the political sciences which tried to demonstrate its existence, appeared by no means definitely secured. It was necessary, therefore, to defend what had grown historically against a historical change which must always be expected and which was even held to be progress. To study history was good as long as the aim of such study was to praise the status quo—bourgeois society in general, or, in Prussian fashion, the throne and the altar. Whatever historical values were destroyed in pursuing this goal were insignificant when compared to the values which obtained there and then. Suddenly, however, somebody declared that it was unworthy of science "to unriddle the meaning and purpose of society and to define its value."[35] This view was like a decree prohibiting thought, but it was a decree to which "men of good will" silently submitted. Yet the urgent question regarding the nature of society—no matter how difficult it was to grasp it objectively and comprehensively—could not be silenced. The older social philosophy—and sociology, too—had once tried to answer it. Simmel gave a new and surprising answer: There is no such thing as society; there are only individuals in interaction.

Men do indeed live in continual interaction with one another, whether they know it or not, and whether they like it or want to protect themselves from it. Nor is there any question that the web of the complex processes of sociation which results from such interaction is comprehensive enough to easily suggest its identity with society. And certainly Simmel was right in rejecting the traditional reification of society. The "psychological microscopy of the interactions of the atoms of society, that is, of the individuals,"[36] which Simmel initiated—casually, as it were—is practiced today with respectable exactitude in the laboratories devoted to "group dynamics."

At the same time, however, Simmel pushed aside as unserious the question of society's course and goal, and he rejected as inadmissible any statement concerning a good or bad society. Simmel helped produce a quiet conscience; it was enough to observe that a certain "form" can be found in a band of robbers, an industrial enterprise, and a religious denomination; and if the inspection of "content" was thus no longer necessary, then the painful awareness that more than formal similarities may be found in the band, the enterprise, and the church disappears.[37]

Durkheim, too, demanded that a concept of society like Comte's be abandoned as too abstract: to Durkheim, groups alone were concrete. Groups may form societies that are different from other societies, but mankind and its progress are merely ideas; they are not facts of sociology. For Durkheim, as for Simmel, sociology is above all a method. Like Simmel, Durkheim was a student of the younger historical school; and perhaps his insistence on social facts and their historically conditioned and historically changing contents has contributed to his having had so little influence on German sociology. For German sociology came into its own precisely by distinguishing itself from history. Although since Hegel one of the components of its development has been the emphasis on historical-social reality,[38] it is another component, one which shows a progressive denial of any determinism, which has achieved respectability. This may be seen in Dilthey's explicit, laudatory reference to Simmel.[39] An inspection of the relevant literature of Simmel's time shows that, despite all appreciation of Simmel the sociologist, writers saw his true importance in his observations concerning the philosophy of history, or, more precisely, concerning the logic of the science of history.

Although historians contributed to Durkheim's *Année sociologique* and men such as Henri Berr, Marcel Bloch, and Lucien Febvre were inspired to research by sociology, the issue concerning the nature of the natural sciences as against the *Geisteswissenschaften* aroused hardly any excitement in France. In Germany, on the contrary, this issue became the central epistemological problem around the turn of the century. It preoccupied, "under the leadership of Dilthey, Windelband, Simmel, and H. Rickert, most of the contemporary philosophers and logicians."[40] In this conflict, Simmel's "speculation," Tönnies wrote, "carefully remains in contact with the achievements of both the natural sciences and historical study,"[41] with psychology mediating between the two. Simmel, according to the vita he appended to his doctoral dissertation, owed his psychology essentially to Lazarus, as well as to Bastian. The aftereffects of Herbartian scientific psychology—the sharp separation of individual phenomena, the initial direction toward *Völkerpsychologie,* and, above all, the position of an "individualistic realism" (which, however, must be understood empirically, not metaphysically)[42]—led Simmel to assume in his sociology that only individuals have reality, while their formations in complex structures are held to be, not products of reality, but of the synthetic understanding. In line with Herbart, Simmel started from the psychological premises of historical study and was able to reduce the contrast between historical and nomothetic science to such an extent (Rickert reproached him for this)[43] that the distinction threatened to lose its logical significance almost completely.

This, at least, was Simmel's position in the first edition of his *Probleme der Geschichtsphilosophie* ("Problems of Philosophy of History," 1892). In the second, completely revised edition, too, the author took his departure from the position that the ideal of historiography might be said "to be applied psychology, so that, if there is psychology as a nomothetic science, historiography would be related to it as astronomy is to mathematics."[44] He continued to insist that psychology seeks to "abstract, to ascertain lawful relations, or relations analogous to laws, valid wherever their conditions are given, even if in reality this situation occurs only once."[45] But in the second edition he clearly separated history from the allegedly abstract atemporality of psychology, because history has to do with meaning and significance, and he emphasized the fact that in contrast to the task of the natural sciences, that of historiography consists in the identification of the "individual," the individual that, because of the qualities that are characteristic of it alone, determines which "laws" are valid for it.[46] If natural science comprehends the given by its laws, historical science seeks specific phenomena of reality which are significant in themselves.

Troeltsch, the critical historian of historicism, called Simmel's contribution "the most profound and fertile achievement in this field": "it is not completed but it sees all problems and throws new light on them. In [Simmel] . . . converge . . . the suggestions of Spencer, Windelband, and Rickert and [in him] they find a new center."[47] This center is the understanding of history itself. Max Weber, also a friend of Simmel's, proclaimed that the logically most advanced beginning of a theory of understanding was found in Simmel: "Simmel has the merit of having clearly distinguished, within the widest area which the concept of 'understanding' . . . can cover, between the objective 'understanding' of the *meaning* of an utterance and the subjective 'interpretation' of the *motives* of a (speaking or acting) individual."[48] However, Simmel was less concerned with interpreting an individual's speech or action than with uncovering contexts of meaning. He put this in exaggerated and misleading fashion by saying "that historical truth must by no means be considered as the mirror of historical reality."[49]

Simmel turned against the "suffocating . . . historical realism," that is, positivism. He believed he could refute it by demonstrating that every historical picture is the product of selective, classifying, construing, and always subjective thought; this was his "declaration of the sovereignty of the category over the material."[50] He tried to clarify his position by analyzing the concept of progress, on the one hand, and the methodology of historical materialism, on the other. But here, as in his sociology, he played a twofold role: as a destroyer and as an innovator. He did not reject the concept of progress; but those who entertained doubts about progress—doubts that in Simmel's time began to gnaw at the bourgeois tradition—could, thanks to him, believe them to have an epistemological foundation: progress became a manner of speaking. Nor is there anything cavalier in Simmel's rejection of historical materialism: he discussed it on various occasions, and his voluminous *Philosophie des Geldes* ("Philosophy of Money") could hardly have been written without Marx. Like a seismograph, he sensed its historical power, but at the same time he followed the fashion of the times (as did Sombart, among others) and only flirted with it. He referred to Marxian theory as the chief witness of his own intent, "epistemological idealism";[51] but in the same breath he accused it of being an ideology which makes it impossible "to recognize the idea as the *form* of history."[52] However, in this fashion, all kinds of "ideas" and "categories" can be made to order the material of history, and opposing views, even if they are true, can be defamed as ideologies. Simmel was not aware of this consequence of his view; if he had been, he would have opposed it most vigorously.

There is no doubt that Simmel's *Die Probleme der Geschichtsphilosophie,* as well as his properly sociological studies and the essays and fragments on the philosophy of culture, contain a wealth of the most diverse suggestions which even today are still worth exploring. (It is these suggestions which have been plucked out of Simmel's work when it has been quoted since his death.) Simmel's work was, in Herman Schmalenbach's words, "interwoven with all the movements of our total intellectual life in such a way as mere technical philosophy can never be: in its contents, too, Simmel signifies the very philosophic representation of our age."[53] This means that in a singular fashion Simmel reconciled the contradictory tendencies which had already begun to make themselves felt during Wilhelm II's Reich, and which later determined, for good and evil, the intellectual and political history of modern Germany. However, when considering all the fame which came to Simmel during and after his life, one should not overlook the acidly analytical words of a man who, like Simmel, was a member of Max Weber's circle:

> Simmel has the finest mind among all contemporaries. But beyond this, he is wholly empty and aimless, desiring everything except the truth. He is a collector of standpoints which he assembles all around truth without ever wanting or being able to possess it. He consumes himself in many quick and occasional fires and is most of the time nothing but dazzling in an ever repeated methodo-

logical pyrotechnic display, by which we are rapidly bored. He is coquettish without ever showing his true colors, and is, on the whole, entirely unwilling and incompetent to stake his sensitive methodology—which always goes in circles—on a comprehensive, broadly contextual objectivity. He is a psychologist who forever winds himself into everything and out again, and who is not solid enough to deserve the tough designation of a rigorous relativist. Yet it cannot be denied that just in the adaptation and closeness to life which he attempted, in his nervous intimacy with the soul—in the virtues of his vices—Simmel has given to thought nuances and a heightened temperature which, if only taken out of the hands of a man born without a hard core, can indeed be of great service to philosophy, which owes much to Simmel's subtlety.[54]

Perhaps all this is true. But if it is true, it may be because Simmel represented a social reality which is not yet a matter of the past in Germany even today, forty years after his death. Today, however, that sensitivity, that capacity for listening and contemplating, that ability to attend to the singular and specific because it might illuminate the general and the broadly significant—all of that which, around the turn of the century, was condemned as decadent, un-German, and without basis—has become even more rare. Simmel, whose language is like the point of a pencil—not robust, capable of tracing nuances, very breakable, allusive, feverishly sharp—distrusted the great collectivities and insisted on the individual's right to follow his own thoughts, even if they were as playful and inconspicuous as the fleeting strokes of a pencil sketch. He was against big words, but at the end he succumbed to the magic of the so-called philosophy of life. Yet he sought the lived moment in which the past, too, comes to life again; he did not seek a justification of brutality metaphysicized as "life." In an entry in his diary he once characterized his own position in the intellectual life of Germany:

> I know that I shall die without spiritual heirs (and this is good). The estate I leave is like cash distributed among many heirs, each of whom puts his share to use in some trade that is compatible with *his* nature but which can no longer be recognized as coming from that estate.[55]

It is indeed difficult to detail all the heritage he left. He had no "school."

> His effect on historians was and is . . . a very slight one; . . . his influence remained an influence on the general atmosphere, making itself felt in particular among more sophisticated journalists.[56]

In sociology, Theodor Litt, Alfred Vierkandt, and above all Leopold von Wiese were the immediate recipients of his suggestions. The first sketch of a modern social psychology, presented in 1899 in an inaugural address by Franz Eulenburg,[57] was influenced by him. The basic idea of his sociology has become a common possession although there is little awareness of its origin. If in contemporary Germany there is, owing to American influence, more interest in microsociology, in the social psychology of interaction, than in traditional macrosociology, this probably goes back to Simmel. He was published in the *American Journal of Sociology* in the 1890's and 1900's and was given due regard in the classical textbook of sociology, Robert E. Park and Ernest W. Burgess' *Introduction to the Science of Sociology* of 1921.

It is undoubtedly one of Simmel's merits that he gave sociology an autonomous position among the established disciplines by formalizing it, that is, by differentiating it from history, as well as from anthropology, economics, political science, and psychology. Today, when sociology is widely accepted, it is important to reconnect it with its great tradition. Surely, this tradition cannot be simply and uncritically accepted, any more than Durkheim could accept it in this way. For Durkheim, sociology was not only a "new way of looking," not only a method, it had a pedagogical, even a political mission. It aimed at a better social order—as it did for Comte and Hegel and Marx. Today, more than ever, sociology needs to combine Simmelian investigations of minute structures with Durkheimian analyses of comprehensive economic-political historical processes.

Translated by Kurt H. Wolff

1. Parts of Comte's *Système de politique positive* (1824) appeared in the *Neue Monatsschrift für Deutschland* (Berlin). The *Système* was reviewed in the same year in the *Leipziger Literatur-Zeitung.*

2. November 5, 1842, *Lettres d'Auguste Comte à John Stuart Mill* (Paris: Ernest Leroux, 1877), p. 100.

3. J. Heyderhoff, "Rudolf Haym und Karl Twesten. Ein Briefwechsel über positive Philosophie und Fortschrittspolitik (1859-1863)," *Preussische Jahrbücher,* CLXI (1915), 239.

4. *Ibid.,* p. 241.

5. Karl Knies, one of the founders of the so-called younger historical school of German economics, wrote in 1883 in the second edition of his work, *Die Politische Oekonomie vom geschichtlichen Standpunkte* (p. 516): "When in 1852 I wrote on the method of political economy, the *Cours de philosophie positive par Auguste Comte,* published in six volumes between 1830 and 1842, was completely unknown to me, as it probably was to any of my German fellow economists. I was thus very much surprised when I later found a good many significant parallels in Comte's statements on 'the method of sociology.' . . . Of course, I must at once recognize in particular Comte's basic devotion to facts perceived through experience and observation and must go on record as saying that he described, in respect to life as well as science, the actual process of a continuous development (evolution) in no uncertain terms, long before I did." In his professorial language, Knies expresses regret, however, that Comte does not deal more thoroughly with the phenomena of human-individual life, a "mistake by which Comte was necessarily kept from an altogether satisfactory achievement."

6. Wilhelm Dilthey, *Einleitung in die Geisteswissenschaften* (*Gesammelte Schriften,* Band I [Leipzig and Berlin: B. G. Teubner, 1923]), p. 93.

7. *Ibid.,* pp. 104 ff.

8. Cf. Heinz Maus, "Geschichte der Soziologie," *Handbuch der Soziologie,* ed. W. Ziegenfuss (Stuttgart: Ferdinand Enke, 1956), pp. 12 ff.

9. At first, Comte thought that in Hegel he had found a fellow fighter for the common cause, the construction of a scientific basis of politics and history. Through the mediation of the Saint-Simonist G. d'Eichthal, he sent Hegel a copy of his *Système de politique positive,* which had been published in Saint-Simon's *Catéchisme des industriels.*

10. Its head was Savigny. Marx took his courses at the University of Berlin.

11. Cf. Hegel, *Schriften zur Politik und Rechtsphilosophie,* ed. Georg Lasson (Leipzig: Felix Meiner, 1913), p. 199.

12. Ernst Troeltsch, *Der Historismus und seine Probleme* (*Gesammelte Schriften,* Band III [Tübingen: J. C. B. Mohr (Paul Siebeck), 1922]), p. 4.

13. Heinrich von Treitschke, *Die Gesellschaftswissenschaft* ([1859] Halle: Max Niemeyer, 1926), pp. 55, 79.

14. Ferdinand Tönnies, *Soziologische Studien und Kritiken* (Jena: Gustav Fischer, 1929), III, 292.

15. Schmoller's *Jahrbuch,* XXII (1898), 401.

16. Eberhard Gothein, "Gesellschaft und Gesellschaftswissenschaft," in *Handwörterbuch der Staatswissenschaften* (Jena: Gustav Fischer, 1909), IV, 683.

17. Robert Michels, *Soziologie als Gesellschaftswissenschaft* (Berlin: Mauritius-Verlag, 1926), p. 81.

18. Max Frischeisen-Köhler, "Georg Simmel," *Kant-Studien,* XXIV (1919), 1-2.

19. *Ibid.,* p. 2.

20. *Ibid.*

21. *Ibid.,* p. 7.

22. Georg Lukács, "Die deutsche Soziologie der imperialistischen Periode," *Die Zerstörung der Vernunft* (Berlin: Aufbau-Verlag, 1954), pp. 359 ff.

23. Translated from Armand Cuvillier's French translation of Emile Durkheim's paper, "La sociologie et son domaine scientifique," in Cuvillier, *Où va la sociologie française?* (Paris: Librairie Marcel Rivière, 1953), pp. 177-208.

24. *Ibid.,* p. 181.

25. *Ibid.,* p. 182.

26. *Ibid.,* p. 183.

27. *Ibid.,* p. 186.

28. *Ibid.,* p. 190.

29. Cf. Cuvillier, *Où va la sociologie française?* pp. 17 ff.

30. Durkheim, *op. cit.,* p. 190.

31. George M. Marica, *Emile Durkheim. Soziologie und Soziologismus* (Jena: Gustav Fischer, 1932).

32. Gothein, *loc. cit.*

33. Durkheim seems to have attracted attention only recently, and then through American sociology, which has always emphasized the group more than has German sociology. Another reason for this recent concern with his work is the newly awakened interest in social psychology, which has also discovered new significance in Simmel.

34. Leopold von Wiese in his review of Theodore Abel, *Systematic Sociology in Germany* (New York: Columbia University Press, 1929), in *Kölner Vierteljahrshefte für Soziologie,* VIII (1929-30), 145.

35. Gothein, *loc. cit.*

36. *Ibid.*

37. From the standpoint of the sociology of knowledge, Pareto's cold-blooded and naïve equation of the elite of a gang of thieves with that of a monastic order must be appraised differently.

38. To mention a few names: Marx, Dilthey, Freyer, Mannheim, Horkheimer, and Th. W. Adorno.

39. Wilhelm Dilthey, "Soziologie" (1904-6), in *Einleitung in die Geisteswissenschaften* (Leipzig and Berlin: B. G. Teubner, 1933), pp. 421-22.

40. Marianne Weber, *Max Weber ein Lebensbild* (Heidelberg: Lambert Schneider, 1950), p. 351.

41. "Entwicklung der Soziologie in Deutschland im 19. Jahrhundert," *Soziologische Studien und Kritiken* (Jena: Gustav Fischer, 1926), II, 103. This was originally published in the Schmoller-Festgabe, *Entwicklung der deutschen Volkswirtschaftslehre im 19. Jahrhundert* (Leipzig: Duncker und Humblot, 1908).

42. Cf. Frischeisen-Köhler, *op. cit.*, p. 12.

43. Heinrich Rickert, *Die Grenzen der naturwissenschaftlichen Begriffsbildung* ([1902] 5th ed.; Tübingen: J. C. B. Mohr [Paul Siebeck], 1929), p. 272.

44. *Die Probleme der Geschichtsphilosophie. Eine erkenntnistheoretische Studie* (2nd ed.; Leipzig: Duncker und Humblot, 1905), p. 1.

45. *Ibid.*, p. 142.

46. *Ibid.*, p. 137. Simmel adds, "to obviate misunderstandings: historical individuality . . . by no means refers only to individual persons but to individual, qualitatively characterized single phenomena as such, that is, to groups and situations, states of affairs, and over-all developments, as well as to personal being and becoming."

47. Troeltsch, *op. cit.*, p. 594.

48. Max Weber, "Roscher und Knies und die logischen Probleme der historischen Nationalökonomie," in *Gesammelte Aufsätze zur Wissenschaftslehre* ([1906] Tübingen: J. C. B. Mohr [Paul Siebeck], 1922), p. 93.

49. *Geschichtsphilosophie* (2nd ed.), p. 49.

50. *Ibid.*, p. 160.

51. *Ibid.*, p. 166.

52. *Ibid.*, p. 167.

53. "Simmel," *Sozialistische Monatshefte,* LII (1919), 274. (Schmalenbach introduced into German sociology the category of the *Bund,* as intermediate between Tönnies' *Gemeinschaft* and *Gesellschaft.* He was close to Stefan George and his circle.)

54. Ernst Bloch, *Geist der Utopie* (Munich: Duncker und Humblot, 1918), pp. 246-47.

55. Quoted from Maria Steinhoff, "Die Form als soziologische Grundkategorie bei Georg Simmel," *Kölner Vierteljahrshefte für Soziologie,* IV (1924-25), 259.

56. Troeltsch, *op. cit.,* p. 594.

57. Franz Eulenburg, "Ueber die Möglichkeit und die Aufgaben einer Sozialpsychologie," *Schmollers Jahrbuch für Gesetzgebung, Verwaltung und Volkswirtschaft in Deutschland,* Neue Folge, XXIV (1900), 201 ff.

GEORG SIMMEL'S INFLUENCE ON JAPANESE THOUGHT

MASAMICHI SHIMMEI

When we try to assess the influence of Georg Simmel on Japanese thought, we must take into account not only his sociological but also his philosophical ideas. Spykman, in fact, calls him primarily a philosopher.[1] Although he began his scholarly career as a sociologist and gained fame at first through new and acute analyses and the introduction of a formal concept of society, he practiced philosophical habits of thought throughout his life, and in his later days turned away from sociology.

His influence on Japanese thought—as on American thought—is, however, stronger in sociology than in philosophy.[2] There are, of course, differences between the two countries. In general, Japan has been more exposed to German ideas than has the United States; thus Simmel's impact on Japan is far stronger, not only in sociology, but also in philosophy. It is not difficult to understand why this should be so. Japan and the United States began to cultivate academic learning and to import scientific knowledge from European countries at almost the same time. Although French and English influence was greater in Japan at first, from about the end of the last century German influence has grown conspicuously, and the names and works of representative German scholars have become well known to the reading public. And whereas in the United States German thought was accepted only as a supplement to French and British thought, in Japan it was welcomed as almost the supreme model. This development corresponded in time with the ascent of political conservatism, which succeeded in crushing the once triumphant liberalism and resulted in the rise of militaristic regimes. Early in the Meiji era, British and French thought was widely diffused; Spencer's books in particular were much read in translation. After 1889, the year when the Meiji Constitution was promulgated, the situation changed, however, and German thought became dominant.

With this historical background, it is no wonder that the

Japanese were more familiar than the Americans with German ideas. German thought—both good and bad—had become easier to accept in Japan. Thus, when Simmel's work was brought into Japan as a new species of sociology, Japanese scholars were ready to welcome it wholeheartedly, and it soon became a sort of cult among them. Simmel's influence in the United States made itself felt first through John Henry Wilbrandt Stuckenberg, who adopted Simmel's viewpoint in his *Introduction to the Study of Sociology* (1898). Park and Burgess, in their classic *Introduction to the Science of Sociology* (1921), also showed Simmel's impact, although their orientation was not quite free from tendencies toward a synthetic sociology. In Japan, as early as 1907, S. Yoneda was delivering detailed critical lectures on Simmel's sociology at Kyoto University; and Yasuma Takata's monumental *Principles of Sociology* (*Shakaigaku Genri,* 1919), which espoused sociology as a special science with its own rigorous methodology, used and interpreted Simmel's writings. Between 1925 and 1930, four academic works appeared which treated of Simmel's sociology, as well as a number of introductions to sociology which adopted it. We may say that during this period Japanese sociologists, far more than the Americans, were influenced by Simmel.

Simmel's influence on Japanese philosophy has been comparatively meager, however. Simmel failed to find any consistent and faithful disciple in Japan, but his subtle logic and analysis impressed a sympathetic circle of philosophers and essayists. Most of his philosophical writings have been translated into Japanese but are still not available in English. The reason for this may again lie in the difference in the cultural traditions of Japan and the United States. In the United States, saturated as it is with an experimental and pragmatic spirit, speculation is greeted with skepticism, and theoretical thinking is often distrusted, if not rejected, as being metaphysics. There has been no such attitude in Japan, which has shown a readiness to accept every new school of philosophical thought, especially if it is German. Thus Simmel's philosophy has exerted more influence in Japan than in the United States, although its impact even in Japan has not rivaled Kant's or Hegel's.

In discussing Simmel's influence on Japanese thought in general, we shall present an analysis of this influence, first, in the area of philosophy, then in that of sociology.

As mentioned before, German influence on Japanese philosophy has been clearly apparent since about 1890, after the Meiji Constitution—essentially an imitation of the Prussian Constitution—was promulgated. The government, zealous in following the Prussian model, began to send as many students as possible to Germany so that they might bring back and disseminate German thought and learning, which was to bolster the domestic policy. Between 1890 and 1900, German philosophy, especially that of Kant and Hegel, was introduced into Japan and soon became predominant. From 1900 on, American pragmatism and, a little later, Bergson's philosophy were imported by some professors; but the influence of German philosophy was never enfeebled by this, as witness, for instance, the fact that some textbooks in philosophy were largely based on it.

After the First World War, however, as an indirect result of the victory of the allied nations and the popularity of Neo-Kantianism, with its mild cultural liberalism, the Japanese tradition of German philosophy began to lose its highly conservative character and to become more genuinely academic. Moreover, some dissatisfied Japanese philosophers turned elsewhere, particularly to Bergson, on the one hand, and Dilthey and Simmel, on the other. Among these, it was Bergson who gained the widest popularity; compared with his influence, that of Dilthey and Simmel was neither wide nor deep, although Dilthey's was greater than Simmel's. This was also true in Germany, where Dilthey was a full professor, while Simmel never attained a chair at Berlin, their common university. Dilthey had a fairly large following in Japan, but a plan to publish his works was abandoned after one volume had been issued; most of Simmel's philosophical writings are available in Japanese, however. These include his *Die Probleme der Geschichtsphilosophie, Schopenhauer und Nietzsche, Philosophische Kultur, Rembrandt, Kant und Goethe, Zur Philosophie der Kunst, Lebensanschauung,* and two partial translations of *Philosophie des Geldes.*

On the whole, however, Simmel's influence on Japanese

thought has been slight. He is sometimes referred to by academic scholars, but this is hardly more than lip service. There has been no one who could be called his disciple. His relativistic thought on morals, expressed in his *Einleitung in die Moralwissenschaft,* has had some echoes in Western countries, but it was almost wholly disregarded in Japan, presumably because it gave the impression of being too scientific and not philosophical enough. His noteworthy attempt at developing a philosophy of economics, embodied in his *Philosophie des Geldes,* attracted the attention of some economists. K. Tsunedo, professor at Osaka City University, the first of the two translators of the work, thought very highly of it and tried to construct a kind of philosophy of economics which combined Simmel with Marx and R. Stammler; but he left only a fragment, and he had no followers. In the field of the philosophy of art, Simmel has had some effect. K. Onishi, professor of aesthetics at Tokyo University, translated his *Rembrandt,* but, for the rest, was not particularly influenced by Simmel. J. Abe, however, a former professor of aesthetics at Tohoku University, was impressed by Simmel's thoughts on art and literature—especially by his book on Goethe—and utilized Simmelian ideas in his own book on Nietzsche's *Thus Spake Zarathustra,* even though he was a Neo-Kantian and a personalist.

Perhaps the scholar whose thought may be credited with being closest to Simmel's is T. Tanigawa, professor of philosophy at Hosei University and an active journalist. He has written no technically philosophical work, but a collection of his essays attests his deep knowledge of philosophy and reflects a strong influence of the German philosophy of life as represented by Simmel, with whom he has a similarity of style (as well as a similarity of occupations—Simmel, too, had been both a professor and a writer for newspapers and magazines). For Tanigawa, life is, above all, an expression of the critical spirit, which he contrasts with the temper of the present age, particularly with its belief in a conceptual and mechanistic intellect. Tanigawa stresses the importance of intuition as against intellect, of the inner as against the outer world, of the spirit as against the soul, of irrationality as against rationality. Yet this criticism of the intellect and of mechanism is tempered by common sense, and does not fall into radical irrationalism. The exposition of this philosophy of life may be found in such essays as "Sentimentality and Reflection," "Philosophical Literature," "The Japanese Soul," and "Life, Philosophy, and Art." Even their titles suggest that Tanigawa is temperamentally close to Simmel.

Another scholar influenced by Simmel, though one not usually thought of as a philosopher, is I. Shimizu, professor at Gakushuin University and the translator of Simmel's posthumously published *Fragmente und Aufsätze*. Properly speaking, Shimizu is a sociologist. Like Tanigawa, however, he is very active as a journalist. Occasionally, he betrays a view of life which is reminiscent of Simmel's.

The influence of Simmel's philosophy on Japanese philosophy declined even further when Heidegger's existentialism was introduced to Japan where it met with considerable interest.

The fact that Simmel exerted a much greater influence on Japanese sociology than on philosophy is striking in view of the circumstance that Japanese sociology had developed chiefly under French and American auspices, in contrast to the other sciences, many of which were more strongly influenced by Germany. Sociology remained an exception, however, even when governmental policy shifted toward conservatism and German thought and learning came, under government sponsorship, to be almost worshiped in the universities. To be sure, with this change the fervent enthusiasm for Spencer's sociology faded and was replaced by interest in such German and Austrian sociologists as Schäffle and Gumplowicz. However, German sociology took no root at that time. For instance, T. Tatebe, professor at Tokyo University, a leader in Japanese sociology from about 1900 on, constructed a system which was a queer mixture, essentially Confucianism and Comtism; but despite its marked tendency toward conservatism, it showed no trace of German influence. There was also the beginning of the impact of American sociology. Giddings' *Principles of Sociology* was welcomed, and appeared in free translation.

Beginning with the present century, this situation gradually changed. Especially after the First World War, the long-neglected German sociology began to attract the interest of Japanese scholars. Simmel had become known as a sociological name as early as 1898, when N. Kishimoto published a book on sociology in which Simmel was mentioned for the first time. Almost nobody, however, was acquainted with his characteristic conception of formal sociology. R. Higuchi's *A Short History of Sociology (Shakaigaku Shoshi),* which appeared in 1912, did not help to make Simmel better known. It merely made brief mention of him as a sociologist who, with Maurice Hauriou and James Mark Baldwin, belonged to the subjective school, with its emphasis on psychology. In 1907, however, S. Yoneda, lecturer at Kyoto University, who had returned to Japan after some years of study under Giddings and Tarde, began giving lectures in which he introduced and criticized Simmel's and Tarde's sociological theories. He further developed his ideas in a series of articles published in the *Annual* of the Japanese Institute of Sociology in 1914.

Yoneda's program for a sociological system is divided into three parts. The first (systematic sociology) deals with the classification of social phenomena, the nature of social laws, the methods of sociology, and the classification and systematization of the social sciences. The second (pure sociology) treats the genesis of intermental relationships, the social-psychological actions which give rise to them, and the fundamental processes and forms through which they are developed. The third part (synthetic sociology) concerns concrete processes of social formation, social circles and groups, cultural phenomena, social evolution, and cultural development.

This conception appears to have been suggested by Tarde, Simmel, and Giddings, on the one hand, and by Eugéne V. de Roberty, Julio Vanni, René Worms, Raoul de la Grasserie, and Fausto Squillace, on the other. Yoneda's aim was the construction of a large, inclusive system of sociology in which all branches hitherto developed would be synthesized. He supported Simmel's attempt to build up sociology as a special science, but he recognized and supported it as identical with Tarde's pure sociology and as an indispensable part of a sociological system. He opposed Simmel's identification of this formal sociology with the whole of sociology. He understood clearly that a new concept of sociology such as Simmel's had evolved as a critique of encyclopedic or synthetic sociology as developed, for instance, by Comte, whose defects he acknowledged. Yet he also appreciated the fact that the Comtean idea of establishing an inclusive system of sociology which would clarify social life in its totality originated in answer to dissatisfaction with the partial and fragmentary knowledge of the special social sciences; and he realized that since this need had not only persisted but had become more urgent, sociology could not be allowed to abandon the task assigned to it. Hence he rejected Simmel's attempt to limit it to formal sociology.

Consequently, Yoneda also rejected Simmel's conception of sociology as a special science. He affirmed that even if sociology was a science of pure form, as Simmel asserted, it was on a level different from that of the other social sciences because its object of study was the form common to all aspects of social phenomena. For this reason he welcomed Simmel's later conception, developed in his *Grundfragen der Soziologie,* in which Simmel enlarged the sphere of the discipline beyond formal to general and philosophical sociology. In a later article, Yoneda confessed that he was both surprised and happy when he discovered that Simmel's new conception was almost identical with his own. Although he did not complete his system, he contributed greatly to raising the scientific level of Japanese sociology by introducing and criticizing many new sociological theories which had been gaining ground in Western countries since the end of the last century—among them, particularly, was Simmel's. Owing to his effort, the real meaning of Simmel's formal sociology was grasped for the first time, and Simmel himself gradually became popular among Japanese sociologists. A decade or so later, a sociologist appeared who harvested the seeds sown by Yoneda. This was Yasuma Takata.

In 1919, Takata, a student of Yoneda's, published his *Principles of Sociology (Shakaigaku Genri),* a book of 1,385 pages, completed after several years of study and reflection. Although Yoneda's influence was obvious, the system Takata presented was very different from that of his teacher. In contrast to Yoneda, Takata justified Simmel's attempt to delimit the object of sociology on the ground that it might dispel the ambitious but impossible fantasy of an encylopedic sociology, and open the door to the establishment of sociology as an independent science. Like Simmel, he postulated society as his starting point, but not as the proper object of sociology, for which he considered it far too large and multifarious. Instead, sociology, like any other social science, must abstract from "society" a special object of its own on the basis of a particular viewpoint. It must be a special "plebeian," not the encyclopedic "master," science, aloof from the other social sciences and lording it over them.

It is clear that in this respect, Takata definitely departed from his teacher. His system may well be considered the first substantial attempt to build sociology as a special science, not only in Japan, but in the world. Of course, Simmel has priority in proposing the foundation of sociology as a special science in the form of formal sociology, and in establishing this foundation methodologically, but he failed to bring his idea to fruition. His *Soziologie* of 1908 was an unsystematic collection of random essays, even though it was characterized by subtle thought and brilliant logic. By contrast, Takata's *Principles* was excellent in its systematization and minute in its descriptions, although its style was less attractive than Simmel's. Takata was more than a scholar who tried to systematize what was bequeathed to him, unfinished, by Simmel.

Takata was indeed indebted to Simmel, but he was also influenced by Giddings and Durkheim. Giddings provided him with the framework of his system; Durkheim, with the concept of social consciousness. If we examine Takata's theory in detail, we find that in certain important respects his standpoint was not identical with Simmel's. He did not adopt Simmel's concept of form, and he objected to his contention that socialization or interaction should be thought of as forms. Instead, he asserted that, inasmuch as both form and content are concepts abstracted from concrete social phenomena, form considered from one standpoint being content from another, Simmel's attempt generally to define some phenomena as forms and others as content could not be supported. He urged that if we could assume economic and religious phenomena to be contents of social life, we had the right to make the same assumption in respect to interaction. Hence he also repudiated Simmel's view that the relation between sociology and the other social sciences could be compared to that between epistemology and the sciences in general:

sociology could not claim such a privileged position. He suspected a survival of encyclopedic sociology in Simmel's concept of form, and believed that this defect must be eradicated before sociology as a special science could be firmly established.

In 1923, Takata published his *Introduction to Sociology (Shakaigaku Gairon),* a briefer version of his *Principles.* The new work, however, adopted the classification of the sciences into natural and cultural, introduced from German philosophy; as a result of this, sociology, which the author had previously regarded as a natural science, now came to belong to the cultural sciences. A collection of essays, *Classes and the Third Interpretation of History,* published in 1925, is also worth mentioning in connection with Simmel. This third interpretation of history follows the first, which proceeds on the basis of materialistic factors only, and the second, which, on the contrary, is based exclusively on spiritual factors. Takata's own third interpretation was intended as a new synthesis promising adequate understanding, free of the one-sidedness of previous interpretations. His fundamental assumption was that among the many factors of history, socialization was the most effective and decisive—even the economic factor, held by Marxists and others to be predominant, could not exert its influence except in conjunction with some social relationship. Furthermore, the development of social relationships is caused by quantitative and qualitative changes in the composition of the population. Clearly, in this estimation of the demographic factor, Takata was greatly influenced by Durkheim, but the interpretation of history in terms of socialization or social relationships goes back to Simmel. When, in his *Grundfragen der Soziologie,* Simmel extended his conception of sociology beyond the formal to the general, he suggested that the view of man as determined by his interaction with other men would introduce a new perspective into all cultural sciences. To Takata goes the credit for having developed this idea.

In 1926, Takata published a new collection of essays, *A Study of Social Relationships (Shakaikankei no Kenkyu),* in which he analyzed the theories of social relationships as propounded by Simmel, Tönnies, Vierkandt, and von Wiese. By about that time, Simmel's sociology had come to be studied by a wider circle of scholars. As already mentioned, part of Simmel's *Philosophie des Geldes* appeared in translation in 1923. In 1925, S. Sugiyama published a book, *Twelve Lectures on Sociology (Shakaigaku Juniko),* in which he adopted Simmel's concept of society and tried to explain sociology as a special science. In 1926, the first translation of Simmel's *Grundfragen der Soziologie* appeared in Japan (the second, by another translator, was published in 1932). In the same year, M. Hayashi, then professor at Tokyo University, published *The Study of Simmel's Methodology of Sociology,* in which he investigated Simmel's fundamental methodological viewpoint, with special reference to his theories of knowledge and distance. Hayashi was evidently in agreement with Simmel, although he withheld positive judgment. The following year, 1927, R. Imori, professor at Aichi University, published *The Study of Formal Sociology,* in which, like Hayashi, he took up Simmel's formal sociology; but he went a step further by defending the cause of formal sociology, rebutting criticisms of it, and approving even the controversial term "formal sociology." His viewpoint may well be said to be wholly Simmelian. Hardly any other sociologist, even among the supporters of Simmel's conception in principle, accepted that term. Also in 1927, Simmel's *Über sociale Differenzierung* was published in a translation by N. Igarashi of Kyoto University, one of Yoneda's students.

The study of formal sociology, with Simmel at its center, came to full bloom in 1923, when K. Komatsu's *Introduction to Sociology (Shakaigaku Gairon)* and T. Toda's *Plan of Course of Sociology, I (Shakaigaku Kogian, I)* appeared. In 1927, Komatsu, a student of Takata and professor at Doshisha University, wrote *Theory of Social Structure* as a part of his system of sociology. He was the most militant advocate of sociology as a special science, and contributed not a little to its consolidation. Toda, then professor at Tokyo University, studied in the United States and was the first to import modern methods of social research into Japan. While not influenced by German sociology, in his conception of sociology he was an adherent of Simmel's, and did good service in fostering the development of sociology as a special science in Japan.

The trend in favor of Simmel's conception was not without

resistance. In 1927, books appeared which criticized Simmel's and related views. In my own work, *On Formal Sociology (Keishiki Shakaigaku Ron),* I tried to present formal sociology following a review of the sociological theories of Simmel and others. I suggested the possibility and necessity of basing sociology on a broader concept of society, which would be free from the vague and extravagant assumptions of encyclopedic sociology, but which would differ from the overly narrow and formalized approaches which had followed Simmel's formal sociology. In his *Introduction to Sociology (Shakaigaku Gairon),* published in 1928, T. Kada, then professor at Keio University, also opposed Simmel. Evidently under the influence of Marxism—at that time gaining ground among the Japanese as a kind of sociology—he defended synthetic sociology with an emphasis on the economic factor. In contrast to Shimmei and Kada, U. Iwasaki, president of Kansai University, who, in 1928, wrote *Prolegomenon to Sociology (Shakaigaku Josetsu),* was not wholly in disagreement with Simmel, though critical of his original intention of delimiting sociology to formal sociology. Instead, Iwasaki proposed to establish a system of sociology which included historical, practical, and theoretical (that is, formal) sociology. His viewpoint was similar to Yoneda's, and may be considered as a reaction to Simmel's narrower concept.

Simmel's influence, however, was not completely lost. Many sociologists followed his example in considering sociology a special science. Among them is J. Usui, professor at Kyoto University, whose methodological views were affected not only by Simmel but also by Vierkandt and Heidegger. Another is K. Kurauchi, professor at Osaka University, whose special interest lies in cultural sociology, which in his view is based on sociology conceived of as a special science; like Usui, Kurauchi has introduced phenomenological ideas into his position, notably Theodor Litt's concept of the reciprocity of perspectives.

Nevertheless, during the period under discussion, which lasted to the end of the Second World War, the trend against formal sociology, or sociology as a special science, was more challenging and commanded wider attention. In 1929, I again criticized the sociology of Simmel and his followers in my *German Sociology;* and in *Sociology* I first presented a plan for a synthetic sociology divided into two parts dealing with social groups and with social phenomena. Later, consolidating my position and replacing the concept of social phenomena with that of social forces (*Outlines of Sociology* [*Shakaigaku Yoko*], 1935), I set out to complete my system of sociology in *Fundamental Problems of Sociology* (*Shakaigaku no Kisomondai,* 1942). This work offers a broader and more concrete view of society, designed to transcend and correct narrower ones. The basic concept is that of "actional unison," which tries to capture the essence of society as the unity of form and content.

At about the same time, J. Matsumoto began to publish his system of sociology. Following the programmatic *Outlines of Sociology* (*Shakaigaku Yoko,* 1934), he completed this system by publishing in quick succession, between 1935 and 1941, *Introduction to Sociology (Shakaigaku Genron), Principles of Group Sociology (Shudanshakaigaku Genri),* and *Principles of Cultural Sociology (Bunkashakaigaku Genri).* Matsumoto's "total sociology" was to overcome the anarchy caused by the split of sociological theories. It called for a new system of sociology based on a comprehensive rather than a one-sided and partial conception of society. This system, resembling Andreas Walther's *vollständige Soziologie,* includes pure, real, natural, cultural, and practical sociology, the history of sociology, and the logic and methodology of the social sciences. It is critical of formal sociology for its identification of the sociology of groups with the whole of sociology and its neglect of cultural sociology. In Matsumoto's view, the social group is the basis of social processes; its three constructing principles are interaction, *Gemeinschaft,* and *Gesellschaft;* and culture is analyzed by reference to such concepts as social character and social self-consciousness. This view, which includes, but is not limited to, formal sociology, constitutes an extension and qualification of formal sociology rather than its complete refutation.

Simmel's name was not wholly forgotten even after his formal sociology became the object of criticism. However, his influence on Japanese sociology declined steadily until he came to be remembered only as a sociologist whose books were sometimes referred to but seldom read, even by representatives of this field. Among the Germans replacing him were Hans Freyer, who proposed to establish sociology as a "science of reality"; Alfred Weber, who is known for his "cultural sociology"; and Karl Mannheim, who developed the "sociology of knowledge." Thus, German sociologists are still important for Japanese sociology, but Simmel is no longer a significant figure among them.

In the first section of this paper, I suggested that Simmel has exerted a stronger influence on Japanese thought than on American, in both philosophy and sociology, and that his impact on Japanese philosophy has been much weaker than his influence on Japanese sociology. In fact, his conception of sociology brought an important new perspective to Japanese sociological thinking. Between 1920 and 1930, while his influence was at its peak, some Japanese sociologists, notably Takata, produced meritorious works which clearly benefited from it; and thanks to Simmel and Takata, the idea of sociology as a special science found many followers. Yet Simmel's influence, perhaps surprisingly, did not last.

The great change came with the end of the Second World War, the collapse of the militaristic regime, and the democratic reform of government and education. Until then, the government had viewed sociology with suspicion, vaguely associating it with socialism. The end of the war, however, brought greater freedom of investigation in the sciences, including sociology. In addition, the study of sociology was greatly enhanced by the establishment of a large number of new universities. Almost all of the new ones, as well as the old, introduced one or more courses in the field. The content of these courses has shifted, significantly in the direction of the United States, away from the traditional orientation toward Germany. In view of the intimate postwar relationship that Japan has with the United States—politically, economically, and culturally—and the world-wide prestige of modern American sociology, this shift is not surprising. At any rate, Simmel, along with German sociology in general, has lost influence.

Yet there are some exceptions. In his treatment of social groups, I. Shimizu (*Courses of Sociology* [*Shakaigaku Kogi*], 1948) subscribes enthusiastically to Simmel's theory of the subject. In *The Essence and Problem of Sociology, I (Shakaigaku no Honshitsu to Kadai, I,* 1949), K. Odaka, professor at Tokyo University, analyzes Simmel's sociology at length. While largely approving Simmel's position on formal sociology, he is critical of identifying it with sociology as a whole. For Odaka, Simmel's "form," though indispensable for the establishment of sociology as an independent science, is not so much an object as it is a special viewpoint from which the social world in its totality may be observed. While the success of his attempt at consolidating formal and synthetic sociology (with emphasis on the former) may be questioned, Odaka's analysis of Simmel is very penetrating. In this connection, we may also call attention to Y. Atoji's much earlier *Representative* [German] *Sociologists, I (Daihyoteki Shakaigakusha, I),* published in 1931, which indicates the influence of German sociology at that time. In that book, Atoji expounded Simmel's life and work as well as those of Max Weber, Tönnies, and Mannheim, and contributed not a little to increasing interest in German sociology.

If we compare the present state of Japanese sociology with that of American sociology in regard to Simmel's impact, it becomes clear that there is a remarkable contrast. Although in the twenties this impact was stronger in Japan than in the United States, today the opposite is true. Whereas Japanese sociology was once strongly influenced by Simmel and has lost interest in him, American sociologists have recently renewed attention to him which had long been absent or dormant. Some of Simmel's writings in sociology were translated and introduced by Kurt H. Wolff in *The Sociology of Georg Simmel* (1950), and by him and Reinhard Bendix in *Conflict* and *The Web of Group-Affiliations* (1955).

In comparison with Simmel's influence on Japan, his influence on American sociology may be said to have been more consistent, though perhaps not so strong as at times in Japan. An important example of this influence is Homans' recent *The Human Group,*[3] which Robert K. Merton, in his Introduction, praises as the work contributing most to a sociological theory of small groups since Simmel.[4] According to the Hinkles,[5] Simmel's influence in the United States, as compared with that of Pareto, Durkheim, Freud, and Max Weber, has been small. Nevertheless, it appears to be more persistent than in

Japan. If this is true, the reason, perhaps, is that Japanese culture is rather quick to imitate, even in the field of science, and readily changes its model when a new stimulus appears. Japanese postwar preoccupation with American sociology is good since, among other things, it makes up for the previous, almost complete neglect of it. However, it is rather strange that Japanese sociologists should show so little interest in Simmel since this interest is comparatively strong among the Americans, now the supreme model of the Japanese. Under the influence of Homans and others, some Japanese sociologists have begun to analyze small groups, but they do not go back to Simmel. Simmel's influence is not dead, but Japanese sociologists, much to their own loss, have left his precious heritage relatively unexplored.

1. Nicholas J. Spykman, *The Social Theory of Georg Simmel* (Chicago: University of Chicago Press, 1925), p. 3.

2. Kurt H. Wolff (ed.), *The Sociology of Georg Simmel* (Glencoe, Ill.: Free Press of Glencoe, Illinois, 1950), p. xxiv.

3. George C. Homans, *The Human Group* (New York: Harcourt, Brace & Co., 1950).

4. *Ibid.,* p. xxiii.

5. R. C. Hinkle, Jr., and G. J. Hinkle, *The Development of Modern Sociology* (Garden City, N.Y.: Doubleday & Co., Inc., 1954), p. 49.

ON SIMMEL'S *PHILOSOPHY OF MONEY*

HOWARD BECKER

If asked to list a dozen of the thinkers who during the past fifty years have most influenced the development of sociology as a discipline, sociologists the world over would in all probability include, in the majority of these lists, the name of Georg Simmel. Nevertheless, it is astonishing to note that, with few exceptions, sociologists have paid little attention to one of his most profound and stimulating works, the *Philosophie des Geldes.* Granted, the subject of the book may be doubly cursed; to many of us, "philosophy" has bad connotations, and to others, "money" seems a topic for the economist only. To these handicaps has been added the absence of even an abridged translation of the entire work; only bits and pieces—some of them giving little inkling of what it is all about—have been presented in English. Moreover, discussions of Simmel's writings, and commentaries thereon, either omit altogether any reference to the *Philosophie des Geldes* or give only a partial and perhaps distorted impression of what it contains. This seems to be true of even that remarkably able summary, *The Social Theory of Georg Simmel,* by N. J. Spykman (1925), who devotes less than forty pages to the *Philosophie des Geldes,* and who by singling out several aspects of relatively little interest to the sociologist and labeling what he offers as Simmel's "social metaphysics," evokes hostility among readers who are in the field of sociology.

There is one fortunate exception in this dismal history, but it is a work that is apparently little known. In 1903, S. P. Altmann, then lecturing in Berlin, published an article entitled "Simmel's Philosophy of Money" in the *American Journal of Sociology;*[2] this comes closer to giving a reasonably good idea of what Simmel was driving at than anything printed before or since. Few references have ever been made to this article, however; it has remained among the neglected resources of the sociologist who does not read German. But with all its merits, Altmann's article is clearly the work of a man whose field of major interest and competence was economics; and although he does his best to emphasize the primarily sociological character of Simmel's treatise, he does not quite succeed. Nevertheless, what is hereinafter said will occasionally follow up some of Altmann's insights; he really did perceive some of the key sociological issues to which Simmel addressed himself.

It seems best at this point to postpone discussion of these issues. Just now, a translation of the Table of Contents of the *Philosophie des Geldes* is probably most appropriate, for within present space limits the points covered in discussion must be relatively few and their choice somewhat arbitrary. To present so lengthy a translation within the space of an article seems, from the standpoint of literary form, somewhat objectionable, but so little is known of the remarkable range of the *Philosophie des Geldes* that even so brief a sketch may serve a useful purpose. Some alleviation of the repellent schematism may be afforded by the present writer's comments, given within brackets throughout.

PREFACE (pp. v-ix)

Analytic Part

CHAPTER I: Value and Money

[This entire chapter is devoted to laying the foundation for the remainder of the book. The epistemology is Neo-Kantian, which was widely accepted at that time and has recently been in vogue—often in psychologistic form—in the United States, as witness many recent studies of "social perception."]

I. [This section includes, in somewhat diffuse form, the basic definition of value underlying the rest of the study, and also sets forth, without explicit reference, the Neo-Kantian position assumed throughout.]
Reality and value as mutually independent categories, through which the contents of our ideas become images of the world. The psychological fact of objective value. The objective in practice as offering a standard or guarantee for the totality of the subjective. Economic value as the objectification of subjective values by virtue of the distance (or separation) established between (1) the subject enjoying direct gratification, and (2) the object. Analogy: aesthetic value. Economic activity as the establishing of separation (through effort, renunciation, sacrifice) and the simultaneous overcoming thereof. (pp. 3-29)

II. [Here "value as object" is considered at length, largely in preparation for the succeeding section.]

Exchange as occasion for the elevation of the object beyond its mere subjective value-significance: in exchange, things *mutually* express their value. The value of the object becomes objectified in the process of exchange for another object. Exchange as (1) a form of life, and as (2) a condition of economic value, as a primarily economic fact. Refutation of the utility and scarcity theory. The socially determined price as the preliminary stage of the objectively regulated price. (pp. 30-61)

III. [The fundamental relativism characteristic of all Simmel's work in ethics, aesthetics, and sociology finds concise expression at this point; money is viewed merely as a symbol of such relativism.]

The locating of economic value in a relativistic view of the world. This view, from an epistemological standpoint, outlined by means of examples: the projection of proofs in infinite series and their reciprocal legitimation. The objectivity of truth, as well as of value, as the relation of subjective elements. Money as the manifestation, which has become autonomous, of the exchange relation through which desired objects become economic; the substitutability of things. Clarification of this fundamental characteristic of money by reference to its value-constancy, its development, its objectivity. Money as a substantialization of the general form of existence in accordance with which things derive their significance *from one another.* (pp. 62-100)

CHAPTER II: The Value of Money as Substance

[This presentation, organized in terms of the controversy among the economists of that day concerning the necessity for a monetary standard based upon metal—or some similar material of "intrinsic" value—as opposed to one based on fiat money, actually goes far beyond conceptions of money as such. In essence, it represents an effort to reduce substance, or even structure, to function or process, and is in line with the rejection of "society" as an entity in favor of "sociation" as a process.]

I. [The concept of equivalence, developed toward the end of this section, has a general significance which goes beyond its specific meaning for a theory of money.]

The seeming necessity of an intrinsic value for money in order to fulfill its function of measuring value. Refutation of this idea by showing the transmutation of the immediate equivalence between separate goods and separate sums of money into the equivalence of two proportions: on the one hand, between the former and the total quantity of goods effective at the moment, and on the other, between the latter and the total quantity of money effective at the moment. Lack of awareness of the denominators of these proportions. Logical possibility of monetary function independent of all intrinsic value. The original necessity for money's having intrinsic value. Development of the concept of equivalence beyond this original stage toward the purely symbolic character of money. (pp. 101-28)

II. [Here again the argument concerning money serves a general purpose; namely, to illustrate an all-pervasive relativism.]

Renunciation of the non-monetary uses of monetary material. The first argument against money as being symbolic: The relations of money and goods, which would make an intrinsic value for money superfluous, are not accurately determinable; intrinsic value remedies this deficiency. The second argument against money as being symbolic: The unlimited augmentability of monetary symbols; relativistic indifference to the absolute limits of monetary quantity and the errors to which this indifference leads. The uncompletable development of money from the stage in which it has intrinsic value to the one in which it has relative significance as an example of a general phenomenon; the reciprocal nature of the limitation which reality places on pure concepts. (pp. 129-50)

III. [Sociological considerations dominate this section; there is a sustained effort to show that economic activities cannot be adequately comprehended unless placed in a sociological context.]

Historical development of money from substance to function; the sociological conditioning of this development. Social interactions and their crystallization into separate structures; the common relations of buyer and seller to the social unit as the sociological premise of monetary intercourse. Largeness and smallness, diffuseness and concentration of the economic circle in their significance for the intrinsic character of money. The transition to a general functional character as growing out of money's various special functions: its facilitation of trade, its constancy as a measure of value, its mobilization and condensation of values. The declining significance of money as substance and its increasing significance as value. (pp. 151-96)

CHAPTER · III. Money in the Sequence of Ends

[Essentially, this is an extended statement of "the means-ends schema" that is utilized consistently, although often implicitly, throughout.]

I. [In the following, a wide array of highly significant points is offered. For example: (1) a diffuse but important definition of social interaction; (2) a concise sketch of instrumentalism; (3) an explanation of what might be paraphrased by the American colloquial maxim, "Them as has, gits," or by its Biblical precedent, "For he that hath, to him shall be given: and he that hath not, from him shall be taken away even that which he hath" (Mark 4:25); and (4) a survey of "middleman (or marginal) trading peoples," such as Armenians, Parsees, Huguenots, Quakers, Lombards, and Jews.]

Action toward an end as conscious interaction between subject and object. The varying length of teleological series. The tool as intensified means; money as the purest example of the tool. The intensification of the value of money through the unlimitedness of the possibilities of its utilization. The unearned increment of wealth. The difference between the same amount of money as part of a large and of a small fortune; the limitation of price in consumption. Money—because of its character as pure means—as peculiarly congruent with personality types that are not closely united with social groups. (pp. 197-228)

II. [The fact that means may become ends, and vice versa, often advanced as a "novel" criticism of the means-ends schema, is explicitly considered as a demonstration of its utility when placed in the appropriate context. The general phenomenon of ambivalence, constituted in other than narrowly Freudian terms, is also considered, with special reference to the "modern" phenomenon of decadent personality types.]

The psychological growth of means into ends; money as the most extreme example. The dependence of the character of money as an end upon the cultural tendencies of the given epoch. Psychological consequences of the teleological position of money: greed, avarice, wastefulness, ascetic poverty, modern cynicism, and boredom. (pp. 229-66)

III. [The expression generally current in Max Weber's day, "the paradox of consequences," called by Wundt "the heterogony of ends," which has recently been skillfully paraphrased as "the unanticipated consequences of purposive social action," is here considered and illustrated at length, together with several other matters of sociological and social-psychological importance.]

The quantity of money as its quality. Subjective differences in quotas of risk. The general phenomenon of qualitatively disparate consequences of quantitatively altered causes. The threshhold of economic awareness. Differential sensitivity toward economic stimuli. Relations between external stimuli and emotional responses in the field of money. Significance of the personal unity of the possessor. The material and the cultural relation of form and amount, of quantity and quality of things, and the significance of money for this relation. (pp. 267-94)

Synthetic Part

Chapter IV: Individual Freedom

[Much that has recently been said about "urbanization" is shown, by implication, to be nothing more than the consequences of a money economy, regardless of the urban or rural nature of the locale.]

I. [The rise of anonymity and emotional detachment is linked with the increasing prevalence of monetary exchange.]

Freedom existing in conjunction with duties: gradations of this freedom depending on whether the duties are directly personal or apply only to the products of labor; monetary responsibility as the form congruent with the most complete freedom. Connecting this with the problem of maximizing value through change in possession. Cultural development as increasing the number of persons on whom one is dependent and the simultaneous decrease in ties to persons viewed as individuals. Money as responsible for "non-commital" relations between persons, and thus for individual freedom. (pp. 297-321)

II. [The traditional identification of owner with object owned is illustrated, and the breakup of such identification is traced to the mobility that is facilitated by a money economy.]

Possession as activity. The mutual dependence of having and being. Dissolving of this dependence by the possession of money. Lack of liberty as the interweaving of psychical series: this lack at a minimum when the interweaving of either is with the most general of the other series. This formula applied to limitations deriving from economic interests. Freedom as the articulation of the self in the medium of things, that is, freedom as possession. Monetary possession and the self. (pp. 322-56)

III. [Individualism, viewed from the standpoint of both its associative and dissociative consequences, is here related to a money economy.]

Differentiation of person and possession: spatial separation and technical objectification through money. The separation of the total personality from its various achievements, and the results of this separation for the evaluation of these achievements. The development of the individual's independence from the group, and of new forms of association, brought about by money; the association planned for a purpose. General relations between a money economy and the principle of individualism. (pp. 357-86)

CHAPTER V: The Monetary Equivalent of Personal Values

[This chapter is well integrated where the first two sections are concerned, but the third section might more properly have been placed earlier in the treatise, perhaps in the second chapter. The illustrative references are many and varied, attesting to a wide acquaintance with the history of law in all its forms, and with much of the literature of "social problems."]

I. [Here is a parallel to Durkheim's discussion of the kinds of law which are characteristic of societies having "mechanical solidarity," as over against those having "organic solidarity." However, there is no parallel to Durkheim's value judgments about the superior worth of societies of the latter type. A discussion of prostitution, remarkable for its insight, is presented and is closely related, with logical and empirical rigor, to the main argument of the section.]

Wergild. The transition from the utilitarian to the objective and the absolute valuation of the human being. Punishment by fine and the stages of culture. The increasing differentiation of human beings and the increasingly undifferentiated character of money as cause of the latter's increasing inadequacy. Marriage by purchase and the value of women. Division of labor among the sexes, and the dowry. The typical relation between money and prostitution; its development analogous to that of *Wergild*. Mercenary marriage. Bribery. Money and the ideal of the gentleman. (pp. 387-437)

II. [The "rootlessness" of personalities wholly devoted to monetary values, who exercise freedom only in the sense of "freedom from," is here discussed.]

The transmutation of specific rights into monetary claims. The enforcibility of demands. The transformation of thing-values into monetary value: the negative meaning of freedom and the deracination of personality. The difference in value between personal achievement and monetary equivalent. (pp. 438-55)

III. [As noted above, this section might well have been placed at a much earlier point. Basically, it is directed against the cruder versions of the Marxian labor theory of value.]

"Labor money" and its rationale. The unpaid contribution of mental effort. Differences in amounts of labor as quantitative differences. Physical labor as labor unit. The value of physical performance reducible to that of psychical performance. Differences in the utility of labor as argument against "labor money"; the insight into the significance of money thereby afforded. (pp. 456-79)

CHAPTER VI: The Style of Life

[Simmel's essay on "The Metropolis and Mental Life"[3] is foreshadowed here, as is Louis Wirth's article on "Urbanism as a Way of Life."[4] Simmel, however, does not fall into the trap of attributing the characteristics of urbanism, which both he and Wirth point out, to just any population cluster bearing the label "city."]

I. [A social-psychological analysis of certain "modern" personality types, which is astonishingly close to that now current in many quarters, is offered here with a minimum of technicality.]

The preponderance of intellectual over emotional functions that is brought about by the money economy; lack of "character" and objectivity of the style of life. The double roles of both intellect and money: with regard to content they are superpersonal; with regard to function, individualistic and egoistic. Relation to the rationalism of law and logic. The calculating character of modern times. (pp. 480-501)

II. [A strongly pessimistic note with regard to "modern" life is evidenced; Simmel's own value-system, already manifested at many points, here becomes apparent.]

The concept of culture. Increase in material culture, lag of personal culture. Objectification of mind. The division of labor as the cause of the divergence of subjective and objective culture. The occasionally greater weight of the former. Relation of money to the bearers of these opposing tendencies. (pp. 502-33)

III. [Relativism is again expounded and illustrated, with indications of the ultimate reference point, namely, that "life" incorporates and transcends all relative oppositions and inequalities. From this section it is easy to see why Simmel was called "the German Bergson." However, a decision for the values indicated by Bergson's *élan vital* is not explicitly made by Simmel; it can only be inferred. His habit of treating every presumably final question, as even one of his friendly critics put it, "as though it were the question before the last," prevented him from openly proclaiming any ultimate stand. Had he lived longer, he might have expressed in his published writings the "anti-'modern'" position which is abundantly manifested in his correspondence with intimates; he was *not* "a spineless intellectual."]

Alterations of the distance between self and objects as manifestations of varying styles of life. Modern tendencies toward the increase and the diminution of this distance. The part played by money in this dual process. Credit. Pre-eminence of technology. The rhythm or symmetry, and its opposite, of the contents of life. Sequence and simultaneity of both tendencies; developments of money as their analogy and vehicle. The tempo of life, its alterations, and alterations of the money supply. The concentration of monetary activity. The mobilizing of values. Fixity and motion as categories for comprehending the world; their synthesis in the relative character of being, and money as historical symbol of this character. (pp. 534-85)

This, like any table of contents, is informative and, at the same time, tantalizing—if not frustrating. If attention is directed chiefly to the terms used, the impression can easily be gained that the work is in the field of economics. But in his Introduction Simmel flatly states:

> Not one line of these investigations is meant to be a statement about economics. That is to say, the phenomena of valuation and purchase, of exchange and the means of exchange, of the forms of production and the values of possession, which economics views from one standpoint, are here viewed from another . . . . *One* science . . . never exhausts the total of a reality . . . . Exchange can . . . legitimately be handled as a psychological, as a moral-historical, and even as an aesthetic fact . . . . Here money is only a means, material, or example for the depicting of relations that link the most superficial, "realistic," and accidental phenomena . . . with the deepest currents of the life of the individual and of history.[5]

Simmel does not say, however, that the angle from which he is viewing money is a sociological one. As is well known, his conception of sociology virtually excluded what today we would call social psychology of sociological derivation; he was inclined to call this psychology or philosophy. Before he began to publish anything dealing with sociology as he viewed it, he had already established the base lines of the *Philosophie des Geldes* in an article entitled "Psychologie des Geldes," which appeared in 1889. Furthermore, almost a decade before this, he had launched his more strictly epistemological, aesthetic, and ethical studies, which continued concurrently with his rigidly limited sociological investigations and finally pre-empted most of his attention and effort. In brief, a conception of sociology broader than Simmel's would lead to the inclusion of much that he calls psychological and philosophical.

Without attempting to sketch such a broader conception at this time, it may nevertheless be appropriate to note a few of Simmel's analytical and synthetic presentations in the *Philosophie des Geldes* that might justly be viewed as relevant, at the very least, for much of current sociology.

To begin with, take value itself. Those of us who have read the famous *The Polish Peasant in Europe and America* are quite familiar with Thomas and Znaniecki's definition of value as reciprocal with attitude.

> By a social value we understand any datum having an empirical content accessible to the members of some social group and a meaning with regard to which it is or may be an object of activity.[6]

> By attitude we understand a process of individual consciousness which determines real or possible activity of the individual in the social world . . . . The attitude is thus the individual counterpart of the social value; activity, in whatever form, is the bond between them.[7]

> The cause of a value or of an attitude is never an attitude or a value alone, but always a combination of an attitude and a value.[8]

Clearly, Thomas and Znaniecki regard a value as any object of any attitude.

Simmel's literary style is such that a completely self-contained definition of value is nowhere to be found in his writings—not even in the axiological first chapter of *Philosophie des Geldes*. Nevertheless, there are some highly pertinent passages.

> Subject and object are born in the same act: (*a*) logically, in that the purely conceptual, ideal [*ideell*] constituents [*Sachgehalt*] are, on the one hand, given as the content [*Inhalt*] of representation [*Vorstellen*], and, on the other, as the content of objective reality; and (*b*) psychologically, in that the as yet self-unrelated [*noch ichlose*] representation, containing both subject [*Person*] and object [*Sache*] in a neutral state [*Indifferenzzustand*], undergoes internal differentiation and thereby gives rise to a contrast between the self [*Ich*] and its object [*Gegenstand*], through which each of these is first endowed with the character that sets it apart from the other. This process, which eventually brings about our cognitive model of the world [*Weltbild*], also goes on within our volitional experience [*willensmässige Praxis*] . . . . In so far as the human being receives gratification from [*geniesst*] anything [*Gegenstand*], there occurs an entirely unitary act [that is, subject and object are not distinguished] . . . . The possibility of desire [however] is the possibility of the object of desire. Such an object—characterized by contrast with the subject, and constituted as object by that contrast—the desire for which the

> subject simultaneously endeavors to gratify and to set at rest [*überwinden*], is for us a value.[9]

Perhaps it would not be too much to say, then, that for Simmel a value is any object of any desire.

The parallel between Simmel and Thomas and Znaniecki seems close, and given the nature of Znaniecki's early training, it is quite conceivable that the precedent afforded by Simmel influenced him considerably. However, it is possible to derive a great deal more than a definition of value from the passages quoted above: indications are given of the basic pattern of social interaction as developed by George Herbert Mead and others. But let it be hastily added that Mead, in all probability, drew on Hegel rather than on Simmel; whatever parallel may exist would then arise from the familiarity of both writers with Hegel and those who carried his ideas further.

It seems clear that Simmel viewed interaction between subject and object as occurring only when these can be clearly differentiated; before this ability to differentiate appears, it is quite nonsensical to talk about *inter*action between human beings. To be sure, in his treatment of value, Simmel does not talk about subject and object as self and other; the self does represent one pole, but the other is merely one of many possible objects. He lays a foundation for social interaction, but the interaction he has in mind is not fully social in the sense attached to it by Mead or, for that matter, by Max Weber.

Still, Simmel's epistemological position has far-reaching social-psychological and sociological implications—implications, indeed, that Simmel did not himself realize. Had he done so, he would not have committed himself to the untenable position that others are known only by analogical inference.

> Every human being we encounter, as directly experienced, is only a noise-making and gesticulating robot [*Automat*]; that behind these perceivable phenomena there is a mind, and that certain processes are going on within this mind, can be inferred by us solely through analogy with our own internal life, which represents for us the only directly known psychic being. Conversely, knowledge of the self develops only through knowledge of the other; in fact, the fundamental cleavage of the self into observed and observing portions comes about only through its

> analogy with the relation between the self and other personalities.[10]

This is pre-Meadian, and even pre-Hegelian; one might even go so far as to say that it is pre-Kantian. Simmel's own Neo-Kantianism should have saved him from the absurdities of the "conclusion by analogy" *(Analogieschluss)*.

The commentary provided by the present writer for the various parts of the Table of Contents makes it unnecessary—or at least inadvisable under present space limits—to discuss at length most of the matters and topics mentioned there. Furthermore, the general structure of the *Philosophie des Geldes* is adequately indicated by the Table of Contents. Consequently, the balance of this paper will be concerned only with various items not already touched upon in some reasonably clear, albeit superficial, way. The choice of such items, however, is necessarily somewhat arbitrary; for Simmel's presentation abounds in brilliant examples, intricate subtleties, hints at possibilities of further development that remain hints only, and outright digressions. Only a few of the multifarious avenues can be followed.

One item, of considerable interest to systematic sociologists, is the differentiation between the family as a web of concrete interactions, some of which can ordinarily be known only to the family members themselves, and the family as an abstract collectivity, often more readily perceivable by outsiders than by its own members.[11] In other words, Simmel distinguished between the Joneses as they interact with one another, and the Joneses as they are known to those who are trying to keep up with them. There may be relatively little connection between the two constellations, but in certain situations the Joneses as an abstract collectivity may assume tremendous importance for the Joneses as a web of intimately personal relations. It is needless here to call the roll of those who have worked with this and similar distinctions; Leopold von Wiese is but one name among many.

We have long heard man spoken of as *homo faber;* the expression can be paraphrased as "the tool-making animal." Simmel carries such a view to a highly important conclusion: Since all the evidence indicates that man is characteristically a toolmaker, and since any tool is, as a tool, a means to a more or less clearly envisaged end, those who think of man as *homo faber* should also think of him as "the end-setting animal," that is, "the purposive animal."[12] The present writer therefore suggests that man might well be called *homo tendens*. We all know, of course, that a tool may become an end in itself, as in the case of the gun fancier who never fires a shot. In such cases, obviously, the tool is no longer a tool as such. But as long as it retains its character as a tool, it is only an instrument intended to achieve a given purpose. Simmel's rapier[13] may prove a little dangerous to those who swing their broadswords in tumultuous assault on the means-ends schema.

A number of years ago, Willard Waller asserted that when two persons share an intimate relationship, the partner who cares least for the perpetuation of the intimacy can exploit the partner who cares more. This familiar point is developed at some length by Simmel with special reference to the destructive effect of mercenary considerations on "affectively united dyads."[14]

An amazingly insightful longer passage[15] that could readily be expanded into a book on the sociology of contemporary science has to do with the parallels between the mentality often generated by an all-pervasive money economy and the conviction that nothing is real, in any ultimate sense, that cannot be readily measured. A similar point regarding the relations between money and mathematics is made later.[16] That such insistence on quantity as ultimate reality involves a metaphysical commitment, witting or unwitting (and it is usually the latter), is for Simmel beyond doubt.

In virtually all of his writings, many of Simmel's abstract analyses are illustrated in such a way that, for some readers, the illustration is of greater interest than the analysis. Such an illustration occurs in conjunction with a description of the difference in value between personal achievement and monetary equivalent.[17] This passage contains an array of evidence bearing not only on the abstract analysis but also on the point that revolutionary tendencies are rarely manifested by utterly impoverished, underprivileged, or underdeveloped social strata, but rather by those who have begun to rise in the social scale. The same hypothesis has often been stated by students of revolutionary movements, but rarely on the basis of such highly relevant evidence. Those good-hearted but ill-informed advocates of massive aid to underdeveloped areas as a means of forestalling Communist infiltration might well study Simmel; it is perhaps demonstrable that the likelihood of direct revolt against the benefactor, or the rejection of him, is in direct proportion to his beneficent activity. This is, of course, no argument against contemporary foreign-aid programs, but it is to say that many of the arguments that advance and support such programs have no solid base in fact. Those offering aid must be prepared for ingratitude; when dealing with underdeveloped areas, virtue must be its own reward.

In many "principial" societies tending toward normlessness, and in "pronormless" societies, it is widely assumed that self-interested action *(das Handeln in selbstischem Interesse)* is of necessity the only "logical" variety.[18] Simmel shows clearly how thoroughly such an opinion is bound up with the rationalism and individualism that are characteristic of societies of this kind,[19] and how entirely relative the "logic" involved actually is. The sociology of knowledge, unknown by that name in Simmel's day, is not only anticipated as an abstract possibility but is also concretely applied to a world that even then plumed itself on its "modernity." Some recent work on motivation, launched at the behest of hucksters and pitchmen, might have been sounder—if less salable—had its producers been even remotely aware of Simmel's analysis, which, although far from dispassionate, is nevertheless penetrating and probably quite valid.

Reference was made earlier to Simmel's remarks on the family and similar intimate groups, and some of what Simmel had to say about the disorganization of the family as one outcome of a comprehensive money economy was there adumbrated. However, something new is added in a later passage,[20] for it qualifies, in a striking way, the assertions often made by some exponents of "urbanization" as a sufficient explanation of the source of disorganization of any and every kind. Close reading of the passage noted, and of others related to it, shows that Simmel never thought of "urbanization" as an explanatory formula like the Yankee peddler's trousers, "large enough for any man, small enough for any boy." On the contrary, the cities that he had in view were exclusively of the kind manifesting an elaborate division of labor, a money economy, a wage system, marked industrialization, and other characteristics peculiar to the Western world from the fifteenth century until very recent times. Recently, of course, such cities have affected other cities scattered throughout those parts of the world experiencing the direct impact of Westernization. Moreover, even when writing about Western and Westernized cities, Simmel makes several references indicating that they are never fully "urban" in the sense recently assigned to that adjective; many aspects of life in "modern" cities have not yet, at least, been substantially altered by "urbanization." Those who still view Louis Wirth's essay, "Urbanism as a Way of Life," as a sort of revelation which is never to be questioned might well read, ponder, and prayerfully digest Simmel's presentation.

The love of paradox—or, to put it less drastically, the love of startling nuances that apparently reverse the meanings ordinarily assigned to standard formulations—becomes evident in one passage toward the end of Simmel's great book.[21] With a straight face, he points out that the Golden Rule finds its fullest formal realization in a money economy. The injunction to "do as you would be done by" is most readily met when the producer of object A need not directly exchange it for what the producer of object B has to offer. Only in a money economy can the producer of A who wants C instead of B achieve his objective, for in such an economy the producer of B, exchanging his product for money, D, makes it possible for the producer of A to acquire C. The producer of B does this by giving D to the producer of A, who then can lay hands on the coveted C by offering D for it. Formally, then, the producer of B has followed the Biblical injunction, "Therefore all things whatsoever ye would that men should do to you, do ye even so to them."

It is this note of what his harsher critics label willful triviality, as perverse delight in analytic subtlety, that has caused Simmel to be dismissed with the remark, "Only a gifted essayist." We may perhaps regret that Simmel does at times confuse his more simple-minded readers by piling up illustrations and analytic refinements until his main points are obscured. Our regret should not lead us, however, to grant the contention that the main points are not there or that they are of no great importance. Every man has his own mode of thought and his own style, and to impose requirements on him which are utterly foreign to that thought and style is to show oneself incurably egocentric. The thirteenth chapter of First Corinthians is still worth reading, particularly in the King James version. Some of us who find "love" unpalatable in a scientific context may still be able to practice "charity."

1. *Philosophie des Geldes* (Leipzig: Duncker und Humblot, 1900). See the Bibliography for a listing of later editions.

2. Vol. IX, pp. 46-68.

3. H. H. Gerth and C. Wright Mills (trans.), in *The Sociology of Georg Simmel,* ed. Kurt H. Wolff (Glencoe, Ill.: Free Press of Glencoe, Illinois, 1950), pp. 409-24.

4. *American Journal of Sociology,* XLIV (1938), 1-24.

5. *Philosophie des Geldes,* p. vii.

6. William I. Thomas and Florian Znaniecki, *The Polish Peasant in Europe and America* (Boston: Richard G. Badger [Gorham Press], 1918), I, 21.

7. *Ibid.,* p. 22.

8. *Ibid.,* p. 44.

9. *Philosophie des Geldes,* pp. 12-13.

10. *Ibid.,* p. 76.

11. *Ibid.,* p. 107.

12. *Ibid.,* p. 206.

13. *Ibid.,* p. 207.

14. *Ibid.,* pp. 211-12.

15. *Ibid.,* pp. 291-94.

16. *Ibid.,* pp. 498-99.

17. *Ibid.,* pp. 453-55.

18. Cf. Howard Becker, "Current Sacred-Secular Theory and Its Development," in *Modern Sociological Theory in Continuity and Change,* ed. Howard Becker and Alvin Boskoff (New York: Dryden Press, 1957), pp. 133-86.

19. *Philosophie des Geldes,* pp. 492-93.

20. *Ibid.,* p. 541.

21. *Ibid.,* p. 530.

A NOTE FROM A STUDENT OF SIMMEL'S

ARTHUR SALZ

When I enrolled as a Freshman at the University of Berlin in the fall of 1900, it was an unheard-of novelty for a youngster who had graduated from the Gymnasium of a provincial town in Bohemia to study abroad. The proper thing for him to do, of course, was to attend one of the universities of the home country—Prague, Vienna, Graz, Innsbruck—a certificate from which put him on the road toward a position as lawyer, public servant, teacher, or physician, whereas a certificate from a foreign university was useless for all practical purposes.

I felt cast out on the shores of a foreign country, a stranger among strangers. For a better understanding of the predicament in which I found myself, it might be best to outline briefly the environment from which I came. The Gymnasium I had attended for eight years was a convent school, a cloister in fact, under the management of the Order of the Premonstratensians (founded by St. Norbert in 1119), who are closely related to the Benedictines. Discipline was strict as a matter of course, but the monks did not proselytize; they were open-minded and liberal, graduates of Austrian universities. The backbone of the curriculum was Latin and Greek, with French and English as electives. We also got our fill of mathematics and physics.

From the first day, when we were only ten years old, the teachers treated us like gentlemen. For them to call us by our first names was out of the question. The form of address was not the familiar "thou" but the formal "you." This principle of decorum helped to inculcate in us the code of *noblesse oblige,* which rests on reciprocity.

In Berlin, however, neither my scholastic background nor the strange dialect and unfamiliar food accounted for the feeling of strangeness and abandonment, but rather the mental and moral atmosphere. At the turn of the century no *carmen seculare* was intoned. In the aftermath of the Bismarck era, the mood of the population was cheerless rather than festive. The chancellor had cemented the new German empire under the hegemony of

Prussia, but the young, ambitious Wilhelm II (a grandson of Queen Victoria), who had ascended to the throne in 1888, did not share his abilities.

What, then, induced a fledgling to pick out Berlin, where the odds would all be against him from the practical point of view? The reason was primarily Berlin's reputation as a center of learning. The University was not an old institution; in fact, it was an upstart. Established less than a hundred years before by luminaries such as Humboldt and Fichte (with Savigny the first rector) in response to Napoleon's humiliation of Prussia, it had acquired a fine reputation and much good will. It had drawn a galaxy of first-rate men to all departments. Although the political atmosphere was extremely unpleasant, even grim, mainly because of Wilhelm II's erratic policies, the University proved to be an intellectual oasis devoted to learning and transmitting learning to its students and the world at large. Wilhelm Dilthey was the head of the Department of Philosophy—Dilthey, rather than Nietzsche, has been called by Ortega y Gasset the leading philosopher of the modern era. Even then he was known for his *Einleitung in die Geisteswissenschaften* and his studies of the philosophical currents in the fifteenth and sixteenth centuries; also well known were his denial of philosophy of history as a special field of study and his argument that history itself tells its philosophy.

Simmel was then forty-two and an assistant professor without salary. By chance—and a lucky chance it turned out to be—I stumbled into his lecture room in the very first days of my stay in Berlin. (Attendance at lectures was up to the student. The essence of academic freedom, Max Weber has said, is the student's right to cut classes.) I did not know much of Simmel's work then. I had heard his name mentioned and, a few days before in the student reading room, had read an essay of his that had just been published in one of the German monthlies. It dealt with the poet Stefan George, then practically unknown. That essay made a strong impression on me and aroused my curiosity. I did not know that Simmel had published a two-volume work on problems of moral science, another volume on philosophy of history, and that his *Philosophie des Geldes* was about to be issued.

After I had attended one or two of Simmel's lectures as an unauthorized listener, my mind was made up. I registered as a regular student in his course and must admit that no other teacher has had a stronger and more enduring influence in forming my outlook on life. Why was Simmel's exposition a unique experience for a youth in a formative stage of development? Perhaps it was because he who was exposed to him felt himself witnessing a true teacher's soliloquy. Although Simmel seemed to be speaking to himself, his audience was held in suspense. At the end of a lecture, everybody asked himself how the story would go on, what would come next. By this pedagogical method, Simmel crystallized what may be called his idea of dialectic, which differs from the dialectic of Aristotle and Hegel. (In the only interview Hegel had with Goethe, he replied to Goethe's question concerning the nature of dialectics that it was nothing but the perennial spirit of contradiction—a definition which Goethe could not accept.)

Much of Simmel's fascination lay in the way he presented his material. In his search for the bases of knowledge, he seemed to understand how to improvise or, more accurately, he appeared to be improvising. The listener had the impression that he experienced the finding of truth in *statu nascendi*. There was no suggestion of indoctrination. Simmel's delivery struck us as the struggle of an individual, lonely soul with truth, as "creative evolution" in the proper sense of this term, as the skill of midwifery at its best. Simmel dealt with problems *sub specie aeternitatis* while feigning to deal with them *sub specie momenti*.

He made it appear quite plausible that dialectics is the air in which we live and breathe. A paradox, he knew, loses its impact when it is recognized as a statement contrary to accepted opinion, a statement seemingly outrageous although perhaps well founded. ("The very weightiest truths now received amongst men," Thomas De Quincey wrote in 1847, "have nearly all of them, in turn, in some stage of their development, been found strong paradoxes to the popular mind.") We must, Simmel seemed to say, get used to realizing that the coexistence of logical incompatibles is a law of life. Yet for him this realization was no reason for discouragement. On the contrary, the core of his philosophy was the belief that life is a daring adventure, and that in its periods of trial, we must take up the cudgels with vigor and audacity.

Tolerant of the most diverse views and malicious toward none, he freely admitted that life is a medley of material, banal and spiritual, sublime elements; however, he was not a relativist who wavered and talked with tongue in cheek. The truth is that he had a firm hold on Ariadne's thread through the labyrinth. Whatever the subject of his discussion—moral philosophy, sociology, religion—his was not a dogmatic, "high-principled" philosophy. He would hardly have hesitated to affirm Protagoras' "man is the measure of all things." The supremacy and dignity of the individual was for him an established principle, a categorical a priori. He might even have subscribed to Dilthey's dictum that we explain nature, but understand mental life.

Something of the sort applies to Simmel's sociology. He conceived of it as the study of the forms of sociation. But whoever speaks of forms moves in the field of aesthetics. Society, in the last analysis, is a work of art. And where there is form (*forma, eidos, morphé*), there is distance, reluctance to sell out or surrender. "Form" suggests seeing things in perspective, being prepared for the unexpected so that it can be taken in stride.

Simmel's philosophy of life was not vitalism, much less biologism. He was a philosopher of life in the sense that he believed "all things transitory but as symbols are sent." This mental attitude imparted to him the serenity of mind that he obviously possessed. His outlook on life was free from any morbid "tragicism." He knew how to make the polarity of phenomena both plausible and bearable. Thus he put into practice—and his example was contagious—Bacon's axiom that the light of nature should be combined with that of grace.

When, many years later, through one of the many oddities and contingencies of life, I came into rather close personal contact with Simmel, I realized to my surprise that the old master-apprentice relation had continued—and it has to this day.

TRANSLATIONS

Used by permission of Hans Broermann of Duncker und Humblot

GEORG SIMMEL

A LETTER FROM SIMMEL TO MARIANNE WEBER

Almost the only part of Simmel's voluminous correspondence that has been published thus far is to be found in *Buch des Dankes an Georg Simmel*[1] (pp. 67-135), which contains letters to Paul Ernst, Adolf von Harnack, Edmund Husserl, Heinrich Rickert, Rainer Maria Rilke, August Rodin, Margarete Susman, and Max and Marianne Weber. The letter printed below (by courtesy of Else Simmel, M.D., Simmel's daughter-in-law) was addressed to Marianne Weber to whom Simmel had dedicated his *Goethe* (1913), for which she had effusively thanked him. It has been previously published—though neither wholly accurately nor completely—in Marianne Weber's *Lebenserinnerungen* (pp. 384-85) and *in toto* in *Buch des Dankes an Georg Simmel* (pp. 131-32). It is presented here in facsimile, in a transcript that preserves the line arrangement of the original, and in a translation that is as literal as is compatible with understandable English.—Ed.

Transcript

Westend 9 XII 12

Liebe Freundin,

Unmöglich kann ich mir so gute Dinge sagen lassen u. / dasitzen, ohne mich zu rühren. Dass ich für all die herzliche Gesinnung, / die ich von Ihnen erfahren habe, u. für das Bild Ihrer Existenz, / um das ich bereichert bin, die Form eines bescheidnen Dankes suchte, / das scheint mir so natürlich u. einfach, dass ich über die Art, wie / Sie es aufnehmen, fast beschämt bin. Aber Sie gehören nun einmal / zu den Menschen, die, wenn sie geben, es mit vollen Händen tun; / u. so will ich mich auch nicht dagegen wehren, u. froh sein, dass es / gelungen ist. Es gehört eigentlich so wenig dazu, sich gegenseitig eine / Freude zu machen, u. es ist einer der am schwersten erträglichen Gedan- / ken, zu denen mich das Leben gebracht

1. All references contained in this paragraph may be found in the Bibliography by Kurt Gassen in the present volume.

hat: wie leicht die Menschen / es doch hätten, sich die Welt zum Paradies zu machen u. dass sie / statt dessen vorziehen, sie sich zur Hölle zu machen—

Ich fürchte fast, dass Sie in dem Buch ziemlich langsam vor- / wärts kommen werden. Nun ich in dem Gedruckten blättere, sehe ich / doch mancherlei Stellen, die etwas zu dick geraten sind. Es ist eine / Summirung von vielerlei Erlebtem u. Gedachtem u. ich habe vielleicht / nicht immer genug Rücksicht darauf genommen, dass andre Leute / eben von andren Erlebnissen u. Gedanken herkommen und dass ich / [new page] deshalb etwas breitere Zugänge bauen müsste. Es würde mir / leid tun, wenn ich damit eine gewisse kulturelle Wirkung des / Buches, auf die es mir ankommt, verhindert hätte. Ich habe mich / nämlich davon überzeugen müssen, dass nur eine minimale / Anzahl von Menschen Goethe als ganzen, d.h. als die Einheit / aus seinen einzelnen Teilen kennen; diese Teile freilich kennen / viele. Aber ihre Summirung giebt noch keineswegs den / "ganzen" Goethe—den muss man jenseits der Einzelheiten / suchen. Ich habe die Anmassung, dies Buch für das deutsche Volk, / (wenn auch nicht in seiner unmittelbaren Breite) geschrieben zu / haben, als eine Hülfe, diesen unerhörten Schatz zu realisiren, den / es besitzt, fast ohne es zu wissen.—Für mich selbst ist das Buch / eine Art Abschluss, eine letzte Verwendung der bisherigen Begriffs- / bildungen. Ich setze nun die Segel um u. suche ein unbetretnes / Land. Freilich wird die Fahrt wohl noch v o r der Küste ihr / Ende finden. Wenigstens soll mir nicht geschehn, wie so vielen / meiner Genossen: sich auf dem Schiff selbst heimisch einzurichten, / so dass sie schliesslich meinten, das Schiff selbst wäre das / neue Land.—

Wir danken Ihnen u. Ihrem Mann herzlich für die Güte, mit der / Sie den Hans aufgenommen haben. Es war das Glück seiner / Heidelberger Zeit, dass er zu Ihnen kommen durfte. /

Mit allen Grüssen von der Frau u. in der treusten Gesinnung

immer Ihr

G.S.

München 9 XII 12

Liebe Freundin,

Unmöglich kann ich mir so gute Dinge sagen lassen u. dasitzen, ohne mich zu rühren. Dass ich für all die herzliche Schwärmerei die ich von Ihnen erfahren habe, u. für das Licht Ihrer Hoffnung, um das ich bereichert bin, die Form eines besonderen Dankes suche, das scheint mir so unbillig u. einfach, dass ich über die Art, wie Sie es aufnehmen, fast bestürzt bin. Aber Sie gehören nun einmal zu den Menschen, die, wenn sie geben, es mit vollen Händen tun; u. so mache ich mich auch nicht dagegen wehren, u. froh sein, dass es gelungen ist. Es gehört eigentlich so wenig dazu, sich gegenseitig eine Freude zu machen, u. es ist einer der am schwersten erträglichen Gedanken, zu denen mich das Leben gebracht hat: wie leicht die Menschen es doch hätten, sich die Welt zum Paradies zu machen u. dass sie es statt dessen vorziehen, sie sich zur Hölle zu machen — —

Ich fürchte sehr, dass Sie mit dem Buch ziemlich langsam vorwärts kommen werden. Wie ich die geschriebenen Blätter lese, sehe ich doch manchmal Stellen, die etwas zu dick geraten sind. Es ist eine Sammlung von verschiedenen Erlebten u. Gedachten u. ich habe vielleicht nicht immer ganz Rücksicht darauf genommen, dass andere Leute aber von anderen Erlebnissen u. Gedanken herkommen u. dass ich

deshalb etwas breitere Zugänge bauen müßte. Es würde mir
leid tun, wenn ich damit eine gewisse kollektive Wirkung des
Buches, auf die es mir ankommt, verscherzt hätte. Ich habe mich
nämlich davon überzeugen müssen, daß nur eine minimale
Anzahl von Menschen Goethe als ganzen, d. h. als die Einheit
aus seinen einzelnen Teilen, kennen; diese Teile freilich kennen
viele. Aber ihre Summierung ergibt noch keineswegs den
„ganzen" Goethe – den muß man jenseits der Einzelheiten
suchen. Ich habe die Anmaßung, das Buch für das deutsche Volk
(wenn auch nicht in seiner unmittelbaren Breite) geschrieben zu
haben, als eine Hilfe, diesen unerhörten Schatz zu realisieren, den
es besitzt, fast ohne es zu wissen. – Für mich selbst ist das Buch
eine Art Abschluß, eine letzte Anwendung der bisherigen Begriffs-
bildungen. Ich sehe wie die Vögel im Herbst ein unbekanntes
Land. Freilich wird die Fahrt wohl auch vor der Küste ihr
Ende finden. Wenigstens ist mir nicht geschehen, was so vielen
meiner Genossen: sich auf dem Schiff selbst häuslich einzurichten,
so daß sie schließlich meinten, das Schiff selbst wäre das
neue Land. –

Wir danken Ihnen u. Ihrem Mann herzlich für die Güte, mit der
Sie den Sohn aufgenommen haben. Es war das Glück seiner
Heidelberger Zeit, daß er zu Ihnen kommen durfte.

Mit allen Grüßen von der Frau u. in der treuesten Gesinnung

immer Ihr

G. S.

Translation

[Berlin] Westend, December 9, 1912

Dear Friend,

I cannot possibly let myself be told such good things without making a stir. That I [should have] sought the form of a modest thanks for all the cordial attitude that I have experienced from you, and for the image of your existence by which I am enriched—this seems to me so natural and simple that I am almost ashamed by the manner in which you receive it. But, after all, you are among those people who, when they give, do it with full hands; and thus I won't fight against it and will be glad that it succeeded. Actually, it takes so little to give joy to one another; and it is one of the thoughts most difficult to bear to which life has brought me: how easy it would be for men to make the world into paradise for themselves, but instead they prefer to make it into hell—

I almost fear that you will get on with the book rather slowly. Now that I am leafing through the printed [thing], I do see several places that turned out a bit too thick. It is a summation of many things experienced and thought, and perhaps I have not always paid enough attention to [the fact] that other people do come from other experiences and thoughts and that therefore I should build somewhat broader accesses. I should regret it if I had thus prevented a certain cultural effect of the book, [an effect] which is important to me. For I have had to convince myself that only a minimal number of people know Goethe as a whole, that is, as the unity out of his single parts; these parts, to be sure, are known to many. But their summation does not yet by any means yield the "whole" Goethe—for him one must look beyond the particulars. I have the arrogance to have written this book for the German people (even if not in its immediate breadth), as a help in realizing this unheard-of treasure, which they own almost without knowing it. —For myself, the book is a sort of termination, a last employment of the past concept-formations. I am now changing sails and seeking an untrod land. To be sure, the voyage will probably find its end *before* [reaching] the coast. At least, what happens to so many of my colleagues shall not happen to me: to settle down comfortably in the ship itself so that eventually they think that the ship itself is the new land.—

We cordially thank you and your husband for the kindness with which you have received Hans [Simmel's son]. It was the happiness of his stay at Heidelberg that he could come to you.

With all greetings from the wife and in the most faithful attitude

always your

G.S.

THE ADVENTURE[1]

GEORG SIMMEL

Each segment of our conduct and experience bears a twofold meaning: it revolves about its own center, contains as much breadth and depth, joy and suffering, as the immediate experiencing gives it, and at the same time is a segment of a course of life—not only a circumscribed entity, but also a component of an organism. Both aspects, in various configurations, characterize everything that occurs in a life. Events which may be widely divergent in their bearing on life as a whole may nonetheless be quite similar to one another; or they may be incommensurate in their intrinsic meanings but so similar in respect to the roles they play in our total existence as to be interchangeable.

One of two experiences which are not particularly different in substance, as far as we can indicate it, may nevertheless be perceived as an "adventure" and the other not. The one receives the designation denied the other because of this difference in the relation to the whole of our life. More precisely, the most general form of adventure is its dropping out of the continuity of life. "Wholeness of life," after all, refers to the fact that a consistent process runs through the individual components of life, however crassly and irreconcilably distinct they may be. What we call an adventure stands in contrast to that interlocking of life-links, to that feeling that those countercurrents, turnings, and knots still, after all, spin forth a continuous thread. An adventure is certainly a part of our existence, directly contiguous with other parts which precede and follow it; at the same time, however, in its deeper meaning, it occurs outside the usual continuity of this life. Nevertheless, it is distinct from all that is accidental and alien, merely touching life's outer shell. While it falls outside the context of life, it falls, with this same movement, as it were, back into that context again, as will become clear later; it is a foreign body in our existence which is yet somehow connected with the center; the outside, if only by a long and unfamiliar detour, is formally an aspect of the inside.

Because of its place in our psychic life, a remembered adventure tends to take on the quality of a dream. Everyone knows how quickly we forget dreams because they, too, are placed outside the meaningful context of life-as-a-whole. What we designate as "dreamlike" is nothing but a memory which is bound to the unified, consistent life-process by fewer threads than are ordinary experiences. We might say that we localize our inability to assimilate to this process something experienced by imagining a dream in which it took place. The more "adventurous" an adventure, that is, the more fully it realizes its idea, the more "dreamlike" it becomes in our memory. It often moves so far away from the center of the ego and the course of life which the ego guides and organizes that we may think of it as something experienced by another person. How far outside that course it lies, how alien it has become to that course, is expressed precisely by the fact that we might well feel that we could appropriately assign to the adventure a subject other than the ego.

We ascribe to an adventure a beginning and an end much sharper than those to be discovered in the other forms of our experiences. The adventure is freed of the entanglements and concatenations which are characteristic of those forms and is given a meaning in and of itself. Of our ordinary experiences, we declare that one of them is over when, or because, another starts; they reciprocally determine each other's limits, and so become a means whereby the contextual unity of life is structured or expressed. The adventure, however, according to its intrinsic meaning, is independent of the "before" and "after"; its boundaries are defined regardless of them. We speak of adventure precisely when continuity with life is thus disregarded on principle—or rather when there is not even any need to disregard it, because we know from the beginning that we have to do with something alien, untouchable, out of the ordinary. The adventure lacks that reciprocal interpenetration with adjacent parts of life which constitutes life-as-a-whole. It is like an island in life which determines its beginning and end according to its own formative powers and not—like the part of a continent—also according to those of adjacent territories. This factor of decisive boundedness, which lifts an adventure out of the regular course of a human destiny, is not mechanical but organic: just as the organism determines its spatial shape not simply by adjusting to obstacles confining it from right and left but by the propelling force of a life forming from inside out, so does an adventure not end because something else begins; instead, its temporal form, its radical being-ended, is the precise expression of its inner sense.

Here, above all, is the basis of the profound affinity between the adventurer and the artist, and also, perhaps, of the artist's attraction by adventure. For the essence of a work of art is, after all, that it cuts out a piece of the endlessly continuous sequences of perceived experience, detaching it from all connections with one side or the other, giving it a self-sufficient form as though defined and held together by an inner core. A part of existence, interwoven with the uninterruptedness of that existence, yet nevertheless felt as a whole, as an integrated unit—this is the form common to both the work of art and the adventure. Indeed, it is an attribute of this form to make us feel that in both the work of art and the adventure the whole of life is somehow comprehended and consummated—and this irrespective of the particular theme either of them may have. Moreover, we feel this, not although, but because, the work of art exists entirely beyond life as a reality; the adventure, entirely beyond life as an uninterrupted course which intelligibly connects every element with its neighbors. It is because the work of art and the adventure stand over against life (even though in very different senses of the phrase) that both are analogous to the totality of life itself, even as this totality presents itself in the brief summary and crowdedness of a dream experience.

For this reason, the adventurer is also the extreme example of the ahistorical individual, of the man who lives in the present. On the one hand, he is not determined by any past (and this marks the contrast between him and the aged, of which more later); nor, on the other hand, does the future exist for him. An extraordinarily characteristic proof of this is that Casanova (as may be seen from his memoirs), in the course of his erotic-adventurous life, every so often seriously intended to marry a woman with whom he was in love at the time. In the light of his temperament and conduct of life, we can imagine nothing more obviously impossible, internally and externally. Casanova not only had excellent knowledge of men but also rare knowledge of himself. Although he must have said to himself that he could not stand marriage even two weeks and that the most miserable consequences of such a step would be quite unavoidable, his perspective on the future was wholly obliterated in the rapture of the moment. (Saying this, I mean to put the emphasis on the moment rather than on the rapture.) Because he was entirely dominated by the feeling of the present, he wanted to enter into a future relationship which was impossible precisely because his temperament was oriented to the present.

In contrast to those aspects of life which are related only peripherally—by mere fate—the adventure is defined by its capacity, in spite of its being isolated and accidental, to have necessity and meaning. Something becomes an adventure only by virtue of two conditions: that it itself is a specific organization of some significant meaning with a beginning and an end; and that, despite its accidental nature, its extraterritoriality with respect to the continuity of life, it nevertheless connects with the character and identity of the bearer of that life—that it does so in the widest sense, transcending, by a mysterious necessity, life's more narrowly rational aspects.

At this point there emerges the relation between the adventurer and the gambler. The gambler, clearly, has abandoned himself to the meaninglessness of chance. In so far, however, as he counts on its favor and believes possible and realizes a life dependent on it, chance for him has become part of a context of meaning. The typical superstition of the gambler is nothing other than the tangible and isolated, and thus, of course, childish, form of this profound and all-encompassing scheme of his life, according to which chance makes sense and contains some necessary meaning (even though not by the criterion of rational logic). In his superstition, he wants to draw chance into his teleological system by omens and magical aids, thus removing it from its inaccessible isolation and searching in it for a lawful order, no matter how fantastic the laws of such an order may be.

The adventurer similarly lets the accident somehow be encompassed by the meaning which controls the consistent continuity of life, even though the accident lies outside that continuity. He achieves a central feeling of life which runs through the eccentricity of the adventure and produces a new, significant necessity of his life in the very width of the distance between its accidental, externally given content and the unifying core of existence from which meaning flows. There is in us an eternal process playing back and forth between chance and necessity, between the fragmentary materials given us from the outside and the consistent meaning of the life developed from within.

The great forms in which we shape the substance of life are the syntheses, antagonisms, or compromises between chance and necessity. Adventure is such a form. When the professional adventurer makes a system of life out of his life's lack of system, when out of his inner necessity he seeks the naked, external accidents and builds them into that necessity, he only, so to speak, makes macroscopically visible that which is the essential form of every "adventure," even that of the non-adventurous person. For by adventure we always mean a third something, neither the sheer, abrupt event whose meaning—a mere given—simply remains outside us nor the consistent sequence of life in which every element supplements every other toward an inclusively integrated meaning. The adventure is no mere hodgepodge of these two, but rather that incomparable experience which can be interpreted only as a particular encompassing of the accidentally external by the internally necessary.

Occasionally, however, this whole relationship is comprehended in a still more profound inner configuration. No matter how much the adventure seems to rest on a differentiation within life, life as a whole may be perceived as an adventure. For this, one need neither be an adventurer nor undergo many adventures. To have such a remarkable attitude toward life, one must sense above its totality a higher unity, a super-life, as it were, whose relation to life parallels the relation of the immediate life totality itself to those particular experiences which we call adventures.

Perhaps we belong to a metaphysical order, perhaps our soul lives a transcendent existence, such that our earthly, conscious life is only an isolated fragment as compared to the unnamable context of an existence running its course in it. The myth of the transmigration of souls may be a halting attempt to express such a segmental character of every individual life. Whoever senses through all actual life a secret, timeless existence of the soul, which is connected with the realities of life only as from a distance, will perceive life in its given and limited wholeness as an adventure when compared to that transcendent and self-consistent fate. Certain religious moods seem to bring about such a perception. When our earthly career strikes us as a mere preliminary phase in the fulfillment of eternal destinies, when we have no home but merely a temporary asylum on earth, this obviously is only a particular variant of the general feeling that life as a whole is an adventure. It merely expresses the running together, in life, of the symptoms of adventure. It stands outside that proper meaning and steady course of existence to which it is yet tied by a fate and a secret symbolism. A fragmentary incident, it is yet, like a work of art, enclosed by a beginning and an end. Like a dream, it gathers all passions into itself and yet, like a dream, is destined to be forgotten; like gaming, it contrasts with seriousness, yet, like the *va banque* of the gambler, it involves the alternative between the highest gain and destruction.

Thus the adventure is a particular form in which fundamental categories of life are synthesized. Another such synthesis it achieves is that between the categories of activity and passivity, between what we conquer and what is given to us. To be sure, their synthesis in the form of adventure makes their contrast perceptible to an extreme degree. In the adventure, on the one hand, we forcibly pull the world into ourselves. This becomes clear when we compare the adventure with the manner in which we wrest the gifts of the world through work. Work, so to speak, has an organic relation to the world. In a conscious fashion, it develops the world's forces and materials toward their culmination in the human purpose, whereas in adventure we have a nonorganic relation to the world. Adventure has the gesture of the conqueror, the quick seizure of opportunity, regardless of whether the portion we carve out is harmonious or disharmonious with us, with the world, or with the relation between us and the world. On the other hand, however, in the adventure we abandon ourselves to the world with fewer defenses and reserves than in any other relation, for other relations are connected with the general run of our worldly life by more bridges, and thus defend us better against shocks and dangers through previously prepared avoidances and adjustments. In the adventure, the interweaving of activity and passivity which characterizes our life tightens these elements into a coexistence of conquest, which owes everything only to its own strength and presence of mind, and complete self-abandonment to the powers and accidents of the world, which can delight us, but in the same breath can also destroy us. Surely, it is among adventure's most wonderful and enticing charms that the unity toward which at every moment, by the very process of living, we bring together our activity and our passivity—the unity which even in a certain sense *is* life itself—accentuates its disparate elements most sharply, and precisely in *this* way makes itelf the more deeply felt, as if they were only the two aspects of one and the same, mysteriously seamless life.

If the adventure, furthermore, strikes us as combining the elements of certainty and uncertainty in life, this is more than the view of the same fundamental relationship from a different angle. The certainty with which—justifiably or in error—we know the outcome, gives our activity one of its distinct qualities. If, on the contrary, we are uncertain whether we shall arrive at the point for which we have set out, if we know our ignorance of the outcome, then this means not only a quantitatively reduced certainty but an inwardly and outwardly unique practical conduct. The adventurer, in a word, treats the incalculable element in life in the way we ordinarily treat only what we think is by definition calculable. (For this reason, the philosopher is the adventurer of the spirit. He makes the hopeless, but not therefore meaningless, attempt to form into conceptual knowledge an attitude of the soul, its mood toward itself, the world, God. He treats this insoluble problem as if it were soluble.) When the outcome of our activity is made doubtful by the intermingling of unrecognizable elements of fate, we usually limit our commitment of force, hold open lines of retreat, and take each step only as if testing the ground.

In the adventure, we proceed in the directly opposite fashion: it is just on the hovering chance, on fate, on the more-or-less that we risk all, burn our bridges, and step into the mist, as if the road will lead us on, no matter what. This is the typical fatalism of the adventurer. The obscurities of fate are certainly no more transparent to him than to others; but he proceeds as if they were. The characteristic daring with which he continually leaves the solidities of life underpins itself, as it were, for its own justification with a feeling of security and "it-must-succeed," which normally only belongs to the transparency of calculable events. This is only a subjective aspect of the fatalist conviction that we certainly cannot escape a fate which we do not know: the adventurer nevertheless believes that, as far as he himself is concerned, he is certain of this unknown and unknowable element in his life. For this reason, to the sober person adventurous conduct often seems insanity; for, in order to make sense, it appears to presuppose that the unknowable is known. The prince of Ligne said of Casanova, "He believes in nothing, except in what is least believable." Evidently, such belief is based on that perverse or at least "adventurous" relation between the certain and the uncertain, whose correlate, obviously, is the skepticism of the adventurer—that he "believes in nothing": for him to whom the unlikely is likely, the likely easily becomes unlikely. The adventurer relies to some extent on his own strength, but above all on his own luck; more properly, on a peculiarly undifferentiated unity of the two. Strength, of which he is certain, and luck, of which he is uncertain, subjectively combine into a sense of certainty.

If it is the nature of genius to possess an immediate relation to these secret unities which in experience and rational analysis fall apart into completely separate phenomena, the adventurer of genius lives, as if by mystic instinct, at the point where the course of the world and the individual fate have, so to speak, not yet been differentiated from one another. For this reason, he is said to have a "touch of genius." The "sleepwalking certainty" with which the adventurer leads his life becomes comprehensible in terms of that peculiar constellation whereby he considers that which is uncertain and incalculable to be the premises of his conduct, while others consider only the calculable. Unshakable even when it is shown to be denied by the facts of the case, this certainty proves how deeply that constellation is rooted in the life conditions of adventurous natures.

The adventure is a form of life which can be taken on by an undetermined number of experiences. Nevertheless, our definitions make it understandable that one of them, more than all others, tends to appear in this form: the erotic—so that our linguistic custom hardly lets us understand by "adventure" anything but an erotic one. The love affair, even if short-lived, is by no means always an adventure. The peculiar psychic qualities at whose meeting point the adventure is found must be added to this quantitative matter. The tendency of these qualities to enter such a conjuncture will become apparent step by step.

A love affair contains in clear association the two elements which the form of the adventure characteristically conjoins: conquering force and unextortable concession, winning by one's own abilities and dependence on the luck which something incalculable outside ourselves bestows on us. A degree of balance between these forces, gained by virtue of his sense of their sharp differentiation, can, perhaps, be found only in the man. Perhaps for this reason, it is of compelling significance that, as a rule, a love affair is an "adventure" only for men; for women it usually falls into other categories. In novels of love, the activity of woman is typically permeated by the passivity which either nature or history has imparted to her character; on the other hand, her acceptance of happiness is at the same time a concession and a gift.

The two poles of conquest and grace (which manifest themselves in many variations) stand closer together in woman than in man. In man, they are, as a matter of fact, much more decisively separated. For this reason, in man their coincidence in the erotic experience stamps this experience quite ambiguously as an adventure. Man plays the courting, attacking, often violently grasping role: this fact makes one easily overlook the element of fate, the dependence on something which cannot be predetermined or compelled, that is contained in every erotic experience. This refers not only to dependence on the concession on the part of the other, but to something deeper. To be sure, every "love returned," too, is a gift which cannot be "earned," not even by any measure of love—because to love, demand and compensation are irrelevant; it belongs, in principle, in a category altogether different from a squaring of accounts—a point which suggests one of its analogies to the more profound religious relation. But over and above that which we receive from another as a free gift, there still lies in every happiness of love—like a profound, impersonal bearer of those personal elements—a favor of fate. We receive happiness not only from the other: the fact that we do receive it from him is a blessing of destiny, which is incalculable. In the proudest, most self-assured event in this sphere lies something which we must accept with humility. When the force which owes its success to itself and gives all conquest of love some note of victory and triumph is then combined with the other note of favor by fate, the constellation of the adventure is, as it were, preformed.

The relation which connects the erotic content with the more general form of life as adventure is rooted in deeper ground. The adventure is the exclave of life, the "torn-off" whose beginning and end have no connection with the somehow unified stream of existence. And yet, as if hurdling this stream, it connects with the most recondite instincts and some ultimate intention of life as a whole—and this distinguishes it from the merely accidental episode, from that which only externally "happens" to us. Now, when a love affair is of short duration, it lives in precisely such a mixture of a merely tangential and yet central character. It may give our life only a momentary splendor, like the ray shed in an inside room by a light flitting by outside. Still, it satisfies a need, or is, in fact, only possible by virtue of a need which—whether it be considered as physical, psychic, or metaphysical—exists, as it were, timelessly in the foundation or center of our being. This need is related to the fleeting experience as our general longing for light is to that accidental and immediately disappearing brightness.

The fact that love harbors the possibility of this double relation is reflected by the twofold temporal aspect of the erotic. It displays two standards of time: the momentarily climatic, abruptly subsiding passion; and the idea of something which cannot pass, an idea in which the mystical destination of two souls for one another and for a higher unity finds a temporal expression. This duality might be compared with the double existence of intellectual contents: while they emerge only in the fleetingness of the psychic process, in the forever moving focus of consciousness, their logical meaning possesses timeless validity, an ideal significance which is completely independent of the instant of consciousness in which it becomes real for us. The phenomenon of adventure is such that its abrupt climax places its end into the perspective of its beginning. However, its connection with the center of life is such that it is to be distinguished from all merely accidental happenings. Thus "mortal danger," so to speak, lies in its very style. This phenomenon, therefore, is a form which by its time symbolism seems to be predetermined to receive the erotic content.

These analogies between love and adventure alone suggest that the adventure does not belong to the life-style of old age. The decisive point about this fact is that the adventure, in its specific nature and charm, is a *form of experiencing*. The *content* of the experience does not make the adventure. That one has faced mortal danger or conquered a woman for a short span of happiness; that unknown factors with which one has waged a gamble have brought surprising gain or loss; that physically or psychologically disguised, one has ventured into spheres of life from which one returns home as if from a strange world—none of these are necessarily adventure. They become adventure only by virtue of a certain experiential tension whereby their substance is realized. Only when a stream flowing between the minutest externalities of life and the central source of strength drags them into itself; when the peculiar color, ardor, and rhythm of the life-process become decisive and, as it were, transform its substance—only then does an event change from mere experience to adventure. Such a principle of accentuation, however, is alien to old age. In general, only youth knows this predominance of the process of life over its substance; whereas in old age, when the process begins to slow up and coagulate, substance becomes crucial; it then proceeds or perseveres in a certain timeless manner, indifferent to the tempo and passion of its being experienced. The old person usually lives either in a wholly *centralized* fashion, peripheral interests having fallen off and being unconnected with his essential life and its inner necessity; or his center atrophies, and existence runs its course only in isolated petty details, accenting mere externals and accidentals. Neither case makes possible the relation between the outer fate and the inner springs of life in which the adventure consists; clearly, neither permits the perception of contrast characteristic of adventure, viz., that an action is completely torn out of the inclusive context of life and that simultaneously the whole strength and intensity of life stream into it.

In youth, the accent falls on the process of life, on its rhythm and its antinomies; in old age, it falls on life's substance, compared to which experience more and more appears relatively incidental. This contrast between youth and age, which makes adventure the prerogative of youth, may be expressed as the contrast between the romantic and the historical spirit of life. Life in its immediacy—hence also in the individuality of its form at any one moment, here and now—counts for the romantic attitude. Life in its immediacy feels the full strength of the current of life most of all in the pointedness of an experience that is torn out of the normal run of things but which is yet connected with the heart of life. All such life which thrusts itself out of life, such breadth of contrast among elements which are penetrated by life, can feed only on that overflow and exuberance of life which exists in adventure, in romanticism, and in youth. Age, on the other hand—if, as such, it has a characteristic, valuable, and coherent attitude—carries with it a historical mood. This mood may be broadened into a world view or limited to the immediately personal past; at any rate, in its objectivity and retrospective reflectiveness, it is devoted to contemplating a substance of life out of which immediacy has disappeared. All history as depiction in the narrower, scientific sense originates in such a survival of substance beyond the inexpressible process of its presence that can only be experienced. The connection this process has established among them is gone, and must now, in retrospect, and with a view to constructing an ideal image, be re-established by completely different ties.

With this shift of accent, all the dynamic premise of the adventure disappears. Its atmosphere, as suggested before, is absolute presentness—the sudden rearing of the life-process to a point where both past and future are irrelevant; it therefore gathers life within itself with an intensity compared with which the factuality of the event often becomes of relatively indifferent import. Just as the game itself—not the winning of money—is the decisive motive for the true gambler; just as for him, what is important is the violence of feeling as it alternates between joy and despair, the almost touchable nearness of the daemonic powers which decide between both—so the fascination of the adventure is again and again not the substance which it offers us and which, if it were offered in another form, perhaps would receive little heed, but rather the adventurous form of experiencing it, the intensity and excitement with which it lets us feel life in just this instance. This is what connects youth and adventure. What is called the subjectivity of youth is just this: The material of life in its substantive significance is not as important to youth as is the process which carries it, life itself. Old age is "objective"; it shapes a new structure out of the substance left behind in a peculiar sort of timelessness by the life which has slipped by. The new structure is that of contemplativeness, impartial judgment, freedom from that unrest which marks life as being present. It is all this that makes adventure alien to old age and an old adventurer an obnoxious or tasteless phenomenon. It would not be difficult to develop the whole essence of adventure from the fact that it is the form of life which in principle is inappropriate to old age.

Notwithstanding the fact that so much of life is hostile to adventure, from the most general point of view adventure appears admixed with all practical human existence. It seems to be an ubiquitous element, but it frequently occurs in the finest distribution, invisible to the naked eye, as it were, and concealed by other elements. This is true quite aside from that notion which, reaching down into the metaphysics of life, considers our existence on earth as a whole, unified adventure. Viewed purely from a concrete and psychological standpoint, every single experience contains a modicum of the characteristics which, if they grow beyond a certain point, bring it to the "threshold" of adventure. Here the most essential and profound of these characteristics is the singling out of the experience from the total context of life. In point of fact, the meaning of no single part of life is exhausted by its belonging in that context. On the contrary, even when a part is most closely interwoven with the whole, when it really appears to be completely absorbed by onflowing life, like an unaccented word in the course of a sentence—even then, when we listen more closely, we can recognize the intrinsic value of that segment of existence. With a significance which is centered in itself, it sets itself *over against* that total development to which, nevertheless, if looked at from another angle, it inextricably belongs.

Both the wealth and the perplexity of life flow countless times from this value-dichotomy of its contents. Seen from the center of the personality, every single experience is at once something necessary which comes from the unity of the history of the ego, and something accidental, foreign to that unity, insurmountably walled off, and colored by a very deep-lying incomprehensibility, as if it stood somewhere in the void and gravitated toward nothing. Thus a shadow of what in its intensification and distinctness constitutes the adventure really hovers over every experience. Every experience, even as it is incorporated into the chain of life, is accompanied by a certain feeling of being enclosed between a beginning and an end—by a feeling of an almost unbearable pointedness of the single experience as such. This feeling may sink to imperceptibility, but it lies latent in every experience and rises from it—often to our own astonishment. It is impossible to identify any minimal distance from the continuity of life short of which the feeling of adventurousness could not emerge—as impossible, to be sure, as to identify the maximal distance where it must emerge for everyone. But everything could not become an adventure if the elements of adventure did not in some measure reside in everything, if they did not belong among the vital factors by virtue of which a happening is designated a human experience.

Similar observations apply to the relation between the accidental and the meaningful. In our every encounter there is so much of the merely given, external, and occasional that we can, so to speak, decide only on a quantitative basis whether the whole may be considered as something rational and in some sense understandable, or whether its insolubility as regards its reference to the past, or its incalculability as regards its reference to the future, is to stamp its whole complexion. From the most secure civic undertaking to the most irrational adventure there runs a continuous line of vital phenomena in which the comprehensible and the incomprehensible, that which can be coerced and that which is given by grace, the calculable and the accidental, mix in infinitely varied degrees. Since the adventure marks one extreme of this continuum, the other extreme must also partake of its character. The sliding of our existence over a scale on which every point is simultaneously determined by the effect of our strength and our abandonment to impenetrable things and powers—this problematic nature of our position in the world, which in its religious version results in the insoluble question of human freedom and divine predetermination, lets all of us become adventurers. Within the dimensions into which our station in life with its tasks, our aims, and our means place us, none of us could live one day if we did not treat that which is really incalculable as if it were calculable, if we did not entrust our own strength with what it still cannot achieve by itself but only by its enigmatic co-operation with the powers of fate.

The substance of our life is constantly seized by interweaving forms which thus bring about its unified whole. Everywhere there is artistic forming, religious comprehending, the shade of moral valuing, the interplay of subject and object. There is, perhaps, no point in this whole stream where every one of these and of many other modes of organization does not contribute at least a drop to its waves. But they become the pure structures which language names only when they rise out of that fragmentary and confused condition where the average life lets them emerge and submerge and so attain mastery over life's substance. Once the religious mood has created its structure, the god, wholly out of itself, it is "religion"; once the aesthetic form has made its content something secondary, by which it lives a life of its own that listens only to itself, it becomes "art"; once moral duty is fulfilled simply because it is duty, no matter how changing the contents by means of which it is fulfilled and which previously in turn determined the will, it becomes "morality."

It is no different with adventure. We are the adventurers of the earth; our life is crossed everywhere by the tensions which mark adventure. But only when these tensions have become so violent that they gain mastery over the material through which they realize themselves—only then does the "adventure" arise. For the adventure does not consist in a substance which is won or lost, enjoyed or endured: to all this we have access in other forms of life as well. Rather, it is the radicalness through which it becomes perceptible as a life tension, as the rubato of the life process, independent of its materials and their differences—the quantity of these tensions becoming great enough to tear life, beyond those materials, completely out of itself: this is what transforms mere experience into adventure. Certainly, it is only one segment of existence among others, but it belongs to those forms which, beyond the mere share they have in life and beyond all the accidental nature of their individual contents, have the mysterious power to make us feel for a moment the whole sum of life as their fulfillment and their vehicle, existing only for their realization.

Translated by David Kettler

1. "Das Abenteuer," *Philosophische Kultur. Gesammelte Essays* ([1911] 2nd ed.; Leipzig: Alfred Kröner, 1919), pp. 7-24. Used by permission of Else Simmel, M.D.

THE RUIN[1]

GEORG SIMMEL

Architecture is the only art in which the great struggle between the will of the spirit and the necessity of nature issues into real peace, in which the soul in its upward striving and nature in its gravity are held in balance. In poetry, painting, and music, the laws governing the materials must be made dumbly submissive to the artistic conception which, in the perfect work, wholly and invisibly absorbs them. Even in sculpture the tangible piece of marble is not the work of art; what stone or bronze of themselves contribute to the work has its effect only as a means of expressing spirit. Although architecture, too, uses and distributes the weight and carrying power of matter according to a plan conceivable only in the human soul, within this plan the matter works by means of its own nature, carrying out the plan, as it were, with its own forces. This is the most sublime victory of the spirit over nature—a situation like that which obtains when we know how to guide a person so that he realizes our will through his own. His will has not been overpowered; rather, the very tendency of his own nature is made to execute our plan.

This unique balance—between mechanical, inert matter which passively resists pressure, and informing spirituality which pushes upward—breaks, however, the instant a building crumbles. For this means nothing else than that merely natural forces begin to become master over the work of man: the balance between nature and spirit, which the building manifested, shifts in favor of nature. This shift becomes a cosmic tragedy which, so we feel, makes every ruin an object infused with our nostalgia; for now the decay appears as nature's revenge for the spirit's having violated it by making a form in its own image. The whole history of mankind is a gradual rise of the spirit to mastery over the nature which it finds outside, but in a certain sense also within, itself. If in the other arts the spirit bends the forms and events of this nature to its command, in architecture it shapes nature's masses and inherent forces until, as if of their own accord, they yield, and the artistic conception is made visible. But the necessities of matter submit to the freedom of the spirit, and its vitality is expressed without residue in nature's merely weighing and carrying forces, only so long as the building remains perfect. The moment its decay destroys the unity of the form, nature and spirit separate again and reveal their world-pervading original enmity—as if the artistic formation had only been an act of violence committed by the spirit to which the stone unwillingly submitted; as if it now gradually shook off this yoke and returned once more into the independent, lawful order of its own forces.

But this makes the ruin a more meaningful, more significant phenomenon than are the fragments of other destroyed works of art. A painting from which particles of paint have fallen off, a statue with mutilated limbs, an ancient text of poetry from which words or lines are lost—all of these have effect only according to what is still left in them of artistic formation or what the imagination can construe of it from remnants. Their immediate appearance is no artistic unity; it offers us nothing but a work of art imperfect through the reductions it has undergone. The ruin of a building, however, means that where the work of art is dying, other forces and forms, those of nature, have grown; and that out of what of art still lives in the ruin and what of nature already lives in it, there has emerged a new whole, a characteristic unity. To be sure, from the standpoint of that purpose which the spirit has embodied in palace and church, castle and hall, aqueduct and memorial column, the form in which they appear when decayed is a meaningless incident. Yet a new meaning seizes on this incident, comprehending it and its spiritual form in a unity which is no longer grounded in human purposiveness but in that depth where human purposiveness and the working of non-conscious natural forces grow from their common root. For this reason, a good many Roman ruins, however interesting they may be otherwise, lack the specific fascination of the ruin—to the extent, that is, to which one notices in them the destruction *by man;* for this contradicts the contrast between human work and the effect of *nature* on which rests the significance of the ruin as such.

Such a contradiction is engendered not only by man's positive action but also by his passivity when (and because) he strikes us as an element of mere nature. This characterizes a good many urban ruins, like those, still inhabited, often found in Italy off the main road. In these cases, what strikes us is not, to be sure, that human beings destroy the work of man—this indeed is achieved by nature—but that men *let it decay*. From the standpoint of the idea of man, such indifference is, so to speak, a positive passivity, whereby man makes himself the accomplice of nature and of that one of its inherent tendencies which is dramatically opposed to his own essential interests. Here the inhabited ruin loses for us that sensuous-suprasensuous balance of the conflicting tendencies of existence which we see in the abandoned one. This balance, indeed, gives it its problematical, unsettling, often unbearable character. Such places, sinking from life, still strike us as settings of a life.

In other words, it is the fascination of the ruin that here the work of man appears to us entirely as a product of nature. The same forces which give a mountain its shape through weathering, erosion, faulting, and the growth of vegetation, here do their work on old walls. Even the charm of alpine forms—which are, after all, for the most part, clumsy, accidental, artistically insipid—rests on the felt counterplay of two cosmic tendencies: volcanic eruptions or gradual stratification have built the mountain upward; rain and snow, weathering and landslides, chemical dissolution, and the effect of gradually intruding vegetation have sawed apart and hollowed out the upper ledge, have cast downward parts of what had been raised up, thus giving the contour its form. In this form, we feel the vitality of those opposing tendencies, and—instinctively sensing these antitheses in ourselves—we notice, beyond everything merely formal and aesthetic, the signficance of the configuration in whose serene unity they have their synthesis.

In the ruin, these antitheses are distributed over even more widely separated segments of existence. What has led the building upward is human will; what gives it its present appearance is the brute, downward-dragging, corroding, crumbling power of nature. Still, so long as we can speak of a ruin at all and not of a mere heap of stones, this power does not sink the work of man into the formlessness of mere matter. There rises a new form which, from the standpoint of nature, is entirely meaningful, comprehensible, differentiated. Nature has transformed the work of art into material for her own expression, as she had previously served as material for art.

According to its cosmic order, the hierarchy of nature and spirit usually shows nature as the substructure, so to speak, the raw material, or semifinished product; the spirit, as the definitely formative and crowning element. The ruin reverses this order: what was raised by the spirit becomes the object of the same forces which form the contour of the mountain and the bank of the river. If in this way there emerges an aesthetic significance, it ramifies into a metaphysical one in the manner revealed by patina on metal and wood, ivory and marble. In the formation of patina, too, a natural process takes place on the surface of a human product and produces a growth of skin which completely covers up the original one. That the product becomes more beautiful by chemical and physical means; that what has been willed becomes, without intention or force, something obviously new, often more beautiful, and once more self-consistent—this is the mysterious harmony which is the fantastic fascination of patina; and it cannot be wholly accounted for by analyzing our perception of it.

This is the fascination of the ruin, too; but the ruin has an additional fascination which is of the same order: the destruction of the spiritual form by the effect of natural forces, that reversal of the typical order, is felt as a return to the "good mother," as Goethe calls nature. Here, the saying that all that is human "is taken from earth and to earth shall return" rises above its sad nihilism. Between the not-yet and the no-longer lies an affirmation of the spirit whose path, it is true, now no longer ascends to its peak but, satiated by the peak's riches, descends to its home. This is, as it were, the counterpart of that "fruitful moment" for which those riches which the ruin has in retrospect are still in prospect. That the overwhelming of a work of the human will by the power of nature can have an aesthetic effect at all suggests that nature has a never completely extinguished, rightful claim to this work, however much it may be formed by the spirit. In its material, its given state, it has always remained nature; and if now nature becomes once more completely master over it, she is merely exercising a right which until now has remained latent but which she has never, so to speak, renounced.

For this reason, the ruin strikes us so often as tragic—but not as sad—because destruction here is not something senselessly coming from the outside but rather the realization of a tendency inherent in the deepest layer of existence of the destroyed. For this reason, too, the aesthetically satisfying impression, which is associated with the tragedy or secret justice of destruction, is so often lacking when we describe a person as a "ruin." For even when we mean by this that the psychic layers we designate as natural in the narrower sense—the drives or inhibitions connected with the body, the inert, the accidental, that which points toward death—have become master over the specifically human, rationally valuable ones, we still do not feel that a latent right is being realized through these tendencies. Rather, such a right does not exist at all. We believe—rightly or wrongly—that such derogations, inimical to the spirit, do *not* inhere in the nature of man in its deepest sense: they have a right to everything external that is born with him, but not to man himself. Reflections and complexities in other contexts aside, man as a ruin, therefore, is so often more sad than tragic, lacking that metaphysical calm which attaches to the decay of a material work as by virtue of a profound a priori.

When we speak of "returning home," we mean to characterize the peace whose mood surrounds the ruin. And we must characterize something else: our sense that these two world potencies—the striving upward and the sinking downward—are working serenely together, as we envisage in their working a picture of purely natural existence. Expressing this peace for us, the ruin orders itself into the surrounding landscape without a break, growing together with it like tree and stone—whereas a palace, a villa, or a peasant house, even where they fit perfectly into the mood of the landscape, always stem from another order of things and blend with that of nature only as if in afterthought. Very old buildings in open country, and particularly ruins, often show a peculiar similarity of color to the tones of the soil around them. The cause of this phenomenon must be somehow analogous to that which gives charm to old fabrics:

however heterogeneous their colors may have been when new, the long common destinies—dryness and moisture, heat and cold, outer wear and inner disintegration—which they have encountered through the centuries, produce a unity of tint, a reduction to the same common denominator of color which no new fabric can imitate. In a similar way, the influences of rain and sunshine, the incursion of vegetation, heat, and cold must have assimilated the building abandoned to them into the color tone of the ground which has been abandoned to the same destinies. They have reduced its once conspicuous contrast to the peaceful unity of belonging.

The ruin conveys the impression of peace from yet another perspective. On the one side of that typical conflict stood the purely external form or symbolism of peace: the contour of the mountain as defined by the building-up and the breaking-down. But in respect to the other pole of existence, peace lives entirely within the human soul—that battlefield between nature, which the soul is itself, and spirit, which the soul is itself. The forces which one can designate only by the spatial simile of upward-striving are at work continuously in our soul, continuously interrupted, deflected, overcome by other forces which work in us as what is dull, mean, "merely natural." The manner in which, and the extent to which, these two variously mingle, yield, at every moment, the form of our soul. But neither by the most decisive victory of one of these two parties nor by their compromise does it ever arrive at a definitive state. For not only does the restless rhythm of the soul not tolerate such a state, but, more important, behind every single event, every single impulse that comes from one or the other of these two directions, there is something which lives on, and there are claims which the decision just made does not put to rest. This gives the antagonism between the two principles something unfinishable and formless, which breaks every frame.

The unending demands of both principles impose on the soul an interminability of the moral process, a profound absence of well-rounded organization, palpably at rest. In this lies perhaps the ultimate formal ground of the animosity between aesthetic and ethical natures. Wherever we perceive aesthetically, we demand that the contradictory forces of existence be somehow in equilibrium, that the struggle between above and below come to a standstill. But the form which yields only a *perception* is rejected by the ethical-psychic process with its incessant moving up and down, its constant shifting of boundaries, and the playing of the inexhaustible forces in it, one against the other.

By contrast, the profound peace, which, like a holy charmed circle, surrounds the ruin, conveys a sense of this constellation, of the obscure antagonism which determines the form of all existence, now acting among merely natural forces, now occurring only within psychic life, and now, as in the present case, taking place between nature and matter. This antagonism—although here too it is in dis-equilibrium in that it lets one side preponderate as the other sinks into annihilation—nevertheless offers us a quietly abiding image, secure in its form. The aesthetic value of the ruin combines the disharmony, the eternal becoming of the soul struggling against itself, with the satisfaction of form, the firm limitedness, of the work of art. For this reason, the metaphysical-aesthetic charm of the ruin disappears when not enough remains of it to let us feel the upward-leading tendency. The stumps of the pillars of the Forum Romanum are simply ugly and nothing else, while a pillar crumbled—say, halfway down—can generate a maximum of charm.

To be sure, we may well be inclined to ascribe this peacefulness to another motif: the character of the ruin as *past*. It is the site of life from which life has departed—but this is nothing merely negative, added to it only by thought, as it is for the countless things which, once immersed in life and accidentally cast on its bank, are by their very nature capable of being easily caught again by its current. In the case of the ruin, the fact that life with its wealth and its changes once dwelled here constitutes an immediately perceived presence. The ruin creates the present form of a past life, not according to the contents or remnants of that life, but according to its past as such.

This also is the charm of antiquities, of which only a narrow-minded logic can assert that an absolutely exact imitation equals them in aesthetic value. No matter if we are deceived in an individual case: with this piece which we are holding in our hand, we command in spirit the entire span of time since its inception; the past with its destinies and transformations has been gathered into this instant of an aesthetically perceptible present. Here, as in the case of the ruin, with its extreme intensification and fulfillment of the present form of the past, such profound and comprehensive energies of our soul are brought into play that there is no longer any sharp division between perception and thought. Here psychic wholeness is at work—seizing, in the same way that its object fuses the contrast of present and past into one united form, on the whole span of physical and spiritual vision in the unity of aesthetic enjoyment, which, after all, is always rooted in a deeper than merely aesthetic unity.

Thus purpose and accident, nature and spirit, past and present here resolve the tension of their contrasts—or, rather, preserving this tension, they yet lead to a unity of external image and internal effect. It is as though a segment of existence must collapse before it can become unresistant to all currents and powers coming from all corners of reality. Perhaps this is the reason for our general fascination with decay and decadence, a fascination which goes beyond what is merely negative and degrading. The rich and many-sided culture, the unlimited *impressionability,* and the understanding open to everything, which are characteristic of decadent epochs, do signify this coming together of all contradictory strivings. An equalizing justice connects the uninhibited unity of all things that grow apart and against one another with the decay of those men and works of men which now can only yield, but can no longer create and maintain their own forms out of their own strength.

Translated by David Kettler

1. "Die Ruine," *Philosophische Kultur. Gesammelte Essays* ([1911] 2nd ed.; Leipzig: Alfred Kröner, 1919), pp. 125-33. Used by permission of Else Simmel, M.D.

THE HANDLE[1]

GEORG SIMMEL

Modern theories of art strongly emphasize that the essential task of painting and sculpture is the depiction of the spatial organization of things. Assenting readily to this, one may then easily fail to recognize that space within a painting is a structure altogether different from the real space we experience. Within actual space an object can be touched, whereas in a painting it can only be looked at; each portion of real space is experienced as part of an infinite expanse, but the space of a picture is experienced as a self-enclosed world; the real object interacts with everything that surges past or hovers around it, but the content of a work of art cuts off these threads, fusing only its own elements into a self-sufficient unity. Hence, the work of art leads its life beyond reality. To be sure, the work of art draws its content from reality; but from visions of reality it builds a sovereign realm. While the canvas and the pigment on it are parts of reality, the work of art constructed out of them exists in an ideal space which can no more come in contact with actual space than tones can touch smells.

This holds for every utensil, for every vase, in so far as it is looked upon as having an aesthetic value. As a piece of metal which is tangible, weighable, and incorporated into both the ways and contexts of the surrounding world, a vase is a segment of reality. At the same time, its artistic form leads an existence completely detached and self-contained, for which the material reality of the metal is merely the vehicle. A vessel, however, unlike a painting or statue, is not intended to be insulated and untouchable but is meant to fulfill a purpose—if only symbolically. For it is held in the hand and drawn into the movement of practical life. Thus the vessel stands in two worlds at one and the same time: whereas reality is completely irrelevant to the "pure" work of art and, as it were, is consumed in it, reality does make claims upon the vase as an object that is handled, filled and emptied, proffered, and set down here and there.

This dual nature of the vase is most decisively expressed in its handle. The handle is the part by which it is grasped, lifted, and tilted; in the handle the vase projects visibly into that real world which relates it to everything external, to an environment that does not exist for the work of art as such. But then the body of the vase is certainly not alone in being subjugated to the demands of art; for were this the case, the handles would be reduced to mere grips, unrelated to the aesthetic value of their form, like the hooks and eyes of a picture frame. Rather, the handles connecting the vase with the world outside art also become components of the art form; they must be justified purely as shapes and as constituting a *single* aesthetic vision with the body of the vase, irrespective of the fact that they have a practical purpose. By virtue of this double significance, and because of the clear and characteristic way in which this significance emerges, the handle as a phenomenon becomes one of the most absorbing aesthetic problems.

Our unconscious criterion for the aesthetic effect of the handle seems to be the manner in which its shape harmonizes these two worlds—the world on the outside which, with the handle, makes its claim on the vessel, and the world of art which, heedless of the other, demands the handle for itself. Moreover, not only must it be possible for the handle actually to perform its practical function, but the possibility must also be manifest in its appearance, and emphatically so in the case of apparently soldered handles, as opposed to those apparently shaped in one movement with the body of the vase. The first of these types indicates that the handle is attached by external forces and comes from an external order of things; it brings into prominence the meaning of the handle as something reaching outside the pure art form. This contrast between vase and handle is more sharply accentuated when, as frequently happens, the handle has the shape of a snake, lizard, or dragon. These forms suggest the special significance of the handle: it looks as though the animal had crawled on to the vase from the outside, to be incorporated into the complete form only, as it were, as an afterthought.

The fact that the handle belongs to the quite different realm in which it originated, and which now uses the handle to claim the vase for itself, becomes apparent through its visible aesthetic unity with the vase. In complete opposition to this, the strongest accent in some vases is on the tendency toward unity. They appear to have been whole forms first, the material extending to the periphery without a break; only afterward was enough material removed so that what remained constituted the handles. We find such modeling done to perfection in certain Chinese bowls, the handles of which are cut out of the cold metal. A similar incorporation of the handles into the aesthetic unity is more organically accented wherever the handle seems to be driven out of the body of the vessel in an uninterrupted transition, and by the same forces that shaped the body itself. For this is like a man's arms which, having grown as part of the same organizational process as his torso, also mediate the relationship of the whole being to the world outside it.

Sometimes shallow bowls are shaped in such a way that, together with their handles, they produce an effect of leaf and stem. Very beautiful examples of such bowls from ancient Central American culture have been preserved—bowls in which the unity of organic growth palpably connects the two parts. The tool, as such, has been characterized as an extension of the hand or of human organs generally. In effect, just as the hand is a tool of the soul, so too the tool is a hand of the soul. Although the fact that it is a tool divorces the hand from the soul, it does not prevent the process of life from flowing through both in intimate unity; their being both apart and together constitutes the unanalyzable secret of life. But life reaches out beyond the immediate circumference of the body and assimilates the "tool" to itself; or better still, a foreign substance *becomes* a tool in that the soul pulls it into its life, into that zone around it which fulfills its impulses. The distinction between being external to the soul and being within it—simultaneously important for the body and of no significance—is, for the things beyond the body, both retained and resolved in a single act by the great motif of the tool in the stream of a life that is unified and transcends itself. The shallow bowl is nothing but an extension or augmentation of the creative hand bearing it. But the bowl is not simply held in the palm of the hand; it is grasped by the handle. Thus, a mediating bridge is formed, a pliable joining of hand with bowl, which, with a palpable continuity, transmits the impulse of the soul into the bowl, into its manipulation. But then, through the reflux of this energy, the bowl is drawn into the circumference of the life of the soul. This relationship cannot be symbolized more perfectly than by a bowl unfolding from its handle like a leaf from its stem. It is as if man were here utilizing the channels of the natural flow of sap between stem and leaf in order to pour his own impulses into an external object, thereby incorporating it into the order of his own life.

When, in the appearance of the handle, one of its two functions is completely neglected in favor of the other, the impression made strikes a discordant note. This often occurs, for example, when the handles form merely a kind of relief ornament, being fully attached to the body of the vase, leaving no space between vase and handle. Here, the form rules out the purpose of the handle (that with it the vase may be grasped and handled), evoking a painful feeling of ineptness and confinement, similar to that produced by a man who has his arms bound to his body. And in such cases, only rarely can the decorative beauty of its appearance compensate for the fact that the inner tendency of the vase toward unity has negated its relatedness to the outer world.

However, just as the aesthetic form must not become so self-willed as to make impossible perception of the handle's purposiveness (even when, as in the case of the ornamental vase, it is out of the question in practice), so a disagreeable picture results whenever the purposiveness works in so many different directions that the unity of the impression is broken up. There are Greek vases that have three handles: two on the body by which the vase can be grasped with both hands and inclined in one or the other direction, and one at the neck by which it can be tilted to one side only. The decidedly ugly impression of these pieces is not caused by a violation of standards appropriate to either visual form or practical utility. For why shouldn't a vessel be tilted in several directions? The ugliness, it seems to me, can rather be traced to the fact that the movements laid out in this system can take place only one *after* the other, whereas the handles present themselves *simultaneously*. Thus completely confused and contradictory feelings of motion are produced; for although the demands of clarity and of utility do not, so to speak, contradict each other on a primary level, the unity of the vision is broken up indirectly: the handles which are, as it were, potential movements are present simultaneously, whereas any actualizing of these movements in practice must deny this simultaneity.

This imbalance suggests the other aesthetic defect of the handle: its exaggerated separation from the unified impression of the vase. To understand this flaw requires a digression. The most extreme estrangement of the handle from the vessel as a whole—that is, the strongest indication of its practical purpose—is to be found when the handle is not rigidly connected with the body of the vessel at all but is movable. In the language of materials, this is often accentuated by having the substance of the handle different from that of the vessel. Such a design allows for a variety of combinations in appearance.

In some Greek vases and bowls, the handle, rigidly attached to the body of the vessel and made of the same substance, has the character of a broad band. If the handle of this kind of vase retains its unity of form with the vessel, the result can be a happy one. The material of a band which differs greatly in weight, consistency, and flexibility from that of the body of a vase is here symbolized; and, by hinting at these differences, the design sufficiently indicates that the handle belongs to another province of existence. At the same time, because the material is actually the same as that of the vase, the aesthetic coherence of the whole is still maintained. The delicate and unstable balance of the two claims on the handle shifts most unfavorably, however, when the fixed handle is in fact of the same substance as the body of the vase but naturalistically imitates another substance in order to stress its special significance by this different appearance. Particularly among the Japanese, otherwise the greatest masters of the handle, the following abomination can be found: fixed porcelain handles that arch beyond the diameter of the vase and accurately imitate the movable straw handles of tea pots. How much a foreign world obtrudes itself, by means of the handle, upon the independent significance of the vase becomes particularly obvious when the special purpose of the handle imparts a quite unnatural and masklike surface to the material of the vase. Just as the handle which merges with the body of the vase without any gap exaggerates one-sidedly the fact that it belongs to the vase (at the cost of not manifesting its purpose), so this latter type goes to the opposite extreme: the remoteness of the handle from the remainder of the vase cannot be stressed more ruthlessly than when the handle takes on the substance of that remainder but forces upon it the appearance of an entirely dissimilar hoop which seems merely to have been fastened on from the outside.

The principle of the handle—to mediate between the work of art and the world while it remains wholly incorporated in the art form—is finally confirmed by the fact that its counterpart, the opening or spout of the vessel, works according to an analogous principle. With the handle the world approaches the vessel; with the spout the vessel reaches out into the world. Only in receiving its current through the handle and in yielding it again through the opening is the vessel fully integrated into human teleology. Precisely because the spout is an opening of the vessel itself, it is easier to connect its form organically with that of the vessel. Accordingly, such unnatural and self-contradictory degenerations as are found in the case of handles occur only rarely. (The very expressions "snout" and "nozzle," for which the handle offers no parallel, indicate the spout's organic function as a part of the body.)

The fact that handle and spout correspond to each other visually as the extreme points of the vessel's diameter and that they must maintain a certain balance reflects the roles they play: while, of course, they serve as the enclosing boundaries of the vessel, they still connect it with the practical world—one centripetally, the other centrifugally. It is like the relation of man as soul to existence outside him: by means of the sensitivity of the sense organs, the corporeal reaches to the soul; by means of willed innervations, the soul reaches out into the corporeal world. Both activities belong to the soul and to the closed sphere of its consciousness; and although the soul's sphere is the opposite of the corporeal one, it is, nevertheless, interwined with it through these two processes.

The handle belongs to the enclosed unity of the vase and at the same time designates the point of entrance for a teleology that is completely external to that form. It is of the most fundamental interest that the purely formal *aesthetic* demands on the handle are fulfilled when these two symbolic meanings of it are brought into harmony or equilibrium. Yet this is not an example of that curious dogma which makes utility a criterion of beauty. For the point at issue is precisely that utility and beauty come to the handle as two unrelated demands—the first from the world, and the second from the total form of the vase. And now, as it were, a beauty of a higher order transcends both of these claims and reveals that their dualism ultimately constitutes a unity that is not further describable. Because of the great span between its two components, the handle becomes a most significant cue to this higher beauty. Till now, art theory has hardly touched on the kind of beauty which contains beauty in the narrower sense merely as one of its elements. Formal beauty, together with all of the demands of idea and life, is incorporated by what one might call superaesthetic beauty into a new synthetic form. Beauty of this ultimate kind is probably the decisive characteristic of all really great works of art; the fact that we give it recognition divorces our position sharply from any aestheticism.

Besides the approach we have been pursuing, it may perhaps be worth while to apply a second, equally far-reaching interpretation to so unpretentious a phenomenon: we are speaking of the *breadth* of symbolic relations which is revealed by its very validity for things in themselves insignificant. For we are concerned with nothing less than the great human and ideal synthesis and antithesis: a being belongs wholly to the unity of a sphere which encloses it and which at the same time is claimed by an entirely different order of things. The latter sphere imposes a purpose upon the former, thereby determining its form. Nevertheless, the form in no way loses its proper place in the first context but retains it as if the second did not exist at all. A remarkable number of spheres in which we find ourselves—political, professional, social, and familial—are enclosed by further spheres, just as the practical environment surrounds the vessel. This relationship is such that the individual, belonging to a more restricted and closed sphere, thereby projects into a larger one. Whenever the more comprehensive sphere must, as it were, manipulate the smaller one and draw it into its own teleology, the individual, too, is manipulated by the more inclusive sphere. Just as the handle must not destroy the unity of the vase's form for the sake of its readiness to perform its practical task, so the art of living demands that the individual maintain his role in his immediate, organically closed sphere while at the same time serving the purposes of the larger unity. With this service he helps to place the smaller sphere into the order of the more inclusive one.

It is the same with our particular provinces of interest. Whenever we pursue knowledge or are subject to ethical demands or create structures that have objective norms, we enter, with the parts or faculties of our selves that are involved, into ideal orders that are propelled by an inner logic, by a developmental impetus that is superpersonal. These orders always seize the totality of our energy by means of such particular faculties and enlist it into their own service. Everything now depends on our not permitting the integrity of our self-centered being to be destroyed. Every single ability, action, and obligation pertaining to that being must remain tied to the law of its unity, while at the same time we belong to that ideal external realm which makes us into points of transition for *its* teleology. Perhaps this duality formulates the richness of the life of men and things; for, after all, this wealth consists of the diversity of the ways in which men and things belong to each other, of the fact that they are simultaneously inside and outside one another, and that every involvement and fusion in one direction is also a dissolution since it is contrasted with an involvement and fusion in another direction. What is most remarkable in the way man understands and constructs the world is that a single element experiences the self-sufficiency of an organic whole, as if no aspect of it were left outside, while at the same time it can be a channel through which an entirely different life flows into the first, a grip by which the totality of one grasps the totality of the other without either of them being torn to pieces.

The handle is perhaps the most superficial symbol of this category; but precisely because of its superficiality, it reveals the range of the category to the fullest. Thus, that we are granted a plenitude of life both lived and shared is probably a reflection of the destiny of the soul, a soul that has its home in two worlds.

For the soul, too, can perfect itself only to the degree to which it belongs, as a necessary component, to the one world and reaches out into the entangled strands and into the meaning of the other—not in spite of, but by means of, the form which membership in the first world imposes on it. It is as if the soul were an arm which one of the worlds—whether the real or the ideal—stretches out so that it may seize the other and join it to itself, and be grasped by and joined to it.

Translated by Rudolph H. Weingartner

1. "Der Henkel," *Philosophische Kultur. Gesammelte Essays* ([1911] 2nd ed.; Leipzig: Alfred Kröner, 1919), pp. 116-24. Used by permission of Else Simmel, M.D.

THE AESTHETIC SIGNIFICANCE OF THE FACE[1]

GEORG SIMMEL

The human face is of unique importance in the fine arts. This importance, however, is described only in very general and approximate terms when it is said that in the features of the face the soul finds its clearest expression. What is it about the face that makes this possible; and, apart from this question, does the face have certain intrinsic aesthetic qualities that account for its significance as a subject in art?

The essential accomplishment of the mind may be said to be its tranformation of the multiplicity of the elements of the world into a series of unities. In the mind, things separated in space and time converge in the unity of a picture, a concept, a sentence. The closer the interrelation of the parts of a complex, and the livelier their interaction (which transforms their separateness into mutual dependence), the more the whole appears to be pervaded by mind. For this reason, the organism, with the intimate relation of its parts and the involvement of the parts in the unity of the life process, is only once removed from mind itself.

Of all the parts of the human body, the face has the highest degree of this kind of inner unity. The primary evidence of this fact is that a change which is limited, actually or apparently, to one element of the face—a curl of the lips, an upturning of the nose, a way of looking, a frown—immediately modifies its entire character and expression. Aesthetically, there is no other part of the body whose wholeness can as easily be destroyed by the disfigurement of only one of its elements. For this is what unity out of and above diversity means: that fate cannot strike any one part without striking every other part at the same time—as if through the root that binds the whole together. Of the rest of the body, the hand, although closest to the face in organic character, still cannot compare with it. The marvelous interrelation and working together of the fingers give one the impression that each is, in reality, mutually independent. When, in fact, one hand always refers to the other; only the two together realize the idea, as it were, of "hand." The unity of the face is accentuated by the head's resting on the neck, which gives the head a sort of peninsular position vis-à-vis the body and makes it seem to depend on itself alone—an effect intensified by the fact that the body is clothed up to the neck.

Unity has meaning and significance only to the degree to which it contrasts with the multiplicity of whose synthesis it consists. Within the perceptible world, there is no other structure like the human face which merges such a great variety of shapes and surfaces into an absolute unity of meaning. The ideal of human co-operation is that completely individualized elements grow into the closest unity which, though composed of these elements, transcends each of them and comes into being exclusively through their co-operation. Among all perceptible things, this fundamental formula of life comes closest to being realized in the human face. By the spirit of a society we mean the content of those interactions which go beyond the individual—although not the individuals—which is more than their sum, yet still their product. In the same manner, the soul, lying behind the features of the face and yet visible in them, is the interaction, the reference of one to the other, of these separate features. From a purely formal viewpoint, the face, with its variety and diversity of parts, forms, and colors, would really be something quite abstruse and aesthetically unbearable—if, that is, the complexity were not at the same time a complete unity.

In order to make this unity aesthetically effective, it is essential that the spatial relation among the facial elements be allowed to shift only within very narrow limits. For aesthetic effect, a form must embrace its parts and hold them together. Any stretching and spreading of extremities is ugly because it interrupts and weakens their connection with the center of the phenomenon; that is, it weakens the perceivable domination of the mind over the circumference of our being. The large gestures of baroque figures, whose limbs appear to be in danger of breaking off, are repugnant because they disavow what is properly human—the absolute encompassment of each detail by the power of the central ego.

The structure of the face makes such centrifugal movement—that is, despiritualization—almost impossible from the outset.

And when it does to some degree take place, as in gaping and staring, it is not only particularly unaesthetic, but, in addition, it is precisely these two expressions which indicate, as we now understand, the "loss of senses," spiritual paralysis, the momentary absence of spiritual control.

The impression of spirituality is also strengthened by the fact that the face shows the influence of gravity less than the other parts of the body. The human figure is the scene in which psychophysiological impulses struggle with physical gravity. The manner of fighting and resolving this battle repeatedly in each succeeding moment determines the style in which individuals and types present themselves to us. The fact that in the face mere bodily weight need not be overcome to any noticeable degree strengthens the impression of its spirituality. Here, too, suggestions of the opposite—closed eyes, head dropping to the chest, slack lips, lax musculature merely obeying gravity—are at the same time evidences of reduced spiritual life.

Man, however, is not simply the bearer of mind. He is not like a book in which spiritual contents are found, but which, as the mere locus of the contents, is indifferent to their intrinsic nature. His spirituality has the form of individuality. The face strikes us as the symbol, not only of the spirit, but also of an unmistakable personality. This feeling has been extraordinarily furthered in the period since the beginning of Christianity by the covering of the body. The face was the heir of the body; for in the degree to which nakedness was the custom, the body presumably had its share in the expression of individuality. The body's capacity in this respect, however, probably differs from that of the face in several ways.

To begin with, bodies differ to the trained eye just as faces do; but unlike faces, bodies do not at the same time *interpret* these differences. A definite spiritual personality is indeed connected with a definite, unmistakable body, and can at any time be identified in it. Under no circumstances, however, can the body, in contrast to the face, signify the *kind* of personality.

Further, the body by its movements—perhaps equally as well as the face—can certainly express psychological processes. However, only in the face do these movements become visible in features which reveal the soul clearly and ultimately. The flowing beauty we call gracefulness must re-create itself with every movement of the hand, bend of the torso, ease of step: it leaves no lasting form in which the individual movement is crystallized. In the face, on the contrary, the emotions typical of the individual—hate or timorousness, a gentle smile or a restless espying of advantage, and innumerable others—leave lasting traces. In the face alone, emotion first expressed in movement is deposited as the expression of permanent character. By virtue of this singular malleability, only the face becomes the geometric locus, as it were, of the inner personality, to the degree that it is perceptible. In this respect, Christianity, whose tendency to cover the body and permit man's appearance to be represented solely by his face, has been the schoolmaster for those who would seek consciousness of individuality.

Besides these formal means of aesthetic representation of individuality, the face has others which serve it in behalf of the opposite principle. The fact that the face consists of two halves which are similar to one another gives it an inner calm and balance which attenuate the excitement and intensity of the purely individual elements. For the very reason that the two halves usually do not present themselves *exactly* alike (owing to differences in profiling and lighting), each is a preparation for, or a fading-away of, the other. The separateness of the individual features is complemented and balanced by the essential comparability of the two halves.

Like all symmetrical forms, that of the face is in itself anti-individualistic. In the symmetrical structure, either of the two parts can be inferred from the other and each points toward a higher principle which governs them both. In all situations, rationalism strives for symmetry, whereas individuality always involves something irrational, something which eludes every predetermining principle. Sculpture, therefore, which presents the halves of the face symmetrically, is confined to a more general or typical style that lacks ultimate individual differentiation; painting, on the other hand, by virtue of the difference in the immediate appearance of the halves of the face resulting from various positions of the profile and proportions of light and shadow, reveals from the beginning a more individualistic nature. The face is the most remarkable aesthetic synthesis of the formal principles of symmetry and of individuality. As a whole, it realizes individualization; but it does so in the form of symmetry, which controls the relations among the parts.

Finally, there is another formal relationship, already mentioned, which gives the face its aesthetic significance and uniqueness. Much of the aesthetic character of objects which are changeable or which exist in many similar forms is determined by the extent to which a modification of the parts must occur in order to result in a change in the over-all impression. Here, too, the ideal of conservation of energy is exemplified: in principle, an object is aesthetically more impressive or useful, the more sensitively it responds as a whole to the alteration of its smallest element. For this shows the sensitivity and strength of the interrelation of its parts, its inner logic, as it were, which requires that every change in a premise inevitably be followed by a change in the conclusion. Aesthetic contemplation and organization abolish the indifference of elements, a characteristic which belongs only to their theoretical images. Those objects, therefore, in which the mutual indifference of elements is suspended and the fate of each determines that of all others are the most receptive to aesthetic treatment.

The face, in fact, accomplishes more completely than anything else the task of creating a maximum change of total expression by a minimum change of detail. The universal problem of art is to elucidate the formal elements of things by relating them to one another—to interpret the perceptible through its connection with the perceptible. Nothing seems more suited to this than the face in which the character of each feature is integrated with the character of every other—that is, of the whole. The cause and effect of this circumstance is the immense mobility of the face. In an absolute sense, it commands only very slight changes of position; yet because of the influence of each change on its total character, the impression of intensified modifications, so to speak, results. It is as if a maximum of movements were invested even in its state of rest, or as if this state of rest were the non-extended moment toward which innumerable movements have tended, from which innumerable movements will come.

The height of this extraordinarily dynamic effect is achieved with a minimal movement by the eye. In painting, in particular, the eye derives its effect not only from its relation to the totality of the features—a relation it mediates by its potential mobility—but also from the importance of the gaze of the persons portrayed in interpreting and structuring the space in the picture itself. There is no other thing which, staying so absolutely in place, seems to reach beyond it to such an extent; the eye penetrates, it withdraws, it circles a room, it wanders, it reaches as though behind the wanted object and pulls it toward itself. The artist's use of the direction, intensity, and whole formal character of the gaze for purposes of dividing and elucidating pictorial space needs a special study.

The eye epitomizes the achievement of the face in mirroring the soul. At the same time, it accomplishes its finest, purely formal end as the interpreter of mere appearance, which knows no going back to any pure intellectuality *behind* the appearance. It is precisely this achievement with which the eye, like the face generally, gives us the intimation, indeed the guarantee, that the artistic problems of pure perception and of the pure, sensory image of things—if perfectly solved—would lead to the solution of those other problems which involve soul and appearance. Appearance would then become the veiling and unveiling of the soul.

Translated by Lore Ferguson

1. "Die ästhetische Bedeutung des Gesichts" (1901), *Brücke und Tür. Essays des Philosophen zur Geschichte, Religion, Kunst und Gesellschaft,* ed. Michael Landmann in collaboration with Margarete Susman (Stuttgart: K. F. Koehler, 1957), pp. 153-59. Used by permission of K. F. Koehler Verlag, Stuttgart.

ON THE NATURE OF PHILOSOPHY[1]

GEORG SIMMEL

Under the concept of philosophy a large body of thought is collected. If we look for a point of entry into this accumulation, if we seek a determination of this concept from some point in the mental world that is not itself already within the province of philosophy, our need cannot be satisfied, given the structure that our knowledge has. For what philosophy is, is actually decided only within philosophy, that is, only by means of its own concepts and methods. Philosophy is, so to speak, the first of its own problems. Perhaps no other discipline directs its investigation back to its own nature in this way. The object of physics is surely not the science of physics itself, but, perhaps, optical and electrical phenomena; philology is concerned with Plautus' manuscripts and the development of inflections in Anglo-Saxon, but not with the nature of philology. Philosophy, and perhaps only philosophy, moves in the following curious circle: It determines the presuppositions of its method of thinking and of its purposes by the use of its own method of thinking and in accordance with its own purposes. There is no access to the concept of philosophy from the outside; for only philosophy can decide what philosophy is—indeed, whether it is at all, or whether perhaps its name merely conceals a worthless phantasm.

This unique procedure on the part of philosophy is the consequence—or perhaps only the expression—of its fundamental effort: to think without presuppositions. It is impossible for man to begin entirely at the beginning. He always finds, within or outside himself, a reality or a past which supplies a basis for his conduct, a starting point, or at least something which is hostile and must be destroyed. In just this way, our knowing is also conditioned by something which is "already there," by realities or by inner laws. These realities and inner laws, whether they are only the rules of logic and method or the fact of an existing world, cannot be produced by the thought process itself. But since the content and direction of this process depend on them, its sovereignty is limited in various ways. Hence, wherever a thinker nevertheless tries to place himself beyond all presuppositions, he begins to philosophize.

To be sure, the attempt is seldom made to such a radical extent. As a rule what is aspired to instead is a structure of knowledge independent of some *particular* presupposition, such as a structure independent of the immediate impression made by the sensible world, of traditional moral evaluations, of the self-evident validity of experience, or of the equally self-evident reality of divine powers. But even with such a delimitation, thinking without presuppositions in philosophy is distinguished from a similar procedure in other fields by this accompanying state of mind: This autonomy of thought, the fact that its course is not tied to anything external, goes beyond momentary particulars, and concerns the *whole* of knowledge and, indeed, the whole of life.

It is, of course, impossible for thinking to be entirely without presuppositions. Wherever knowing begins, something is already presupposed; it is either something dark and insurmountable which frightens us or something which, on the contrary, lends us support in the relativity, the flux, and the subjectivity of knowledge. Because of this, the goal of being absolutely without presuppositions, though indicating a direction, is not an attainable goal of philosophical thinking. In other areas of knowledge, being without presuppositions is *from the first* a goal only to a limited extent. Whenever philosophy develops into epistemology, the fact of this development has the deeper meaning that philosophy is now seeking out and recognizing the presuppositions of knowing and of philosophizing itself, that in this way it includes what is external to it within its jurisdiction and its forms of knowing.

This thinking without presuppositions which is contained in the very concept of philosophy, this inner autonomy of its thought process, has, understandably enough, the following consequence: Philosophy determines its problems by its own means; the object, goals, and paths of philosophy can be examined only from within it. But this result, in turn, has a more important consequence: The right and duty of philosophy—to fix its object for itself with a greater independence from what is given than is exercised in all the other provinces of knowledge—entail that different philosophical doctrines start from problems which are also posed in fundamentally different ways. In every other discipline there is a general end of knowledge which is recognized in principle and which differentiates itself into the diversity of special tasks, only, as it were, on a higher level. Only in philosophy does every thinker who is at all original determine not only what he wants to answer but also what he wants to ask. He not only determines what to ask in the sense of special problems but what it is that he must ask at all in order to be in accord with the concept of philosophy.

Epicurus, for example, conceives philosophy to be the effort to reach a happy life by meditation and by finding the reasons which underlie things as they are. Schopenhauer considers philosophy to be the endeavor to reach by means of ideas what is not idea, that is, to reach beyond the empirical phenomena with which the other sciences occupy themselves. For the Middle Ages, philosophy is the handmaiden of theology, the foundation of religious truths. For Kantianism, it is the critical reflection of reason on itself. While sometimes the concept of philosophy is determined purely ethically, as the examination of what is significant for the ideals of man's conduct, it appears elsewhere as the logical treatment of the image of the world, so that the world's originally given contradictions may be overcome.

From this diversity of philosophic goals—a diversity that can be increased at will—what we can unequivocally conclude is this: The individual philosopher raises a problem which seems to be quite general and still neutral in respect to all possible answers, but he raises it in such a way that, from the beginning, it suits the *answer* that he wants to give. This personal character of philosophical thinking prevents the setting of a general goal of knowledge, a goal that would reach beyond the autonomous immanence of thought. One could almost say that the production of original thought in philosophy is something in itself so unified, so much the intellectual expression of a self-enclosed being, that question and answer signify an after-the-fact division of thought. Here the problem is common and the solution special to a much lesser extent, at least, than it is in other fields. Correctly speaking, if in each case the answer is to be a certain determined one, then the problem must be raised in an appropriately pointed way from the beginning.

But if each definition of philosophy holds only for the particular philosophy of each particular thinker, what is left to justify a common name for such divergent tendencies? To reach an answer it is necessary, perhaps, to pursue another line of questioning. As long as the definition of philosophy is determined by its purpose and content, the works which make up the whole subject seem to lack a common characteristic. Yet a common characteristic may lie in the attitude of philosophers themselves, not in the results of their thinking, but in a basic condition necessary for all results, which, because of the way they ramify, cannot afterward be brought together again. We are concerned with a formal, inner quality of the philosopher as such. By this quality is meant not a psychological "attitude toward life" but the objective condition of all philosophizing, which, to be sure, is operative only when it is realized in a psyche. One can perhaps designate the philosopher as the man who has an organ which is receptive and reactive to the totality of being. In general, men are always turned toward particular things—the practical aspect of life alone makes sure of that. Whether these particulars are very small or very great—one's livelihood or a church dogma, a love affair or the discovery of the periodicity of the chemical elements—it is always particulars which awaken contemplation, interest, and activity. Philosophers, however, have a sense for the collectivity of things and of life, though naturally to greatly varying degrees and never perfectly. Moreover, to the extent to which a philosopher is productive, he has the ability to convert such an intuition or feeling of the whole into concepts and their connections. He need not, of course, always speak of the whole; indeed, he may be completely unable to do so in the exact sense. But whatever special problem of logic or ethics, of aesthetics or religion, he may be treating, he will do so as a philosopher only if that relationship to the totality of being is a vital element in his discussion.

Naturally, the whole of existence in the real sense is accessible to no one and can act upon no one. It must first be assembled from those fragments of reality which are the sole data—given, if you wish, as "idea" or perhaps only as desire. Only then can the totality of existence evoke a reaction from the philosophic intellect. Of course, this amounts to discounting a bank note which will never be redeemed at its full value. But this philosophical production of an objective whole out of the fragments of objectivity, and the continued building on what is produced, is only the extreme case of a general procedure. Thus, for a historian, for example, the totality of a character shines forth from the fragments of the record of tradition, and on this totality he builds his presentation. Indeed, even the most complete record *cannot* contain this intuition of a complete being. It results instead from the spontaneous action of a remarkable energy which, just to give it a name, one might call the mind's ability to "totalize," in spite of the fact that its acts are stimulated and directed by external particulars. And this ability, when it exceeds a certain magnitude, becomes the common condition for all philosophizing whatsoever, irrespective of the degree of individuality to which philosophical structures may develop. This individuality has been already expressed by the definitions of philosophy cited earlier.

However, two principal attempts have been made to grasp, in a more real way, the totality of all being and to make intelligible the fact that the philosopher is somehow affected by this totality and responds to it intellectually. Needless to say, these efforts were not directed by an explicit consciousness of this goal, nor by an intention to pursue it. One is the way of mysticism; the other, that of Kant. I leave it undecided whether mysticism—I here choose that of Meister Eckhart as typical—can be maintained, without reservations, as belonging to philosophy. Perhaps it is a self-sufficient mental structure, beyond both science and religion. But Eckhart's speculation goes on in what might be called an ultimate depth that is so universally human that philosophy can immediately transfer the themes of his speculation into its forms. The first member of the sequence into which his thoughts must be ordered for our present purpose is the absolute inclusion of all things in God. So integrated, they are all *one* being; in itself, each particular thing has no individuality. Only through the event which Eckhart designates by the mystical symbol of God begetting the Son in eternity, do things *become* in their diversity. But in their root and substance, they remain a part of the Divine Being. God flows into all creatures, and therefore all creation is God; were God to turn away for a moment, they would be annihilated. In itself, however, this divinity is absolute unity. God, who is everything, is "neither this nor that" but "one and simple in himself." First, then, the totality of the world is gathered into *one* point. And this gives Eckhart the opportunity to transfer this totality into the soul. Of course the soul itself has manifold abilities, but within it there is a central point that is not touched by any of the diversity that pertains to creatures. Eckhart calls this central point the "spark," something absolutely "one and simple," the true spirit of the soul. In it, God speaks without mediation; indeed, it is no longer divorced from God at all. It is "one and (not merely) united" with him: "here God's substance is my substance and my substance God's substance." In this point we recognize all things in their true essence because we have, or, more correctly, we *are,* their unity in God. "My eye and God's eye are one eye and one sight."

This expresses most clearly, perhaps, the innermost reason for the connection that has always existed between religion and philosophy. In the representation of God, the believer has the whole of the world, even if he lacks all of its countless particulars. Mysticism attempts to make this in some way intuitive by gathering the essence of the soul into an ultimate, simple, living point that is no longer separated from the unity of the divine essence. In the most diverse forms, the following theme runs through the religious mysticism and the philosophical speculation of all times: The deepest submersion into ourselves, overcoming all diversity, leads us at the same time into the absolute unity of things. There is a point at which this unity, expressed in the idea of God, reveals itself as the essence and unity of ourselves. The philosophical attitude which signifies a relation of the mind to the whole of the world, and which, considering the dimension of the individual and that of the world, could appear as a contradiction—indeed, as insanity—thereby attains a metaphysical justification. It appears as the intellectual manifestation of that feeling which, it would seem, emerges in all the epochs of human life in which some profundity is achieved: the feeling, that is, that we reach into the foundation of the world when we submerge ourselves into the foundation of our own souls.

From the opposite viewpoint, the fundamental theme of Kant provides a possibility for giving a basis to this knowledge of the totality of things which the philosopher's feeling for the world anticipates. Kant's chief work does not find its object in existence conceived as a whole or immediately experienced but in existence in so far as existence has become science. This is the form which that totality of things takes for him and through which it may be questioned as to its nature and conditions. For him, the world is reality in so far as it is the content of a science which is already established or is at least possible. Whatever does not conform to the conditions of science is not "real." Before we can follow Kant's path to the goal under consideration, more extensive deliberation about this point is required.

There is perhaps no necessity of thought which is so hard to cast off as the analysis of things into content and form, even though this analysis has neither logical force nor the force of sensibly given data. In countless modifications, under this and other names, this division cuts across our image of the world. It is one of the organizers and flexible instruments with which the mind gives structure to the mass of all that is, a mass which, in its immediate unity, is structureless. Finally, above all particular contents and varying forms, there arises the supreme contrast between the world as content, as existence determined in itself—but not apprehensible by us in its immediacy—on the one hand, and, on the other, the fact that this world is nevertheless made apprehensible in that it is articulated in a diversity of forms, each of which assumes in principle the totality of the world as its content. Science and art, religion and the inner assimiliation of the world, sense perception and the coherence of things according to a given principle and value—these, and perhaps still others, are the great forms through which, as it were, each particular part of the content of the world can, or should, pass. As our world is given to us, it shows at each point a content-element which is taken up in one of these categories. Our reflection believes that it sees the very same content now under this, then under that, category. We can have precisely the same man as the object of knowledge and of artistic creation, precisely the same event as a moment of our inner destiny and as proof of divine intervention, precisely the same object purely as a sense impression and as an exemplification of the metaphysical construction of existence.

Now the very meaning of these great forms is that each can take up any given content whatever. Art, according to its principle, can claim to shape the entire sphere of existence; and, similarly, no segment of the world can escape knowledge. One can ask about the place of anything in a scale of values, a perfect emotional life must be able to react to everything, and so on. Yet while according to the *idea* of these forms, each can translate the entire world into its language, reality nevertheless does not allow a form to express itself so completely. This is because these forms are never operative in abstract purity and absolute perfection, but only within the boundaries and particularities which the intellectual attitude of any given era permits them. We have no absolute art, but only the arts, artistic means, and styles of the culture of a period. And since these are different today from what they were yesterday and from what they will be tomorrow, they suffice to give artistic shape only to certain contents; other contents that cannot be accommodated by the artistic form available can in principle become the content of art. Similarly, we have no absolute religion which permits us to give religious meaning to each thing—the lowest and most contingent as well as the highest—to connect each thing with all things in the unity of the fundamental religious theme. We have instead only historical religions, each of which permeates only a certain part of the contents of the world, the soul and destiny, while another part remains outside and eludes this forming activity of religion. It is always the same: the ideal right of each one of these great forms to construct an entire world out of the collectivity of contents is realized only with the inevitable imperfection of a historical structure. Only in this way can these forms live: with all the contingencies, adaptations, lags, or deviations of development and individual one-sidedness—in short, with all of the peculiarities and deficiencies exhibited by a historical reality that is bound to the conditions of an epoch —in contrast to the idea and principle of a form.

It cannot be any different with scientific knowledge. The formation of concepts and the method of collecting and ordering experiences, the transformation of what is given to sense into an image which conforms to the laws of nature or of history, the criteria of truth and error—in short, all the forms and methods which, if the contents of the world are taken up into them, allow these contents of the world to become contents of science—have developed in the course of the history of the human mind, and will doubtless develop further. As to the ideal of science, in which all the contents of the world are contained without leaving anything outside, we lack not only the ability to master this content empirically (that is, to actually apply the scientific form to the immeasurableness of things), but we also lack the absolute perfection of the form itself that would make it equal to every task. For we possess this form only in shapes which are constantly modified and never completed in any particular epoch of knowledge, and which for man—a historical, evolutionary being—can never be completed. All probabilities, all analogies, and countless facts would be contradicted by the assumption that the form of any actual science, dependent as it is on incalculably manifold historical conditions, would ever be capable of taking up in itself the totality of existence. When Fichte says that the kind of philosophy a man will have depends on the kind of man he is, what he says is valid far beyond philosophy and far beyond the individual man. The kind of science humanity has at any given moment depends on the kind of humanity it is at that moment. Moreover, just as the imperfection and historical contingency of its being are related to the idea of its perfection, so, manifestly, the forms and categories that signify science for humanity at any point in time are related to those which would be sufficient for shaping the entire content of the world into science.

What has just been said contradicts Kant's conviction in so far as the basic forms with which any existing science grasps the material of existence seem to him to be sufficient for the entire content of existence and are not subject to evolution. Nevertheless, the point of view here presented is possible only on a Kantian foundation. For his position, Kant has found a most concise and certainly most paradoxical expression: The understanding prescribes for nature the laws of nature. The fundamental theme is that the cognitive representations of things are not poured into us like nuts into a sack, that as knowers we are not passive recipients of sense impressions like the indifferent wax tablet that is given form from the outside by the impression of a stamp. All knowing is, rather, an activity of the mind. Sense impressions, toward which we are simply receptive are not yet knowledge, and the complex of the contents of sense impressions is not nature. On the contrary, these impressions must be given forms and connections which are not inherent in them but which are imposed on them precisely by the knowing mind as such. Only thus does the chaos or the mere spatial and temporal succession of sense impressions become what we call nature: a meaningful, intelligible coherence in which the diversity of things appears as a principled unity, knitted together by laws. Once these laws are related to particular given things, they are, of course, given to us only through experience, that is, through a co-operation of sensible receptivity with the shaping understanding. However, the most general rules forming the multiplicity of phenomena into a uniform nature (the principle of causality, for example) do not stem from phenomena but from the mind's own ability to connect, to unify. Kant calls this ability "the understanding," the ability which prescribes for nature the laws of nature. For only these laws—the mind's own connecting forms for the given contents of the world—bring about nature from the world contents.

This more exact sense of the popular formula of Kant's doctrine that "the world is my idea" places the mind in such a relation to the world that it encompasses the world in its entirety despite the inexhaustibility of the world's particulars. We know absolutely nothing of things except in so far as they are in our consciousness, that is, in so far as they are formed into objects of knowledge by the activity of our mind. Because of this, the laws of the mind are the laws of things; no content of knowledge of which we can speak at all can escape formation by the forms of the mind. And this may be perfectly suitable for scientific knowledge—but it must be remembered that the forms of this knowledge are themselves historical creations that can therefore never adequately take up the totality of world contents. If, on the contrary, these forms were developed as completely as Kant simply assumes, and if the development were as perfect as it no doubt could be according to the idea of knowledge in principle, there certainly would be a possibility of a mental contact between man and the totality of existence. Yet the paradox contained in the quantitative discrepancy between the particular being of a psyche and the immeasurability of all existence seemed to defeat this contact altogether, and with it the philosophical attitude. The paradox is resolved through the fabulous daring of the Kantian revolution: the whole of existence owes its form as an object of knowledge precisely to the constitution of the psyche. The particular contents of existence may, so to speak, remain in the world, awaiting their gradual reception into experience. But the forms which bring about experience and nature in the first place (in which the entire compass of the world is potentially contained) are in the mind and only in the mind. They are its functions, which we call its knowing. The mind is related to the totality of the world just because this totality is its product.

Curious relations thus obtain between the foundation which mysticism gives to the principle of the philosophical attitude and that which can be derived from the major theme of Kant's philosophy. In the former, the content of the world is, as it were, gathered into one point in so far as its differences are held to be insubstantial and only the unity of the Divine Being really exists. Hence, the soul, which also belongs to the Divine Being, succeeds in permeating the world without mediation, a world which then makes itself explicit, so to speak, in the philosophical development of thought. This way of viewing things has something formless about it: it is merely a question of the substance of being and of an immersion in that substance, while reality forfeits all individuality—that is, all form. Kant's thought, on the other hand, has its pivot in the notion of form. There are a few forms which shape the material of the world into a world and offer themselves to an infinity of diverse contents. All that matters for Kant is the world of knowledge, and knowing does not take place anywhere except in consciousness. Hence it is the forms of consciousness which prejudge or embrace the world on the basis of everything that is for them a principle, of everything which makes the world into an object of knowledge. It is clear that the philosophical grasp of the world as a whole is accomplished by the reduction of that whole either to mere formless substance or to contentless form. For the concrete phenomenon, that is, formed matter, is the immensity, the infinity, of being which cannot be encompassed by any thought. No thought can know itself to be affected by the totality of being all at once.

Only when the mind abstracts the content by itself or the form by itself, thus exercising its own formative activity on existence, does it seem to achieve, by virtue of this activity, an access to the totality of existence.

In spite of the fact that these two views of the world are infinitely different in disposition and content, there is, then, an analogy between them with respect to the present problem. This analogy will become clear when we consider the importance which both these views attach to knowledge of ourselves as a means to knowledge of the world. All the forms which make up the world of knowledge converge, for Kant, in a central, really creative, exemplary form: in *unity*. The diverse representations become objective instances of knowledge in that they flow together into the unity of an object, a sentence, a train of thought, an image of the world. For the ordering of the chaos of spatially and temporally jumbled elements, that is, for the formative principle of an intelligible world, we have no other expression except "unity of diversity." The fact that this is the form of our world of knowledge is both conditioned and realized by the form of consciousness by which and for which this world exists. This form is *unity*. I am conscious of the contents of my consciousness as belonging to *one* personality, as the sensations, thoughts, impulses, and sufferings of a self which knows itself as one and identical at every point in this diversity, a self which cannot be torn apart by the discordance of its contents and products, a self whose feeling of being torn apart, when it occurs, is possible precisely because of the existence of its unity. For without this unity there would be no tearing apart, only an indifferent simultaneous juxtaposition of contents. At this ultimate point of the self in us the world enters. Looking at it in another way, from that same point emanate those rays which, as they encompass the world, make the world a world. This ultimate point has the same significance for the problem of our present concern as the "spark" of Meister Eckhart. In both cases the mind's absolute, central unity is precisely that by which the mind enters into relation with the absolute wholeness of existence.

The fact that the basic philosophical attitude is realized in this way—by means of the innermost unity of the mind—allows us to explain the peculiarities of the attitude as an intelligible consequence of the attitude itself. First, there is the consequence which has been expressed by means of the very ambiguous concept of the "subjectivity" of philosophical theories in contrast to the objectivity of exact knowledge, empirical or mathematical. The more inclusive one makes the circle of things to which the intellect reacts in uniform fashion, the more freely can the intellect express its individuality in the reaction; for the intellect will have a correspondingly greater field from which to choose the decisive element, or combination of elements, than when only a single element or a few of them evoke the reaction. As the size of the circle of different objects increases, the necessity of reacting in a way that is equally valid for all individuals approaches the limit of zero. Precisely what is called a view of the *world* depends most of all on the different constitutions of the personalities holding that view. The very image of the *whole,* which seems to imply the fullest and purest objectivity, reflects the peculiarity of its possessor much more than the objective image of any *particular* thing usually reflects it. If art is, as it is said to be, an image of the world seen through a temperament, then philosophy is a temperament seen through an image of the world. The remarkable thing is that in the latter case this particularity does not produce a multiplicity of philosophies. The particularity does not refer to those aspects in which every man is simply different from every other; for not only are there not so many philosophies as there are men philosophizing, but the number of fundamental philosophical themes which determine a world view is very limited. The same themes turn up again and again in the course of millenia. They divide, unite, appear in different shadings and in changing guises, but their number increases very slowly indeed. One wonders whether humanity should be considered poverty-stricken because it has succeeded in achieving only a minimum of real conceptions of the whole and of thoughts which unify all existence when compared to the infinite diversity of individualities and fortunes, of experiences and dispositions; or whether mankind should be considered rich because it has been able to derive satisfaction for incalculably diversified mental demands from this small range of fundamental philosophical conceptions, and has been able to fructify, to the very center of their personalities, the most widely different psychic complexions. But the fact that there is such a very small number of distinct philosophical reactions to the world and to life shows that, although these reactions are determined by the personal moment and by their "subjectivity," the determination is not arbitrary, the result of a submission to the vacillations of subjective moods, or even of the singularity of an individual psychic career.

Here a mental category becomes operative which is deep-rooted and not easily described by traditional concepts. On the one hand, it is completely erroneous to look for the source of philosophy in the "personal acts of its creators." For what one usually calls the "personal"—temperament, fortunes, environment—is precisely the universal that the philosopher has in common with countless others. It cannot, therefore, explain his creation, which has come to be absolutely within him alone and in no one else. On the contrary, the truly personal, the only personal aspect of the creative man is his work, or, rather, the process which pertains to this work alone and does not and cannot pertain to anything else. But neither is the point of uniqueness and incomparability in the individual a sufficient basis for his creation, for in that case his creation could not be comprehensible to, and valid for, others. It could not be objectively conceivable, nor could it enter into countless interpersonal relationships. The mental factor which reacts to existence is, then, by no means the completely immediate individuality, but must be sought in some special level or modification of that individuality. On the other hand, neither logical concatenations nor factual knowledge and its methods determine the origin of a philosophy. The thinkers of a cultural period may have all of this in common, and therefore not allow any contradictions among concrete items of knowledge to persist; yet their philosophical images of the world may diverge in the sharpest way, even to the point of complete mutual contradiction. There must therefore be a third something in man, beyond his individual subjectivity and the logical, objective thinking which is universally convincing. And this third something must be the soil in which philosophy takes root. Indeed, the existence of philosophy demands as its presupposition that there be such a third thing.

To use an approximate characterization, this third level in

us might be designated the *typical* mentality. For type is the kind of structure which neither coincides with particular, real individuality nor represents an objectivity beyond men and their lives. It is a fact that mental energies are manifested in us, the activity-contents of which are not of an individual and subjective nature, although this does not make them copies of something objective which confronts the subject. A feeling in us distinguishes, often with great instinctive sureness, between those convictions and dispositions which we modestly recognize as purely personal and subjective and those which we believe to be shared by some—or perhaps all—other men. To be sure, we could not cite any objective evidence for this phenomenon, but it seems as if something universal spoke in us, as if this thought or that sensation emerged from a more universal foundation in us which itself justifies its own content.

It may be that this is also the seeding ground of art. Certainly the artist works from a purely personal necessity, so that each artist who is faced with the same model produces a work of art that is different from all others. Yet each of these works, assuming that it has artistic worth, has something which is called artistic "truth" and carries with it the demand that it be generally recognized as such. This individual productivity that emerges from the personality is, then, evidently a *typical* one. The particular form has a validity which goes beyond particularity. This validity does not come from the object; it exists because what here expresses itself is that curious psychic level within the creator in which the human type, or a human type, becomes operative in the individual phenomenon.

It might also be that in this soil the proselytism of religious creation flourishes. Inasmuch as the religious genius expresses his innermost life and the mystically subjective element of his ecstasies and illuminations, these expressions take on, for countless others, the dignity of a truth, even though they cannot be legitimized by any objective counterpart or, indeed, in many cases even by logical norms. The somewhat extravagant saying that the "genius of humanity" speaks through these inspired men expresses, nevertheless, a somehow correct instinct; namely, that energies which are rooted in that aspect of the soul which is more than individual, or which represent this aspect in a mysterious way, are expressed in the individual and immediately by him. What characterizes all great philosophical achievements is the remarkable fact that, on the one hand, each is a combination of a presentation of a conception of the world and of life which is resolutely one-sided and has a distinct personality that cannot be confused with any other; and, on the other hand, an expression which, proceeding from a personal necessity that goes beyond the individual, is universally human and is rooted in life in general. This combination presupposes that what is operative here is the typical aspect of a mental individuality, namely, the immanent objectivity of a personality which is obedient exclusively to its own law.

Furthermore, this circumstance enables us to recognize that the concept of truth in philosophy, in so far as it includes these ultimate decisions about all existence and total reactions to it, departs from that of the other sciences. Here truth does not copy the objectivity of things—this is done by the sciences in the narrower sense—but rather the types of human mentality that are revealed in every particular view of all things. In philosophical assertions there is no question of correspondence (however understood) with an "object"; the question is whether the assertions are an adequate expression of the being of the philosopher himself or of the human type that lives within him. It does not matter whether the type is characteristic of a certain category of individuals or whether it constitutes an element which is to some degree present in every individual. However, philosophy is not to be conceived as psychological confession or as autobiography, for then it would have an object, like any psychology, and it would have to be true or false depending on whether it did or did not correspond to that object. The content of the assertions of a philosopher is not his personality, for these assertions refer to various objective realities; but his personality *is expressed in them.* The special type of human being who possesses this personality does not disappear in the assertion itself, as in the other sciences, but is retained. This content is not the mind as mirrored by itself, but the world as it is pictured in the mind—not according to the mind's subjective, contingent reality—but corresponding to that type of man. The human kind of mentality in general implies certain contents and forms of the image of the world which would be replaced by different ones for beings that are differently organized. In the same way, the particular types of human mentality demand those special colorations, combinations, and orientations, the principles of which can be found in the great philosophical theories. This conception of philosophy could be summed up in the following formula: Philosophical thinking objectifies the personal and personalizes the objective. For philosophy expresses the most profound and ultimate aspect of a personal attitude toward the world in the language of an image of the world. And just because of this, it depicts an image of the world according to certain directional lines and a certain total significance. Choosing among these will always be a matter of the differences among essential human traits and types.

Now it is entirely possible that when these types and traits are expressed and developed with full clarity, impressiveness, and convincing force, the expression is accomplished by means of assertions which are completely false as far as their objects are concerned, that is, in so far as they are judged from an objective, scientific standpoint—or, if one wishes, from a universally human one. Indeed, from time to time, the objective falsity of a doctrine can reveal, all the more profoundly and clearly, that other truth of the mental type which holds the doctrine. It may be, therefore, that truth is not at all the most appropriate concept with which to express the value of a philosophy. For truth, after all, is bound up with a product of thought to which a real or ideal being is compared, and the truth of that product consists in its somehow corresponding to that being. In philosophy, however, the character of the product of thought itself is decisive. It carries with it its own value as *being;* that is, its value is measured by the significance of the mental direction and disposition immediately evinced by that product, and by the convincing honesty, profundity, and clarity of the evidence itself.

Only because the ultimate criterion of philosophical value is not the truth of an assertion as determined by an object but the typical being which lives and is revealed in these assertions, does it become understandable why certain minds today still find decisions and solutions for the problem of their relation to the world in Socrates and Plato, in Thomas Aquinas and Giordano Bruno, in Spinoza and Leibnitz. The development of intellectual history brings about, in an observable way, a reduction of the truth value that is oriented toward objects to the significance of the mental being that is objectified in the great philosophers. As soon as philosophical assertions are presented as assertions about the factual character of things, the tone naturally falls to the factual level, both as regards the persuasive power of the assertion and as regards any criticism of it. Gradually, however, this becomes a matter of indifference, whereas the inner significance of the doctrine perseveres as the expression of a real position that is not affected by the question of objective truth. Is there anyone, nowadays, who still asks whether Plato's theory of ideas or the pantheism of the Stoics is "correct," whether Nicholas of Cusa's concept of God as the "coincidence of contradictions" or Fichte's world-creating self "correspond to the facts," or whether Schelling's doctrine of the identity of nature and mind or Schopenhauer's metaphysics of will is "true"? All these views have been frequently and conclusively "refuted." Yet in each case, the human type which set down its reactions to existence in these "errors" has survived all refutations and, in its own way, has lent those doctrines an immortal significance. In any case, the criterion of truth of these doctrines is not to be obtained from the point to which the factual assertion refers but from the point from which it comes.

The content which is embodied in this philosophical reaction to the impression made by being as such is constructed in the following way: From among the given phenomena of existence, or from among the conceptual representations in which our ability to abstract grasps the aspects, the parts, the movements of existence, a single one is chosen (as it were) to function as the real nucleus or sense of the whole of existence. This one-sidedness of individual philosophies is grounded in their inmost essence; for, as regards this essence, it has been shown that what is most general is represented in the form of a typical individuality. It is therefore quite comprehensible that what is most general can be experienced as an expanding of the individuality to the entire world. The world is given to us as a sum of fragments, and it is the effort of philosophy to substitute the whole for the part. It accomplishes this in substituting the part for the whole. A countless number of threads make up the web of reality; their totality sets the problem for the philosopher. From among these threads, the peculiarity of the philosopher's mental type allows him to grasp a single one. He declares it to be the one which holds the totality together, the one from which all the others are derived. This is the thread which he pursues, even though it may appear on the surface only in fragments and is concealed by others. He pursues it as the only thread that continues throughout the entire web. He spins it out beyond the relative measure of its finite appearance into the infinite and absolute. This is the formal possibility which enables an individuality to imprint its inner sensible and creative relationship to the universe on an objective image of the universe: an individuality grasps a trait of the whole which is also individual and which corresponds to the individual's peculiar type. The individual allows this trait to grow to the dimensions of the whole, reducing everything that is different and discordant to the status of a non-essential or an appearance, to something which is not really there or which is merely a disguised form of that which alone is real.

This, as is evident, is the attitude which gives rise to the same complaint against philosophy which is made against religion: that it anthropomorphizes the world. The image of the world as the reaction of a psyche determined by the peculiar type of that psyche, and the structure of this image arrived at by an exclusive emphasis on *one* of its possible traits considered as the objective correlative of this peculiar type—all of this, after all, makes the world, more or less explicitly, into man "writ large." This appears most unmistakably in the doctrines that identify the essential nature of being in general with the human soul and its determinations. It is the case, for example, with Leibnitz. For him, all existence is an aggregate of souls; matter, according to its true essence, consists of the same soul-elements as do men, but what is awake in the latter is asleep in the former. The same is true for Kant, who sees the purpose of the existence of the whole of the world in man, in so far as he is subject to moral laws. It also holds for Schopenhauer, who declares the will to be the metaphysical essence of all reality; that is, its essence is the very same restless and ultimately purposeless state of being driven which we find in us as conscious acts of the will tending to given particulars.

It is a complete misunderstanding to see in all of this a

misuse of poetic analogies, a relapse into that primitive animism for which the essence of the wind could be nothing but the blowing of Aeolus and the movement of the stars an expression of the forces of the spirits living in them. Certainly, these images of the whole world are determined by the structure of the psyche which receives the impression of the whole that produces the images. Yet the thought process of the metaphysician does not take the following course: I am constituted in such and such a way; therefore, this is also the aspect of the world. Instead, he asks, What is the most fundamental coherent basis on which the world can rest, and I with it and in it? The metaphysician finds himself in the world as an objective, most certain fact. He asks—no matter how the question is formulated —How must the world be constituted so that this fact may be possible in it, making an intelligible, harmonious unity? Leibnitz' declaration that all the elements of being are souls in ordered grades of perfection or consciousness is therefore no naïve projection of the human soul into the universe, but inversely, the soul is seen from the point of view of the universe. The question is asked, How must we assume the *whole* to be constituted, so that the human soul as it is known does not introduce into it a break or an anomaly, but permits the thoroughgoing order and relatedness of all elements to remain intact?

In the case of Schopenhauer, this same intention leads into a dimension which is not very different. When he interprets all existence as the appearance of a "will," it would be a childish anthropomorphization of the world if he were seeing in nature the will that appears in us as an empirical fact of consciousness. On the contrary, he takes first of all what underlies the phenomena of the will in our consciousness, the metaphysical nucleus of all things, which is the same for non-psychic phenomena as for psychic ones, except that it shines through more clearly and is more easily designated in the latter. The will that we recognize in ourselves remains for Schopenhauer, too, a particular fact of psychological experience. But it is only in this experience that the metaphysical reality—the restless becoming and striving, the dark fate of being driven without end, the infinite changing—acquires its most unequivocal symbol and is felt most immediately by us. This absolute reality stands beyond the relativity of our own appearances, as well as of any other appearance. It is so far from being drawn into human forms that these, together with all other phenomena, are built on the metaphysical foundation. Whether such thoughts are correct in their particular content, whether they are logically necessary or even possible, remains quite undecided. We are here concerned only with what holds in principle: The reaction of the philosophical mind to the total impression made by being does not signify, either in fact or in intention, that the world is drawn into the individual and anthropomorphized in his image. On the contrary, it means that a typical image of the world comes to be into which the individual is drawn. A whole is shaped in the way in which this type of man simply must conceive it, so that he, who knows himself to be an indubitable reality, can be adjoined to the unity of this whole and understood in it.

With this last consideration, the principle that underlies the form of the philosophical image of the world is designated: What matters is the achievement of the *unity* that the mind needs in the face of the immeasurable multiplicity, the variegated and unreconciled shreds, of the world. Philosophical thought states what it considers the totality of the world to be under various categories. It may believe that it recognizes the world's sense or its substance, its value or its purpose. Under whatever categories, the assertion always fulfills, in addition, formal requirements. It offers a point of unity in all the confusions and oppositions of the phenomenal world, a place where the aloofness of the realities gives way to their kinship. For even if the mutual animosity of things were to become a metaphysical interpretation of the world, it would be presented as the uniform character of the whole, realized in the mutual relations of all the elements.

The fact that the multiplicity of the world becomes a mental unity is precisely what indicates that philosophy is a reaction of psyches to the totality of being. For the psyche knows itself as a unity; in it—and at first *only* in it—the rays of existence intersect, as it were, at one point. Everything that consciousness finds as something external to it, as objective elements of being, is condemned to an irreducible separateness which takes the form of the spatial or temporal succession of particular representations or of their logical separation. But because of the fact that all things come together in consciousness, they achieve an otherwise unattainable unity. For instance, in the expression "to live is to suffer" both concepts unite into one meaning. That meaning is found in neither of the two, not even *pro rata*. From the complete interpenetration of the two concepts a unified structure results. No analogy can be found for it anywhere in the conditions of space or time. Such unification is an absolutely unique ability of the mind; indeed, its true constitutive essence is the carrying out of this unification. Subject and predicate penetrate each other in a judgment which has its place only in the mind, resulting in a unity that things in space could never attain, or even approach or hint at. For each thing in space occupies a separate place which can be changed but never lost. Because of this, the unification of the world is the truly philosophical act, an act which expresses the fact that here the psyche responds to the impression of the totality of being. But if this totality is to affect the psyche and really enter into it, then the psyche must impart to this totality its own form, and must attempt to grasp the diversity of its content in one concept, one meaning, one value.

The peculiar way in which the concept of truth which is inherent in the fundamental essence of philosophy is detached from the factual content of its assertions has been exhibited. This detachment results from the fact that philosophical assertions express not the general, objective image of the world but the relation which exists between typical individual mentalities and the world. This being so, the peculiarity of this concept of truth can be recognized once more in the image which came to be in this way. This image, as a consequence of its origin, takes the form of the unification of the totality. It assumes this form by means of a biased selection of one element from the totality, which is then enthroned absolutely. In no way except by paying the price of such one-sidedness can our intellect bring about a total unity. To see the whole as a unity, while giving equal consideration to each facet and direction of reality and to each possible interpretation, would require the power of a divine mind. This, then, is the reason behind one of the distinctive characteristics of philosophic "truth": A proposition which belongs to the sphere of philosophy and which is held at that level of abstraction can be held and experienced as an entirely conclusive truth, but it cannot be applied to all the particulars to which, as a general assertion, it should really relate. The most profound thoughts of philosophy, which claim to be valid for the sum total of phenomena and which seem to achieve their profundity because of this validity, are the very ones which become inadequate, meager, and contradictory as soon as their validity is tested in relation to particular phenomena and problems.

Perhaps the reason for this lies in that deep contradiction with which our kind of mentality is confronted in any philosophical effort: Our mentality demands absolute generality and uniformity, but it can realize this only in a content which is one-sided and designated individually. Often enough, general ideas are found among philosophical ideas. These general ideas, however, are not generalizations of particulars; for when they descend from their heights, they lose the validity which we attribute to them as long as they remain in their own sphere. In that sphere they are measured by the criteria of that sphere and not by the criteria of particular experience. This is such a remarkable relation, one which is so contradictory to the logical representation of the universal and the particular, of the super-individual unity and individual reality to which it refers, that it can be legitimized only by its inclusion within a wide range of related phenomena.

Let us suppose that in some, or perhaps all, fields there is some elementary material, some fundamental and ultimate phenomena, which can be reached by our objective sense. In such a case, if we take our stand at one of the points which are removed at a certain distance from these phenomena, we obtain an image of them which is different from the image of these phenomena looked at from another distance, an image which is obedient to other norms, and displays different relations within itself and to all other images. And if one were to add a part of the image seen from the second distance to the image seen from the first distance, the first image would be falsified and rendered meaningless, and the reverse is also true. The optical representation of a house at a distance of thirty meters is completely ordered, uniform, and comprehensible. However, if one were suddenly to introduce into this picture a segment of the representation that would be received if the same house were seen from a distance of three meters (which in itself is just as correct and meaningful), then the resulting representation would be quite incomprehensible and contradictory.

All the mental structures in which we assemble the data of things are obtained according to the norm of this simple relation. Our painting, for example, is bound to a specific acuteness of vision. We form images of spatial objects only from those distances at which we are placed by practical life, which is itself determined by our organization, so that we speak of "seeing" them only in the case of distances that differ relatively little. But if we had the acuteness of vision of the eagle, we should need an entirely different art; and if we imagined a specimen of this art next to our own, we should designate it as "false," even though it would perhaps be much more "accurate" and much closer to the ultimate, objective, constitutive parts of things.

The same thing is true of the figurative sense of "distance" in art. The various elements of life which flow together in a lyric poem have, from the point of view of empirical existence, an exactitude of outline, a richness of relations to all sorts of other things, and an intelligible coherence. All these features are completely transformed just as soon as we assume toward them the distance of lyric art. Each of these two measures of the accuracy of inner images yields a coherent, total representation. This is the reason why it is a complete misunderstanding to attack the content of a poem, beyond a very limited degree, with criticism from the standpoint of empirical truth and logical analysis. The laws of artistic truth relate, so to speak, to the outlines of things as they are seen from a much greater distance; they allow, therefore, entirely different relations among them from those which the truth of science or practical experience demands.

The interval at which religion stands is quite different from the preceding one. The believer forsakes his style, as it were, when he wishes to transfer the meanings and expectations, connections and profundities, which are attached to things within the religious sphere, to their concrete images which are seen directly from near at hand. This is the case, for example, when in connection with the banal interests and needs of every day he expects the "help of God." That help has a genuinely religious significance only in the most sublime sense, that is, in reference to the deepest and most general relation to life and destiny. In this sense a philosopher of religion has said, "God does not fill either the spoon or the plate, but only the bowl." Interpreted logically, the content of the spoon surely comes from that of the bowl and would seem therefore to share its qualities directly. Even so, the spoon standpoint is still a different one from the bowl standpoint, and what is true for the former becomes untrue as soon as it is carried over to the images of the latter, images that result from a completely different distance. Thus one should not demand from what is called "the sense of existence" that it make every moment intelligible for us because it holds good not for the hour, nor for the year, but for life—even though life consists of hours and years.

Our mental structure has the following peculiarity: A universal which, it would seem, should be realized in the particular and the proximate is nevertheless not immediately applicable thereto. The universal develops its images and norms according to its distance, but these norms cannot be constructed from those which hold for its "more real" foundation. The same peculiarity also determines the character of metaphysical structures. Such structures do synthesize existence uniformly. Nevertheless, the universality proclaimed by a metaphysical structure is not of such a kind that the synthesized particulars belong to the universal in the same sense as the oak, the pine, and the lime are among the specifications of the concept "tree," in which their common attributes are unified. We are sure of the essential traits of our character as a fixed reality that determines our life; still we find that our particular actions, though directed by this reality, are by no means always in accord with it. By no means do the details of our being always confirm the profound unity of that being in which they seem to be included, and yet they do not mislead us about this unity, which is somehow fixed from the inside. In the same way, we are permeated by the truth of certain ultimate universals and maxims, and we remain so even when the particulars to which they should really be applied seem to evade their legislative activity. I shall cite two examples.

The theme of pantheism runs through the entire development

of philosophy. Again and again there appears the conviction that all the diversity and contrariety of existence do not affect its true essence. The world is not set in opposition to the Divine Being but lives the very life of the Divinity itself—or, conversely, God lives the life of the world. All parts and moments of reality are thereby grasped in a deeper insight, one which penetrates into their substance, and for which they become an undifferentiated unity of essence and value. This thought transcends all particulars and determines their aspect from its point of view. In it, clearly, philosophical form is given to an emotional element that is inherent in every human psyche in greatly varying degrees and manifestations. But in some philosophical minds it has become the sole determinant of the image of the world.

No matter how sincerely one is convinced of the complete unity of things or of their essential identity, one may nevertheless fail in applying this notion to all the particulars of experience. To be sure, Xenophon, one of the first to proclaim the pantheistic doctrine, affirms that "wherever I allow my mind to roam, everything dissolves for me into a unity." Yet, in reality, this thought does not reach down from the lofty level of abstraction, where it is valid, to the level of phenomena. Socrates and the inkwell standing before me, or the German state and a mosquito in the Indian jungles, will scarcely be conceived successfully as being metaphysically one and the same.

Now the objection will certainly be raised that the pantheistic unification is not intended to hold for two arbitrarily chosen things but for *all* things. What corresponds to this universal is the *totality* of particulars, not just any particular by itself. This correspondence is very similar to the way in which the overlapping of two colors of the rainbow yields white light; they are a specific pair, however, not just any two colors chosen arbitrarily. Nonetheless, if it is true that only in the totality of things as such does this divine unity operate freely, then what permeates us is precisely the meaning and the value of that totality. At the same time, we are confronted with the impossibility of applying this meaning and value to the particulars collected in this whole. Because of the fact that our minds are able to conceive the unity in God of *all* things, but not of *particular* things, a difference of distances is fixed. The philosophical universal has its own laws, and is no longer applicable to the particulars that were seen from a different distance, even though as a universal it seemed to include them.

The same is the case with the conviction, quite the opposite of pantheism, that the world about which man is able to say anything at all exists only as his idea. How could consciousness possibly reach out of itself in order to grasp things as they are in and for themselves? All it can ever be filled with is its own content, and whatever it represents can never be produced except by itself, by the process of representation. However convinced of this one may be, it may not be easy, in practice, to have a genuine realization of this purely subjective production, in view of the particular phenomenon which irresistibly obtrudes itself and is absolutely foreign to one's own self. In the sphere of philosophical universals, this reduction of all the existence that there is for us to the producing self has the mark of a logical inevitability or of a self-evident axiom which holds together the totality of our world from a dominating central point. But if we look at the starry heavens and the dreadful might of our destinies, at the swarm of micro-organisms and the fortuitous yet irresistible way in which, hour after hour, life etches its images upon us, the idea that all this is created by the receiving subject itself has something insurmountably paradoxical about it. This thought has, so to speak, a truth of its own that cannot be employed or made conclusive in connection with those particulars of which the world consists when seen from a lesser distance.

The paradox of all great philosophical concepts of the world consists in the fact that they pronounce an absolutely general assertion with which the particular that is *logically* contained in it is at variance. Nevertheless, we cannot deny the assertion a truth value, as we normally do when a would-be universal fails to be verified in the particulars of which it is a generalization. This peculiar kind of philosophical universal is differentiated from that which holds in science, logic, and practical life in the following way: Here the universal is not obtained from particular things, but is an expression concerning the totality of things, an expression of the manner in which each of the great mental types reacts to the impression made by life and the world. We are dealing here, not with a universal derived from things seen one at a time, but with a universal that stems from an individual, mental, yet at the same time typical, reaction to these things. However, this reaction must be objectified intelligibly and by the use of concepts (in contrast to the practice of an artist or a person engaged in religious activity), and this objectification can take place only if a single, one-sided concept is stressed and rendered absolute. In this way, the concept translates the reaction or attitude into the language of objective representations.

Because of this one-sidedness, which nevertheless expresses a basic kind of essence that in principle is open to the whole world, there arises a strange contradiction between the universality of metaphysical assertions and their inability to be realized in the particular. For it seems as if the objective particular, observed from the closest proximity, is always the focus of all sorts of ideas and principles. When we look at an isolated segment of existence, we find in it fragmentary realizations, simultaneous intimations of opposing fundamental concepts. It is one and many, it is action and passion, it is being and becoming, it is somehow absolute and at the same time somehow relative, it shows traces of connection with the creative whole of the cosmos or of the Divinity and of the fact that our human conceiving has bestowed upon it its determinations. In such a close relation to things, their image seems to include all metaphysical realities, undifferentiated or in embryo. Only when we step back do we obtain an image that is dominated by a *single* point of view. But the choice of this point of view inevitably depends on the mental type that is involved. And with equal inevitability, the consequent unified conviction about the constitution of being cannot be applied to the particulars which are viewed at close range. Thus the structure of metaphysical universals is explained: they do not hold for the very particulars of which they seem to be generalizations.

Translated by Rudolph H. Weingartner

1. "Vom Wesen der Philosophie" (1910), *Hauptprobleme der Philosophie* (7th unrevised ed.; Berlin: de Gruyter, 1950). The last paragraph of the chapter is omitted since it serves as a transition to the second chapter. Simmel's long sentences and paragraphs have been broken up wherever it served to clarify his text. Used by permission of Else Simmel, M.D.

THE PROBLEM OF SOCIOLOGY[1]

GEORG SIMMEL

Knowledge of truth is a weapon in the struggle for existence —as much in the struggle with nature as with other men. If it is true that human knowledge originated in practical needs, it is no longer very closely tied to those origins. It is no longer merely a means to action; human knowledge has become an ultimate end in itself. However, even in science, which seems to be autonomous, cognition has not entirely detached itself from practical interest. Nevertheless, science is no longer thought to result merely from a practical interest but rather from an interaction with it; science and practical life are conceived as two equally legitimate spheres. For not only does scientific cognition (as in technology) contribute to the realization of external ends, but practical situations themselves require the insight which is gained from theory. Sometimes new, quite abstract currents of thought do no more than move us to new modes of feeling and willing by formulating questions and developing new intellectual forms.

The science of sociology usually claims to continue and reflect in its theories the actual, practical power gained in the nineteenth century by the masses over the interests of the individual. The sense of importance and the attention which the lower wrested from the higher classes are expressed precisely by the concept "society," the reason being that social distance makes the lower appear to the higher, not as individuals, but as a unified mass. Furthermore, this very distance creates the impression that the two classes are really not connected with each other except that together they constitute a society. As a consequence of this actual shift in power, the fact of classes— whose characteristic is not to be composed of individuals but to form a society—attracted the attention of theorists. It was suddenly discovered that all individual phenomena are determined by innumerable influences stemming from their human environments. This thought even gained retroactive force, so to speak: when compared to present society, past society appeared as the substance within which individual existence matured—as a wave is created by the sea. Only a conception such as this seemed to promise the establishment of terms in which it would be possible to explain the particular forms adopted by individuals. And this conception was reinforced by modern relativism, that is, by the tendency to resolve what is individual and substantial into effects of reciprocity. The individual was merely the point where social forces join; personality, merely the particular manner in which this occurs. To remember that all human actions take place within society and that none of them can stay outside its influence entailed the conclusion that everything which was not science of external nature must be science of society. The science of society appeared as the all-inclusive discipline, covering ethics, history of civilization, aesthetics, demography, political science, and ethnology. Since the subject matters of these disciplines were realized in a social framework, the science of man became the science of society.

This conception of sociology as the science of everything human was supported by the fact that it was a new science. All kinds of problems not adequately treated elsewhere crowded into it—in the beginning, a newly opened territory is always the El Dorado of the homeless and rootless; the unavoidable uncertainty and defenselessness of the boundaries give everybody the right of asylum.

However, if we examine more closely this throwing together of all traditional fields of knowledge, we note that it creates no new field; all it does is to dump all historical, psychological, and normative sciences into one great pot labeled "sociology." All that is gained is a new name. Everything this name designates is already defined in its content and in its relations or is already produced by the traditional branches of study. To be sure, human thought and action occur in society and are determined by it, but this does not make sociology the all-embracing science of society. After all, the subject matters of chemistry, botany, and astronomy are realized only in human consciousness and therefore depend on its structure; but this does not make these disciplines mere contents of psychology.

The basis of this error is a misunderstood but very important fact—the insight that man, in his whole nature and in all his expressions, is determined by living in interaction with other men. And this insight must indeed lead to a new way of thinking in all so-called human studies.[2] It is no longer possible to explain historical facts (in the broadest sense of this term), contents of culture, types of economic systems, and norms of morality, by referring solely to the individual, his intellect, and his interests, and by resorting to metaphysical or magical causes where this fails. For instance, we no longer think we have to choose between the alternative explanations of language, according to which it is either the invention of individuals of genius or God's gift to men; nor must we explain religious phenomena as being either the invention of shrewd priests or direct revelation. We now believe we can understand historical phenomena in terms of interaction and co-action, in terms of the aggregation and sublimation of innumerable individual contributions, in terms of the embodiment of social energies into structures that exist and develop outside the individual. In its relation to the existing sciences, sociology is therefore a new *method,* an instrument of investigation, a new way of getting at the subject matters of all those sciences. It thus presents a parallel to induction, which, introduced as a new principle of investigation, invaded all the sciences, became acclimated (as it were) in each of them, and greatly contributed to the discovery of new solutions for tasks that had already been well defined. But induction is no more a special science—much less an all-embracing one—than sociology. In so far as sociology is based on the facts that man must be understood as a social being and that society is the medium of all historical process, it contains no subject matter not already treated in one of the existing sciences. It only proposes a new *way* for all of them, a method which, because of its very applicability to all problems, does not constitute a science on its own.

What is the particular new subject matter whose study would make sociology an independent and clearly delimited science? Obviously, it is not the discovery of a new, previously unknown object that is required for its legitimation. What we designate as "object" is a complex of characteristics and relations, each of which can be shown to manifest itself in a large number of concrete things and can be made the subject matter of a special science. Every science rests upon an abstraction inasmuch as it considers the totality of some given thing in one of its aspects and from the viewpoint of a particular conception. No one science can grasp this totality as a whole. Confronted by the totality (of one thing or of things generally), every science grows by virtue of a decomposition of this totality into specific qualities and functions, the investigation of which is carried on by a division of labor. This decomposition is possible once a conception has been found that lends itself to the isolation of these qualities and functions and to the methodical ascertainment of their occurrence in concrete things. For instance, the linguistic facts that are now treated by the discipline of comparative linguistics had long existed in phenomena that, moreover, had received scientific study. But the specific science of comparative linguistics originated only with the discovery of the conception under which these facts, previously scattered throughout various linguistic complexes, are unified and recognized as subject to specific laws. Similarly, sociology, as a special science, might find its specific subject matter merely by drawing a new line through facts which are quite well known. Perhaps the only difficulty here is that what has not yet become clear and widely adopted is the conception which allows us to recognize the relevant aspects of these facts as something common to all of them, something which constitutes a methodological and scientific unit. The concepts of politics, economics, culture, and so on, engender such lines of thought in regard to the exceedingly complex facts of historical society (facts which cannot be brought together under any one scientific viewpoint). They do so either by integrating certain parts of these facts into unique historical sequences (and eliminating or reducing other parts) or by grouping together elements which, aside from any considerations of time, exhibit timeless, necessary relations. If, then, we want a sociology as a special science, we need a concept of society which subjects sociohistorical data to a new mode of abstraction and co-ordination that is not dependent on any external relations among them. And this concept must be constructed upon recognition of the fact that certain characteristics of these data (thus far noted only in a variety of miscellaneous connections) actually belong together and therefore constitute the subject matter of one science.

Such a point of view is attained by analyzing the concept of society in a way that may be characterized as distinguishing between its form and its content. We must stress the fact, however, that this distinction is, properly speaking, merely an analogy employed in an effort to find approximate labels for the elements to be distinguished; we must grasp at once the specific significance of the contrast between "form" and "content" without being misled by the connotations of these preliminary terms. I shall begin, therefore, with the broadest conception of society (trying, as far as possible, to avoid quarrels over definitions).

Society exists where a number of individuals enter into interaction.[3] This interaction always arises on the basis of certain drives or for the sake of certain purposes. Erotic, religious, or merely associative impulses; and purposes of defense, attack, play, gain, aid, or instruction—these and countless others cause man to live with other men, to act for them, with them, against them, and thus to correlate his condition with theirs. In brief, he influences and is influenced by them. The significance of these interactions among men lies in the fact that it is because of them that the individuals, in whom these driving impulses and purposes are lodged, form a unity, that is, a society. For unity in the empirical sense of the word is nothing but the interaction of elements. An organic body is a unity because its organs maintain a more intimate exchange of their energies with each other than with any other organism; a state is a unity because its citizens show similar mutual effects. In fact, the whole world could not be called *one* if each of its parts did not somehow influence every other part, or if at any one point the reciprocity of effects, however indirect it may be, were cut off.

This unity, or sociation,[4] may be of very different degrees, according to the kind and the intimacy of the interaction which obtains. Sociation ranges all the way from the momentary getting together for a walk to the founding of a family, from relations maintained "until further notice" to membership in a state, from the temporary aggregation of hotel guests to the intimate bond of a medieval guild. I designate as the content—

the materials, so to speak—of sociation everything that is present in individuals (the immediately concrete loci of all historical reality)—drive, interest, purpose, inclination, psychic state, movement—everything that is present in them in such a way as to engender or mediate effects upon others or to receive such effects. In themselves, these materials which fill life, these motivations which propel it, are not social. Strictly speaking, neither hunger nor love, work nor religiosity, technology nor the functions and results of intelligence, are social. They are factors in sociation only when they transform the mere aggregation of isolated individuals into specific forms of being with and for one another, forms that are subsumed under the general concept of interaction. Sociation is the form (realized in innumerably different ways) in which individuals grow together into a unity and within which their interests are realized. And it is on the basis of their interests—sensuous or ideal, momentary or lasting, conscious or unconscious, causal or teleological—that individuals form such unities.

In any given social phenomenon, content and societal form constitute one reality. A social form severed from all content can no more attain existence than a spatial form can exist without a material whose form it is. Any social phenomenon or process is composed of two elements which in reality are inseparable: on the one hand, an interest, a purpose, or a motive; on the other, a form or mode of interaction among individuals through which, or in the shape of which, that content attains social reality.

It is evident that that which constitutes society in every current sense of the term is identical with the kinds of interaction discussed. A collection of human beings does not become a society because each of them has an objectively determined or subjectively impelling life-content. It becomes a society only when the vitality of these contents attains the form of reciprocal influence; only when one individual has an effect, immediate or mediate, upon another, is mere spatial aggregation or temporal succession transformed into society. If, therefore, there is to be a science whose subject matter is society and nothing else, it must exclusively investigate these interactions, these kinds and forms of sociation. For everything else found within "society" and realized through it and within its framework is not itself society. It is merely a content that develops or is developed by this form of coexistence, and it produces the real phenomenon called "society" in the broader and more customary sense of the term only in conjunction with this form. To separate, by scientific abstraction, these two factors of form and content which are in reality inseparably united; to detach by analysis the forms of interaction or sociation from their contents (through which alone these forms become social forms); and to bring them together systematically under a consistent scientific viewpoint—this seems to me the basis for the only, as well as the entire, possibility of a special science of society as such. Only such a science can actually treat the facts that go under the name of sociohistorical reality upon the plane of the purely social.

Abstractions alone produce science out of the complexity or the unity of reality. Yet however urgently such abstractions may be demanded by the needs of cognition itself, they also require some sort of justification of their relation to the structure of the objective world. For only some functional relation to actuality can save one from sterile inquiries or from the haphazard formulation of scientific concepts. Certainly, naïve naturalism errs in assuming that the given itself contains the analytic or synthetic arrangements through which it becomes the content of a science. Nevertheless, the characteristics of the given are more or less susceptible to such arrangements. An analogy may help here. A portrait fundamentally transforms the natural human appearance, but one face is better suited than another to such a transformation into something radically alien. Remembering this helps us to appraise the greater or lesser appropriateness of various scientific problems and methods. The right to subject sociohistorical phenomena to an analysis in terms of form and content (and to synthesize the forms) rests upon two conditions which must be verified on a factual basis. On the one hand, we must demonstrate that the same form of sociation can be observed in quite dissimilar contents and in connection with quite dissimilar purposes. On the other hand, we must show that the same content is realized in using quite dissimilar forms of sociation as its medium or vehicle. A parallel is found in the fact that the same geometric forms may be observed in the most heterogeneous materials and that the same material occurs in the most heterogeneous spatial forms. Similar relations obtain between logical forms and the material contents of cognition.

Both of these conditions are undeniable facts. We do find that the same form of interaction obtains among individuals in societal groups that are the most unlike imaginable in purpose and significance. Superiority, subordination, competition, division of labor, formation of parties, representation, inner solidarity coupled with exclusiveness toward the outside, and innumerable similar features are found in the state as well as in a religious community, in a band of conspirators as in an economic association, in an art school as in a family. However diverse the interests that give rise to these sociations, the forms in which the interests are realized are identical. On the other hand, the identical interest may take on form in very different sociations. Economic interest is realized both in competition and in the planned organization of producers, in isolation from other groups and in fusion with them. Although the religious contents of life remain identical, at one time they demand an unregulated, at another time a centralized, form of community. The interests upon which the relations between the sexes are based are satisfied by an almost endless variety of family forms. The educational interest may lead to a liberal or to a despotic relation between teacher and pupil, to individualistic interaction between them, or to a more collectivistic type of interaction between the teacher and the totality of his pupils. Hence, not only may the form in which the most widely different contents are realized be identical, but a content too may persist while its medium—the interactions of the individuals—moves in a variety of forms. We see, then, that the analysis in terms of form and content transforms the facts—which in their immediacy present form and content as an indissoluble unity of social life—in such a way as to furnish the legitimation of the sociological problem. This problem demands that the pure forms of sociation be identified, ordered systematically, explained psychologically, and studied from the standpoint of their historical development.

To found sociology on the basis of this problem is to proceed in a manner which is the direct antithesis of that in which the traditional social sciences have been created. For the division of labor among them was determined entirely by differences in content. The study of political economy, of church policy, of the history of pedagogy, of the history of morals, of political science, of theories of sexual life, and so on, have appropriated to themselves the realm of social phenomena. A sociology designed to cover the totality of these phenomena, with all their interpenetrations of form and content, could only result in a summation of these sciences. As long as historical reality is divided by types of content into separate fields of research, it will not be amenable to sociology as a special science. The organization of such a science depends on the detachment of the pure fact of sociation, in all its manifold forms, from its connection with the most diverse contents. Sociology will thus become a special science in the same sense (in spite of all obvious differences in method and result) as epistemology. Epistemology abstracts the categories or functions of cognition as such from the multitude of cognitions of individual objects. There are sciences whose special character consists in the fact that their subject matter, along with the subject matters of other sciences, are covered by a more general discipline (like classical philology, the study of German literature, optics, and acoustics). Sociology is not this type of science. Its special character derives from the circumstance that it brings a whole realm of objects under a specific viewpoint. Not its subject matter but its approach—the specific abstraction which it makes—differentiates it from the other sociohistorical sciences.

The concept "society" has two denotations which scientific treatment must keep strictly distinct. The first designates society as the complex of societalized individuals, the societally formed human material as it has been shaped by the totality of historical reality. The second denotes society as the sum of those forms of relationship by virtue of which individuals are transformed into "society" in the first sense of the term. In a parallel way, we use the word "sphere," first to designate material of a certain form, and second to designate (in mathematics) the shape or form by virtue of which material is transformed into a "sphere" in the first sense. When using "society" in the first sense, the social sciences indicate that their subject matter includes everything that occurs in and with society. But when using the term in the second sense, social science indicates that its subject matter is the forces, relations, and forms through which human beings become sociated. Studied separately, these forces, relations, and forms show society in the strictest sense of the term. And this, of course, is not altered by the fact that the content of sociation (that is, the special modifications of its material purpose and interest) often if not always determines its specific form.

It would be a grave mistake to object here that all forms of sociation—hierarchies, corporations, competitions, marriage, friendship, societal customs, monocracy, and polycracy—are merely constellations occurring in already existing societies. It would be erroneous, that is, to argue that if a society were not already present, preconditions and opportunities for such forms would be lacking. This fallacious notion arises from the fact that, in every society known to us, a great number of such forms of combination—that is, of sociation—are operative, and if one of them disappeared, "society" would still be left intact. Because of this, it may seem as if each form were added to a society already completely constituted, or as if each of them emerged within such a society. But if we imagine *all* of these forms eliminated, we can see that we would have no society left. Only when interactions (brought forth as they are by certain motives and interests) come into being does society emerge. To be sure, the history and the laws of the development of total phenomena are the business of social science in the wider sense of this term. But inasmuch as social science has already split up into special branches—the social sciences—there remains for a sociology in the strict sense (in a sense, that is, which presents it with a definite task) nothing but the treatment of the forms abstracted. These forms do not *make for* sociation; they *are* sociation. "Society," then, in the sense that is of any use to sociology, is either the abstract general concept under which all these forms are subsumed (that is, the genus of which they are the species), or else it is their sum as it operates at one given time.

This conception of society implies a further proposition: A given number of individuals may be a society to a greater or a smaller degree. With each formation of parties, with each joining for common tasks or in a common feeling or way of thinking, with each articulation of the distribution of positions of submission and domination, with each common meal, with each self-adornment for others—with every growth of new synthesizing phenomena such as these, the same group becomes "more society" than it was before. There is no such thing as society "as such"; that is, there is no society in the sense that it is the condition for the emergence of all these particular phenomena. For there is no such thing as interaction "as such"—there are only specific kinds of interaction. And it is with their emergence that society too emerges, for they are neither the cause nor the consequence of society but are, themselves, society. The fact that an extraordinary multitude and variety of interactions operate at any one moment has given a seemingly autonomous historical reality to the general concept of society. Perhaps it is this hypostatization of a mere abstraction that is the reason for the peculiar vagueness and uncertainty involved in the concept of society and in the customary treatises in general sociology. We are here reminded of the fact that not much headway was made in formulating a concept of "life" as long as it was conceived of as an immediately real and homogeneous phenomenon. The science of life did not establish itself on a firm basis until it investigated specific processes within organisms—processes whose sum or web life is; not until, in other words, it recognized that life consists of these particular processes.

Only if we follow the conception here outlined can we grasp what in "society" really *is* society. Similarly, it is only geometry that determines what the spatiality of things in space really is. Sociology, the discipline that deals with the purely social aspects of man (who, of course, can be an object of scientific inquiry in innumerable other respects), is related to the other special sciences of man as geometry is related to the physicochemical sciences. Geometry studies the forms through which any material becomes an empirical body, and these forms as such exist, of course, in abstraction only, precisely like the forms of sociation. Both geometry and sociology leave to other sciences the investigation of the contents realized in the forms, that is, the total phenomena whose forms they explore.

It is hardly necessary to point out that this analogy with geometry does not go beyond the clarification of the fundamental problem of sociology. It was only in attempting this clarification that we made use of this analogy. Above all, geometry has the advantage of having at its disposal extremely simple structures into which it can resolve the more complicated figures. Geometry can construe the whole range of possible formations from a relatively few fundamental definitions. Not even a remotely similar resolution into simple elements is to be hoped for in the foreseeable future as regards the forms of sociation. Sociological forms, if they are to be even approximately definite, can apply only to a limited range of phenomena. Even if we say, for instance, that superordination and subordination are forms found in almost every human sociation, we gain very little from this general knowledge. What is needed is the study of specific kinds of superordination and subordination, and of the specific forms in which they are realized. Through such a study, of course, these forms would lose in applicability what they would gain in definiteness.

In our day, we are used to asking of every science whether it is devoted to the discovery of timelessly valid laws or to the presentation and conceptualization of real, unique historical processes. Generally, this alternative ignores innumerable intermediate phenomena dealt with in the actual practice of science. It is irrelevant to our conception of the problem of sociology because this conception renders a choice between the two answers unnecessary. For, on the one hand, in sociology the object abstracted from reality may be examined in regard to laws entirely inhering in the objective nature of the elements. These laws must be sharply distinguished from any spatiotemporal realization; they are valid whether the historical actualities enforce them once or a thousand times. On the other hand, the forms of sociation may be examined, with equal validity, in regard to their occurrence at specific places and at specific times, and in regard to their historical development in specific groups. In this latter case, ascertaining them would be in the service of history, so to speak; in the former case, it would provide material for the induction of timeless uniformities. About competition, for instance, we learn something from a great many fields—political science, economics, history of religion, history of art, and so on. The point is to ascertain from all the facts what competition is as a pure form of human behavior; under what circumstances it emerges and develops; how it is modified by the particular character of its object; by what contemporaneous formal and material features of a society it is increased or reduced; and how competition between individuals differs from that between groups. In short, we must ascertain what competition is as a form of relation among individuals. This form may involve all sorts of contents. But in spite of the great variety of these contents, the form maintains its own identity and proves that it belongs to a sphere which is governed by its own laws and which may legitimately be abstracted from other spheres or from total reality. What we are suggesting, in brief, is that similar elements be singled out of the complex phenomena so as to secure a cross-section, whereby dissimilar elements—in our case the contents—reciprocally paralyze each other, as it were.

We have to proceed in this fashion with respect to all the great situations and interactions that form society—the formation of parties; imitation; the formation of classes and circles; secondary subdivisions; the embodiment of types of social interaction in special structures of an objective, personal, or ideal nature; the growth and the role of hierarchies; the representation of groups by individuals; the bearing of common hostility on the inner solidarity of the group. In addition to such major problems, there are others which no less regularly involve the form of the group and which are either more specialized or more complex than these. Among the more specialized questions, there are those such as the significance of the non-partisan, the role of the poor as organic members of society, the numerical determination of group elements, and the phenomena of *primus inter pares* and *tertius gaudens*. Among more complex processes are the intersection of various social circles in the individual; the special significance of the secret for the formation of groups; the modification of the character of groups by a membership composed of individuals who belong together geographically, or by the addition of elements who do not; and innumerable other processes.

In this whole discussion, as I have already indicated, I waive the question of whether there ever occurs an *absolute* identity of forms along with a difference in content. The *approximate* identity that forms exhibit under materially dissimilar circumstances (and vice versa) is enough to conceive, in principle, of an affirmative answer to this question. The fact that absolute identity is not actually realized shows the difference between historical-psychological and geometrical phenomena. Historical-psychological processes, in their fluctuations and complexities, can never be completely rationalized. Geometry, by contrast, does have the power to isolate absolutely pure forms out of their material realizations. It should always be remembered that this identity of the kinds of interaction in the face of the simultaneously existing variety of human or objective material (and vice versa) is nothing primarily but a device to make and legitimate the scientific discrimination between form and content in the treatment of empirical phenomena. Methodologically speaking, this discrimination would be required even if the actual constellations did not call for the inductive procedure of crystallizing the like out of the unlike. In the same way, the geometrical abstraction of the spatial form of a body would be justified even if a body with such a particular form occurred only once empirically.

It cannot be denied, however, that this discussion suggests a difficulty in methodology. For instance, toward the end of the Middle Ages, extended trade relations forced certain guild masters to employ apprentices and to adopt new ways of obtaining materials and attracting customers. All of this was inconsistent with traditional guild principles, according to which every master was to have the same living as every other. Through these innovations, every master sought to place himself outside this traditional narrow unity. Now, what about the purely sociological form which is abstracted from the special content of this whole process? The process seems to indicate that the expansion of the circle with which the individual is connected through his actions is accompanied by a greater articulation of individuality, an expansion of the freedom of the individual, and a greater differentiation of the members of the circle. Yet, as far as I can see, there is no sure method of distilling this sociological significance out of our complex fact which is, after all, real only along with all its contents. In other words, there is no sure method for answering the question of what purely sociological configurations and what specific interactions of individuals (irrespective of the interests and impulses residing in the individual, and of purely objective conditions) are involved in the historical process. On the contrary, all this can be interpreted in more than one way, and, furthermore, the historical facts that attest to the reality of the specific sociological forms must be presented in their material totality. In brief, there is no means of teaching and, under certain conditions, even of performing, the analysis of form and content into sociological elements. The case is comparable to the proof of a geometrical theorem by means of figures drawn in the unavoidably accidental and crude way of all drawings. The mathematician can feel quite safe in assuming that, in spite of the imperfect drawing, the concept of the ideal geometrical figure is known and understood, and that it is regarded as the essential significance of the chalk or ink marks. The sociologist, however, may not make the corresponding assumption; the isolation of truly pure sociation out of the complex total phenomenon cannot be forced by logical means.

Here we must take upon ourselves the odium of talking about intuitive procedures (however far these are removed from speculative, metaphysical intuition). We admit that we are discussing a particular viewpoint that helps to make the distinction between form and content. This viewpoint, for the time being, can be conveyed only by means of examples. Only much later may it be possible to grasp it by methods that are fully conceptualized and are sure guides to research. The difficulty is increased by two factors. Not only is there no perfectly clear technique for applying the fundamental sociological concept itself (that is, the concept of sociation), but, in addition, where this concept can be effectively applied, there are still many elements in the phenomena to be studied whose subsumption under the concept of form and content remains arbitrary. There will be contrary opinions, for instance, concerning the extent to which the phenomenon of the poor is a matter of form or content; the extent to which it is a result of formal relations within the group, a result which is determined by general currents and shifts that are the necessary outcome of contacts among human beings; or the extent to which poverty is to be regarded as a merely material characteristic of certain individuals, a characteristic that must be studied exclusively from the viewpoint of economic interests (that is, as regards its content).

On the whole, historical phenomena may be examined from three fundamental viewpoints. First, one may focus one's attention upon individual existences—these are the true bearers of conditions. Second, one may concentrate on the formal types of interaction. To be sure, these types too are exhibited only by individuals, but from this second viewpoint they are examined not with reference to these individuals but with reference to their own complexes, convergences, and reciprocal relations. Third, one may study the contents of conditions and events which can be formulated in concepts. Here the inquiry is no longer into the bearers of conditions or into the interrelations of the bearers but into the purely objective significance of the conditions and events themselves—into economics, technology, art, science, legal norms, and the products of the life of the emotions. These three viewpoints constantly overlap. The methodological necessity of keeping them apart is always threatened both by the difficulty of finding for each of them an avenue of investigation independent of the others, and by the longing for an all-embracing picture of reality which would comprehend all such viewpoints. It will never be possible in all cases to determine to what extent one of them overlaps the other—which one justifies another and by which one it is justified in turn. Consequently, although questions are posed with methodological clarity and precision, it will be impossible to avoid ambiguity. The treatment of a particular problem will appear to belong now in one category, now in another; and even within its proper category, it will not always be possible to prevent its receiving treatment characteristic of another viewpoint.

For the rest, I hope that the methodology of the sociology here presented will emerge more distinctly, perhaps even more clearly, from the exposition of its particular problems than from the present abstract outline. After all, the situation is not too rare in intellectual matters—and when it comes to the most general and the most profound problems, it is as a matter of fact the rule—that what by an inevitable metaphor must be called "the foundation" is less secure than the superstructure erected upon it. Scientific practice, especially when it works in new areas, cannot do without a certain measure of groundwork which is intuitional. Only later are students able to become fully conscious of the motives and norms of this primary stage and to elucidate it conceptually. Certainly, scientific labor must never be satisfied solely by such vague, intuitive procedures. They are applicable to monographic studies only. However, one would condemn science to sterility if before assuming new tasks one made a completely formulated methodology the condition for taking the first step.[5]

Certain portions of the investigations offered here of the problem area that is marked off by isolating the forms of societalized interaction from the totality of the social phenomenon, lie—even quantitatively, so to speak—outside the province of the tasks commonly considered the business of sociology. For once one inquires into the mutual influences that play back and forth between individuals and whose sum results in society, one immediately comes upon a whole series, even a whole world, as it were, of forms of relation, the study of which has thus far either not been included in social science at all or has been included without realizing the fundamental and vital significance of the forms. On the whole, sociology has confined itself to those social phenomena in which interactional forces already present themselves in isolation from their individual bearers, or, at least, in the form of conceptual unities. Great organs and systems like states, labor unions, priesthoods, family forms, economic systems, military organizations, guilds, communities, class formations, and industrial divisions of labor, seem to constitute society and therefore appear to be the subject matter of the science of society. It is obvious that the greater, the more significant, and the more dominant a sector of social interest and a direction of social action are, the more readily will they make for this exaltation of the immediate interindividual life.

This limitation of the subject matter of sociology must be qualified in two ways. In addition to the phenomena which are widely visible and very imposing in their magnitude and external importance, there are an immeasurable number of minor forms of relation and of kinds of interaction among men. Although each of these taken separately may appear trivial, it is one of a mass that can scarcely be estimated. By inserting themselves between the comprehensive, official, so to speak, social formations, it is really these minor forms that bring about society as we know it. To confine ourselves to the major social formations is to work in a way which is analogous to that of the older anatomy which limited its study to the major, definitely circumscribed organs such as heart, liver, lungs, and stomach, and neglected the innumerable, unnamed or unknown tissues without which these more obvious organs could never make up a living body. On the basis of these major formations—which constitute the traditional subject matter of social science—it would be entirely impossible to piece together the real life of society as we encounter it in our experience. Without the interspersed effects of innumerable minor systheses (to whose study the following investigations are largely devoted), society would break up into a multitude of discontinuous systems. What renders the scientific determination of such obscure social forms difficult is the very thing that makes them eminently important for the deeper understanding of society—the fact that as a rule they are not yet fixated as rigid, superindividual structures, but exhibit society, as it were, *statu nascendi.* They do so not, of course, in the sense that they are the very first beginnings—these are historically untraceable—but in the sense that they originate each day and each hour. Sociation among men continuously emerges and ceases and emerges again; eternal flux and pulsation link individuals even where they do not rise to form organizations as such.

We are dealing here with microscopic-molecular processes within human material, so to speak. These processes are the actual occurrences that are concatenated or hypostatized into those macrocosmic, solid units and systems. That people look at one another and are jealous of one another; that they exchange letters or have dinner together; that apart from all tangible interests they strike one another as pleasant or unpleasant; that gratitude for altruistic acts makes for inseparable union; that one asks another to point out a certain street; that people dress and adorn themselves for each other—these are a few casually chosen illustrations from the whole range of relations that play between one person and another. They may be momentary or permanent, conscious or unconscious, ephemeral or of grave consequence, but they incessantly tie men together. At each moment such threads are spun, dropped, taken up again, displaced by others, interwoven with others. These interactions among the atoms of society are accessible only to psychological microscopy, as it were. They explain all the toughness and elasticity, all the colorfulness and consistency of social life, which is so striking and yet so mysterious.

To social simultaneity must be applied that principle which examines the innumerable and minute effects that has been so successfully applied in the sciences of sequence—geology, biological evolution, history. Immeasurably small steps constitute the structure of historical unity; equally unpretentious interactions between persons constitute the structure of societal unity. What incessantly occurs in the form of physical and psychical contacts, of reciprocal stimulations of joy and sorrow, of talk and silence, of common and conflicting interests—only this makes for the wonderful indissolubility of society, the fluctuation of its life, which constantly attains, loses, and shifts the equilibrium of its elements. Perhaps this sort of insight will do for social science what the beginnings of microscopy did for the science of organic life. Research, prior to the use of the microscope, was confined to the large, clearly articulated organs of the body whose differences in form and function are discerned without much difficulty. With the microscope it saw the life process in its smallest bearers, the cells, and it discovered the identity of this process with the innumerable and incessant interactions among the cells. Only by the study of the destruction of cells, their adhesion to one another, and their assimilation and chemical modification of each other are we gradually enabled to understand how the body develops and maintains and changes its form. If we did not know that these innumerable processes, which obtain among the most minute elements and which are merely put together, as it were, by the microscopic structures, are fundamental to life, we should not know that it is in the major organs that these basic life-bearers are synthesized as specific macrocosmic structures and functions.

However, we are not discussing any sociological or metaphysical analogy between the reality of society and that of the organism. We are merely pointing out an analogy in method and suggesting a further development of it. We want to discover trifling threads, the minima of relations among individuals, the continuous occurrence of which establishes and sustains all major structures that have become objectified and that offer the material for history proper. These quite primary processes, which form society out of the immediate, individual material—and not only the higher and more complex processes and structures—must be subjected to formal scrutiny. The specific interactions which appear in the perspective suggested here (a perspective not quite in line with traditional social theory) must be examined as society-building forms, as parts of sociation in general. In fact, the more these seemingly insignificant types of relations have been neglected by established sociology, the more appropriate will it be to study them thoroughly.

This turn in the discussion seems to make the following investigations into chapters in psychology or, at best, in social psychology, rather than in sociology. Certainly, there is no doubt that all societal processes and instincts have their seat in minds and that sociation is, as a consequence, a psychical phenomenon. In the world of bodies, not even an analogy to the fundamental fact of sociation exists, to the fact, that is, that a plurality of elements becomes a unity. In the world of bodies everything remains fixed in its unbridgeable separation in space. Whatever external occurences we might designate as societal would be a puppet show, no more understandable and significant than the merging of clouds or the entanglements of tree branches, if we did not, as a matter of course, recognize psychic motivations—feelings, thoughts, and needs—and recognized them not merely as bearers of those external relations but also as their essence, as what really and solely interests us. An understanding of the cause of any social event would be possible if the event could be deduced wholly from psychological propositions and from the development of events according to "psychological laws" (however problematical such a notion is to us). Nor is there any doubt that the aspects of the sociohistorical life that we can understand are nothing but psychic concatenations which we reconstruct by means of an instinctive or methodical psychology. In this way, we make these aspects plausible; we get the feeling that the development under study is psychologically necessary.

To this extent, any history or description of a social situation is an exercise of psychological knowledge. But it is of extreme methodological relevance—even of decisive importance—to the principles of human studies in general to note that the scientific treatment of psychic data is not thereby automatically psychological. Even where we constantly use psychological rules and knowledge, even where the explanation of every single fact is possible only psychologically (as is true in sociology), the sense and intent of our activities do not have to be psychological. They do not have to aim, that is, at an understanding of the law of the psychic process itself (which, to be sure, has its content), but can aim rather at this content and its configurations. There is only a difference in degree between the studies of man and the sciences of external nature. After all, the natural sciences too, inasmuch as they are phenomena of the intellectual life, have their locus in the mind. The discovery of every astronomical or chemical truth, as well as the rethinking of each of them, is an event occurring in consciousness, an event which a perfect psychology could deduce without residue from psychical conditions and developments alone. The procedure followed by the natural sciences in choosing the contents and interrelations of psychological processes—rather than the processes themselves—for their subject matter is similar to the procedure which determines the significance of a painting from its aesthetic relevance and from its place in the history of art, rather than from the physical oscillations which produce its colors and which constitute and carry its whole, actual existence. There is always one reality and we cannot grasp it scientifically in its immediacy and wholeness but must consider it from a number of different viewpoints and thereby make it into a plurality of mutually independent scientific subject matters. This applies, too, to those psychological phenomena whose contents fail to combine into an autonomous spatial world and which are not strikingly set apart from their psychic reality. Language, for instance, is certainly constructed out of psychological forces and for psychological purposes. But its forms and laws are treated by the science of linguistics with complete neglect of the realization (a realization which alone is given) that this is the object; they are treated exclusively through the presentation and analysis of the construction of the content and the forms that result from it.

The facts of sociation offer a similar picture. That people influence one another—that an individual does something, suffers something, shows his existence or his development because there are others who express themselves, act, or feel—is, of course, a psychological phenomenon. And the only way to grasp the historical emergence of each particular instance of this general phenomenon is to re-create it psychologically, to construct plausible psychological series, to interpret the externally observable by means of psychological categories. Yet from the particular scientific viewpoint conceived by the notion of sociation, this psychological phenomenon as such may be entirely ignored, and attention may be focused rather upon tracing, analyzing, and connecting its contents. Suppose, for example, that it is noted that the relation of a stronger to a weaker individual, which has the form of *primus inter pares,* tends to lead to a possession of absolute power by the stronger party and a gradual elimination of any elements of equality. This, in terms of historical reality, is certainly a psychological process. Yet from the sociological viewpoint, we are interested only in such questions as: How do the various phases of superordination and subordination follow one another? To what extent is superordination in a given relation compatible with co-ordination in other relations? How much superordination is required in the initial phase of the relation to destroy co-ordination completely? Has combination or co-operation a greater chance to occur in an earlier or in a later stage of such a development? Or, as a further example, let us suppose it is noted that those hostilities are the bitterest that arise on the basis of a previous and somehow still felt communion or solidarity (hatred between blood relatives has been called the most burning hatred). As an occurrence, this can only be understood, or even described, psychologically. However, looking at this phenomenon as a sociological formation, we are not interested in the psychological processes that occur in each of the two individuals but in their subsumption under the categories of union and discord. We are interested in such problems as: Up to what point can the relation between two individuals or parties contain hostility and solidarity before depriving the relation of the character of solidarity or giving it that of hostility? What sort of solidarity—that which arises from remembered communion or that which is based on inextinguishable instinct—furnishes the means for more cruel, more profoundly wounding injury than is ever possible when the original relation was one of relatively great distance? In brief, how is our observation to be presented as the realization of forms of relation between people—what specific combination of social categories does it present? This is the point, and it is so in spite of the fact that the concrete description of the process, or the description of it as a typical process, can be nothing but psychological. Returning to an earlier illustration, we may (ignoring all differences) compare the procedure of sociology with the performance of a geometrical deduction using a figure drawn on a blackboard. All that is given and seen here is the physically produced chalk marks, but it is not in them that we are interested but in their significance from the viewpoint of geometry, which has nothing whatever to do with that physical figure as a deposit of chalk particles. (On the other hand, this figure, precisely as a physical structure, may be brought under scientific categories; its physiological genesis, its chemical composition, or its optical impression may become the object of special investigations.)

In this sense, then, the givens of sociology are psychological processes whose immediate reality presents itself first of all under psychological categories. But these psychological categories, although indispensable for the description of the facts, remain outside the purpose of sociological investigation. It is to this end that we direct our study to the objective reality of sociation, a reality which, to be sure, is embodied in psychic processes and can often be described only by means of them. Similarly, a drama, from beginning to end, contains only psychological processes and can be understood only psychologically; but its purpose is not to study psychological cognitions but to examine the syntheses which result when the contents of the psychic processes are considered from the viewpoints of tragedy and artistic form, or as symbolic of certain aspects of life.[6]

The theory of sociation, abstracted from all the social sciences which are determined by a special content of societal life, appears to be the only basis for a science that is entitled to the unqualified name of "science of society." Yet, the important point, of course, is not the naming but the discovery of that new complex of specific problems. As long as the quarrel about what sociology really is only concerns the assignment of a name to problem areas that already exist and already receive scientific treatment, the quarrel seems entirely irrelevant. If, on the other hand, the label "sociology" is selected for a collection of tasks which is claimed to cover the idea of sociology completely and exclusively, then this claim must justify itself vis-à-vis still another problem area. For this problem area, no less than sociology, undeniably seeks to make valid statements about society as such and in its entirety, far beyond any pretension on the part of any social science that is determined by considerations of content.

Like every other exact science which aims at the immediate understanding of the given, social science, too, is surrounded by two philosophical areas. One of these covers the conditions, the fundamental concepts, and the presuppositions of concrete research that cannot be taken care of in research itself because it is based upon them. In the other area, research is carried to completions, ordered through systematic connections, and put in relation to questions and concepts which have no place within experience and immediately objective knowledge. The former is the epistemology; the latter, the metaphysics of the particular discipline. Properly speaking, metaphysics involves two problems. Yet actual practice proceeds as if they were undifferentiated—and rightly so. In the first place, dissatisfaction with the fragmentary character of particular cognitions and the rapid exhaustion of what can be objectively ascertained and demonstrated leads to the supplementation of these imperfections by means of speculation. This very same means satisfies the parallel need for overcoming the disconnection and inner heterogeneity of individual fragments by the unity of a total picture. In the second place, there exists, along with this first function of metaphysics which is concerned with the degree of cognition, an additional function which aims at another dimension of existence, the dimension that contains the metaphysical significance of the contents of existence. This dimension is called meaning or purpose and is characterized as the absolute substance underlying the relative phenomena, as value or religious significance.

The attitude that responds to the recognition of the metaphysical area sketched results in such questions as these regarding society: Is society the purpose of human existence or a means for the individual? Or is it not a means for the individual but, on the contrary, a hindrance? Does the value of society lie in the functions of social life itself, in the development of an objective mind, or in the ethical qualities it evokes in the individual? Do the typical stages in the development of societies reveal a cosmic analogy, so that man's social relations must be subsumed under a general form or rhythm which cannot itself be ascertained but is the basis of all phenomena and even determines the root forces of material facts? And can speaking of a metaphysical-religious significance of collectivities be justified or must such a significance be reserved for individuals only?

These and countless similar questions do not seem to me to possess that categorial autonomy or that unique relation between subject matter and method which would enable them to ground sociology as a new science, co-ordinate with extant sciences. For all these are philosophical questions, and the fact that they deal with society as their object merely indicates the application of an already existing type of cognition to a new field. Aside from the question of whether or not philosophy is a science, the philosophy of society certainly has no right to escape the advantages or disadvantages that result from its belonging to philosophy in general by constituting itself a special science of sociology.

The same is true in regard to the type of philosophical problems which do not, as the former do, presuppose society, but which rather inquire into the very presuppositions of society. They do not do so in the historical sense, that is, in an effort to describe the rise of a given concrete society, or the physical or anthropological conditions surrounding the rise of society in general. Nor do they study the particular drives or motives which move the individual, as he comes into contact with other individuals, to engage in the interactions whose types are described by sociology. Rather the question is this: If there are such individuals, what are the conditions for their consciousness that they are social beings? Society is not yet given with the individuals as such—and in the forms of interaction society is already real. What, then, are the intrinsic and fundamental conditions on the basis of which individuals, who are equipped with such drives, produce society at all? What is the a priori condition which makes possible and which determines the empirical structure of the individual in so far as he is a social being? We do not ask merely: How is it possible that there are the empirically developing, particular formations which are brought together under the general concept of "society"? We ask beyond this: How is society as such possible, as an objective form of subjective minds?

Translated by Kurt H. Wolff

1. "Das Problem der Soziologie" (Chap. i), *Soziologie. Untersuchungen über die Formen der Vergesellschaftung* ([1908] 3rd ed.; Munich and Leipzig: Duncker und Humblot, 1923), pp. 1-21. Used by permission of Hans Broermann of Duncker und Humblot.—TR.

2. *Geisteswissenschaften.* This translation of the term is Hodges' coinage. Cf. H. A. Hodges, *Wilhelm Dilthey: An Introduction* (New York: Oxford University Press, 1944), esp. p. 157.—TR.

3. *Wechselwirkung.* On the choice of "interaction" as the translation of this, one of Simmel's key terms, cf. Kurt H. Wolff (ed.), *The Sociology of Georg Simmel* (Glencoe, Ill.: Free Press of Glencoe, Illinois, 1950), p. lxiv. —TR.

4. *Vergesellschaftung.* For a discussion of the translation of this even more important term, see *ibid.*, p. lxiii.—TR.

5. If we compare the infinite complexity of social life with the initial crudeness that the concepts and methods employed to master this complexity are only now beginning to leave behind, we realize that it would be sheer megalomania to expect, at this juncture, complete clarity in the posing of questions and absolute correctness in answering them. It seems to me more dignified to admit this from the start (since by so doing a decisive first step can at least be taken) than to pretend to be definitive and to jeopardize thereby the significance of our pioneering efforts. In other words, the chapters of this volume are intended as examples (methodologically speaking) and mere fragments (as far as their content is concerned) of what I hold to be the science of society. In both respects it seems indicated that themes be chosen that are as heterogeneous as possible and

that the most general and the most specific be mixed. The less the present offering can be rounded out into a systematic whole and the further apart its elements are, the more comprehensive is the circumference within which the future perfection of sociology will be able to connect the isolated points that can now be identified. If I myself stress the wholly fragmentary and incomplete character of this book, I do not do so in order to protect myself in a cheap manner against objections to this character. For when measured by the ideal of objective perfection, the selection of the particular problems and examples contained in this work doubtless presents a haphazard character. If this character strikes one as a defect, this serves only to prove that I have not been able to clarify the fundamental idea of the present volume. According to this idea, nothing more can be attempted than the establishment of the beginning and the direction of an infinitely long road—the pretension to any systematic and definitive completeness would be, at the very least, illusory. Perfection can be obtained here by the individual student only in the subjective sense that he communicates everything he has been able to see.

6. The introduction of a new way of looking at facts must clarify the various aspects of its method by resorting to analogies taken from recognized fields of study. Nevertheless, it is only the process (perhaps never completed) by which the new principle becomes realized, clearly defined, and legitimated as fruitful through concrete research that can purify such analogies of the confusion of material differences that in the beginning cover up the decisive identity of form. However, to the same degree that the process frees these analogies from their ambiguity, it makes the analogies themselves superfluous.

HOW IS SOCIETY POSSIBLE?[1]

GEORG SIMMEL

Kant asked and answered the fundamental question of his philosophy, "How is nature possible?" He could do so only because nature for him was nothing but the representation of nature. It was so not merely in the sense that "the world is my representation" and that we can therefore speak of nature too as only a content of consciousness, but also in the sense that what we call nature is the special way in which the mind assembles, orders, and shapes sense perceptions. These given perceptions of color, taste, tone, temperature, resistance, and smell pass through our consciousness in the accidental sequence of our subjective experience. In themselves, they are not yet nature. They rather become nature, and they do so through the activity of the mind which combines them into objects and series of objects, into substances and attributes, and into causal connections. In their immediate givenness, Kant held, the elements of the world do not have the interdependence which alone makes them intelligible as the unity of nature's laws. It is this interdependence which transforms the world fragments—in themselves incoherent and unstructured—into nature.

The Kantian image of the world grows from a most peculiar play of contrasts. On the one hand, sense impressions are purely subjective: they depend upon a physicopsychical organization (which may differ from individual to individual) and upon the contingency of their provocations. They become objects as they are absorbed by the forms of our intellects and are transformed thereby into fixed regularities and into a consistent picture of "nature." On the other hand, these perceptions are what is really "given," the content of the world which we must simply accept, and the guarantee of an existence that is independent of us. Thus it is precisely the fact that our intellect forms perceptions into objects, systems, and uniformities which strikes us as subjective, that is, as something which *we* add to the given, as intellectual functions which, though unchangeable themselves, would have constructed a nature with a different content had they had different sense materials to work upon. For Kant, nature is a particular way of cognizing, a picture growing through and in our cognitive categories. Therefore, the question, "How is nature possible?"—that is, "What conditions are necessary for nature to be?"—is resolved by means of an inquiry into the forms which constitute the essence of our intellect. It is they which call forth nature itself.

It is very suggestive to treat as an analogous matter the question of the aprioristic conditions under which society is possible. Here, also, we find individual elements. In a certain sense, they too, like sense perceptions, stay forever isolated from one another. They, likewise, are synthesized into the unity of society only by means of a conscious process which correlates the individual existence of the single element with that of the other, and which does so in certain forms and according to certain rules. However, there is a decisive difference between the unity of a society and the unity of nature. It is this: In the Kantian view (which we follow here), the unity of nature emerges in the observing subject exclusively; it is produced exclusively by him in the sense materials, and on the basis of sense materials, which are in themselves heterogeneous. By contrast, the unity of society needs no observer. It is directly realized by its own elements because these elements are themselves conscious and synthesizing units. Kant's axiom that connection, since it is the exclusive product of the subject, cannot inhere in things themselves, does not apply here. For societal connection immediately occurs in the "things," that is, the individuals. As a synthesis, it too, of course, remains something purely psychological. It has no parallels with spatial things and their interaction. Societal unification needs no factors outside its own component elements, the individuals. Each of them exercises the function which the psychic energy of the observer exercises in regard to external nature: the consciousness of constituting with the others a unity is actually all there is to this unity. This does not mean, of course, that each member of a society is conscious of such an abstract notion of unity. It means that he is absorbed in innumerable, specific relations and in the feeling and the knowledge of determining others and of being determined by them. On the other hand, it should be noted that it is quite possible for an observing outsider to perform an additional synthesis of the persons making up the society. This synthesis would proceed as if these persons were spatial elements, but it is based only upon the observer himself. The determination of which aspect of the *externally* observable is to be comprehended as a unity depends not only on the immediate and strictly objective content of the observable but also upon the categories and the cognitive requirements of the subjective psyche. Again, however, society, by contrast, is the objective unit which needs no outside observer.

Things in nature are further apart than individuals are. In the spatial world, each element occupies a place it cannot share with any other. Here, there is nothing analogous to human unity, which is grounded in understanding, love, or common work. On the other hand, spatial elements fuse in the observer's consciousness into a unity that is not attained by the assemblage of individuals. For here, the objects of the synthesis are independent beings, psychic centers, personal units. They therefore resist the absolute fusion (in an observer's mind) to which, by contrast, the "self-lessness" of inanimate things must yield. Thus, a number of people is a unit to a much greater extent, really, but to a much lesser extent, ideally, than are the units "décor," which is formed by table, chairs, couch, carpet, and mirror, or "landscape" (or its "picture" in a painting), which is made up of river, meadow, trees, and house.

Society is "my representation"—something dependent upon the activity of consciousness—in quite a different sense from that in which the external world is. For the other individual has for me the same reality which I have myself, and this reality is very different from that of a material thing. Kant insists that I am precisely as certain of the existence of spatial objects as I am of my own existence. But by "my own existence" he can understand only the particular contents of my subjective life. For its basis, the very basis of representation, the feeling of the existing ego, is unconditional and unshakable to a degree not attained by any representation of a material object. This very certainty, however, whether we can account for it or not, also extends to the *you*. And as the cause or as the effect of this certainty, we feel the *you* as something independent of our representation of it, as something that exists with exactly the same autonomy as does our own existence. And yet, this selfness of the other does not preclude his being made our representation. In other words, something which can by no means be resolved into our representation, nevertheless becomes its content, and thus its product.

This phenomenon is the fundamental psychologico-epistemological paradigm and problem of sociation. Within our own consciousness we very clearly distinguish between two things. One is the basic character of the ego, the precondition of all representing, which does not have the problematic nature of its contents, a nature which can never be completely eliminated; and the other is these contents themselves. In their coming and going, in their doubtfulness and corrigibility, all of these contents always present themselves as the mere products of the former, products of that absolute and ultimate force and existence which is our psychic being. And although we also *think* the other *mind,* we must nevertheless ascribe to it the very conditions, or rather freedom from conditions, of our own ego. We think that the other mind has the same maximum degree of reality, as distinguished from its mere contents, which our own self possesses, as distinguished from its contents.

Owing to these circumstances, the question of how society is possible implies a methodology which is wholly different from that for the question of how nature is possible. The latter question is answered by the forms of cognition, through which the subject synthesizes the given elements into nature. By contrast, the former is answered by the conditions which reside a priori in the elements themselves, through which they combine, in reality, into the synthesis, society. In a certain sense, the entire content of this book [*Soziologie*], as it is developed on the basis of the principle enunciated, is the beginning of the answer to this question. For it inquires into the processes—those which, ultimately, take place in the individuals themselves—that condition the existence of the individuals as society. It investigates these processes, not as antecedent causes of this result, but as part of the synthesis to which we give the inclusive name of "society."

But the question of how society is possible must be understood in a still more fundamental sense. I said that, in the case of nature, the achieving of the synthetic unity is a function of the observing mind, whereas, in the case of society, that function is an aspect of society itself. To be sure, consciousness of the abstract principle that he is forming society is not present in the individual. Nevertheless, every individual knows that the other is tied to him—however much this knowledge of the other as fellow sociate, this grasp of the whole complex as society, is usually realized only on the basis of particular, concrete contents. Perhaps, however, this is not different from the "unity of cognition." As far as our conscious processes are concerned, we proceed by arranging one concrete content alongside another, and we are distinctly conscious of the unity itself only in rare and later abstractions. The questions, then, are these: What, quite generally and a priori, is the basis or presupposition which lies behind the fact that particular, concrete processes in the individual consciousness are actually processes of sociation? Which elements in them account for the fact that (to put it abstractly) their achievement is the production of a societal unit out of individuals?

The sociological apriorities envisaged are likely to have the same twofold significance as those which make nature possible. On the one hand, they more or less completely determine the actual processes of sociation as functions or energies of psychological processes. On the other hand, they are the ideational, logical presuppositions for the perfect society (which is perhaps never realized in this perfection, however). We find a parallel in the law of causation. On the one hand, it inheres and is effective in the actual processes of cognition. On the other hand, it constitutes truth as the ideal system of perfect cognition. And it does so irrespective of whether or not this truth obtains in the temporal and relatively accidental psychological dynamics in which causation actually operates—irrespective, that is, of the greater or lesser degree to which the actual, consciously held truth approximates the ideally valid truth.

To ask whether such an inquiry into the conditions of the process of sociation should or should not be called an epistemological inquiry is merely a question of terminology. The phenomenon which arises from these conditions and which receives its norms from their forms does not consist of cognitions but of concrete processes and actual situations. Nevertheless, what I have in mind here and what (as the general idea of sociation) must be examined in regard to its conditions *is* something cognitive, namely, the consciousness of sociating or of being sociated. This consciousness is perhaps better called a "knowing" than a "cognizing." For here, the subject is not confronting an object of which he will gradually gain a theoretical picture. The consciousness of sociation is, rather, the immediate agent, the inner significance, of sociation itself. It is the processes of interaction which signify the fact of being sociated to the individual—not the abstract fact, to be sure, but a fact capable of abstract expression. What forms must be at the basis of this fact? What specific categories are there that man must bring along, so to speak, so that this consciousness may arise? And what, therefore, are the forms which come to the fore in the consciousness once this consciousness has arisen (namely, society as a fact of knowledge)? The discussion of these questions may well be called the epistemology of society. In what follows, I shall try to give an example of such epistemological studies by sketching some of these a priori effective conditions or forms of sociation (which cannot, however, in contrast to the Kantian categories, be designated by a single word).

(1) The picture of another man that a man gains through personal contact with him is based on certain distortions. These are not simple mistakes resulting from incomplete experience, defective vision, or sympathetic or antipathetic prejudices. They are fundamental changes in the quality of the actual object perceived, and they are of two types. We see the other person generalized, in some measure. This is so, perhaps, because we cannot fully represent to ourselves an individuality which deviates from our own. Any re-creation of a person is determined by one's similarity to him. To be sure, similarity is by no means the only condition of psychological insight, for dissimilarity, too, seems required in order to gain distance and objectivity. In addition, aside from the question of similarity or dissimilarity, an intellectual capacity is needed. Nevertheless, *perfect* cognition presupposes perfect identity. It seems, however, that every individual has in himself a core of individuality which cannot be

re-created by anybody else whose core differs qualitatively from his own. And the challenge to re-create is logically incompatible with psychological distance and objective judgment which are also bases for representing another. We cannot know completely the individuality of another.

All relations among men are determined by the varying degrees of this incompleteness. Whatever the cause of this incompleteness, its consequence is a generalization of the psychological picture that we have of another, a generalization that results in a blurring of contours which adds a relation to other pictures to the uniqueness of this one. We conceive of each man—and this is a fact which has a specific effect upon our practical behavior toward him—as being the human type which is suggested by his individuality. We think of him in terms not only of his singularity but also in terms of a general category. This category, of course, does not fully cover him, nor does he fully cover it. It is this peculiarly incomplete coincidence which distinguishes the relation between a human category and a human singularity from the relation which usually exists between a general concept and the particular instance it covers. In order to know a man, we see him not in terms of his pure individuality, but carried, lifted up or lowered, by the general type under which we classify him. Even when this transformation from the singular to the typical is so imperceptible that we cannot recognize it immediately; even when all the ordinary characterological concepts such as "moral" or "immoral," "free" or "unfree," "lordly" or "slavish," and so on, clearly appear inadequate, we privately persist in labeling a man according to an unverbalized type, a type which does not coincide with his pure, individual being.

This leads to a further step. It is precisely because of the utter uniqueness of any given personality that we form a picture which is not identical with its reality but which at the same time does not coincide with a general type. The picture we form is the one the personality would show if the individual were truly himself, so to speak, if he realized, toward a good or toward a bad side, for better or worse, his ideal possibility, the possibility which lies in every individual. All of us are fragments, not only of general man, but also of ourselves. We are outlines not only of the types "man," "good," "bad," and the like but also of the individuality and uniqueness of ourselves. Although this individuality cannot, on principle, be identified by any name, it surrounds our perceptible reality as if traced in ideal lines. It is supplemented by the other's view of us, which results in something that we never are purely and wholly. It is impossible for this view to see anything but juxtaposed fragments, which nevertheless are all that really exist. However, just as we compensate for a blind spot in our field of vision so that we are no longer aware of it, so a fragmentary structure is transformed by another's view into the completeness of an individuality. The practice of life urges us to make the picture of a man only from the real pieces that we empirically know of him, but it is precisely the practice of life which is based on those modifications and supplementations, on the transformation of the given fragments into the generality of a type and into the completeness of the ideal personality.

In practice, this fundamental process is only rarely carried to completion. Nevertheless, within an existing society it operates as the a priori condition of additional interactions that arise among individuals. Every member of a group which is held together by some common occupation or interest sees every other member not just empirically, but on the basis of an aprioric principle which the group imposes on every one of its participants. Among officers, church members, employees, scholars, or members of a family, every member regards the other with the unquestioned assumption that he is a member of "my group." Such assumptions arise from some common basis of life. By virtue of it, people look at one another as if through a veil. This veil does not simply hide the peculiarity of the person; it gives it a new form. Its purely individual, real nature and its group nature fuse into a new, autonomous phenomenon. We see the other not simply as an individual but as a colleague or comrade or fellow party member—in short, as a cohabitant of the same specific world. And this inevitable, quite automatic assumption is one of the means by which one's personality and reality assume, in the imagination of another, the quality and form required by sociability.

Evidently, this is true also of the relations of members who belong to different groups. The civilian who meets an officer cannot free himself from his knowledge of the fact that this individual is an officer. And although his officership may be a part of this particular individuality, it is certainly not so stereotypical as the civilian's prejudicial image would have it. And the same goes for the Protestant in regard to the Catholic, the businessman in regard to the bureaucrat, the layman in regard to the priest, and so on. In all these cases, reality is veiled by social generalization, which, in a highly differentiated society, makes discovering it altogether impossible. Man distorts the picture of another. He both detracts and supplements, since generalization is always both less and more than individuality is. The distortions derive from all these a priori, operative categories: from the individual's type as man, from the idea of his perfection, and from the general society to which he belongs. Beyond all of these, there is, as a heuristic principle of knowledge, the idea of his real, unconditionally individual nature. It seems as if only the apprehension of this nature could furnish the basis for an entirely correct relation to him. But the very alterations and new formations which preclude this ideal knowledge of him are, actually, the conditions which make possible the sort of relations we call social. The phenomenon recalls Kant's conception of the categories: they form immediate data into new objects, but they alone make the given world into a knowable world.

(2) There is another category under which the individual views himself and others and which transforms all of them into empirical society. This category may be suggested by the proposition that every element of a group is not only a societal part but, in addition, something else. However trivial it may seem, this fact nevertheless operates as a social a priori. For that part of the individual which is, as it were, not turned toward society and is not absorbed by it, does not simply lie beside its socially relevant part without having a relation to it. It is not simply something outside society to which society, willingly or unwillingly, submits. Rather, the fact that in certain respects the individual is not an element of society constitutes the positive condition for the possibility that in other respects he is: the way in which he is sociated is determined or codetermined by the way in which he is not. The chapters of this book discuss, among

other things, several types whose essential sociological significance lies in the very fact that in some fashion or other they are excluded from society (for which their existence, nevertheless, is important). Such types are the stranger, the enemy, the criminal, even the pauper. But this peculiar relationship to society not only holds for such generalized types as these but, albeit with innumerable modifications, for any individual whatever. The proposition is not invalidated by the fact that at every moment we are confronted, as it were, by relations which directly or indirectly determine the content of every moment: for the social environment does not surround all of the individual. We know of the bureaucrat that he is not only a bureaucrat, of the businessman that he is not only a businessman, of the officer that he is not only an officer. This extrasocial nature —a man's temperament, fate, interests, worth as a personality— gives a certain nuance to the picture formed by all who meet him. It intermixes his social picture with non-social imponderables—however little they may change his dominant activities as a bureaucrat or businessman or officer.

Man's interactions would be quite different if he appeared to others only as what he is in his relevant societal category, as the mere exponent of a social role momentarily ascribed to him. Actually, individuals, as well as occupations and social situations, are differentiated according to how much of the non-social element they possess or allow along with their social content. On this basis, they may be arranged in a continuum. One pole of the continuum is represented by an individual in love or friendship. What this individual preserves for himself after all the developments and activities devoted to the friend or beloved are taken care of is almost nothing. In his case, there is only a single life that can be viewed or lived from two sides, as it were: from the inside, from the *terminus a quo* of the subject and in the direction of the beloved, and from the *terminus ad quem,* by which, too, this life is covered without residue. A very different tendency is illustrated by the formally identical phenomenon of the Catholic priest, where the clerical function entirely supersedes and absorbs his individual existence. In the first of these two extreme subtypes, the non-social element, which exists in addition to the social, disappears, because its content has completely vanished in the individual's turning toward another person. In the second case, it disappears because the corresponding type of content itself has completely disappeared.

The opposite pole of the continuum is found in certain phenomena characteristic of modern culture with its money economy. Here the individual, inasmuch as he produces, buys, sells, and in general performs anything, approaches the ideal of absolute objectivity. Except in the highest leading positions, the individual life and the tone of the total personality is removed from the social action. Individuals are merely engaged in an exchange of performance and counter-performance that takes place according to objective norms—and everything that does not belong to this pure objectivity has actually disappeared from it. The personality itself, with its specific coloration, irrationality, and inner life, has completely absorbed the non-social element and, in a neat separation, has left to the social activities only those energies which are specifically appropriate for them.

Actually, social individuals move between these two extremes. They do so in such a way that the energies and characteristics which are directed back toward the individual have significance at the same time for the actions and attitudes which are directed toward another. There is an extreme case, namely, the notion that this social activity or mood is something separate from the rest of the personality, that the personality's non-social existence and significance do not enter into social relations. Clearly, even this notion, however, has its effect upon the attitude which the subject holding it adopts toward others and upon the attitude which others adopt toward him. The a priori of empirical social life consists of the fact that life is not entirely social. The reservation of a part of our personalities so as to prevent this part from entering into interaction has an effect upon our interactions which is twofold. In the first place, through general psychological processes it has its effect upon the social structure of the individual. In the second place, the formal fact itself, the part that exists outside the individual, affects this structure.

A society is, therefore, a structure which consists of beings who stand inside and outside of it at the same time. This fact forms the basis for one of the most important sociological phenomena, namely, that between a society and its component individuals a relation may exist as if between two parties. In fact, to the degree that it is more open or more latent, this relation, perhaps, always does exist. Society shows possibly the most conscious, certainly the most general, elaboration of a fundamental form of general life. This is that the individual can never stay within a unit which he does not at the same time stay outside of, that he is not incorporated into any order without also confronting it. This form is revealed in the most transcendent and general as well as in the most singular and accidental contexts. The religious man feels himself fully seized by the divine, as if he were merely a pulse-beat of its life. His own substance is given over unreservedly, if not in a mystical, undifferentiated fusion, to that of the absolute. But in spite of this, in order to give this fusion any significance whatever, he must preserve some sort of self-existence, some sort of personal counter, a differentiated ego, for whom the absorption in this divine all-being is a never ending task. It is a process that neither would be possible metaphysically, nor could be felt religiously, if it did not start from the existence of the individual: to be one with God is conditioned in its very significance by being other than God.

We do not have to adduce this experience of the transcendental. The same form of life is expressed in the idea that man's relation to nature is as a part of the totality of nature, an idea which the human mind has vindicated throughout its history. We view ourselves as incorporated into nature, as one of its products, as an equal of all other natural products, as a point which the stuffs and forces of nature reach and leave just as they circulate through flowing water and a blossoming plant. Yet we have the feeling of being independent and separate from all these entanglements and relationships, a feeling that is designated by the logically uncertain concept "freedom." We have a feeling that we represent a counter and contrast to this process, whose elements we nevertheless are. The most radical formulation of this feeling is found in the proposition that nature is merely a human imagination. In this formulation, nature, with all its undeniable autonomy and hard reality is made part of the individual self, although this self, with all its freedom and separate existence and contrast to "mere" nature, is nevertheless a link in it. In its most general form, the very essence of the relation between nature and man is that man comprises nature in spite of the fact that it is independent and very often hostile; that which is, according to man's innermost life-feeling, outside of him, must necessarily be his medium and element.

This formula is no less valid in regard to the relation between individuals and the groups to which they are socially tied or, if these groups are subsumed under the over-all concept or feeling of sociation, in regard to the relation among individuals in general. On the one hand, we see ourselves as products of society. The physiological succession of our ancestors, their adaptations and peculiarities, the traditions of their work and knowledge and belief—the whole spirit of the past as it is crystallized in objective forms determines the pattern and content of our lives. The question has even been raised as to whether the individual is anything more than a vessel in which elements existing before him are mixed in varying measures. For even if these elements ultimately are produced by the individual himself, his contribution is only minimal; only as individuals converge in species and society do the factors arise whose synthesis results in any discernible degree of individuality. On the other hand, we see ourselves as members of society. In this capacity we depend on it. By our life and its meaning and purpose, we are as inextricably woven into society, as a synchronic, coexisting phenomenon, as we are, as products, into diachronic, successive society.

In our capacity as natural objects we have no self-existence. The circulation of natural forces passes through us as through completely self-less structures, and our equality before the laws of nature resolves our existence without residue into a mere example of the necessity of these laws. Analogously, as social beings we do not live around any autonomous core. Rather, at any given moment, we consist of interactions with others. We are thus comparable to a physical body which consists merely of the sum of numerous sense impressions and does not have its own existence. Yet we feel that this social diffusion does not entirely dissolve our personalities. We feel this, not only because of the reservations already mentioned, that is, because of particular contents whose significance and development inhere exclusively in the individual and find no room whatever in the social sphere; nor only because the unifying center, the individual phenomenon, in the formation of social contents is not itself social (just as the artistic form, though composed of color spots on canvas, cannot be derived from the chemical nature of the colors); but also because, although it may be possible to explain the whole content of life completely in terms of social antecedents and interactions, this content must also be considered under the category of the individual life, as the individual's experience, as something exclusively oriented toward the individual. The two—social and individual—are only two different categories under which the same content is subsumed, just as the same plant may be considered from the standpoint of its biological development or its practical uses or its aesthetic significance. In the same way, the standpoint from which the life of the individual is conceived and structured may be taken from within as well as from without the individual. With all its socially derivable contents, a total life may be interpreted as the centripetally directed fate of its bearer as legitimately as—with all the elements that are reserved for the individual—it may be conceived of as the product and component of social life.

We thus see how the fact of sociation puts the individual into the dual position which I discussed in the beginning: The individual is contained in sociation and, at the same time, finds himself confronted by it. He is both a link in the organism of sociation and an autonomous organic whole; he exists both for society and for himself. The essence and deepest significance of the specific sociological a priori which is founded on this phenomenon is this: The "within" and the "without" between individual and society are not two unrelated definitions but define together the fully homogeneous position of man as a social animal. His existence, if we analyze its contents, is not only partly social and partly individual, but also belongs to the fundamental, decisive, and irreducible category of a unity which we cannot designate other than as the synthesis or simultaneity of two logically contradictory characterizations of man—the characterization which is based on his function as a member, as a product and content of society; and the opposing characterization which is based on his functions as an autonomous being, and which views his life from its own center and for its own sake.[2] Society consists not only of beings that are partially nonsociated, as we saw earlier, but also of beings which, on the one hand, feel themselves to be complete social entities, and, on the other hand—and without thereby changing their content at all—complete personal entities. And we do not deal here with two unrelated, alternative standpoints such as we adopt, for instance, when we look at an object in regard to either its weight or its color; for we are dealing with two elements that together form the unit we call the social being, that is, with a synthetic category. The phenomenon parallels the concept of causation. It, too, is an a priori unit, in spite of the fact that it covers two elements which are heterogeneous in content, cause and effect. We do perform the synthesis "social being." We are capable of constructing the notion of society from the very idea of beings, each of whom may feel himself as the *terminus a quo* and the *terminus ad quem* of his developments and destinies and qualities. And we do construct this concept of society, which is built up from that of the potentially autonomous individual, as the *terminus a quo* and the *terminus ad quem* of the individual's very life and fate. This capacity constitutes an a priori of empirical society. It makes possible the form of society as we know it.

(3) Society is a structure composed of unequal elements. The "equality" toward which democratic or socialistic efforts are directed—and which they partly attain—is actually an equivalence of people, functions, or positions. Equality in people is impossible because of their different natures, life contents, and destinies. On the other hand, the equality of everybody with everybody else in an enslaved mass, such as we find in the great oriental despotisms, applies only to certain specific aspects of existence—political or economic aspects, for example—never to the total personality. For innate qualities, personal relations, and decisive experiences inevitably make for some sort of uniqueness and irreplaceability in both the individual's self-evaluation and his interactions with others.

Society may be conceived as a purely objective system of contents and actions connected by space, time, concepts, and values. In such a scheme, personality, the articulation of the ego (in which, nevertheless, the dynamics of society is located) may be ignored. However, the elements of this system are heterogeneous. Every action and quality within it is individual and is irrevocably located in its specific place. Society appears as a cosmos whose complex nature and direction are unlimited, but in which every single point can be fixed and can develop only in a particular way because otherwise the structure of the whole would change. What has been said of the structure of the world in general—that not a single grain of sand could have a shape different from what it has or be in a position different from its actual position without first conditioning the alteration by a change of the whole and without entailing such a change in the whole—is true of the structure of society, of society considered as a web of qualitatively differentiated phenomena.

This image of general society finds a small-scale analogy (infinitely simplified and stylized) in bureaucracy. A bureaucracy consists of a certain order of positions, of a predetermined system of functions. It exists as an ideal structure, irrespective of the particular occupants of these positions. Every new entrant finds within it a clearly defined place which has waited for him, so to speak, and to which his individual talents must be suited. In society at large, what here is a conscious, systematic determination of functions is a deeply entangled play and counterplay of them. Positions within society are not planned by a constructive will but can be grasped only through an analysis of the creativity and experience of the component individuals. Empirical, historical society is therefore vastly different from a bureaucracy because of its irrational and imperfect elements. From certain value standpoints, some of these elements must be condemned. Nevertheless, the phenomenological structure of society is the sum of the objective existences and actions of its elements and the interrelations among these existences and actions. It is a system of elements each of which occupies an individual place, a co-ordination of functions and function-centers which have objective and social significance, although they are not always valuable. Purely personal and creative aspects of the ego, its impulses and reflexes, have no place in this system. To put it otherwise: The life of society (considered not psychologically but phenomenologically, that is, exclusively in regard to its social contents) takes its course as if each of its elements were predestined for its particular place in it. In spite of all discrepancies between it and ideal standards, social life exists as if all of its elements found themselves interrelated with one another in such a manner that each of them, because of its very individuality, depends on all others and all others depend on it.

We are thus in a position to see the a priori which we must now discuss. This a priori provides the individual with the basis for, and offers the "possibility" of, his being a member of a society. An individual is directed toward a certain place within his social milieu by his very quality. This place which ideally belongs to him actually exists. Here we have the precondition of the individual's social life. It may be called the general value of individuality. It is independent both of its development into a clear, consciously formed conception and of its realization in the empirical life-process. In the same way, the apriority of causality as a determining precondition of cognition depends neither on its conscious formulation in specific concepts nor on the behavior of reality, as we grasp it psychologically, in accord or discord with it. For our cognition is based on the premise of a pre-established harmony that exists between our psychological energies, however individualized they may be, and external, objective existence. This existence always remains immediate, no matter how many attempts there have been to show, metaphysically or psychologically, that it is the intellect's own product. In a similar fashion, social life presupposes an unquestionable harmony between the individual and society as a whole. This harmony, of course, does not preclude violent ethical and eudaemonistic dissonances. If social reality were determined by this presupposition of harmony alone, without the interference of other factors, it would result in the perfect society. It would be perfect, however, not in the sense of ethical or eudaemonistic perfection, but of conceptual perfection; it would be not the *perfect* society but the perfect *society*. The a priori of the individual's social existence is the fundamental correlation between his life and the society that surrounds him, the integrative function and necessity of his specific character, as it is determined by his personal life, to the life of the whole. In so far as he does not realize this a priori or does not find it realized in society, the individual is not sociated and society is not the perfect system of interactions called for by its definition.

This situation is shown with particular sharpness in the phenomenon of vocation. Antiquity, to be sure, did not know this concept in its connotation of personal differentiation in a society articulated by a division of labor. But even antiquity knew its root, the idea that socially effective action is the unified expression of the inner qualification of the individual, the idea that by functioning in society the wholeness and permanence of subjectivity becomes practically objective. Yet in antiquity this relationship was exemplified by contents that were much less heterogeneous than they are today. Its principle is expressed in the Aristotelian axiom that some individuals are by nature destined to slavery; others, to domination. The more highly developed concept of vocation refers to a peculiar phenomenon: On the one hand, society within itself produces and offers to the individual a place which—however different in content and delimitation it may be from other places—can be filled by many individuals, and which is, for this reason, something anonymous, as it were. On the other hand, this place, in spite of its general character, is nevertheless taken by the individual on the basis of an inner calling, a qualification felt to be intimately personal. For such a thing as vocation to be possible, there must exist that harmony, whatever its origin, between the structure and development of society, and individual qualities and impulses. It is this general premise that constitutes the ultimate basis of the idea that for every personality there exist a position and a function in society to which he is called and which he must seek and find.

Empirical society becomes possible because of the a priori that finds its most obvious expression in the concept of vocation. Nevertheless, like the other a prioris thus far discussed, it cannot be designated by a simple slogan like those which it is possible to use for the Kantian categories. The processes of consciousness which formulate sociation—notions such as the unity of the many, the reciprocal determination of the individuals, the significance of the individual for the totality of the others and vice versa—presuppose something fundamental which finds expression in practice although we are not aware of it in its abstractness. The presupposition is that individuality finds its place in the structure of generality, and, furthermore, that in spite of the unpredictable character of individuality, this structure is laid out, as it were, for individuality and its functions. The nexus by which each social element (each individual) is interwoven with the life and activities of every other, and by which the external framework of society is produced, is a causal nexus. But it is transformed into a teleological nexus as soon as it is considered from the perspective of the elements that carry and produce it—individuals. For they feel themselves to be egos whose behavior grows out of autonomous, self-determined personalities. The objective totality yields to the individuals that confront it from without, as it were; it offers a place to their subjectively determined life-processes, which thereby, in their very individuality, become necessary links in the life of the whole. It is this dual nexus which supplies the individual consciousness with a fundamental category and thus transforms it into a social element.

It is a rather irrelevant question to ask whether the epistemological analyses of society exemplified in these sketches belong to social philosophy or to sociology proper. Perhaps they are tangential to both. At any rate, the nature of the sociological problem, as outlined earlier, and its delimitation from philosophical problems do not suffer from this question. They no more suffer from it than do the notions of day and night from the phenomenon of dawn, or the concepts of man and animal from the possibility that one day perhaps we may find intermediate stages in which the characteristics of both are fused in a way that we can no longer separate them conceptually. The sociological inquiry is directed toward abstracting from the complex phenomenon called social life that which is purely society, that is, sociation. It eliminates from the purity of this concept everything which does not constitute society as a unique and autonomous form of existence, although it can be realized only historically in society. It thus has its clearly defined problem area, whose center does not shift its position, although its periphery may, at present or forever, touch on other areas so that it becomes blurred.

I shall now proceed to show, by means of specific investigations, the fruitfulness of this central concept and problem. I am far from claiming that I can do justice, even remotely, to the variety of forms of interaction that constitute society. These investigations merely point the way which may lead to the scientific isolation from the totality of life of the phenomenon "society" in its full range. They try to do this by taking the first steps on this way.

Translated by Kurt H. Wolff

1. "Exkurs über das Problem: Wie ist Gesellschaft möglich?" *Soziologie. Untersuchungen über die Formen der Vergesellschaftung* ([1908] 3rd ed.; Munich and Leipzig: Duncker und Humblot, 1923), pp. 21-31. Used by permission of Hans Broermann of Duncker und Humblot.—Tr.

2. It is true, of course, that in given cases these may actually develop as two unrelated characteristics and that they may even be in mutual conflict.

BIBLIOGRAPHY OF WRITINGS ON GEORG SIMMEL

KURT GASSEN

The two available Simmel bibliographies—Nicholas J. Spykman's in his *The Social Theory of Georg Simmel* (1925) and Erich Rosenthal and Kurt Oberlaender's in the *American Journal of Sociology,* LI (1945)—are both American in origin. Although both list the great majority of Simmel's own writings (especially the later one), both pay only minor attention to the literature *on* Simmel (Spykman's contains twelve items; Rosenthal-Oberlaender's, twenty-four). However, except for fuller referencing and the addition of some relatively minor entries—especially translations, book reviews, and the like—Rosenthal-Oberlaender has not been significantly enlarged by subsequent bibliographical publications. These include Kurt H. Wolff's in *The Sociology of Georg Simmel* (1950) and my own in *Buch des Dankes an Georg Simmel* (1958). Parts A through D of the latter list Simmel's books (including reviews of them), his papers and essays, translations of his writings, and the university courses and seminars which he conducted. What follows is Part E of this bibliography. It contains everything that has come to my attention during the many years that I have devoted to assembling it. It omits the listing of purely incidental mentions of Simmel in some other context; it does include, however, biographical material and descriptions of the man, for these may be valuable to a better understanding of Simmel the thinker.

1894 BOUGLÉ, CHARLES. "Les sciences sociales en Allemagne: G. Simmel," *Revue de métaphysique et de morale,* II (1894), 329-55. On Simmel's *Über sociale Differenzierung* (1890), *Einleitung in die Moralwissenschaft* (1892-93), and *Die Probleme der Geschichtsphilosophie* (1893). Almost completely reprinted in the next entry.

1896 BOUGLÉ, CHARLES. "G. Simmel. La science de la morale" (Chap. ii), *Les sciences sociales en Allemagne: Les méthodes actuelles.* Paris: Alcan, 1896. pp. 43-70. (2nd ed., 1902.)

1899 a. *Darvinizm i teorija poznanija.* Vyp. 1. *Georg Simmelja i Fridricha Nicse* ["Darwinism and Epistemology. 1. Georg Simmel and Friedrich Nietzsche"]. Petrograd: 1899. Pp. 86.

b. KISTIAKOWSKI, THEODOR. *Gesellschaft und Einzelwesen: eine methodologische Studie.* Berlin: Liebmann, 1899. Esp. pp. 74-80.

1900 DURKHEIM, EMILIO. "La sociologia ed il suo dominio scientifico," *Rivista italiana di sociologia,* IV (1900), 127-48. See 1953, b., and 1959.

1901 a. GALLINGER, AUGUST. "Simmel über die Möglichkeit einer allgemeingültigen Norm, *Kantstudien,* VI (1901), 406-21. On Simmel's *Einleitung in die Moralwissenschaft.*

b. JOËL, KARL. "Eine Zeitphilosophie," *Neue deutsche Rundschau,* XII (1901), 812-26. On Simmel's *Philosophie des Geldes.*

c. SCHMIDT, CONRAD. "Eine Philosophie des Geldes," *Sozialistische Monatshefte,* V (1901), 180-85. On Simmel's *Philosophie des Geldes.*

1902 a. BOUGLÉ, CHARLES. See 1896.

b. ERNST, PAUL. *Die Badia von Fiesole* (Altitalienische Novellen. Ausgewählt und übersetzt). Leipzig: Insel-Verlag, 1902. pp. 1-36. (2nd ed., 1907.) Ernst's introductory story to his translation. The figure of the "philosopher" is Simmel; that of the "actress," Louise Dumont.

1903 ALTMANN, S. P. "Simmel's Philosophy of Money," *American Journal of Sociology,* IX (1903), 46-68.

1903-1904 ALTMANN, SALOMON PAUL. "Die Philosophie des Geldes," *Deutschland: Monatsschrift für die gesamte Kultur,* III (1903-4), 88-104, 213-19. On Simmel's *Philosophie des Geldes.*

1905 a. KOIGEN, DAVID. "Georg Simmel als Geldapologet," *Dokumente des Sozialismus,* V (1905), 317-23.

b. KOPPEL, AUGUST. "Von Marx zu Simmel" (Chap. i), *Für und wider Karl Marx. Prolegomena zu einer Biographie.* ("Volkswirtschaftliche Abhandlungen der Badischen Hochschulen," Vol. VIII, No. 1.) Karlsruhe: Braun, 1905. pp. 1-21. See also pp. 22, 35, 56, 83 f., 91 f., 115 f., 131 ff. (Doctoral dissertation, University of Heidelberg, 1905.)

1907 a. ERNST, PAUL. See 1902, b.

b. RAUH, FRÉDÉRIC. "Idéalisme et réalisme historique. A propos d'un livre de M. Simmel," *Revue de Synthèse historique,* Vol. XIV, No. 1 (1907), pp. 1-20. On Simmel's *Die Probleme der Geschichtsphilosophie.*

c. ZOCCOLI, ETTORE. *La concezione formale della sociologia secondo Giorgio Simmel.* Bologna: Emiliano, 1907. Pp. 20.

1909 a. EULENBURG, FRANZ. "Simmels Probleme der Geschichtsphilosophie," *Archiv für Sozialwissenschaft und Sozialpolitik,* XXIX (1909), 169-97.

b. MASARYK, THOMAS G. "Simmels Soziologie," *Zeitschrift für Sozialwissenschaft,* XII (1909), 600-7.

1910 a. WIESE, LEOPOLD VON. "Neuere soziologische Literatur," *Archiv für Sozialwissenschaft und Sozialpolitik,* XXXI (1910), 882-907. On Simmel, pp. 897-900.

b. KOIGEN, DAVID. "Georg Simmels soziologischer Rationalismus," *ibid.,* pp. 908-24.

1911 a. ALAFBERG, FRIEDRICH. "Georg Simmel," *Die Grenzboten,* LXX (1911), 187-90.

b. JANKÉLÉVITCH, S. "La théorie sociologique de M. Simmel," *Revue de Synthèse historique,* XXII (1911), 129-39. On Simmel's *Soziologie.*

1912 a. BOUGLÉ, CHARLES. "La sociologie de G. Simmel," in CHARLES ANDLER, and others, *La philosophie allemande au XIXe siècle.* Paris: Alcan, 1912. pp. 189-203.

b. SOMLÓ, FELIX. "Das Wertproblem, II. Polemische Bemerkungen. 6. Simmel," *Zeitschrift für Philosophie und philosophische Kritik,* CXLVI (1912), 95-98. On Simmel's *Einleitung in die Moralwissenschaft.*

1912-1913 MAMELET, ALBERT. "La philosophie de Georges Simmel," *Revue de métaphysique et de morale,* XX (1912), 567-612, 682-717, 825-77; XXI (1913), 390-435.

1913 a. BLÁHA, ARNOŠT (ERNST). "O některých směrech současné sociologie. 1. Sociologický subjektivism" ["On Some Tendencies of Present-Day Sociology. 1. Sociological Subjectivism"], *Česká Mysl* ["Czech Thought"], XIII (1913), 289-305 (esp. 299-302).

b. SCHUMANN, FRIEDRICH KARL. "Die Wirklichkeitsfrage in der Religion bei Nivellierung des Immanenz-Transzendenz-Gegensatzes (Simmel)" (Chap. iv), *Religion und Wirklichkeit.* Leipzig: Quelle und Meyer, 1913. pp. 99-145. (Doctoral dissertation, University of Greifswald, 1913.)

c. SPANN, OTHMAR. "Soziologie," *Jahrbücher der Philosophie,* I (1913), 301-21 (esp. 302-6, 317-19).

1914 a. BERNHARD, ERNST. "Georg Simmel als Soziologe und Sozialphilosoph," *Die Tat,* V (1914), 1080-86.

b. FRIEDEMANN, HERMANN. "Georg Simmel," *Strassburger Post,* January 18, 1914.

c. HAVENSTEIN, MARTIN. "Chamberlains und Simmels 'Goethe,'" *Preussische Jahrbücher,* Vol. CLV, No. 1 (1914), pp. 27-70.

d. LESSING, THEODOR. "Gestalten. Georg Simmel. Betrachtungen und Exkurse 1912-13" (Book II), *Philosophie als Tat.* Göttingen: Hapke, 1914. pp. 303-42.

e. LUDWIG, EMIL. "Simmel auf dem Katheder," *Die Schaubühne,* X (1914), 411-13.

f. MAMELET, ALBERT. *Le relativisme philosophique chez Georg Simmel.* Préface de VICTOR DELBOS. Paris: Alcan, 1914. Pp. ix + 215.

Reviews:

Année philosophique, XXIV (1913), 260-63 (L.D.).

Journal of Philosophy, Psychology and Scientific Methods, XI (1914), 526-29 (GEORGE CLARKE COX).

Polybiblion [Paris], CXXX (1914), 402 (LOUIS MAISONNEUVE).

Revue des Sciences philosophiques et théologiques, VIII (1914).

Rivista di filosofia, VI (1914), 125 f.

Die Philosophie der Gegenwart, V (1913 [1915]), 111.

g. SPANN, OTHMAR. *Kurzgefasstes System der Gesellschaftslehre.*

Berlin: Guttentag, 1914. pp. 9-19, 254 f., etc. (Text modified in second [1923] and third [1930] editions, entitled *Gesellschaftslehre* [pp. 25-30].)

h. TAGGER, THEODOR (pseud. "FERDINAND BRUCKNER"). "Georg Simmel," *Die Zukunft,* Vol. LXXXIX, No. 4 (1914), pp. 36-41.

i. VEIL, GERHARD. "Georg Simmels 'negativer Unterricht auf dem Gebiete der Moral,'" *Strassburger Post,* March 10, 1914.

1917 LEWINSOHN, RICHARD. "Simmels 'Rembrandt,'" *Die Gegenwart,* XLVI (1917), 204-7.

1918 a. ALTARAZ, ISAAK. "Georg Simmel" (Chap. ii), "Reine Soziologie: Darstellung und Kritik der typischen Versuche zur Schaffung einer philosophischen Sozialwissenschaft." Doctoral dissertation, University of Berlin, 1918. pp. 30-46.

b. FECHTER, [PAUL]. "Georg Simmel," *Norddeutsche Allgemeine Zeitung,* September 28, 1918.

c. FISCHER, ALOYS. "Georg Simmel (geb. 1 März 1856 [*sic*], gest. 27. [*sic*] September 1918)," *Deutscher Wille,* XXXII (October, 1918), 43-47.

d. HERMANN, GEORG (pseud. of GEORG BORCHARDT). "Erinnerungen an Simmel," *Vossische Zeitung,* September 29, 1918.

e. HOEBER, FRITZ. "Georg Simmel, der Kulturphilosoph unserer Zeit," *Neue Jahrbücher für das klassische Altertum, Geschichte und deutsche Literature und für Pädagogik,* XLI=*Neue Jahrbücher für das klassische Altertum,* XXI (1918), 475-77.

f. ———. "Der Kulturphilosoph unserer Zeit Georg Simmel," *Die Umschau,* XXII (1918), 593 f. An abridged version of the preceding entry.

g. ———. "Georg Simmel," *Rheinisch-Westfälische Zeitung,* November 16, 1918. Except for minor changes, this is identical with the preceding entry.

h. JOËL, KARL. "Georg Simmel," *Neue Zürcher Zeitung,* October 16, 1918.

i. KUBSCH, HUGO. "Zum Tode Georg Simmels," *Tägliche Rundschau,* September 28, 1918.

j. LEWINSOHN, RICHARD. "Georg Simmel," *Frankfurter Zeitung,* October 5, 1918.

k. LUDWIG, EMIL. "Simmels Vortrag," *Vossische Zeitung,* October 22, 1918.

l. LUKÁCS, GEORG. "Georg Simmel," *Pester Lloyd,* October 2, 1918.

m. MANNHEIM, KÁROLY. "Georg Simmel mint filozófus," *Huszadik Század* ["The Twentieth Century"], XXXVIII (1918), 364-66.

n. MAUTHNER, FRITZ. "Georg Simmel," *Berliner Tageblatt,* October 18, 1918.

o. [Obituary] "Georg Simmel," *Vossische Zeitung,* September 28, 1918.

p. TH., P. "Georg Simmel," *Basler Nachrichten,* October 10, 1918.

q. THIESS, FRANK. "Zu Füssen Simmels. Ein Wort der Erinnerung," *Berliner Tageblatt,* September 28, 1918.

r. TÖNNIES, FERDINAND. "Simmel als Soziologe," *Frankfurter Zeitung,* October 9, 1918.

1919 a. ADLER, MAX. *Georg Simmels Bedeutung für die Geistesgeschichte.* Vienna and Leipzig: Anzengruber-Verlag, 1919. Pp. 44.

Reviews:

Der Bibliothekar. Monatsschrift für Arbeiterbibliotheken, XI (1919), 1273 (F.P.).

Der Kampf [Vienna], XII (1919), 452 (H. KAPPER).

Der Zwiebelfisch, X (1919), 165.

Literarisches Zentralblatt, Vol. LXXI (1920), col. 149 (HANS FREYER).

b. FRISCHEISEN-KÖHLER, MAX. "Georg Simmel," *Kantstudien,* XXIV (1919), 1-51 (with portrait). Published as a book—Berlin: Reuther und Reichard, 1919. Pp. 53 (with portrait).

Reviews:

Literarischer Handweiser, LVI (1920), cols. 113 f. (JOSEF WEIGER).

Literarisches Zentralblatt, LXXII (1921), col. 308 (PAUL MÜLLER).

c. HURWICZ, ELIAS. "Georg Simmel als jüdischer Denker," *Neue jüdische Monatshefte,* III (1919), 196-98.

d. JOËL, KARL. "Georg Simmel, ein Nachruf," *Die Neue Rundschau= Die Freie Bühne,* XXX (1919), 241-47.

e. KNEVELS, WILHELM. "Das Religiöse Problem in besonderer Beziehung auf Simmels Religionstheorie." Doctoral dissertation, University of Heidelberg, 1919. Pp. iv + 107.

f. SCHMALENBACH, HERMAN. "Simmel," *Sozialistische Monatshefte,* LII (1919), 283-88.

g. TIDEMANN, WILHELM. "Simmels Philosophie der Mode," *Weser-Zeitung,* October 6, 1919.

1919-1920 a. HOEBER, FRITZ. "Der deutsche Kulturphilosoph unserer Zeit: Georg Simmel," *Die Hochschule: Blätter für akademisches Leben und studentische Arbeit,* III (1919-20), 25-27.

b. WAGNER, WALTHER. "Georg Simmels Geschichtsphilosophie," *Philosophische Mitteilungen: Monatsschrift zur Förderung philosophischer Bildung und Kultur,* II (1919-20), 39 f.

1920 a. HOEBER, FRITZ. "Georg Simmel," *Feuer* [Saarbrücken], I (1920), 63.

b. KNEVELS, WILHELM. *Simmels Religionstheorie, ein Beitrag zum religiösen Problem der Gegenwart.* Leipzig: Hinrichs, 1920. Pp. vi+107. Knevel's dissertation published as a book; see 1919, e.

Reviews:

Bayerische Blätter für das Gymnasialschulwesen, LVII (1921), 178 (MARKUS REDENBACHER [?]).

Geisteskultur und Volksbildung. Monatschefte der Co-

menius-Gesellschaft, XXX (1921), 31 f. (AUGUST WOLFSTIEG).

Literarisches Zentralblatt, Vol. LXXII (1921), col. 738 (ERNST BERGMANN).

Theologischer Literaturbericht, XLV (1922), 19 f. (GERHARD HEINZELMANN).

Theologisches Literaturblatt, Vol. XLIII (1922), col. 93 f. (KARL GIRGENSOHN).

c. RICKERT, HEINRICH. *Die Philosophie des Lebens. Darstellung und Kritik der philosophischen Modeströmungen unserer Zeit.* Tübingen: Mohr, 1920. pp. 64-72, etc. (2nd ed., 1922.)

d. UTITZ, EMIL. "Georg Simmel und die Philosophie der Kunst," *Zeitschrift für Ästhetik und allgemeine Kunstwissenschaft,* XIV (1920), 1-41.

e. WUST, PETER. "Die Bahnbereiter einer neuen Synthese: Ernst Troeltsch und Georg Simmel" (Chap. v), *Die Auferstehung der Metaphysik.* Leipzig: Meiner, 1920. pp. 204-56.

1920-1921 a. KRACAUER, SIEGFRIED. "Georg Simmel," *Logos,* IX (1920-21), 307-38.

b. SINGER, KURT. "Die Krisis der Soziologie," *Weltwirtschaftliches Archiv,* XVI (1920-21), 246-61 (esp. 255 f.).

1921 a. DIETRICH, OTTO. "Georg Simmel und seine Bedeutung für die Nationalökonomie." Doctoral dissertation, University of Freiburg, 1921. Pp. 142.

b. SCHOLZ, HEINRICH. *Religionsphilosophie.* Berlin: Reuther und Reichard, 1921. pp. 378-84. (Rev. 2nd ed., 1922 [pp. 265-73].)

c. STERN, ERICH. *Über den Begriff der Gemeinschaft.* Langensalza: Beyer und Mann, 1921. Pp. 46.

d. TROELTSCH, ERNST. "Der historische Entwicklungsbegriff in der modernen Geistes- und Lebensphilosophie. II. Die Marburger Schule, die Südwestdeutsche Schule, Simmel," *Historische Zeitschrift,* CXXIV (1921), 421-47. Later modified in *Der Historismus und seine Probleme.* Tübingen: Mohr, 1922. pp. 572-95.

e. UTITZ, EMIL. *Die Kultur der Gegenwart.* Stuttgart: Enke, 1921. Esp. pp. 266-69. (2nd ed., entitled *Die Kultur in der Epoche des Weltkrieges,* 1927.)

1922 a. BANFI, ANTONIO. "Il relativismo critico e l'intuizione filosofica della vita nel pensiero di G. Simmel," Introduction to *I problemi fondamentali della filosofia* [an Italian translation of Simmel's *Hauptprobleme der Philosophie* by Banfi]. Florence: Vallecchi, 1922. pp. 5-30.

b. KLEMMT, ALFRED. "Georg Simmel. Eine kritische Charakterstudie und Erläuterung der Grundprobleme der gegenwärtigen Philosophie." Doctoral dissertation, University of Berlin, 1922. Pp. ii + 156. An abstract appears in *Jahrbuch der Dissertationen der Philosophischen Fakultät Berlin,* 1921-22, pp. 12 f.

c. KRACAUER, SIEGFRIED. *Soziologie als Wissenschaft.* Dresden: Sibyllen-Verlag, 1922. On Simmel, esp. pp. 108-10.
d. LEWKOWITZ, ALBERT. "Zur Religionsphilosophie der Gegenwart. II. Philosophie des Lebens: Darwin, Bergson, Simmel," *Monatsschrift für Geschichte und Wissenschaft des Judentums,* LXVI (1922), 260-65.
e. MOOG, WILLY. *Die deutsche Philosophie des 20. Jahrhunderts in ihren Hauptrichtungen und ihren Grundproblemen.* Stuttgart: Enke, 1922. pp. 77-88, etc.
f. RICKERT, HEINRICH. See 1920, c.
g. SCHOLZ, HEINRICH. See 1921, b.
h. SPANN, OTHMAR. "Der Streit um die Möglichkeit und das Wesen der Gesellschaftslehre," *Zeitschrift für Volkswirtschaft und Sozialpolitik,* N. F., II (1922), esp. pp. 209-14. Included in the second edition (1923) of Spann's *Gesellschaftslehre,* pp. 25-30; see 1914, g.
i. TROELTSCH, ERNST. See 1921, d.
j. WIESE, LEOPOLD V. "Zu Spanns Kritik der empirischen Soziologie," *Kölner Vierteljahrshefte für Sozialwissenschaften,* Vol. II, No. 4 (1922), pp. 70-75. Comment on Spann's critique of Simmel.

1923 a. BOHLIN, TORSTEN. *Das Grundproblem der Ethik. Über Ethik und Glauben.* Uppsala: Almqvist & Wiksell; Leipzig: Harrassowitz, 1923. pp. 342-86.
b. HELLMUTH, O. "Professor Georg Simmel als Pädagog," *Erziehung und Bildung: Wissenschaftliche Beilage zur Preussischen Lehrerzeitung,* IV (1923), 37-40.
c. KEYSERLING, Count HERMANN. In: *Die Philosophie der Gegenwart in Selbstdarstellungen,* Vol. IV. Leipzig: Meiner, 1923. pp. 99-125, *passim.*
d. MÜLLER-FREIENFELS, RICHARD. *Die Philosophie des 20. Jahrhunderts in ihren Hauptströmungen.* Berlin: Mittler, 1923. Esp. pp. 80 f., 100 f., etc.
e. OESTERREICH, TRAUGOTT KONSTANTIN. *Die deutsche Philosophie des XIX. Jahrhunderts und der Gegenwart.* ("Friedrich Überwegs Grundriss der Philosophie, Vierter Teil," 12th ed.) Berlin: Mittler, 1923. pp. 467-71.
f. PERTICONE, GIACOMO. *La filosofia di Giorgio Simmel.* Turin: Paravia, 1923. Pp. ii + 32.
g. SPANN, OTHMAR. See 1914, g.
h. ZIEGLER, LEOPOLD. In: *Die Philosophie der Gegenwart in Selbstdarstellungen,* Vol. IV. Leipzig: Meiner, 1923. pp. 163-217, *passim.*

1923-1924 SUSMAN, MARGARETE. "Pole jüdischen Wesens—Hermann Cohen und Georg Simmel," *Die Tat,* XV (1923-24), 385-89.

1924 a. RICHTER, FRIEDRICH. "Der Begriff des Lebens in der Philosophie Georg Simmels." Doctoral dissertation, University of Giessen,

1924. Pp. 28. Published in abstract—Berlin: Ebering, 1924. Pp. 4.

b. WIESE, LEOPOLD V. *Allgemeine Soziologie als Lehre von den Beziehungen und Beziehungsgebilden der Menschen.* Munich and Leipzig: Duncker und Humblot, 1924. (2nd ed., entitled *System der Allgemeinen Soziologie als Lehre von den sozialen Prozessen und den sozialen Gebilden der Menschen (Beziehungslehre),* 1933; 3rd ed., 1955.) See 1932, e.

1924-1925 GROSCHE, ROBERT. "Georg Simmel," *Die Schildgenossen,* V (1924-25), 191-98.

1925 a. COHN, JONAS. *Die Philosophie im Zeitalter des Spezialismus.* ("Geschichte der Philosophie," Vol. VII.) Leipzig and Berlin: Teubner, 1925. pp. 124-30.

b. FROST, WALTER. "Die Soziologie Simmels," *Acta Universitatis Latviensis* [Riga], XII (1925), 219-313; XIII (1926), 149-225.

c. GRÜNEWALD, MAX. "Die Philosophie Simmels mit besonderer Berücksichtigung ihrer Beziehung zum Pragmatismus." Doctoral dissertation, University of Breslau, 1925. Pp. 65. Published in abstract—Breslau: Hochschulverlag, 1925.

d. HEUSCHELE, OTTO. "Georg Simmel. Brief an einen Toten," *Kölnische Zeitung,* August 18, 1925.

e. JANKÉLÉVITCH, VLADIMIR. "Georg Simmel, philosophe de la vie," *Revue de métaphysique et de morale,* XXXII (1925), 213-57, 373-86.

f. SPYKMAN, NICHOLAS J. *The Social Theory of Georg Simmel.* Chicago: University of Chicago Press, 1925. Pp. xxix + 297. Biography and Bibliography on pp. 277-92. (Ph. D. dissertation, University of Chicago, 1925.)

Reviews:

American Journal of Sociology, XXXI (1925), 84-87 (ALBION W. SMALL).

International Journal of Ethics, XXXVI (1925-26), 324 (W. L. DORN).

Revue de métaphysique et de morale, XXXIII (supplement to July-September issue, 1926), 12 f.

Literarische Wochenschrift [Weimar], (1926), cols. 307 f. (ANDREAS WALTHER).

Kantstudien, XXXV (1930), 379 (HORST GRUENEBERG).

g. STEINHOFF, MARIA. "Die Form als soziologische Grundkategorie bei Georg Simmel," *Kölner Vierteljahrshefte für Soziologie,* IV (1925), 214-59. (Doctoral dissertation, University of Cologne, 1925, with the subtitle, "Ihre Bedeutung für Begründung und Aufbau der Soziologie als selbständiger Einzelwissenschaft.")

h. WOBBERMIN, GEORG. *Systematische Theologie nach religionspsychologischer Methode.* 2nd ed. Leipzig: Hinrichs, 1925. pp. 441-44.

1925-1926 NISSEN, INGJALD. "Vergesellschaftung als Einstellung. Eine Betrachtung zu Simmels Soziologie," *Annalen der Philosophie und philosophischen Kritik*, V (1925-26), 77-108.

1926 a. BENTLEY, ARTHUR F. "Simmel, Durkheim, and Ratzenhofer," *American Journal of Sociology*, XXXII (1926), 250-56.

b. FABIAN, WILHELM. "Kritik der Lebensphilosophie Georg Simmels." Doctoral dissertation, University of Breslau, 1926. Published as a book—Breslau: Trewendt und Granier, 1926. Pp. 34.

c. JARISLOWSKY, MARGARETE. "Das 'Individuelle Gesetz' in seiner Anwendung auf die Kunst des Porträts." Doctoral dissertation, University of Berlin, 1926. See esp. pp. 5-11.

d. NOBS, MAX. "Der Einheitsgedanke in der Philosophie Georg Simmels." Doctoral dissertation, University of Bern, 1926. Pp. 67.

e. PRZYWARA, ERICH. *Gott. 5 Vorträge über das religionsphilosophische Problem.* ("Der Katholische Gedanke," No. 17.) Cologne, Munich, and Vienna: Oratoriums-Verlag, 1926. On Simmel, *passim.*

f. WEBER, MARIANNE. *Max Weber. Ein Lebensbild.* Tübingen: Mohr, 1926. (New ed.; Heidelberg: Lambert Schneider, 1950.) In several places, discusses the relations between the Webers and the Simmels.

g. WIESE, LEOPOLD V. *Soziologie: Geschichte und Hauptprobleme.* ("Sammlung Göschen," No. 101.) Berlin: de Gruyter, 1926. Esp. pp. 82-88. (2nd, enlarged ed., 1931 [pp. 115-20]; 3rd, slightly modified ed., 1947 [pp. 137-43]; 4th ed., 1950 [pp. 46 ff., 120 ff.]; 5th ed., 1954.)

1926-1927 STERN, ERICH. "Soziologie," *Pädagogische Rundschau*, III (1926-1927), 390-92.

1927 a. BOTEZ, OCTAV. "Über Simmels Ästhetik," *Minerva* [Rumanian], (1927).

b. CRON, HELMUT. "Georg Simmel als Philosoph der modernen Kultur," *Preussische Jahrbücher*, CCVII (1927), 292-316.

c. LEVY, HEINRICH. "Georg Simmels Weg zu einer hegelianischen Metaphysik" (Chap. v), *Die Hegel-Renaissance in der deutschen Philosophie.* ("Philosophische Vorträge, veröff. von der Kant-Gesellschaft," No. 30.) Charlottenburg: Pan-Verlag Rolf Heise, 1927. pp. 25-30.

d. LITT, THEODOR. *Ethik der Neuzeit.* Munich and Berlin: Oldenbourg, 1927. Esp. pp. 174-77.

e. TROMNAU, ERICH. "Georg Simmels Schopenhauerauffassung. Darstellung und Nachprüfung ihrer Eigenheiten." Doctoral dissertation, University of Königsberg, 1927. Pp. 66.

f. UTITZ, EMIL. See 1921, e.

1928 a. COHN, JONAS. "Georg Simmels Lebensphilosophie," *Badische Schulzeitung*, LXVI (1928), 615-18. (Radio broadcast, August 17, 1928.)

b. ———. "Georg Simmel," *Deutsches Biographisches Jahrbuch. Überleitungsband II (1917-20)* [1928], pp. 326-33.

c. Marcuse, Ludwig. "Georg Simmels Gegenwart," *Hannoverscher Kurier,* September 26, 1928.

d. Matthias, Leo. "Georg Simmel in memoriam," *Berliner Tageblatt,* September 4, 1928.

e. ———. "In memoriam Georg Simmel, gest. am 26. September 1918," *Thüringer Allgemeine Zeitung; Erfurter Allgemeiner Anzeiger,* September 26, 1928.

f. Sorokin, Pitirim. *Contemporary Sociological Theories.* New York and London: Harper & Brothers, 1928. Esp. pp. 496-98, 500-2.

1929 a. Abel, Theodore. "The Formal Sociology of Georg Simmel" (Chap. i), *Systematic Sociology in Germany: A Critical Analysis of Some Attempts to Establish Sociology as an Independent Science.* ("Studies in History, Economics, and Public Law," No. 310.) New York: Columbia University Press, 1929. pp. 13-49. (Ph.D. dissertation, Columbia University, 1929.)

b. Heinemann, Fritz. "Der Durchbruch eines neuen Verständnisses der historisch-geistigen Welt und die Gewinnung einer von der Ratio unabhängigen Grundschicht. Georg Simmel," *Neue Wege der Philosophie.* Leipzig: Quelle und Meyer, 1929. pp. 230-50, etc.

c. Liebert, Artur. *Geist und Welt der Dialektik.* Berlin: Pan-Verlag, 1929. pp. 408-15.

d. Marcard, Karl-Alfred v. "Der Begriff des Kunstwerks bei Georg Simmel." Doctoral dissertation, University of Leipzig, 1929. Pp. 60.

1930 a. Bauhofer, Oskar. *Das Metareligiöse. Eine kritische Religionsphilosophie.* Leipzig: Hinrichs, 1930. pp. 60, 198-200.

b. Bohner, Hellmuth. "Untersuchungen zur Entwicklung der Philosophie Georg Simmels." Doctoral dissertation, University of Freiburg, 1930. Pp. 85.

c. Brock, Erich. "Georg Simmels Weiterwirken," *Neue Zürcher-Zeitung,* July 13, 1930.

d. Freyer, Hans. "Logische Grundlegung des Systems der Soziologie. I, 5. Formale Soziologie (G. Simmel)," *Soziologie als Wirklichkeitswissenschaft.* Leipzig and Berlin: Teubner, 1930. pp. 46-57.

e. Galecki, Jerzy. "Pragmatyzm Simmla" ["Simmel's Pragmatism"], *Kvartalnik filozoficzny* ["Philosophical Quarterly" (Cracow)], (1930).

f. Loewenberg, J. "Problematic Realism," in *Contemporary American Philosophy: Personal Statements,* Vol. II, ed. George P. Adams and William Pepperell Montague. London: Allen and Unwin; New York: Macmillan Co., 1930. pp. 80 f.

g. Niemeier, Gottfried. *Die Methoden und Grundauffassungen der Religionsphilosophie der Gegenwart.* ("Beiträge zur Philosophie und Psychologie," No. 6.) Stuttgart: Kohlhammer, 1930. pp. 161-65.

h. Spann, Othmar. See 1914, g.

i. Wolters, Friedrich. *Stefan George und die Blätter für die Kunst. Deutsche Geistesgeschichte seit 1890.* Berlin: Bondi, 1930. pp. 115-17, 157-60, etc.

1931 a. Banfi, Antonio. "Il pensiero filosofico e pedagogico di G. Simmel," *Rivista pedagogica* (1931), pp. 43-??.

b. Ernst, Paul. *Jünglingsjahre.* Munich: G. Müller, 1931. pp. 318-20.

c. Gothein, Marie Luise. *Eberhard Gothein. Ein Lebensbild, seinen Briefen nacherzählt.* Stuttgart: Kohlhammer, 1931. pp. 211-15, 216 f.

d. Kaufmann, Fritz. *Geschichtsphilosophie der Gegenwart.* ("Philosophische Forschungsberichte," No. 10.) Berlin: Junker und Dünnhaupt, 1931. pp. 42-55, etc.

e. Ludwig, Emil. *Geschenke des Lebens. Ein Rückblick.* Berlin: Rowohlt, 1931. pp. 153 f.

f. Marck, Siegfried. "Georg Simmel: Die Idee des Lebens und das Leben der Idee" (Chap. iii, 1, a), *Die Dialektik in der Philosophie der Gegenwart,* Vol. II. Tübingen: Mohr, 1931. pp. 117-22.

g. Menzer, Paul. *Deutsche Metaphysik der Gegenwart.* Berlin: Mittler, 1931. pp. 61-63.

h. Sorokin, Pitirim. *Soziologische Theorien im 19. und 20. Jahrhundert. Deutsche Bearbeitung von Hans Kasspohl.* Munich: Beck, 1931. Esp. pp. 160 f.

i. Wiese, Leopold v. See 1926, g.

j. Woyslawski, Hersch-Leib. "Georg Simmels Philosophie des kapitalistischen Geistes." Doctoral dissertation, University of Berlin, 1931. Pp. 54 (Teildruck).

1932 a. "Bk." "Georg Simmel, Goethe und das Elsass. Auch ein Beitrag zum Goethejahr," *Elsass-Lothringen. Heimatstimmen,* X (1932), 225-29.

b. Gerson, Hermann. "Die Entwicklung der ethischen Anschauungen bei Georg Simmel." Doctoral dissertation, University of Berlin, 1932. Pp. 81.

c. Leese, Kurt. "Geistesleben und Lebensschwungkraft (Idealismus und Vitalismus), 3. Georg Simmel (1858-1918)" (Chap. iv), *Die Krisis und Wende des christlichen Geistes. Studien zum anthropologischen und theologischen Problem der Lebensphilosophie.* Berlin: Junker und Dünnhaupt, 1932. pp. 280-92.

d. Lersch, Philipp. "Leben und Form (G. Simmel)" (Chap. iv), *Lebensphilosophie der Gegenwart.* ("Philosophische Forschungsberichte," No. 14.) Berlin: Junker und Dünnhaupt, 1932. pp. 47-60.

e. Wiese, Leopold v., and Becker, Howard. *Systematic Sociology on the Basis of the* Beziehungslehre *and* Gebildelehre. New York: John Wiley & Sons, Inc., 1932. pp. 44-47. See 1924, b.

1933 a. LOOSE, GERHARD. "Die Religionssoziologie Georg Simmels." Doctoral dissertation, University of Leipzig, 1933. Pp. 79. Published as a book—Dresden: Risse, 1933. Pp. 79.

b. POVIÑA, ALFREDO. "El relativismo formal de Jorge Simmel," *Cursos y Conferencias,* Vol. II, Nos. 8 and 12 (1933).

c. WIESE, LEOPOLD V. See 1924, b.

1934 a. NITZSCHKE, HEINZ. "Three German Sociologists [Ferdinand Tönnies, Georg Simmel, Leopold v. Wiese]," *Calcutta Review,* LI (1934), 186-96. Based on a lecture delivered in the Bangiya German-Vidya Samsad ("Bengali Society of German Culture") in Calcutta on March 27, 1934.

b. VIERKANDT, ALFRED. "Simmel," *Encyclopaedia of the Social Sciences,* XIV (1934).

c. WACH, JOACHIM. *Das Problem des Todes in der Philosophie unserer Zeit.* ("Philosophie und Geschichte," No. 49.) Tübingen: Mohr, 1934. pp. 29-39.

1935 a. ARON, RAYMOND. *La sociologie allemande contemporaine.* ("Nouvelle encyclopédie philosophique," No. 7.) Paris: Alcan, 1935. Esp. pp. 6-10. (2nd ed.; Paris: Presses Universitaires de France, 1950.) See 1953, a., and 1957, a.

b. LEPSIUS, SABINE. *Stefan George. Geschichte einer Freundschaft.* Berlin: Verlag Die Runde, 1935. pp. 25, 26-28, 52, 81 f.

c. LESSING, THEODOR. *Einmal und nie wieder. Lebenserinnerungen.* Prague: Mercy, 1935. pp. 350 f., etc.

d. MÜLLER, HERWIG. "Georg Simmel als Deuter und Fortbildner Kants." Doctoral dissertation, University of Leipzig, 1935. Pp. 68.

e. POVIÑA, ALFREDO. "El relativismo formal de Jorge Simmel," *Notas de Sociología* [Córdoba, Argentina], (1935).

1937 a. NOME, JOHN. *Filosofisk kultur. Georg Simmel som moderne tenker.* Oslo: Gyldendal Norsk Forlag, 1937. Pp. 328. See 1938, d.

b. WEISBACH, WERNER. *Und alles ist zerstoben. Erinnerungen aus der Jahrhundertwende.* Vienna, Leipzig, and Zurich: Reichner, 1937. pp. 382-84. See 1956, g.

1938 a. ARON, RAYMOND. "Philosophie de la vie et logique de l'histoire (Simmel)" (Chap. iii), *Essai sur la théorie de l'histoire dans l'Allemagne contemporaine. La philosophie critique de l'histoire.* Paris: Librairie Philosophique J. Vrin, 1938. pp. 159-218; n. J, "Simmel et Bergson," pp. 307 f.; Bibliography, pp. 318-20. (2nd ed., entitled *La philosophie critique de l'histoire. Essai sur une théorie Allemande de l'histoire,* 1950.)

b. BARNES, HARRY ELMER, and BECKER, HOWARD. *Social Thought from Lore to Science,* Vol. II. 2 vols. Boston: D. C. Heath & Co., 1938. Esp. pp. 889-90, 913-17. (2nd ed.; Washington: Harren Press, 1952.)

c. MANDELBAUM, MAURICE. *The Problem of Historical Knowledge:*

An Answer to Relativism. New York: Liveright Publishing Corp., 1938. pp. 101-9, 166-70.

d. NOME, JOHN. *Mennesket og kulturen.* Oslo: Gyldendal Norsk Forlag, 1938. Pp. 314. A continuation of 1937, a.

e. SASSEN, FERDINAND. *Wijsbegeerte van onzen tijd.* Nijmegen: Dekker & Van de Vogt, 1938. pp. 171-75. (2nd ed., 1940 [pp. 175-79]; 3rd ed., 1944 [pp. 162-66].)

f. TODORAN, ISIDOR. "Georg Simmel," *Istoria filosofici moderne* (1938), 325-38.

1939 BALTHASAR, HANS URS. *Die Vergöttlichung des Todes. (Apokalypse der deutschen Seele. Studien zu einer Lehre von letzten Haltungen,* Vol. III.) Salzburg and Leipzig: Pustet, 1939. pp. 231-34, etc.

1940 a. FLEXNER, ABRAHAM. *I Remember: The Autobiography of Abraham Flexner.* New York: Simon and Schuster, Inc., 1940. p. 108.

b. SASSEN, FERDINAND. See 1938, e.

1941 TREVES, RENATO. *Sociología y filosofía social.* Buenos Aires: Editorial Losada, 1941. pp. 47-59.

1943 ERMATINGER, EMIL. *Richte des Lebens.* Frauenfeld and Leipzig: Huber, 1943. pp. 258 f.

1944 a. GIUSSO, LORENZO. *Lo storicismo tedesco: Dilthey, Simmel, Spengler.* ("Storia universale della filosofia," No. 84.) Milan: Bocca, 1944. pp. 133-236.

b. SASSEN, FERDINAND. See 1938, e.

1945 a. BEERLING, REINIER FRANCISCUS. "De dood als vormingsbeginsel van het leven (G. Simmel)" (Chap. ii), "Moderne doodsproblematiek. Een vergelijkende studie over Simmel, Heidegger en Jaspers." Doctoral dissertation, University of Amsterdam, 1945. pp. 49-87. Published as a book—Delft: Delftsche Uitgever Maatschappij, 1946. pp. 49-87.

b. NAWIASKY, HANS. *Allgemeine Staatslehre.* Einsiedeln/Cologne: Benziger, 1945. pp. 88-92. Discussion of Simmel's conception of the "social."

c. ROSENTHAL, ERICH, and OBERLAENDER, KURT. "Books, Papers, and Essays by Georg Simmel," *American Journal of Sociology,* LI (1945), 238-47.

d. SALOMON, ALBERT. "German Sociology," in *Twentieth Century Sociology,* ed. GEORGES GURVITCH and WILBERT E. MOORE. New York: Philosophical Library, Inc., 1945. pp. 604-9. See 1947, c.

1946 a. BUSTAMENTE, NORBERTO RODRÍGUEZ. "Jorge Simmel y el problema de la sociología," *Revista de la Universidad Nacional de Córdoba,* XXXIII (1946), 193-205.

b. COLLINGWOOD, ROBIN GEORGE. *The Idea of History.* Oxford: Clarendon Press, 1946. pp. 170 f., 174 f. Published as a Galaxy Book in New York: Oxford University Press, 1956. See 1955, a.

c. DESSOIR, MAX. *Buch der Erinnerung.* Stuttgart: Enke, 1946. p. 164, etc.

d. TJALSMA, PIETER DOUWES. "De religie zonder God van Georg Simmel," *Vox theologica,* XVII (1946), 54-62.

1947 a. AYALA, FRANCISCO. *Sociología.* Buenos Aires: Editorial Losada, 1947. pp. 191 f.

b. RUGGIERO, GUIDO DE. *La filosofia contemporanea.* 5th ed. Bari: Laterza, 1947. pp. 88-90.

c. SALOMON, ALBERT. "La sociologie allemande," in *La Sociologie au XXe siècle,* ed. GEORGES GURVITCH. Paris: Presses Universitaires de France, 1947. pp. 611-16. A French translation of 1945, d.

d. WIESE, LEOPOLD V. See 1926, g.

1948 a. FECHTER, PAUL. *Menschen und Zeiten. Begegnungen aus fünf Jahrzehnten.* Gütersloh: Bertelsmann, 1948. pp. 52-56. (Reprinted, Berlin and Darmstadt: Deutsche Buchgemeinschaft, 1949; 2nd ed., 1951 [pp. 49-53].)

b. ———. "Der Philosoph Georg Simmel," *Die Zeit. Wochenzeitung für Politik, Wirtschaft, Handel und Kultur* [Hamburg], September 30, 1948.

c. HEBERLE, RUDOLF. "The Sociology of Georg Simmel: The Forms of Social Interaction," in *An Introduction to the History of Sociology,* ed. HARRY ELMER BARNES. Chicago: University of Chicago Press, 1948. pp. 249-73.

d. TRNKA, HELGA. "Inwieweit bedeuten Simmels *Philosophie des Geldes* und Molls *Logik des Geldes* eine Förderung der modernen Geldtheorie?" Dissertation, Hochschule für Welthandel, Vienna, 1948. Pp. 160.

e. VANNATTA, THOMAS A. "A Study in Polarities in the Writings of George Simmel." Unpublished Ph.D. dissertation, Ohio State University, 1948. Pp. v + 163.

f. WEBER, MARIANNE. *Lebenserinnerungen.* Bremen: Storm, 1948. pp. 375-409. More on Gertrud Simmel, Simmel's wife, than on Simmel himself.

g. WORRINGER, WILHELM. *Abstraktion und Einfühlung.* 11.-13. Taus. Munich: Piper, 1948. pp. 6-11. The earlier editions do not contain these reminiscences of Simmel which are reprinted, however, in Worringer's *Fragen und Gegenfragen, Schriften zum Kunstproblem.* Munich: Piper, 1956. pp. 23-28.

1949 a. BONNER, HUBERT. "Georg Simmel: Field Theory and Sociology," *Sociology and Social Research,* XXXIII (1949), 171-79.

b. FECHTER, PAUL. See 1948, a.

c. GASSEN, KURT. "Georg Simmels Vorlesung 'Ethik und Probleme der modernen Kultur' (1913). Nachschrift," *Philosophische Studien,* I (1949), 310-44.

d. LANDMANN, MICHAEL. *Problematik. Nichtwissen und Wissensverlangen im philosophischen Bewusstsein.* Göttingen: Vandenhoeck und Ruprecht, 1949. pp. 374-80.

e. M. L. [MICHAEL LANDMANN]. "Georg Simmel. Vorbereitung eines Archivs und einer Ausgabe," *Zeitschrift für philosophische Forschung,* Sonderheft 1 (1949). ["Philosophische Vorträge und Diskussionen. Bericht über den Mainzer Philosophen-Kongress 1948."] pp. 204 f.

f. MEINECKE, FRIEDRICH. *Strassburg—Freiburg—Berlin 1901-1919. Erinnerungen.* Stuttgart: K. F. Koehler, 1949. pp. 102 f.

g. MEYER, HANS. "Die Lebensphilosophie" (Chap. iv, b), *Die Weltanschauung der Gegenwart. (Geschicte der abendländischen Weltanschauung,* Vol. V.) Würzburg: Schöningh, 1949. pp. 300-306.

1950 a. ARON, RAYMOND. See 1935, a., and 1938, a.

b. CURTIUS, LUDWIG. *Deutsche und antike Welt. Lebenserinnerungen.* Stuttgart: Deutsche Verlags-Anstalt, 1950. p. 138.

c. NEWMAN, K. J. "Georg Simmel and Totalitarian Integration," *Theoria* [Natal University, Pietermaritzburg], III (1950), 39-47.

d. PUCCIARELLI, EUGENIO. "Goethe visto por Simmel," *La Nación* [Buenos Aires], Suplemento literario, February 26, 1950.

e. RUPP, KARL. "Geisteskampf um Goethe. Die geistesgeschichtlichen Grundlagen des lebensphilosophischen Goethe-Bildes Georg Simmels und Friedrich Gundolfs." Doctoral dissertation, University of Innsbruck, 1950. Pp. 486.

f. WEBER, MARIANNE. See 1926, f.

g. WIESE, LEOPOLD V. See 1926, g.

h. WOLFF, KURT H. Introduction to *The Sociology of Georg Simmel.* Translated and edited by KURT H. WOLFF. Glencoe, Ill.: Free Press of Glencoe, Illinois, 1950. pp. xvii-lxiv.

i. ZIEGENFUSS, WERNER, and JUNG, GERTRUD. *Philosophen-Lexikon. Handwörterbuch der Philosophie nach Personen,* Vol. II. Berlin: de Gruyter, 1950. pp. 539-46.

1951 a. BOEHRINGER, ROBERT. *Mein Bild von Stefan George.* Munich and Düsseldorf: Küpper, vormals Bondi, 1951. pp. 66, 91 f.

b. FECHTER, PAUL. See 1948, a.

c. GABRIEL, LEO. *Existenzphilosophie von Kierkegaard bis Sartre.* Vienna: Herold, 1951.

d. NEWMAN, K. J. "Georg Simmel and Totalitarian Integration," *American Journal of Sociology,* LVI (1951), 348-53. Identical with 1950, c. [?].

1951-1952 LANDMANN, MICHAEL. "Konflikt und Tragödie. Zur Philosophie Georg Simmels," *Zeitschrift für philosophische Forschung,* VI (1951-52), 115-33.

1952 a. BARNES, HARRY ELMER, and BECKER, HOWARD. See 1938, b.

b. CHIKAMATSU, YOSHIYUKI. "On G. Simmel—from the Standpoint of 'Lebensphilosophie,'" *The Scientific Reports of the Saikyo University.* ("Humanistic Science," No. 1 [February, 1952].) pp. 126-73.

c. SCIACCA, MICHELE FEDERICO. "Le origini della filosofia attuale" (Chap. i), "Il relativismo di G. Simmel e il finzionismo di H. Vaihinger" (Sezione 6), *La filosofia oggi.* 2nd ed. Rome and Milan: Bocca, 1952. pp. 46-48.

d. THIEME, KARL. *Philosophenbilder.* ("Sammlung Birkhäuser," No. 18.) Basel: Birkhäuser, 1952. pp. 284 f. (with portrait).

1953 a. ARON, RAYMOND. *Die deutsche Soziologie der Gegenwart, eine systematische Einführung.* Übersetzt und bearbeitet von IRING FETSCHER. ("Króners Taschenausgabe," No. 214.) Stuttgart: Kröner, 1953. A German translation of 1935, a.

b. DURKHEIM, EMILE. "La sociologie et son domaine scientifique," in *Où va la sociologie française?* by ARMAND CUVILLIER. Paris: Marcel Rivière, 1953. pp. 177-208 [On Simmel, pp. 179-86, and elsewhere]. A French translation of the 1900 entry.

1954 a. FISCHL, JOHANN. "Leben als Transzendenz (Georg Simmel)" (Chap. ii, 1, B), *Idealismus, Realismus und Existenzialismus der Gegenwart.* (*Geschichte der Philosophie,* Vol. V.) Graz, Vienna, and Cologne: Styria, 1954. pp. 29-31.

b. LUKÁCS, GEORG. "Die Lebensphilosophie in der Vorkriegszeit (Simmel)," *Die Zerstörung der Vernunft. Der Weg des Irrationalismus von Schelling zu Hitler.* Berlin: Aufbau-Verlag, 1954. pp. 350-64, etc. (2nd ed., 1955.)

c. LUONGO, MARIA ROSARIA. *Il relativismo di Simmel e di Pirandello. L'opposizione della forma e della vita.* Con prefazione di ANTONIO ALIOTTA. Naples: Edizione Libreria scientifica editrice, 1954. Pp. 63.

d. NASO, ECKART v. *Ich liebe das Leben. Erinnerungen aus fünf Jahrzehnten.* Hamburg: Wolfgang Krüger, 1954. pp. 325 f.

e. SEMERARI, GIUSEPPE. "Kant interpretato da Simmel," *Rivista internazionale di filosofia del diritto,* Ser. 3, No. 31 (1954), pp. 289-96.

f. WIESE, LEOPOLD v. See 1926, g.

1955 a. COLLINGWOOD, ROBIN GEORGE. *Philosophie der Geschichte.* Stuttgart: Kohlhammer, 1955. pp. 181 f. A German translation of 1946, b.

b. FREUND, LUDWIG. "Simmels unvermeidlicher 'Streit,'" *Politik und Ethik. Möglichkeiten und Grenzen ihrer Synthese.* Frankfurt am Main and Berlin: Metzner, 1955. pp. 102-5, etc.

c. HUGHES, EVERETT CHERRINGTON. Foreword to Georg Simmel's *Conflict* and *The Web of Group-Affiliations.* Glencoe, Ill.: Free Press of Glencoe, Illinois, 1955. pp. 7-9. "Conflict" translated by KURT H. WOLFF; "The Web of Group-Affiliations" translated by REINHARD BENDIX.

d. LUKÁCS, GEORG. See 1954, b.

e. PRZYWARA, ERICH. "Simmel—Husserl—Scheler" [1954], *In und Gegen. Stellungnahmen zur Zeit.* Nuremberg: Glock und Lutz, 1955. pp. 33-54.

f. Steffen, Albert. *Begegnungen mit Rudolf Steiner.* Dornach (Switzerland): Verlag für schöne Wissenschaften, 1955. p. 13.

g. Wiese, Leopold v. See 1924, b.

1956 a. Coser, Lewis A. *The Functions of Social Conflict.* ("International Library of Sociology and Social Reconstruction.") London: Routledge and Kegan Paul, 1956. Pp. 203. Based largely on Simmel; many references are made to him.

b. Ekhart, Leonhard. "Georg Simmels philosophische Begründung seiner Soziologie." Graz, 1956. (Doctoral dissertation, University of Graz, 1957. Pp. iv + 121.)

c. Hawthorn, H. B. "A Test of Simmel on the Secret Society: the Doukhobors of British Columbia," *American Journal of Sociology,* LXII (1956), 1-7.

d. Honigsheim, Paul. "Georg Simmel," *Handwörterbuch der Sozialwissenschaften,* IX (1956), 270-72.

e. Mannheim, Karl. *Essays on the Sociology of Culture,* ed. Ernest Manheim in co-operation with Paul Kecskemeti. London: Routledge and Kegan Paul, 1956. pp. 18, 45, 56, 141, 207.

f. Rossi, Pietro. "L'ereditá del neocriticismo e la filosofia della vita (Georg Simmel)" (Part III), *Lo storicismo tedesco contemporaneo.* ("Studi e Ricerche," No. 4.) Turin: Einaudi, 1956. pp. 211-72.

g. Weisbach, Werner. *Geist und Gewalt.* Vienna and Munich: Schroll, 1956. pp. 87 f. A continuation of 1937, b.

h. Worringer, Wilhelm. See 1948, g.

1957 a. Aron, Raymond. *German Sociology.* Translated by Mary and Thomas Bottomore. Melbourne, London, and Toronto: William Heinemann, 1957. pp. 5-8. An English translation of 1935, a.

b. Becker, Howard, and Boskoff, Alvin (eds.). *Modern Sociological Theory in Continuity and Change.* New York: Dryden Press, 1957. pp. 15, 16, 20, 24-28, 54, 62, 65, 74, 81, 82, 87, 92, 178, 181, 264, 286, 306, 310 f., 336, 339, 482, 486-88, 505, 551, 658, 663 f., 692, 714 f.

c. Landmann, Michael. Einleitung zu Georg Simmels *Brücke und Tür: Essays des Philosophen zur Geschichte, Religion, Kunst und Gesellschaft.* Stuttgart: K. F. Koehler, 1957. pp. v-xxiii.

d. Levine, Donald N. "Simmel and Parsons: Two Approaches to the Study of Society." Unpublished Ph.D. dissertation, University of Chicago, 1957. Pp. vii + 239.

e. Mathieu, Vittorio. "Georg Simmel," *Enciclopedia filosofica,* Vol. IV. Venice and Rome: Istituto per la Collaborazione culturale, 1957. cols. 629-31.

1958 a. *American Journal of Sociology,* LXIII (May, 1958). ["Durkheim-Simmel Commemorative Issue."]

Relevant articles:

ROSSI, PETER H. "Emile Durkheim and Georg Simmel," p. 579.

NAEGELE, KASPAR D. "Attachment and Alienation: Complementary Aspects of the Work of Durkheim and Simmel," pp. 580-89.

WOLFF, KURT H. "The Challenge of Durkheim and Simmel," pp. 590-96.

COSER, LEWIS A. "Georg Simmel's Style of Work: A Contribution to the Sociology of the Sociologist," pp. 635-40.

MILLS, THEODORE M. "Some Hypotheses on Small Groups from Simmel," pp. 642-50.

b. FAHRENKRUG, ARTHUR. "Wiederentdecktes Werk ohne Erben. Vor 100 Jahren wurde der Philosoph und Soziologe Georg Simmel geboren," *Darmstädter Echo,* March 1, 1958. p. 15.

c. GASSEN, KURT, and LANDMANN, MICHAEL (eds.). *Buch des Dankes an Georg Simmel. Briefe, Erinnerungen, Bibliographie.* Berlin: Duncker und Humblot, 1958.

Contents:

(1) SIMMEL, GEORG. "Anfang einer unvollendeten Selbstdarstellung"

(2) LANDMANN, MICHAEL. "Bausteine zur Biographie"

(3) GAUGLER, ANDREAS. "Graphologische Analyse"

(4) LIEBER, HANS-JOACHIM, and FURTH, PETER. "Zur Dialektik der Simmelschen Konzeption einer formalen Soziologie"

(5) MÜLLER, HORST. "Plan einer Gesamtausgabe der Werke Georg Simmels"

(6) Simmel's letters to Paul Ernst, Adolf von Harnack, Edmund Husserl, Heinrich Rickert, Rainer Maria Rilke, Auguste Rodin, Margarete Susman, and Max and Marianne Weber.

(7) Reminiscences of Simmel by Karl Berger, Ernst Bloch, Ferdinand Bruckner, Martin Buber, Ludwig Curtius, Max Dessoir, Emil Ermatinger, Paul Ernst, Paul Fechter, Kurt Gassen, Eberhard Gothein, Friedrich Gundolf, Charles Hauter, Georg Hermann, Otto Heuschele, Kurt Hiller, Paul Honigsheim, Fritz Jacobs, Karl Joël, Otto Klemperer, Richard Kroner, Gertrud Kupffer, Edith Landmann, Sabine Lepsius, Theodor Lessing, Richard Lewinsohn, Emil Ludwig, Georg Lukács, Hugo Marcus, Ludwig Marcuse, Leo Matthias, Friedrich Meinecke, Ernst Morwitz, Eckart von Naso, Rudolf Pannwitz, Erich Przywara, Ilse Reicke, Sophie Rickert, Albert Salomon, Gottfried Salomon de la Tour, Herman Schmalenbach, Albert Schweitzer, Kurt Singer, Nicholas J. Spykman, Albert

Steffen, Margarete Susman, Frank Thiess, Marianne Weber, Werner Weisbach, Friedrich Wolters, and Wilhelm Worringer.

(8) GASSEN, KURT. Bibliographie.

d. HONIGSHEIM, PAUL. "Georg Simmel: Ein Wort zum 100. Geburtstag." A mimeographed copy of a radio broadcast from RIAS, Berlin, on March 1, 1958. Pp. 9.

e. MARCUSE, LUDWIG. "Auf den einzelnen Lebenden kam es ihm an. Zum 100. Geburtstag des Philosophen Georg Simmel," *Die Zeit. Wochenzeitung für Politik, Wirtschaft, Handel und Kultur* [Hamburg], February 27, 1958.

f. SUSMAN, MARGARETE. "Zum 100. Geburtstag von Georg Simmel," *Neue Zürcher Zeitung,* February 28, 1958.

1959 a. DURKHEIM, EMILE. "Sociology and Its Scientific Field," translated by KURT H. WOLFF, in *Emile Durkheim, 1858-1917: A Collection of Essays, with Translations and a Bibliography,* ed. KURT H. WOLFF. Columbus, Ohio: Ohio State University Press, 1959. An English translation of the 1900 entry.

b. WEINGARTNER, RUDOLPH H. "Experience and Culture: The Philosophy of Georg Simmel." Unpublished Ph.D. dissertation, Columbia University, 1959. Pp. iv + 315.

BIBLIOGRAPHY OF SIMMEL'S BOOKS IN GERMAN AND HIS WRITINGS WHICH ARE AVAILABLE IN ENGLISH

KURT H. WOLFF

In view of the relatively easy accessibility of the bibliographies of writings *by* Simmel to which Kurt Gassen refers in the introductory note to his bibliography *on* Simmel, I have found it appropriate to list here only Simmel's books in German and those writings which have appeared in English translation. For a much more comprehensive bibliography, the reader is referred to Gassen's contribution to *Buch des Dankes an Georg Simmel* (1958), which is mentioned in the same introductory note.

A. Simmel's Books in German

1881 *Das Wesen der Materie nach Kants physischer Monadologie.* Inaugural-Dissertation zur Erlangung der Doktorwürde von der philosophischen Fakultät der Friedrich-Wilhelms Universität zu Berlin genehmigt und Freitag den 25ten Februar 1881 öffentlich verteidigt. Contains an autobiography. Berlin: Druck der Norddeutschen Buchdruckerei, 1881. Pp. 34.

1890 *Über sociale Differenzierung. Sociologische und psychologische Untersuchungen.* ("Staats- und socialwissenschaftliche Forschungen," ed. Gustav Schmoller, Zehnter Band, Erstes Heft.) Leipzig: Duncker und Humblot, 1890. Pp. vii + 147. (2nd ed., 1905; 3rd ed., 1910.)

1892 *Die Probleme der Geschichtsphilosophie. Eine erkenntnistheoretische Studie.* Leipzig: Duncker und Humblot, 1892. Pp. x + 109. (2nd rev. ed., 1905; 3rd ed., 1907; 4th ed., Munich and Leipzig, 1922; 5th ed., 1923.)

1892-1893 *Einleitung in die Moralwissenschaft. Eine Kritik der ethischen Grundbegriffe.* Berlin: Hertz (Besser), Vol. I, 1892 (Pp. viii + 467); Vol. II, 1893 (Pp. viii + 526). (2nd ed., Stuttgart and Berlin: Cotta, 1904; 3rd ed., 1911.)

1900 *Philosophie des Geldes.* Leipzig: Duncker und Humblot, 1900. Pp. xvi + 554. (2nd ed., 1907; 3rd ed., 1920; 4th ed., Munich and Leipzig, 1922; 5th ed., Munich, 1930; 6th ed., Berlin, 1958.)

1904 *Kant. Sechzehn Vorlesungen gehalten an der Berliner Universität.* Leipzig: Duncker und Humblot, 1904. Pp. vi + 181. (2nd ed., 1905; 3rd enlarged ed., Munich and Leipzig, 1913; 4th ed., 1918; 5th ed., 1921; 6th ed., 1924.)

1905 *Philosophie der Mode.* ("Moderne Zeitfragen," No. 11.) Berlin: Pan-Verlag, 1905. Pp. 41. (2nd ed., 1905; slightly revised and enlarged under the title "Die Mode" in the 1911 entry, pp. 25-57.)

1906 a. *Kant und Goethe.* ("Die Kultur, Sammlung illustrierter Einzeldarstellungen," ed. CORNELIUS GURLITT, Vol. X.) Berlin: Marquardt, 1906. Pp. 71. (2nd ed., Leipzig: Wolff, 1907; 3rd rev. ed., titled *Kant und Goethe; zur Geschichte der modernen Weltanschauung,* 1916; 4th ed., 1918; 5th ed., Munich and Leipzig, 1924.)

b. *Die Religion.* ("Die Gesellschaft, Sammlung sozialpsychologischer Monographien," ed. MARTIN BUBER, Vol. II.) Frankfurt am Main: Rütten und Loening, 1906. Pp. 79. (2nd rev. and enlarged ed., 1912; 3rd ed., 1922.)

1907 *Schopenhauer und Nietzsche. Ein Vortragszyklus.* Leipzig: Duncker und Humblot, 1907. Pp. xii + 263. (2nd ed., Munich and Leipzig, 1920; 3rd ed., 1923.)

1908 *Soziologie. Untersuchungen über die Formen der Vergesellschaftung.* Leipzig: Duncker und Humblot, 1908. Pp. 782. (2nd ed., Munich and Leipzig, 1922; 3rd ed., 1923; 4th ed., Berlin, 1958.)

1910 *Hauptprobleme der Philosophie.* ("Sammlung Göschen," No. 500.) Leipzig: Göschen, 1910. Pp. 175. (2nd ed., 1911; 3rd ed., 1913; 4th ed., Berlin and Leipzig: de Gruyter, 1917; 5th ed., 1920; 6th ed., 1927; 7th ed., Berlin, 1950.)

1911 *Philosophische Kultur. Gesammelte Essays.* ("Philosophisch-soziologische Bücherei," Vol. XXVII.) Leipzig: Kröner, 1911. Pp. 319. (2nd enlarged ed., 1919.)

1913 *Goethe.* Leipzig: Klinkhardt und Biermann, 1913. Pp. vii + 364. (4th ed., 1921; 5th ed., 1923.)

1914 *Deutschlands innere Wandlung.* Rede, gehalten . . . am 7. November 1914. Strasbourg: Trübner, 1914. Pp. 14.

1916 a. *Das Problem der Historischen Zeit.* ("Philosophische Vorträge veröffentlicht von der Kantgesellschaft," No. 12.) Berlin: Reuther und Reichard, 1916. Pp. 31. (Reprinted in 1922, a., pp. 152-69; and in the 1957 entry, pp. 43-58.)

b. *Rembrandt. Ein kunstphilosophischer Versuch.* Leipzig: Wolff, 1916. Pp. viii + 205. (2nd ed., 1919.)

1917 a. *Grundfragen der Soziologie (Individuum und Gesellschaft).* ("Sammlung Göschen," No. 101.) Berlin and Leipzig: de Gruyter, 1917. Pp. 103. (2nd ed., 1920.)

b. *Der Krieg und die geistigen Entscheidungen. Reden und Aufsätze.* Munich and Leipzig: Duncker und Humblot, 1917. Pp. 72. (2nd ed., Leipzig, 1920.)

1918 a. *Der Konflikt der modernen Kultur. Ein Vortrag.* Munich and Leipzig: Duncker und Humblot, 1918. Pp. 48. (2nd ed., 1912; 3rd ed., 1926.)

b. *Lebensanschauung. Vier metaphysische Kapitel.* Munich and

Leipzig: Duncker und Humblot, 1918. Pp. 245. (2nd ed., 1922.)

c. *Vom Wesen des historischen Verstehens.* ("Geschichtliche Abende im Zentralinstitut für Erziehung und Unterricht," Fünftes Heft.) Berlin: Mittler, 1918. Pp. 31. (Reprinted in the 1957 entry, pp. 59-85.)

(Published Posthumously)

1922 a. *Zur Philosophie der Kunst. Philosophische und kunstphilosophische Aufsätze,* ed. GERTRUD SIMMEL. Potsdam: Kiepenheuer, 1922. Pp. 175.

b. *Schulpädagogik.* Vorlesungen, ed. KARL HAUTER. Osterwieck/Harz: Zickfeldt, 1922. Pp. iv + 134.

1923 *Fragmente und Aufsätze aus dem Nachlass und Veröffentlichungen der letzten Jahre,* ed. GERTRUD KANTOROWICZ. Munich: Drei Masken Verlag, 1923. Pp. x + 304.

1953 *Rembrandtstudien.* Basel: Schwabe, 1953. Pp. 72. (Reprints of 1914, "Rembrandtstudie," *Logos,* V [1914-15], 1-32; and 1915, "Studien zur Philosophie der Kunst, besonders der Rembrandtschen," *ibid.,* pp. 221-38. Also published as *Rembrandtstudien.* Sonderausgabe. ["Libelli," No. 7.] Darmstadt: Wissenschaftliche Buchgemeinschaft, 1953. Pp. 72.)

1957 *Brücke und Tür. Essays des Philosophen zur Geschichte, Religion, Kunst und Gesellschaft.* Im Verein mit MARGARETE SUSMAN herausgegeben von MICHAEL LANDMANN. Stuttgart: Koehler, 1957. Pp. xxiii + 281.

B. SIMMEL'S WRITINGS AVAILABLE IN ENGLISH[1]

1893 "Moral Deficiencies as Determining Intellectual Functions" [translator not indicated], *International Journal of Ethics,* Vol. III, No. 4 (July, 1893), pp. 490-507. "This article is part of the second volume of the author's 'Einleitung in die Moralwissenschäft [*sic*],' which is shortly to appear. The reader finds here hardly more than a general outline of the original article. From want of space, it has been considerably shortened without being able to consult the author."

1895 "The Problem of Sociology" [translator not indicated], *Annals of the American Academy of Political and Social Science,* Vol. VI, No. 3 (November, 1895), pp. 412-23. Presumably a translation of "Das Problem der Soziologie," *Jahrbuch für Gesetzgebung, Verwaltung und Volkswirtschaft im Deutschen Reich,* Vol. XVIII, No. 4 (1894), pp. 1301-7.

1896 "Superiority and Subordination as Subject-Matter of Sociology," trans. ALBION W. SMALL, *American Journal of Sociology,* Vol. II, No. 2 (September, 1896), pp. 167-89; and Vol. II, No. 3 (November, 1896), pp. 392-415. A translation of an earlier and much shorter draft of Chap. iii of *Soziologie* (1908).

1898 "The Persistence of Social Groups," trans. ALBION W. SMALL, *ibid.,* Vol. III, No. 5 (March, 1898), pp. 662-98; Vol. III, No. 6 (May, 1898), pp. 829-36; and Vol. IV, No. 1 (July, 1898), pp. 35-50. A translation of an earlier and much shorter draft of Chap. viii of *Soziologie* (1908).

1900 "A Chapter in the Philosophy of Value" [translator not indicated], *ibid.,* Vol. V, No. 5 (March, 1900), pp. 577-603. "A fragment from a volume entitled *The Philosophy of Money* to be published this year by Duncker und Humblot, Leipzig. Translated for this JOURNAL from the author's manuscript."

1902 a. "Tendencies in German Life and Thought since 1870," trans. W. D. BRIGGS, *International Monthly,* Vol. V, No. 1 (January, 1902), pp. 93-111; and Vol. V, No. 2 (February, 1902), pp. 166-84.

b. "The Number of Members as Determining the Sociological Form of the Group," trans. ALBION W. SMALL, *American Journal of Sociology,* Vol. VIII, No. 1 (July, 1902), pp. 1-46; and Vol. VIII, No. 2 (September, 1902), pp. 158-96. A translation of an earlier and shorter draft of Chap. ii of *Soziologie* (1908).

1904 a. "The Sociology of Conflict," trans. ALBION W. SMALL, *ibid.,* Vol. IX, No. 4 (January, 1904), pp. 490-525; Vol. IX, No. 5 (March, 1904), pp. 672-89; and Vol. IX, No. 6 (May, 1904), pp. 798-811. A translation of an earlier and shorter draft of Chap. iv of *Soziologie* (1908).

b. "Fashion" [translator not indicated], *International Quarterly,* Vol. X, No. 1 (October, 1904), pp. 130-55.

1905 "A Contribution to the Sociology of Religion," trans. W. W. ELWANG, *American Journal of Sociology,* Vol. XI, No. 3 (November, 1905), pp. 359-76.

1906 "The Sociology of Secrecy and of Secret Societies," trans. ALBION W. SMALL, *ibid.,* Vol. XI, No. 4 (January, 1906), pp. 441-98. A translation of an earlier and shorter draft of Chap. v of *Soziologie* (1908).

1909 "The Problem of Sociology," trans. ALBION W. SMALL, *ibid.,* Vol. XV, No. 3 (November, 1909), pp. 289-320. "This is a portion of the first chapter of Simmel's *Soziologie,* a brief notice of which appeared in this *Journal,* Vol. XIV, p. 544. The translation is as literal as possible. The notes, unless otherwise indicated, are my own.—Albion W. Small."

1910 "How Is Society Possible?" trans. ALBION W. SMALL, *ibid.,* Vol. XVI, No. 3 (November, 1910), pp. 372-91. "This is a translation of the passage entitled, 'Exkurs über das Problem: Wie ist Gesellschaft möglich?' in Simmel's *Soziologie* (pp. 27-45). Although I have often argued (e.g., *General Sociology,* pp. 183-85, 504-8, etc.) that the term 'society' is too vague to be made into an instrument of precision, I am glad to assist in getting a hearing for Simmel's efforts to prove the contrary. I have therefore done my best to render his essay literally as far as possible, and in all cases faithfully. A.W.S."

1921 PARK, ROBERT E., and BURGESS, ERNEST W. *Introduction to the Science of Sociology*. Chicago: University of Chicago Press, 1921. Contains, in addition to numerous short passages reprinted from several of the preceding translations, three new translations, presumably by Park and Burgess: "The Sociological Significance of the 'Stranger,'" pp. 322-27 (from *Soziologie,* pp. 685-91); "Sociology of the Senses," pp. 356-61 (from *Soziologie,* pp. 646-51); and "Money and Freedom," pp. 552-53 (from *Philosophie des Geldes,* pp. 351-52).

1936 "The Metropolis and Mental Life," trans. EDWARD A. SHILS, *Syllabus and Selected Readings, Second-Year Course in the Study of Contemporary Society (Social Science II).* 5th ed. [and later eds.] Chicago: University of Chicago Bookstore, 1936. pp. 221-38. A translation of "Die Grossstädte und das Geistesleben," in *Die Grossstadt,* Vorträge und Aufsätze zur Städteausstellung von K. BÜCHER, F. RATZEL, G. v. MAYR, H. WAENTIG, G. SIMMEL, TH. PETERMANN und D. SCHÄFER. Gehe-Stiftung zu Dresden, Winter 1902-1903. (*Jahrbuch der Gehe-Stiftung zu Dresden,* Band IX.) Dresden: von Zahn und Jaensch, 1903. Pp. 185-206.

(no date) "The Metropolis and Mental Life," trans. H. H. GERTH with the assistance of C. WRIGHT MILLS. Department of Sociology, University of Wisconsin, n.d. Pp. 10 (mimeographed).

1949 "The Sociology of Sociability," trans. EVERETT C. HUGHES, *American Journal of Sociology,* LV (November, 1949), 254-61. A translation of "Soziologie der Geselligkeit, Vortrag, gehalten am Begrüssungsabend des ersten deutschen Soziologentages in Frankfurt, 19. Oktober 1910," *Verhandlungen des ersten deutschen Soziologentages.* Tübingen: Mohr, 1911. pp. 1-16.

1950 *The Sociology of Georg Simmel.* Translated, edited, and with an Introduction by KURT H. WOLFF. Glencoe, Ill.: Free Press of Glencoe, Illinois, 1950. Part I: "Fundamental Problems of Sociology (Individual and Society)," a translation of *Grundfragen der Soziologie (Individuum und Gesellschaft).* Part II: "Quantitative Aspects of the Group," a translation of Chap. ii of *Soziologie.* Part III: "Superordination and Subordination," a translation of Chap. iii of *Soziologie.* Part IV: "The Secret and the Secret Society," a translation of Chap. v of *Soziologie.* Part V, Chap. i: "Faithfulness and Gratitude," a translation of *Soziologie,* 3rd ed., pp. 438-47; Chap. ii: "The Negative Character of Collective Behavior," a translation of *Soziologie,* 3rd ed., pp. 359-62; Chap. iii: "The Stranger," a translation of *Soziologie,* 3rd ed., pp. 509-12.

1955 *Conflict* and *The Web of Group-Affiliations.* With a Foreword by EVERETT C. HUGHES. Glencoe, Ill.: Free Press of Glencoe, Illinois. "Conflict," trans. KURT H. WOLFF, pp. 11-123 (a translation of Chap. iv of *Soziologie*); "The Web of Group-Affiliations," trans. REINHARD BENDIX, pp. 125-95 (a translation of Chap. vi of *Soziologie*).

1959 The translations in the present volume.

(Reprints)

1950 "The Metropolis and Mental Life," Part V, Chap. iv, in the 1950 entry. A reprint of the entry under "no date."

1955 a. "A Contribution to the Sociology of Religion," *American Journal of Sociology*, Vol. LX, Part II (May, 1955), pp. 1-18. A reprint of the 1905 entry.

b. "The Significance of Numbers for Social Life," in *Small Groups: Studies in Social Interaction,* ed. PAUL A. HARE, EDGAR F. BORGATTA, and ROBERT F. BALES. New York: Alfred A. Knopf, Inc., 1955. A reprint of pp. 87, 105-6, 118-20, 122-23, and 135-36 of the 1950 entry.

1956 BORGATTA, EDGAR F., and MEYER, HENRY J. *Sociological Theory: Present-Day Sociology from the Past.* New York: Alfred A. Knopf, 1956. Contains "The Number of Persons as Determining the Form of the Group," pp. 126-58 (a reprint, abridged, of 1902, b.); "Superiority and Subordination in Social Relationships," pp. 180-204 (a reprint, abridged, of the 1896 entry); "Knowledge and Ignorance," pp. 205-26 (a reprint, abridged, of the 1906 entry); and "The Persistence of Social Groups," pp. 364-98 (a reprint, abridged, of the 1898 entry).

1957 a. "Fashion," *American Journal of Sociology,* Vol. LXII, No. 6 (May, 1957), pp. 541-58. A reprint of 1904, b.

b. COSER, LEWIS A., and ROSENBERG, BERNARD. *Sociological Theory: A Book of Readings*. New York: Macmillan Co., 1957. Contains "The Dyad and the Triad," pp. 66-76 (a reprint of pp. 122-25, 143-53 of the 1950 entry); "Forms of Domination," pp. 124-29 (a reprint of pp. 181-86 of the 1950 entry); and "Conflict as Sociation," pp. 193-97 (a reprint of pp. 13-17 of the 1955 entry).

1. This is based on Kurt H. Wolff (ed.), *The Sociology of Georg Simmel* (Glencoe, Ill.: Free Press of Glencoe, Illinois, 1950), pp. lvii-lix.

NOTES ON THE CONTRIBUTORS

HOWARD BECKER teaches sociology at the University of Wisconsin. His *Systematic Sociology on the Basis of the* Beziehungslehre *and* Gebildelehre *of Leopold von Wiese* (1932), *German Youth: Bond or Free* (1946), and numerous other publications attest to his long-standing interest in German intellectual and social life.

HUGH DALZIEL DUNCAN, born in Scotland and trained in philosophy, literature, and sociology at Drake University and the University of Chicago, has written *Language and Literature in Society* (1953) and *Social Hierarchy: Communication of Hierarchy in Art and Society* (forthcoming).

LORE FERGUSON is a graduate student of German at the Ohio State University.

KURT GASSEN, librarian at the Deutsche Staatsbibliothek in Berlin, studied with Simmel from 1912 to 1914 and edited the course in ethics and the problems of modern culture that Simmel taught in 1913. He is co-editor, with Michael Landmann, of *Buch des Dankes an Georg Simmel* (1958).

PAUL HONIGSHEIM studied at the universities of Bonn, Berlin, and Heidelberg, and has taught at the University of Cologne, the National University of Panama, and Michigan State University. While in Cologne, he was also the director of the People's University. He has published widely in many fields, including the history of sociology and anthropology; the sociology of religion, art, and knowledge; and adult education.

GERTRUD KANTOROWICZ was a close friend of Simmel's. She died at Theresienstadt in 1945.

DAVID KETTLER is a student of social and political philosophy. He teaches political science at the Ohio State University.

CONTRIBUTORS

DONALD N. LEVINE wrote his doctoral dissertation on "Simmel and Parsons: Two Approaches to the Study of Society" (University of Chicago, 1957). He is currently doing field research in Ethiopia as a fellow of the Ford Foundation.

MATTHEW LIPMAN studied at Stanford University, Columbia University, the University of Vienna, and the Sorbonne. He teaches philosophy at Columbia University, College of Pharmacy, and is the author of articles in learned periodicals and journals of opinion.

HEINZ MAUS, trained at the universities of Frankfurt and Kiel, teaches sociology at the Pädagogische Hochschule Weilburg (Lahn). He is the author of monographs and papers on the history of sociology, a translator, an editor, and a contributor to encyclopedias and other collections.

ARTHUR SALZ was educated at the University of Berlin, where he studied with Simmel, and at the University of Munich. He has taught at the University of Heidelberg, Cambridge University, and Ohio State University. Among his widespread interests are philosophy, theory of imperialism, formation and utilization of capital, and wage-fund theory. He has contributed to these and other fields.

MASAMICHI SHIMMEI teaches sociology at Tohoku University in Japan. He is the author of several works in Japanese: *On Formal Sociology* (1928), *Fundamental Problems of Sociology* (1939), *Treatise on the Nature of Society* (1942), *Dictionary of Sociology* (1944), and *History of Sociology* (1951).

F. H. TENBRUCK was trained at the University of Marburg and taught sociology and philosophy in Germany prior to joining the Sociology Department at Hobart and William Smith Colleges. He has published in professional journals and collections in both philosophy and sociology.

E. V. WALTER received his education at the University of Minnesota. He teaches political science at Brandeis University and has contributed articles on political and legal theory to academic journals. He has also written for literary magazines and journals of opinion.

RUDOLPH H. WEINGARTNER teaches philosophy at Columbia University. During the academic year 1957-58, he held a fellowship, awarded by the Social Science Research Council under its program in political theory and legal philosophy, so that he could further his study of Georg Simmel.

KURT H. WOLFF, who studied at the universities of Frankfurt, Munich, and Florence, teaches sociology at the Ohio State University. He is the editor and translator of *The Sociology of Georg Simmel* (1950).

INDEX

Page numbers in italics indicate passages in the translations.

Abe, J., 204
Abel, Theodore, 61, 74
Achenwall, Gottfried, 168
Adornment as enhancing the individual, 105, 137
Adventure; *see also* the Adventurer
comparison of, with the work of art, *245*
defined, *243, 244-45, 246*
dreamlike quality of, *243-44*
as a form, *247, 248-49, 257-58*
life as, *247-48*
the love affair as, *250-53*
as a prerogative of youth, *253-55*
as an ubiquitous element, *255-57*
Adventurer, the; *see also* Adventure
as the ahistorical individual, *245-46*
and the artist, *245*
Casanova as, *245-46, 250*
the fatalism of, *249-50*
and the gambler, *246-47*
the philosopher as, *249*
Alienation
explanation of, by Simmel's theory of "factoring," 147
Simmel's idea of, as a tragic concept, 140-46
Altmann, S. P., 216-17
Analogy
as a means of knowing another person, 227-28
Simmel's use of, 152-55, 161, *320-21, 323, 324, 332, 336* (n. 6)
Ankermann, Bernhard, 176
Année sociologique, 188, 191
Anti-Semitism, effects of, on Simmel's career, 167, 169-70
Aquinas, St. Thomas, 149-50, *298*
Architecture, *259-60*
Simmel's analogies from, 152-55
Aristocracy, sociological form of, 13-14
Aristotle, 25, 119, 150, 163, 235
Art
beauty in, *273*
nature of space in, *267*
relation of, to reality, 109-10
Simmel's philosophy of, 6-7
society as a work of, 236
universal problem of, *280*
Atoji, Y., 214

Bachofen, Johann Jacob, 175, 177, 178
Baldwin, James Mark, 206
Barth, Paul, 186
Bastian, Adolf, 176, 192
Bebel, August, 178
Becker, Howard, 107
Bendix, Reinhard, 214
Benedict, Ruth, 24
Bergson, Henri, 36, 120-21, 203, 224
Berlin in Simmel's time, 167-69, 233-34
Berr, Henri, 191
Bismarck, Otto von, 167, 169
Bjornson, Bjornstjerne, 169
Bloch, Marcel, 191
Böcklin, Arnold, 11
Bonald, Louis Gabriel Amboise de, 182
Boskoff, Alvin, 86, 87
Bouglé, Célestin, 187
Bruno, Giordano, *298*
Burgess, Ernest W., 107, 113, 196, 202
Burke, Kenneth, 115

Casanova de Seingalt, Giovanni Giacomo, *245-46, 250*

INDEX

Causal resolution, Simmel's method of analysis described as, 24-27
Collingwood, R. C., 107
Comte, Auguste, 180-82, 183, 184, 191, 206
Condorcet, Marie Jean Antoine, 183
Conflict and *The Web of Group-Affiliations,* 153; *see also* "Web of Group-Affiliations, The"
Coquetry as a form of sociation, 106-7
Coser, Lewis, 16
Culture, Simmel as a philosopher of, 33-34

Dargun, Lothar von, 178
Darwin, Charles, 114
De la division du travail social, 189
De Quincey, Thomas, 235
Dewey, John, 114
Dilthey, Wilhelm, 107, 120, 168, 181, 191, 192, 203, 234, 236
Distance as a principle in interaction, 23
Division of labor, 17-18, 130
Domination; *see* Superordination and subordination
Driesch, Hans Adolf, 172
Drobisch, Moritz Wilhelm, 168
Dualism
  of the forms of sociation, 88-89
  of life, 54
  as a principle in Simmel's social thought, 21-22, 29-30
Durkheim, Emile, 77, 130, 180, 196, 208, 209, 214, 222
  his criticism of Simmel, 188-89
  the place of, in German sociology, 189-91
Dyad, the, as a form of sociation, 25-27

Eckhart, Meister, *286-87, 292-93*
Economics in Simmel's time, 168
Einleitung in die Moralwissenschaft, 170, 176, 187, 204
Einstein, Albert, 114
Engels, Friedrich, 177, 178
Epicurus, *284*
Epistemology, Simmel's and Bergson's, compared, 120-23
Erleben, 43-46
Ethics
  conflict with aesthetics of, *264-65*
  as divorced from sociology, 162
  the young Simmel's conception of, 172
Ethnology
  in Germany, 175-76
  Simmel's interest in, 176-78
Eulenburg, Franz, 196
Expressionism, 6

Factoring, Simmel's theory of, 147
Family, the, Simmel's remarks on, 228
Fashion, 12-13
Febvre, Lucien, 191
Fichte, Johann Gottlieb, 234, *290, 299*
Figure-ground opposition in Simmel's method of analysis, 124
Form and content; *see also* Forms of sociation
  autonomous form, 48-50, 125
  definitions of, 37-43, 149
  distinction between, in Simmel's philosophy, 34-35, 124-25, *288*
  genesis of form, 45
  historical limitations on form, *289-90*
  world-forms, 50-53
Formal sociology; *see also* Forms of sociation; Sociology
  basic assumptions in, 19-22
  criticisms of, 61-63
  formal entities and analogies in, 28-29
  methodology of, 74-76, 80
  and modern sociology, 76-78, 86-89

Formal sociology—*Continued*
principle of dualism in, 21-22, 24, 29-30
problem of freedom in, 16-18
subject matter of, 12-19, 22-24, *312-23, 326-29*
subjective approach to phenomena in, 27-28
Formes élémentaires de la vie religieuse, Les, 189
Forms of sociation
abstraction of, 74-75, 151, 161
ambiguities in the concept of, 110-15
analogical nature of, 64, *314*
autonomy of, 101-2, 125, 159
changes of, 159-60
as constituting society, *315-16, 319-20*
contents of, 70, *314-15*
coquetry, 106-7
criticism of the concept of, 64, 74, 188-89, 208-9
defined, 20-21, 22, 69-71
the dyad, 25-27
independence of, from content, 125
kinds of, 21
legitimation of, *316-17*
methodology of, *323-26*
minor, 88, *326-29*
as the object of sociology, 25, 71, 86-88, 101, *321-23*
ontological status of, 83-86
origin of, in interaction, 88-89
play, 21, 159
predictive value of, 86, 89-90
provisional nature of the concept of, 64-65
as restraining the expression of content, 160
sociability, 102-7
superordination and subordination, 72-73, 155
and the theory of social structure, 77-78
Fouilée, A., 186
Fragmente und Aufsätze, 205
Freedom, increase of, with the development of society, 16-18
Freud, Sigmund, 110, 113, 114, 214
Freyer, Hans, 212-13
Frischeisen-Köhler, Max, 187

Geometry, Simmel's analogies from, 152-55, 161, *320-21, 323, 324, 332*
George, Stefan, 169, 234
Giddings, Franklin H., 205, 206, 208
Goethe, Johann Wolfgang von, 27, 33, 103, 133, 204, 235, *262*
Gothein, Eberhard, 190
Graebner, Fritz, 176
Group, the, and the individual, 15-16, 104, 126-27
Grundfragen der Soziologie, 103, 108, 207, 209, 210
Gumplowicz, Ludwig, 205

Handwörterbuch der Staatswissenschaften, 186
Hauriou, Maurice, 206
Hayashi, M., 210
Haym, Rudolf, 181
Hegel, Georg Wilhelm, 142, 181, 182, 191, 196, 202, 203, 227, 235
Heidegger, Martin, 205, 211
Heilborn, Ernst, 176
Hellwald, Friedrich von, 176
Herbart, Johann Friedrich, 168, 175-76, 192
Herder, Johann Gottfried von, 130, 181
Higuchi, R., 206
Hinkle, G. J., 214
Hinkle, R. C., 214
Historical change, Simmel's theories of, 90-92
Historical school of jurisprudence, 181-82
History
philosophies of, as antecedents of German sociology, 181-83
Simmel's philosophy of, 7, 90-92, 150-52, 161, 191-94

Homans, George C., 214, 215
Hooker, Thomas, 150
Humboldt, Wilhelm von, 234

Ibsen, Henrik, 169
Ideal-types, Max Weber's conception of, 80-81
Igarashi, N., 210
Imori, R., 210
Individual, the
  boundaries of, 134
  conceptions of, 119-20
  eighteenth- and nineteenth-century conceptions of, 128-31
  enhancement of, by adornment, 105, 137
  freedom of, under despotism, 162
  and the group, 15-16, 104, 126-27
  interpretations of, 132-34
  and the larger sphere, *273-75*
  in a money economy, 17-18, 127, 177
  Simmel's definition of, 123-26
  Simmel's epistemological framework for, 120-23
  and society, 111, 131-32, 140-45
  uniqueness of, 120, 135-37, 172
  and universals, 127-28
Individuality; *see also* the Individual
  the face as symbol of, *278-80*
Interaction; *see also* Forms of sociation
  common conception of, 66-68
  as explaining society, *311-12*
  principle of distance in, 23
  Simmel's principle of, 19-20
  Simmel's use of dualisms in defining, 21-22
  social action as, 68-70
Iwasaki, U., 211

Jhering, Rudolf von, 185
Jones, Ernest, 113

Kada, T., 211
Kant, Immanuel, 11, 27, 33, 42, 63, 129, 131, 154, 178, 202, 203, *300, 339, 345*
  concept of the *Ding an sich* of, 39, 122, 156
  concept of progress of, 143-44
  influence of, on Simmel's political theory, 150-51, 155-58, 161
  philosophy of, *287-93, 337-38*
Kant und Goethe, 203
Kautsky, Karl, 180
Kishimoto, N., 206
Knowledge, Simmel's approach to the problem of, 120-23
Köhler, Max Frischeisen-; *see* Frischeisen-Köhler, Max
Komatsu, K., 210
Kurauchi, K., 211

La Grasserie, Raoul Guérin de, 206
Labriola, Antonio, 180
Langbehn, Julius, 169
Lange, Friedrich Albert, 168
Lazarus, Moritz, 192
Le Bon, Gustave, 146
Lebensanschauung, 108, 203
Leibnitz, Gottfried Wilhelm von, *298, 300, 301*
Life
  as adventure, *247-48*
  level of freedom in, 48-50
  as more-life, 35-37
  as more-than-life, 53-54
  Simmel's philosophy of, 3-7, 235-36
  state of *Erleben* in, 43-46
  teleological phase of, 46-48
  tragic nature of Simmel's philosophy of, 7-8
Lilienfeld, P. von, 186
Lippert, Julius, 169, 170, 176, 178
Litt, Theodor, 196, 211
Locke, John, 150
Lotze, Rudolf Hermann, 112
Love in Simmel's philosophy of life, 7

INDEX

Lukács, Georg, 188
Luschan, Felix von, 176

Maistre, Joseph de, 181
Mannheim, Karl, 9, 213, 214
Marica, George M., 189
Marx, Karl, 114, 177, 181, 193-94, 196, 204
Mass behavior, Simmel's explanation of, 146-48
Matsumoto, J., 212
Mead, George Herbert, 114, 115, 135, 227
Merton, Robert K., 214
Michelangelo, 11
Mill, John Stuart, 132, 181
Mind and the creation of unity, *276, 302-3*
Mohl, Robert von, 183
Mommsen, Theodor, 175
Money
  effects of, 29-30
  and individuality, 17-18, 127, 177
Morgan, Lewis Henry, 177
Mysticism, *286-87, 292-93*

Nicholas of Cusa, *299*
Nietzsche, Friedrich, 11, 131, 133, 169, 182, 204, 234

Odaka, K., 214
Onishi, K., 204
Ortega y Gasset, José, 234

Pareto, Vilfredo, 214
Park, Robert E., 107, 113, 196, 202
Parsons, Talcott, 9-10, 16, 24, 27, 77, 110, 112
Patina, 262
"Persistence of Social Groups, The," 80, 84
Philosopher, the; *see also* Philosophy
  basic attitude of, *285-86*
  typical mentality of, as reflected in his work, *293-302*
Philosophie der Geschicht als Soziologie, Die, 186
Philosophie des Geldes, 17, 27, 80-81, 83, 90, 171, 177, 178, 194, 203, 204, 210, 234
  Table of Contents of, 217-24
Philosophische Kultur, 203
Philosophy; *see also* the Philosopher
  inapplicability of, to particulars, *303-9*
  as its own problem, *282*
  of Kant, *287-93, 337-38*
  the object of, *283-84*
  relation of mysticism to, *286-87, 292-93*
  and religion, connection between, *287*
  as thinking without presuppositions, *282-83*
  and the typical mentality of the philosopher, *293-302*
  as a unification of the world, *302-3*
Plato, *298, 299*
Political theory of Simmel
  classical formulations in, 149-50
  influence of Kant on, 150-51, 155-58, 161
Post, Albert Hermann, 178
Preuss, Heinrich, 176
"Problem of Sociology, The," 64-70, 188
Probleme der Geschichtsphilosophie, Die, 84, 85, 192-93, 194, 203
Progress, Simmel's view of the idea of, 151, 171, 193
Protagoras, 236
Psychology
  the German tradition in, at Simmel's time, 168, 171-72
  Simmel's views on, 172, 192-93

Ranke, Leopold von, 168
Ratzel, Friedrich, 176
Reciprocal orientations; *see* Forms of sociation
Reciprocity; *see* Forms of sociation
Règles de la méthode sociologique, Les, 189
Relativism in Simmel's thought, 122
Religion
  as a form, 28-29
  and philosophy, connection between, *287*
  in preliterate cultures, 178
Rembrandt, 27, 33, 124
Rembrandt, 203, 204
Rickert, Heinrich, 82-83, 192, 193
Riehl, W. H., 184
Roberty, Eugéne V. de, 206
Rodin, Auguste, 11
Rousseau, Jean Jacques, 130, 150
Royce, Josiah, 130
Rümelin, Gustav, 185
Ruin, the
  the peace of, *263-66*
  as a product of nature, *261-63*
  tragic nature of, *259-60, 263*
  as a unity, *260*

Savigny, Friedrich Karl von, 234
Schäffle, Albert Ebenhard Friedrich, 184, 205
Schelling, Friedrich Wilhelm von, *299*
Schlegel, Friedrich Wilhelm, 130
Schleiermacher, Friedrich Daniel Ernst, 130
Schlözer, August Ludwig von, 168
Schmalenbach, Herman, 194
Schmidt, Father Bernhardt, 176
Schmoller, Gustav, 168, 185, 186, 189
Schopenhauer, Arthur, 11, 154, 169, *284, 299, 300, 301-2*
Schopenhauer und Nietzsche, 203
Schurtz, Heinrich, 176, 178
Science, distinction between natural and cultural, 82-83
Seler, Eduard Georg, 176
Shimizu, I., 205, 213
Shimmei, Masamichi, 211-12
Sighele, Scipio, 146
Sociability as a form of sociation, 102-7
Social action
  and formal sociology, 76-77
  interaction as, 68-70
Social change and formal sociology, 87-88, 89-91
Social Darwinism, Simmel's views on, 170-71
Social structure, theory of, and formal sociology, 77-78
Socialists of the chair, the, influence of, on German sociology, 184-85
Sociation defined, *314-15; see also* Forms of sociation
Society
  a priori conditions of, *340-56*
  increase of freedom with the development of, 16-18
  and the individual, 111, 131-32, 140-45
  as "my representation," *339-40*
  as the object of sociology, 86-87, *310-11*
  Simmel's conception of, 19-20, *314-16, 318-20, 326-29*
  the unity of, *338-39*
Sociology; *see also* Formal sociology; Forms of sociation
  American, 9-10, 24
  analogy of, to geometry, 152-55, 161, *320-21, 323, 324, 332*
  of the crowd, 146-47
  differentiated from psychology, *329-33*
  in Germany, 180-85
  as a method, *312*
  methodology of, 24-27, *323-26*
  philosophical, and historical change, 90-92
  as the philosophy of society, *333-335*
  as the science of society, *310-11*

Sociology—*Continued*
as a special rather than a general social science, 10, 62-63, 68, 206-207, 208-9, *317-18*
Socrates, *298, 307*
Sombart, Werner, 194
Sorokin, Pitirim, 64, 74
Soul, the, *264-65*
Soziologie, 13, 27, 65, 83, 103, 140, 152, 169, 188, 208
"Soziologie der Geselligkeit," 103, 110
Spencer, Herbert, 170, 180, 183, 184, 193, 201, 205
Spengler, Oswald, 175
Spinoza, Baruch, *298*
Spykman, Nicholas J., 201, 216
Squillace, Fausto, 206
Stammler, R., 204
Statistics
in Germany of Simmel's youth, 168, 185
Simmel's interest in, 171
Stein, Lorenz von, 183-84
Steinen, Karl von den, 176
Stuckenberg, John Henry Wilbrandt, 202
Stumpf, Carl, 168, 172
Subordination; *see* Superordination and subordination
Sudermann, Hermann, 169
Sugiyama, S., 210
Sumner, William Graham, 170
Superordination and subordination
as explained by Simmel's theory of "factoring," 147-48
as a form of sociation, 72-73, 155
as a structural necessity, 148
"Superordination and Subordination," 78
Synthesis; *see* Unity

Taine, Hippolyte Adolphe, 146
Takata, Yasuma, 202, 207-9, 213
Tanigawa, T., 204-5
Tarde, Gabriel, 146, 206
Tatebe, T., 205
Thomas, William I., 225-26, 227
Time, Simmel's conception of, 36-37
Tocqueville, Alexis Henri de, 132
Toda, T., 210
Tönnies, Ferdinand, 90, 184, 186, 189, 192, 209, 214
Tragedy
conflict between the individual and society as, 140-45, 158-59
life as, 7-8
the ruin as, *259-60, 263*
Treitschke, Heinrich von, 168, 183, 184
Truth, the concept of, in philosophy, *297-99*
Tsunedo, K., 204
Twesten, Karl, 181

Über sociale Differenzierung, 90, 170, 176, 186, 210
Unity
creation of, by mind, *276, 302-3*
nature of, *276-77, 280, 314*
of the ruin, *260*
of social action, 69-70
of society, *338-39*
University of Berlin in Simmel's time, 168, 169-70, 234
Urbanism, Simmel's discussion of, 230-31
Usui, J., 211

Valien, Bonita, 61
Valien, Preston, 61
Value
personal as against social, 131-32
Simmel's definition of, 226-27
Vanni, Julio, 206
Verstehende sociology
in America, 62
compared with formal sociology, 80-82

Vico, Giovanni Battista, 163
Vierkandt, Alfred, 189, 196, 209, 211
Virchow, Rudolf, 169
Vitalism in Simmel's later thought, 172
Vollgraf, Karl Friedrich, 175
Voltaire, François Marie Arouet de, 183

Waller, Willard, 229
Walther, Andreas, 212
Ward, L. F., 186
"Web of Group-Affiliations, The," 153; *see also Conflict* and *The Web of Group-Affiliations*
Weber, Alfred, 213
Weber, Max, 16, 62, 84, 168, 178, 185, 193, 194, 214, 221, 227, 234
  community of ideas between Simmel and, 81-83
  conception of ideal-types of, 80-81
Wenckster, Adolph von, 186
Westermarck, Edward Alexander, 178
Wiese, Leopold von, 62, 107, 189, 196, 209, 228
Wilhelm II, 194, 234
Windelband, Wilhelm, 192, 193
Wirth, Louis, 223, 231
Wölfflin, Heinrich, 134
Wolff, Kurt H., 29, 77, 107, 110, 214
Worms, René, 186, 206
Wundt, Wilhelm Max, 168, 172, 221

Xenophon, 307

Yoneda, S., 202, 206-7, 211

Znaniecki, Florian, 76-77, 225-26, 227
Zola, Emile, 169
Zur Philosophie der Kunst, 203

Revised February 1966

harper torchbooks

HUMANITIES AND SOCIAL SCIENCES

American Studies: General

THOMAS C. COCHRAN: The Inner Revolution: *Essays on the Social Sciences in History* TB/1140

EDWARD S. CORWIN: American Constitutional History. *Essays edited by Alpheus T. Mason and Gerald Garvey* TB/1136

CARL N. DEGLER, Ed.: Pivotal Interpretations of American History TB/1240, TB/1241

A. HUNTER DUPREE: Science in the Federal Government: *A History of Policies and Activities to 1940* TB/573

OSCAR HANDLIN, Ed.: This Was America: *As Recorded by European Travelers in the Eighteenth, Nineteenth and Twentieth Centuries. Illus.* TB/1119

MARCUS LEE HANSEN: The Atlantic Migration: 1607-1860. *Edited by Arthur M. Schlesinger. Introduction by Oscar Handlin* TB/1052

MARCUS LEE HANSEN: The Immigrant in American History. *Edited with a Foreword by Arthur M. Schlesinger* TB/1120

JOHN HIGHAM, Ed.: The Reconstruction of American History TB/1068

ROBERT H. JACKSON: The Supreme Court in the American System of Government TB/1106

JOHN F. KENNEDY: A Nation of Immigrants. *Illus. Revised and Enlarged. Introduction by Robert F. Kennedy* TB/1118

RALPH BARTON PERRY: Puritanism and Democracy TB/1138

ARNOLD ROSE: The Negro in America: *The Condensed Version of Gunnar Myrdal's* An American Dilemma TB/3048

MAURICE R. STEIN: The Eclipse of Community: *An Interpretation of American Studies* TB/1128

W. LLOYD WARNER and Associates: Democracy in Jonesville: *A Study in Quality and Inequality* || TB/1129

W. LLOYD WARNER: Social Class in America: *The Evaluation of Status* TB/1013

American Studies: Colonial

BERNARD BAILYN, Ed.: The Apologia of Robert Keayne: *Self-Portrait of a Puritan Merchant* TB/1201

BERNARD BAILYN: The New England Merchants in the Seventeenth Century TB/1149

JOSEPH CHARLES: The Origins of the American Party System TB/1049

LAWRENCE HENRY GIPSON: The Coming of the Revolution: 1763-1775. † *Illus.* TB/3007

LEONARD W. LEVY: Freedom of Speech and Press in Early American History: *Legacy of Suppression* TB/1109

PERRY MILLER: Errand Into the Wilderness TB/1139

PERRY MILLER & T. H. JOHNSON, Eds.: The Puritans: *A Sourcebook of Their Writings* Vol. I TB/1093; Vol. II TB/1094

EDMUND S. MORGAN, Ed.: The Diary of Michael Wigglesworth, 1653-1657: *The Conscience of a Puritan*

EDMUND S. MORGAN: The Puritan Family: *Religion and Domestic Relations in Seventeenth-Century New England* TB/1227

RICHARD B. MORRIS: Government and Labor in Early America TB/1244

KENNETH B. MURDOCK: Literature and Theology in Colonial New England TB/99

WALLACE NOTESTEIN: The English People on the Eve of Colonization: 1603-1630. † *Illus.* TB/3006

LOUIS B. WRIGHT: The Cultural Life of the American Colonies: 1607-1763. † *Illus.* TB/3005

American Studies: From the Revolution to 1860

JOHN R. ALDEN: The American Revolution: 1775-1783. † *Illus.* TB/3011

MAX BELOFF, Ed.: The Debate on the American Revolution, 1761-1783: *A Sourcebook* TB/1225

RAY A. BILLINGTON: The Far Western Frontier: 1830-1860. † *Illus.* TB/3012

EDMUND BURKE: On the American Revolution: *Selected Speeches and Letters.* ‡ *Edited by Elliott Robert Barkan* TB/3068

WHITNEY R. CROSS: The Burned-Over District: *The Social and Intellectual History of Enthusiastic Religion in Western New York, 1800-1850* TB/1242

GEORGE DANGERFIELD: The Awakening of American Nationalism: 1815-1828. † *Illus.* TB/3061

CLEMENT EATON: The Freedom-of-Thought Struggle in the Old South. *Revised and Enlarged. Illus.* TB/1150

CLEMENT EATON: The Growth of Southern Civilization: 1790-1860. † *Illus.* TB/3040

LOUIS FILLER: The Crusade Against Slavery: 1830-1860. † *Illus.* TB/3029

DIXON RYAN FOX: The Decline of Aristocracy in the Politics of New York: 1801-1840. ‡ *Edited by Robert V. Remini* TB/3064

FELIX GILBERT: The Beginnings of American Foreign Policy: *To the Farewell Address* TB/1200

FRANCIS J. GRUND: Aristocracy in America: *Social Class in the Formative Years of the New Nation* TB/1001

ALEXANDER HAMILTON: The Reports of Alexander Hamilton. ‡ *Edited by Jacob E. Cooke* TB/3060

THOMAS JEFFERSON: Notes on the State of Virginia. ‡ *Edited by Thomas P. Abernethy* TB/3052

JAMES MADISON: The Forging of American Federalism: *Selected Writings of James Madison. Edited by Saul K. Padover* TB/1226

† The New American Nation Series, edited by Henry Steele Commager and Richard B. Morris.

‡ American Perspectives series, edited by Bernard Wishy and William E. Leuchtenburg.

* The Rise of Modern Europe series, edited by William L. Langer.

|| Researches in the Social, Cultural, and Behavioral Sciences, edited by Benjamin Nelson.

§ The Library of Religion and Culture, edited by Benjamin Nelson.

Σ Harper Modern Science Series, edited by James R. Newman.

° Not for sale in Canada.

BERNARD MAYO: Myths and Men: *Patrick Henry, George Washington, Thomas Jefferson* TB/1108

JOHN C. MILLER: Alexander Hamilton and the Growth of the New Nation TB/3057

RICHARD B. MORRIS, Ed.: The Era of the American Revolution TB/1180

R. B. NYE: The Cultural Life of the New Nation: 1776-1801. † *Illus.* TB/3026

FRANCIS S. PHILBRICK: The Rise of the West, 1754-1830. † *Illus.* TB/3067

TIMOTHY L. SMITH: Revivalism and Social Reform: *Protestantism on the Eve of the Civil War* TB/1229

FRANK THISTLETHWAITE: America and the Atlantic Community: *Anglo-American Aspects, 1790-1850* TB/1107

A. F. TYLER: Freedom's Ferment: *Phases of American Social History from the Revolution to the Outbreak of the Civil War. 31 illus.* TB/1074

GLYNDON G. VAN DEUSEN: The Jacksonian Era: 1828-1848. † *Illus.* TB/3028

LOUIS B. WRIGHT: Culture on the Moving Frontier TB/1053

American Studies: The Civil War to 1900

THOMAS C. COCHRAN & WILLIAM MILLER: The Age of Enterprise: *A Social History of Industrial America* TB/1054

W. A. DUNNING: Essays on the Civil War and Reconstruction. *Introduction by David Donald* TB/1181

W. A. DUNNING: Reconstruction, Political and Economic: 1865-1877 TB/1073

HAROLD U. FAULKNER: Politics, Reform and Expansion: 1890-1900. † *Illus.* TB/3020

HELEN HUNT JACKSON: A Century of Dishonor: *The Early Crusade for Indian Reform.* ‡ *Edited by Andrew F. Rolle* TB/3063

ALBERT D. KIRWAN: Revolt of the Rednecks: *Mississippi Politics, 1876-1925* TB/1199

ROBERT GREEN MC CLOSKEY: American Conservatism in the Age of Enterprise: 1865-1910 TB/1137

WHITELAW REID: After the War: *A Tour of the Southern States, 1865-1866.* ‡ *Edited by C. Vann Woodward* TB/3066

CHARLES H. SHINN: Mining Camps: *A Study in American Frontier Government.* ‡ *Edited by Rodman W. Paul* TB/3062

VERNON LANE WHARTON: The Negro in Mississippi: 1865-1890 TB/1178

American Studies: 1900 to the Present

RAY STANNARD BAKER: Following the Color Line: *American Negro Citizenship in Progressive Era.* ‡ *Illus. Edited by Dewey W. Grantham, Jr.* TB/3053

RANDOLPH S. BOURNE: War and the Intellectuals: *Collected Essays, 1915-1919.* ‡ *Ed. by Carl Resek* TB/3043

A. RUSSELL BUCHANAN: The United States and World War II. † *Illus.* Vol. I TB/3044; Vol. II TB/3045

ABRAHAM CAHAN: The Rise of David Levinsky: *a documentary novel of social mobility in early twentieth century America. Intro. by John Higham* TB/1028

THOMAS C. COCHRAN: The American Business System: *A Historical Perspective, 1900-1955* TB/1080

FOSTER RHEA DULLES: America's Rise to World Power: 1898-1954. † *Illus.* TB/3021

JOHN D. HICKS: Republican Ascendancy: 1921-1933. † *Illus.* TB/3041

SIDNEY HOOK: Reason, Social Myths, and Democracy TB/1237

ROBERT HUNTER: Poverty: *Social Conscience in the Progressive Era.* ‡ *Edited by Peter d'A. Jones* TB/3065

WILLIAM L. LANGER & S. EVERETT GLEASON: The Challenge to Isolation: *The World Crisis of 1937-1940 and American Foreign Policy* Vol. I TB/3054; Vol. II TB/3055

WILLIAM E. LEUCHTENBURG: Franklin D. Roosevelt and the New Deal: 1932-1940. † *Illus.* TB/3025

ARTHUR S. LINK: Woodrow Wilson and the Progressive Era: 1910-1917. † *Illus.* TB/3023

GEORGE E. MOWRY: The Era of Theodore Roosevelt and the Birth of Modern America: 1900-1912. † *Illus.* TB/3022

RUSSEL B. NYE: Midwestern Progressive Politics: *A Historical Study of its Origins and Development, 1870-1958* TB/1202

WALTER RAUSCHENBUSCH: Christianity and the Social Crisis. ‡ *Edited by Robert D. Cross* TB/3059

PHILIP SELZNICK: TVA and the Grass Roots: *A Study in the Sociology of Formal Organization* TB/1230

GEORGE B. TINDALL, Ed.: A Populist Reader ‡ TB/3069

TWELVE SOUTHERNERS: I'll Take My Stand: *The South and the Agrarian Tradition. Intro. by Louis D. Rubin, Jr. Biographical Essays by Virginia Rock* TB/1072

WALTER E. WEYL: The New Democracy: *An Essay on Certain Political Tendencies in the United States.* ‡ *Edited by Charles B. Forcey* TB/3042

Anthropology

JACQUES BARZUN: Race: *A Study in Superstition. Revised Edition* TB/1172

JOSEPH B. CASAGRANDE, Ed.: In the Company of Man: *Twenty Portraits of Anthropological Informants. Illus.* TB/3047

W. E. LE GROS CLARK: The Antecedents of Man: *Intro. to Evolution of the Primates.* ° *Illus.* TB/559

CORA DU BOIS: The People of Alor. *New Preface by the author. Illus.* Vol. I TB/1042; Vol. II TB/1043

RAYMOND FIRTH, Ed.: Man and Culture: *An Evaluation of the Work of Bronislaw Malinowski* ‖ ° TB/1133

DAVID LANDY: Tropical Childhood: *Cultural Transmission and Learning in a Rural Puerto Rican Village* ‖ TB/1235

L. S. B. LEAKEY: Adam's Ancestors: *The Evolution of Man and His Culture. Illus.* TB/1019

ROBERT H. LOWIE: Primitive Society. *Introduction by Fred Eggan* TB/1056

EDWARD BURNETT TYLOR: The Origins of Culture. *Part I of "Primitive Culture."* § *Intro. by Paul Radin* TB/33

EDWARD BURNETT TYLOR: Religion in Primitive Culture. *Part II of "Primitive Culture."* § *Intro. by Paul Radin* TB/34

W. LLOYD WARNER: A Black Civilization: *A Study of an Australian Tribe.* ‖ *Illus.* TB/3056

Art and Art History

WALTER LOWRIE: Art in the Early Church. *Revised Edition. 452 illus.* TB/124

EMILE MÂLE: The Gothic Image: *Religious Art in France of the Thirteenth Century.* § *190 illus.* TB/44

MILLARD MEISS: Painting in Florence and Siena after the Black Death: *The Arts, Religion and Society in the Mid-Fourteenth Century. 169 illus.* TB/1148

ERICH NEUMANN: The Archetypal World of Henry Moore. *107 illus.* TB/2020

DORA & ERWIN PANOFSKY: Pandora's Box: *The Changing Aspects of a Mythical Symbol. Revised Edition. Illus.* TB/2021

ERWIN PANOFSKY: Studies in Iconology: *Humanistic Themes in the Art of the Renaissance. 180 illustrations* TB/1077

ALEXANDRE PIANKOFF: The Shrines of Tut-Ankh-Amon. *Edited by N. Rambova. 117 illus.* TB/2011

JEAN SEZNEC: The Survival of the Pagan Gods: *The Mythological Tradition and Its Place in Renaissance Humanism and Art. 108 illustrations* TB/2004

OTTO VON SIMSON: The Gothic Cathedral: *Origins of Gothic Architecture and the Medieval Concept of Order. 58 illus.* TB/2018

HEINRICH ZIMMER: Myths and Symbols in Indian Art and Civilization. *70 illustrations* TB/2005

Business, Economics & Economic History

REINHARD BENDIX: Work and Authority in Industry: *Ideologies of Management in the Course of Industrialization* TB/3035
GILBERT BURCK & EDITORS OF FORTUNE: The Computer Age: *And Its Potential for Management* TB/1179
THOMAS C. COCHRAN: The American Business System: *A Historical Perspective, 1900-1955* TB/1080
THOMAS C. COCHRAN: The Inner Revolution: *Essays on the Social Sciences in History* TB/1140
THOMAS C. COCHRAN & WILLIAM MILLER: The Age of Enterprise: *A Social History of Industrial America* TB/1054
ROBERT DAHL & CHARLES E. LINDBLOM: Politics, Economics, and Welfare: *Planning & Politico-Economic Systems Resolved into Basic Social Processes* TB/3037
PETER F. DRUCKER: The New Society: *The Anatomy of Industrial Order* TB/1082
EDITORS OF FORTUNE: America in the Sixties: *The Economy and the Society* TB/1015
ROBERT L. HEILBRONER: The Great Ascent: *The Struggle for Economic Development in Our Time* TB/3030
FRANK H. KNIGHT: The Economic Organization TB/1214
FRANK H. KNIGHT: Risk, Uncertainty and Profit TB/1215
ABBA P. LERNER: Everybody's Business: *Current Assumptions in Economics and Public Policy* TB/3051
ROBERT GREEN MCCLOSKEY: American Conservatism in the Age of Enterprise, 1865-1910 TB/1137
PAUL MANTOUX: The Industrial Revolution in the Eighteenth Century: *The Beginnings of the Modern Factory System in England* ° TB/1079
WILLIAM MILLER, Ed.: Men in Business: *Essays on the Historical Role of the Entrepreneur* TB/1081
RICHARD B. MORRIS: Government and Labor in Early America TB/1244
HERBERT SIMON: The Shape of Automation: *For Men and Management* TB/1245
PERRIN STRYKER: The Character of the Executive: *Eleven Studies in Managerial Qualities* TB/1041
PIERRE URI: Partnership for Progress: *A Program for Transatlantic Action* TB/3036

Contemporary Culture

JACQUES BARZUN: The House of Intellect TB/1051
JOHN U. NEF: Cultural Foundations of Industrial Civilization TB/1024
NATHAN M. PUSEY: The Age of the Scholar: *Observations on Education in a Troubled Decade* TB/1157
PAUL VALÉRY: The Outlook for Intelligence TB/2016

Historiography & Philosophy of History

JACOB BURCKHARDT: On History and Historians. *Intro. by H. R. Trevor-Roper* TB/1216
WILHELM DILTHEY: Pattern and Meaning in History: *Thoughts on History and Society.* ° *Edited with an Introduction by H. P. Rickman* TB/1075
J. H. HEXTER: Reappraisals in History: *New Views on History & Society in Early Modern Europe* TB/1100
H. STUART HUGHES: History as Art and as Science: *Twin Vistas on the Past* TB/1207
RAYMOND KLIBANSKY & H. J. PATON, Eds.: Philosophy and History: *The Ernst Cassirer Festschrift. Illus.* TB/1115
GEORGE H. NADEL, Ed.: Studies in the Philosophy of History: *Selected Essays from* History and Theory TB/1208
JOSE ORTEGA Y GASSET: The Modern Theme. *Introduction by Jose Ferrater Mora* TB/1038
KARL R. POPPER: The Open Society and Its Enemies
Vol. I: The Spell of Plato TB/1101
Vol. II: The High Tide of Prophecy: Hegel, Marx and the Aftermath TB/1102
KARL R. POPPER: The Poverty of Historicism ° TB/1126
G. J. RENIER: History: Its Purpose and Method TB/1209
W. H. WALSH: Philosophy of History: *An Introduction* TB/1020

History: General

L. CARRINGTON GOODRICH: A Short History of the Chinese People. *Illus.* TB/3015
DAN N. JACOBS & HANS H. BAERWALD: Chinese Communism: *Selected Documents* TB/3031
BERNARD LEWIS: The Arabs in History TB/1029

History: Ancient

A. ANDREWES: The Greek Tyrants TB/1103
ADOLF ERMAN, Ed.: The Ancient Egyptians: *A Sourcebook of Their Writings. New material and Introduction by William Kelly Simpson* TB/1233
MICHAEL GRANT: Ancient History ° TB/1190
SAMUEL NOAH KRAMER: Sumerian Mythology TB/1055
NAPHTALI LEWIS & MEYER REINHOLD, Eds.: Roman Civilization. *Sourcebook I: The Republic* TB/1231
NAPHTALI LEWIS & MEYER REINHOLD, Eds.: Roman Civilization. *Sourcebook II: The Empire* TB/1232

History: Medieval

P. BOISSONNADE: Life and Work in Medieval Europe: *The Evolution of the Medieval Economy, the 5th to the 15th Century.* ° *Preface by Lynn White, Jr.* TB/1141
HELEN CAM: England before Elizabeth TB/1026
NORMAN COHN: The Pursuit of the Millennium: *Revolutionary Messianism in Medieval and Reformation Europe* TB/1037
G. G. COULTON: Medieval Village, Manor, and Monastery TB/1022
HEINRICH FICHTENAU: The Carolingian Empire: *The Age of Charlemagne* TB/1142
F. L. GANSHOF: Feudalism TB/1058
EDWARD GIBBON: The Triumph of Christendom in the Roman Empire *(Chaps. XV-XX of "Decline and Fall," J. B. Bury edition).* § *Illus.* TB/46
W. O. HASSALL, Ed.: Medieval England: *As Viewed by Contemporaries* TB/1205
DENYS HAY: The Medieval Centuries ° TB/1192
J. M. HUSSEY: The Byzantine World TB/1057
FERDINAND LOT: The End of the Ancient World and the Beginnings of the Middle Ages. *Introduction by Glanville Downey* TB/1044
G. MOLLAT: The Popes at Avignon: 1305-1378 TB/308
CHARLES PETIT-DUTAILLIS: The Feudal Monarchy in France and England: *From the Tenth to the Thirteenth Century* ° TB/1165
HENRI PIERENNE: Early Democracies in the Low Countries: *Urban Society and Political Conflict in the Middle Ages and the Renaissance. Introduction by John H. Mundy* TB/1110
STEVEN RUNCIMAN: A History of the Crusades.
Volume I: *The First Crusade and the Foundation of the Kingdom of Jerusalem. Illus.* TB/1143
Volume II: *The Kingdom of Jerusalem and the Frankish East, 1100-1187. Illus.* TB/1243
FERDINAND SCHEVILL: Siena: *The History of a Medieval Commune. Intro. by William M. Bowsky* TB/1164
SULPICIUS SEVERUS et al.: The Western Fathers: *Being the Lives of Martin of Tours, Ambrose, Augustine of Hippo, Honoratus of Arles and Germanus of Auxerre. Edited and translated by F. R. Hoare* TB/309
HENRY OSBORN TAYLOR: The Classical Heritage of the Middle Ages. *Foreword and Biblio. by Kenneth M. Setton* TB/1117
F. VAN DER MEER: Augustine the Bishop: *Church and Society at the Dawn of the Middle Ages* TB/304
J. M. WALLACE-HADRILL: The Barbarian West: *The Early Middle Ages, A.D. 400-1000* TB/1061

History: Renaissance & Reformation

JACOB BURCKHARDT: The Civilization of the Renaissance in Italy. *Intro. by Benjamin Nelson & Charles Trinkaus. Illus.* Vol. I TB/40; Vol. II TB/41

JOHN CALVIN & JACOPO SADOLETO: A Reformation Debate. *Edited by John C. Olin* TB/1239

ERNST CASSIRER: The Individual and the Cosmos in Renaissance Philosophy. *Translated with an Introduction by Mario Domandi* TB/1097

FEDERICO CHABOD: Machiavelli and the Renaissance TB/1193

EDWARD P. CHEYNEY: The Dawn of a New Era, 1250-1453. * *Illus.* TB/3002

R. TREVOR DAVIES: The Golden Century of Spain, 1501-1621 ° TB/1194

DESIDERIUS ERASMUS: Christian Humanism and the Reformation: *Selected Writings. Edited and translated by John C. Olin* TB/1166

WALLACE K. FERGUSON et al.: Facets of the Renaissance TB/1098

WALLACE K. FERGUSON et al.: The Renaissance: *Six Essays. Illus.* TB/1084

JOHN NEVILLE FIGGIS: The Divine Right of Kings. *Introduction by G. R. Elton* TB/1191

JOHN NEVILLE FIGGIS: Political Thought from Gerson to Grotius: 1414-1625: *Seven Studies. Introduction by Garrett Mattingly* TB/1032

MYRON P. GILMORE: The World of Humanism, 1453-1517.* *Illus.* TB/3003

FRANCESCO GUICCIARDINI: Maxims and Reflections of a Renaissance Statesman *(Ricordi). Trans. by Mario Domandi. Intro. by Nicolai Rubinstein* TB/1160

J. H. HEXTER: More's Utopia: *The Biography of an Idea. New Epilogue by the Author* TB/1195

HAJO HOLBORN: Ulrich von Hutten and the German Reformation TB/1238

JOHAN HUIZINGA: Erasmus and the Age of Reformation. *Illus.* TB/19

ULRICH VON HUTTEN et al.: On the Eve of the Reformation: *"Letters of Obscure Men." Introduction by Hajo Holborn* TB/1124

PAUL O. KRISTELLER: Renaissance Thought: *The Classic, Scholastic, and Humanist Strains* TB/1048

PAUL O. KRISTELLER: Renaissance Thought II: *Papers on Humanism and the Arts* TB/1163

NICCOLÒ MACHIAVELLI: History of Florence and of the Affairs of Italy: *from the earliest times to the death of Lorenzo the Magnificent. Introduction by Felix Gilbert* TB/1027

ALFRED VON MARTIN: Sociology of the Renaissance. *Introduction by Wallace K. Ferguson* TB/1099

GARRETT MATTINGLY et al.: Renaissance Profiles. *Edited by J. H. Plumb* TB/1162

MILLARD MEISS: Painting in Florence and Siena after the Black Death: *The Arts, Religion and Society in the Mid-Fourteenth Century. 169 illus.* TB/1148

J. E. NEALE: The Age of Catherine de Medici ° TB/1085

ERWIN PANOFSKY: Studies in Iconology: *Humanistic Themes in the Art of the Renaissance. 180 illustrations* TB/1077

J. H. PARRY: The Establishment of the European Hegemony: 1415-1715: *Trade and Exploration in the Age of the Renaissance* TB/1045

J. H. PLUMB: The Italian Renaissance: *A Concise Survey of Its History and Culture* TB/1161

CECIL ROTH: The Jews in the Renaissance. *Illus.* TB/834

A. L. ROWSE: The Expansion of Elizabethan England. ° *Illus.* TB/1220

GORDON RUPP: Luther's Progress to the Diet of Worms ° TB/120

FERDINAND SCHEVILL: The Medici. *Illus.* TB/1010

FERDINAND SCHEVILL: Medieval and Renaissance Florence. *Illus.* Volume I: *Medieval Florence* TB/1090
Volume II: *The Coming of Humanism and the Age of the Medici* TB/1091

G. M. TREVELYAN: England in the Age of Wycliffe, 1368-1520 ° TB/1112

VESPASIANO: Renaissance Princes, Popes, and Prelates: *The Vespasiano Memoirs: Lives of Illustrious Men of the XVth Century. Intro. by Myron P. Gilmore* TB/1111

History: Modern European

FREDERICK B. ARTZ: Reaction and Revolution, 1815-1832. * *Illus.* TB/3034

MAX BELOFF: The Age of Absolutism, 1660-1815 TB/1062

ROBERT C. BINKLEY: Realism and Nationalism, 1852-1871. * *Illus.* TB/3038

ASA BRIGGS: The Making of Modern England, 1784-1867: *The Age of Improvement* ° TB/1203

CRANE BRINTON: A Decade of Revolution, 1789-1799. * *Illus.* TB/3018

D. W. BROGAN: The Development of Modern France. °
Volume I: *From the Fall of the Empire to the Dreyfus Affair* TB/1184
Volume II: *The Shadow of War, World War I, Between the Two Wars. New Introduction by the Author* TB/1185

J. BRONOWSKI & BRUCE MAZLISH: The Western Intellectual Tradition: *From Leonardo to Hegel* TB/3001

GEOFFREY BRUUN: Europe and the French Imperium, 1799-1814. * *Illus.* TB/3033

ALAN BULLOCK: Hitler, A Study in Tyranny. ° *Illus.* TB/1123

E. H. CARR: The Twenty Years' Crisis, 1919-1939: *An Introduction to the Study of International Relations* ° TB/1122

GORDON A. CRAIG: From Bismarck to Adenauer: *Aspects of German Statecraft. Revised Edition* TB/1171

WALTER L. DORN: Competition for Empire, 1740-1763. * *Illus.* TB/3032

FRANKLIN L. FORD: Robe and Sword: *The Regrouping of the French Aristocracy after Louis XIV* TB/1217

CARL J. FRIEDRICH: The Age of the Baroque, 1610-1660. * *Illus.* TB/3004

RENÉ FUELOEP-MILLER: The Mind and Face of Bolshevism: *An Examination of Cultural Life in Soviet Russia. New Epilogue by the Author* TB/1188

M. DOROTHY GEORGE: London Life in the Eighteenth Century TB/1182

LEO GERSHOY: From Despotism to Revolution, 1763-1789. * *Illus.* TB/3017

C. C. GILLISPIE: Genesis and Geology: *The Decades before Darwin* § TB/51

ALBERT GOODWIN: The French Revolution TB/1064

ALBERT GUERARD: France in the Classical Age: *The Life and Death of an Ideal* TB/1183

CARLTON J. H. HAYES: A Generation of Materialism, 1871-1900. * *Illus.* TB/3039

J. H. HEXTER: Reappraisals in History: *New Views on History & Society in Early Modern Europe* TB/1100

STANLEY HOFFMANN et al.: In Search of France: *The Economy, Society and Political System in the Twentieth Century* TB/1219

A. R. HUMPHREYS: The Augustan World: *Society, Thought, and Letters in 18th Century England* ° TB/1105

DAN N. JACOBS, Ed.: The New Communist Manifesto *& Related Documents. Third edition, Revised* TB/1078

HANS KOHN: The Mind of Germany: *The Education of a Nation* TB/1204

HANS KOHN, Ed.: The Mind of Modern Russia: *Historical and Political Thought of Russia's Great Age* TB/1065

FRANK E. MANUEL: The Prophets of Paris: *Turgot, Condorcet, Saint-Simon, Fourier, and Comte* TB/1218

KINGSLEY MARTIN: French Liberal Thought in the Eighteenth Century: *A Study of Political Ideas from Bayle to Condorcet* TB/1114

L. B. NAMIER: Personalities and Powers: *Selected Essays* TB/1186

L. B. NAMIER: Vanished Supremacies: *Essays on European History, 1812-1918* ° TB/1088

JOHN U. NEF: Western Civilization Since the Renaissance: *Peace, War, Industry, and the Arts* TB/1113

FREDERICK L. NUSSBAUM: The Triumph of Science and Reason, 1660-1685. * *Illus.* TB/3009

JOHN PLAMENATZ: German Marxism and Russian Communism. ° *New Preface by the Author* TB/1189

RAYMOND W. POSTGATE, Ed.: Revolution from 1789 to 1906: *Selected Documents* TB/1063

PENFIELD ROBERTS: The Quest for Security, 1715-1740. * *Illus.* TB/3016

PRISCILLA ROBERTSON: Revolutions of 1848: *A Social History* TB/1025

ALBERT SOREL: Europe Under the Old Regime. *Translated by Francis H. Herrick* TB/1121

N. N. SUKHANOV: The Russian Revolution, 1917: *Eyewitness Account. Edited by Joel Carmichael* Vol. I TB/1066; Vol. II TB/1067

A. J. P. TAYLOR: The Habsburg Monarch, 1809-1918: *A History of the Austrian Empire and Austria-Hungary* ° TB/1187

JOHN B. WOLF: The Emergence of the Great Powers, 1685-1715. * *Illus.* TB/3010

JOHN B. WOLF: France: 1814-1919: *The Rise of a Liberal-Democratic Society* TB/3019

Intellectual History & History of Ideas

HERSCHEL BAKER: The Image of Man: *A Study of the Idea of Human Dignity in Classical Antiquity, the Middle Ages, and the Renaissance* TB/1047

R. R. BOLGAR: The Classical Heritage and Its Beneficiaries: *From the Carolingian Age to the End of the Renaissance* TB/1125

RANDOLPH S. BOURNE: War and the Intellectuals: *Collected Essays, 1915-1919.* ‡ *Edited by Carl Resek* TB/3043

J. BRONOWSKI & BRUCE MAZLISH: The Western Intellectual Tradition: *From Leonardo to Hegel* TB/3001

ERNST CASSIRER: The Individual and the Cosmos in Renaissance Philosophy. *Translated with an Introduction by Mario Domandi* TB/1097

NORMAN COHN: The Pursuit of the Millennium: *Revolutionary Messianism in Medieval and Reformation Europe* TB/1037

C. C. GILLISPIE: Genesis and Geology: *The Decades before Darwin* § TB/51

G. RACHEL LEVY: Religious Conceptions of the Stone Age and Their Influence upon European Thought. *Illus. Introduction by Henri Frankfort* TB/106

ARTHUR O. LOVEJOY: The Great Chain of Being: *A Study of the History of an Idea* TB/1009

FRANK E. MANUEL: The Prophets of Paris: *Turgot, Condorcet, Saint-Simon, Fourier, and Comte* TB/1218

PERRY MILLER & T. H. JOHNSON, Editors: The Puritans: *A Sourcebook of Their Writings* Vol. I TB/1093; Vol. II TB/1094

MILTON C. NAHM: Genius and Creativity: *An Essay in the History of Ideas* TB/1196

ROBERT PAYNE: Hubris: *A Study of Pride. Foreword by Sir Herbert Read* TB/1031

RALPH BARTON PERRY: The Thought and Character of William James: *Briefer Version* TB/1156

GEORG SIMMEL et al.: Essays on Sociology, Philosophy, and Aesthetics. || *Edited by Kurt H. Wolff* TB/1234

BRUNO SNELL: The Discovery of the Mind: *The Greek Origins of European Thought* TB/1018

PAGET TOYNBEE: Dante Alighieri: *His Life and Works. Edited with Intro. by Charles S. Singleton* TB/1206

ERNEST LEE TUVESON: Millennium and Utopia: *A Study in the Background of the Idea of Progress.* || *New Preface by the Author* TB/1134

PAUL VALÉRY: The Outlook for Intelligence TB/2016

PHILIP P. WIENER: Evolution and the Founders of Pragmatism. *Foreword by John Dewey* TB/1212

Literature, Poetry, The Novel & Criticism

JAMES BAIRD: Ishmael: *The Art of Melville in the Contexts of International Primitivism* TB/1023

JACQUES BARZUN: The House of Intellect TB/1051

W. J. BATE: From Classic to Romantic: *Premises of Taste in Eighteenth Century England* TB/1036

RACHEL BESPALOFF: On the Iliad TB/2006

R. P. BLACKMUR et al.: Lectures in Criticism. *Introduction by Huntington Cairns* TB/2003

ABRAHAM CAHAN: The Rise of David Levinsky: *a documentary novel of social mobility in early twentieth century America. Intro. by John Higham* TB/1028

ERNST R. CURTIUS: European Literature and the Latin Middle Ages TB/2015

GEORGE ELIOT: Daniel Deronda: *a novel. Introduction by F. R. Leavis* TB/1039

ADOLF ERMAN, Ed.: The Ancient Egyptians: *A Sourcebook of Their Writings. New Material and Introduction by William Kelly Simpson* TB/1233

ÉTIENNE GILSON: Dante and Philosophy TB/1089

ALFRED HARBAGE: As They Liked It: *A Study of Shakespeare's Moral Artistry* TB/1035

STANLEY R. HOPPER, Ed.: Spiritual Problems in Contemporary Literature § TB/21

A. R. HUMPHREYS: The Augustan World: *Society, Thought and Letters in 18th Century England* ° TB/1105

ALDOUS HUXLEY: Antic Hay & The Giaconda Smile. ° *Introduction by Martin Green* TB/3503

ALDOUS HUXLEY: Brave New World & Brave New World Revisited. ° *Introduction by Martin Green* TB/3501

HENRY JAMES: Roderick Hudson: *a novel. Introduction by Leon Edel* TB/1016

HENRY JAMES: The Tragic Muse: *a novel. Introduction by Leon Edel* TB/1017

ARNOLD KETTLE: An Introduction to the English Novel.
Volume I: *Defoe to George Eliot* TB/1011
Volume II: *Henry James to the Present* TB/1012

ROGER SHERMAN LOOMIS: The Development of Arthurian Romance TB/1167

JOHN STUART MILL: On Bentham and Coleridge. *Introduction by F. R. Leavis* TB/1070

KENNETH B. MURDOCK: Literature and Theology in Colonial New England TB/99

SAMUEL PEPYS: The Diary of Samuel Pepys. ° *Edited by O. F. Morshead. Illus. by Ernest Shepard* TB/1007

ST.-JOHN PERSE: Seamarks TB/2002

GEORGE SANTAYANA: Interpretations of Poetry and Religion § TB/9

HEINRICH STRAUMANN: American Literature in the Twentieth Century. *Third Edition, Revised* TB/1168

PAGET TOYNBEE: Dante Alighieri: *His Life and Works. Edited with Intro. by Charles S. Singleton* TB/1206

DOROTHY VAN GHENT: The English Novel: *Form and Function* TB/1050

E. B. WHITE: One Man's Meat. *Introduction by Walter Blair* TB/3505

MORTON DAUWEN ZABEL, Editor: Literary Opinion in America Vol. I TB/3013; Vol. II TB/3014

Myth, Symbol & Folklore

JOSEPH CAMPBELL, Editor: Pagan and Christian Mysteries. *Illus.* TB/2013

MIRCEA ELIADE: Cosmos and History: *The Myth of the Eternal Return* § TB/2050

MERCEA ELIADE: Rites and Symbols of Initiation: *The Mysteries of Birth and Rebirth* § TB/1236

C. G. JUNG & C. KERÉNYI: Essays on a Science of Mythology: *The Myths of the Divine Child and the Divine Maiden* TB/2014

DORA & ERWIN PANOFSKY: Pandora's Box: *The Changing Aspects of a Mythical Symbol. Revised Edition. Illus.* TB/2021

ERWIN PANOFSKY: Studies in Iconology: *Humanistic Themes in the Art of the Renaissance. 180 illustrations* TB/1077
JEAN SEZNEC: The Survival of the Pagan Gods: *The Mythological Tradition and its Place in Renaissance Humanism and Art. 108 illustrations* TB/2004
HELLMUT WILHELM: Change: *Eight Lectures on the I Ching* TB/2019
HEINRICH ZIMMER: Myths and Symbols in Indian Art and Civilization. *70 illustrations* TB/2005

Philosophy

G. E. M. ANSCOMBE: An Introduction to Wittgenstein's Tractatus. *Second edition, Revised.* ° TB/1210
HENRI BERGSON: Time and Free Will: *An Essay on the Immediate Data of Consciousness* ° TB/1021
H. J. BLACKHAM: Six Existentialist Thinkers: *Kierkegaard, Nietzsche, Jaspers, Marcel, Heidegger, Sartre* ° TB/1002
CRANE BRINTON: Nietzsche. *New Preface, Bibliography and Epilogue by the Author* TB/1197
ERNST CASSIRER: The Individual and the Cosmos in Renaissance Philosophy. *Translated with an Introduction by Mario Domandi* TB/1097
ERNST CASSIRER: Rousseau, Kant and Goethe. *Introduction by Peter Gay* TB/1092
FREDERICK COPLESTON: Medieval Philosophy ° TB/376
F. M. CORNFORD: Principium Sapientiae: *A Study of the Origins of Greek Philosophical Thought. Edited by W. K. C. Guthrie* TB/1213
F. M. CORNFORD: From Religion to Philosophy: *A Study in the Origins of Western Speculation* § TB/20
WILFRID DESAN: The Tragic Finale: *An Essay on the Philosophy of Jean-Paul Sartre* TB/1030
A. P. D'ENTRÈVES: Natural Law: *An Historical Survey* TB/1223
HERBERT FINGARETTE: The Self in Transformation: *Psychoanalysis, Philosophy and the Life of the Spirit* || TB/1177
PAUL FRIEDLÄNDER: Plato: *An Introduction* TB/2017
ÉTIENNE GILSON: Dante and Philosophy TB/1089
WILLIAM CHASE GREENE: Moira: *Fate, Good, and Evil in Greek Thought* TB/1104
W. K. C. GUTHRIE: The Greek Philosophers: *From Thales to Aristotle* ° TB/1008
F. H. HEINEMANN: Existentialism and the Modern Predicament TB/28
ISAAC HUSIK: A History of Medieval Jewish Philosophy JP/3
EDMUND HUSSERL: Phenomenology and the Crisis of Philosophy. *Translated with an Introduction by Quentin Lauer* TB/1170
IMMANUEL KANT: The Doctrine of Virtue, *being Part II of* The Metaphysic of Morals. *Trans. with Notes & Intro. by Mary J. Gregor. Foreword by H. J. Paton* TB/110
IMMANUEL KANT: Groundwork of the Metaphysic of Morals. *Trans. & analyzed by H. J. Paton* TB/1159
IMMANUEL KANT: Lectures on Ethics. § *Introduction by Lewis W. Beck* TB/105
IMMANUEL KANT: Religion Within the Limits of Reason Alone. § *Intro. by T. M. Greene & J. Silber* TB/67
QUENTIN LAUER: Phenomenology: *Its Genesis and Prospect* TB/1169
GABRIEL MARCEL: Being and Having: *An Existential Diary. Intro. by James Collins* TB/310
GEORGE A. MORGAN: What Nietzsche Means TB/1198
PHILO, SAADYA GAON, & JEHUDA HALEVI: Three Jewish Philosophers. *Ed. by Hans Lewy, Alexander Altmann, & Isaak Heinemann* TB/813
MICHAEL POLANYI: Personal Knowledge: *Towards a Post-Critical Philosophy* TB/1158
WILLARD VAN ORMAN QUINE: Elementary Logic: *Revised Edition* TB/577
WILLARD VAN ORMAN QUINE: From a Logical Point of View: *Logico-Philosophical Essays* TB/566
BERTRAND RUSSELL et al.: The Philosophy of Bertrand Russell. *Edited by Paul Arthur Schilpp*
Vol. I TB/1095; Vol. II TB/1096
L. S. STEBBING: A Modern Introduction to Logic TB/538
ALFRED NORTH WHITEHEAD: Process and Reality: *An Essay in Cosmology* TB/1033
PHILIP P. WIENER: Evolution and the Founders of Pragmatism. *Foreword by John Dewey* TB/1212
WILHELM WINDELBAND: A History of Philosophy
Vol. I: *Greek, Roman, Medieval* TB/38
Vol. II: *Renaissance, Enlightenment, Modern* TB/39
LUDWIG WITTGENSTEIN: The Blue and Brown Books ° TB/1211

Political Science & Government

JEREMY BENTHAM: The Handbook of Political Fallacies. *Introduction by Crane Brinton* TB/1069
KENNETH E. BOULDING: Conflict and Defense: *A General Theory* TB/3024
CRANE BRINTON: English Political Thought in the Nineteenth Century TB/1071
EDWARD S. CORWIN: American Constitutional History: *Essays edited by Alpheus T. Mason and Gerald Garvey* TB/1136
ROBERT DAHL & CHARLES E. LINDBLOM: Politics, Economics, and Welfare: *Planning and Politico-Economic Systems Resolved into Basic Social Processes* TB/3037
JOHN NEVILLE FIGGIS: The Divine Right of Kings. *Introduction by G. R. Elton* TB/1191
JOHN NEVILLE FIGGIS: Political Thought from Gerson to Grotius: 1414-1625: *Seven Studies. Introduction by Garrett Mattingly* TB/1032
F. L. GANSHOF: Feudalism TB/1058
G. P. GOOCH: English Democratic Ideas in Seventeenth Century TB/1006
J. H. HEXTER: More's Utopia: *The Biography of an Idea. New Epilogue by the Author* TB/1195
SIDNEY HOOK: Reason, Social Myths and Democracy TB/1237
ROBERT H. JACKSON: The Supreme Court in the American System of Government TB/1106
DAN N. JACOBS, Ed.: The New Communist Manifesto & *Related Documents. Third edition, Revised* TB/1078
DAN N. JACOBS & HANS BAERWALD, Eds.: Chinese Communism: *Selected Documents* TB/3031
ROBERT GREEN MCCLOSKEY: American Conservatism in the Age of Enterprise, 1865-1910 TB/1137
KINGSLEY MARTIN: French Liberal Thought in the Eighteenth Century: *Political Ideas from Bayle to Condorcet* TB/1114
ROBERTO MICHELS: First Lectures in Political Sociology. *Edited by Alfred De Grazia* || ° TB/1224
JOHN STUART MILL: On Bentham and Coleridge. *Introduction by F. R. Leavis* TB/1070
BARRINGTON MOORE, JR.: Political Power and Social Theory: *Seven Studies* || TB/1221
BARRINGTON MOORE, JR.: Soviet Politics—The Dilemma of Power: *The Role of Ideas in Social Change* || TB/1222
JOHN B. MORRALL: Political Thought in Medieval Times TB/1076
JOHN PLAMENATZ: German Marxism and Russian Communism. ° *New Preface by the Author* TB/1189
KARL R. POPPER: The Open Society and Its Enemies
Vol. I: *The Spell of Plato* TB/1101
Vol. II: *The High Tide of Prophecy: Hegel, Marx, and the Aftermath* TB/1102
HENRI DE SAINT-SIMON: Social Organization, The Science of Man, and Other Writings. *Edited and Translated by Felix Markham* TB/1152
JOSEPH A. SCHUMPETER: Capitalism, Socialism and Democracy TB/3008

CHARLES H. SHINN: Mining Camps: *A Study in American Frontier Government.* ‡ *Edited by Rodman W. Paul* TB/3062

Psychology

ALFRED ADLER: The Individual Psychology of Alfred Adler. *Edited by Heinz L. and Rowena R. Ansbacher* TB/1154
ALFRED ADLER: Problems of Neurosis. *Introduction by Heinz L. Ansbacher* TB/1145
ANTON T. BOISEN: The Exploration of the Inner World: *A Study of Mental Disorder and Religious Experience* TB/87
HERBERT FINGARETTE: The Self in Transformation: *Psychoanalysis, Philosophy and the Life of the Spirit* || TB/1177
SIGMUND FREUD: On Creativity and the Unconscious: *Papers on the Psychology of Art, Literature, Love, Religion.* § *Intro. by Benjamin Nelson* TB/45
C. JUDSON HERRICK: The Evolution of Human Nature TB/545
WILLIAM JAMES: Psychology: *The Briefer Course. Edited with an Intro. by Gordon Allport* TB/1034
C. G. JUNG: Psychological Reflections TB/2001
C. G. JUNG: Symbols of Transformation: *An Analysis of the Prelude to a Case of Schizophrenia. Illus.* Vol. I: TB/2009; Vol. II TB/2010
C. G. JUNG & C. KERÉNYI: Essays on a Science of Mythology: *The Myths of the Divine Child and the Divine Maiden* TB/2014
JOHN T. MC NEILL: A History of the Cure of Souls TB/126
KARL MENNINGER: Theory of Psychoanalytic Technique TB/1144
ERICH NEUMANN: Amor and Psyche: *The Psychic Development of the Feminine* TB/2012
ERICH NEUMANN: The Archetypal World of Henry Moore. *107 illus.* TB/2020
ERICH NEUMANN: The Origins and History of Consciousness Vol. I *Illus.* TB/2007; Vol. II TB/2008
C. P. OBERNDORF: A History of Psychoanalysis in America TB/1147
RALPH BARTON PERRY: The Thought and Character of William James: *Briefer Version* TB/1156
JEAN PIAGET, BÄRBEL INHELDER, & ALINA SZEMINSKA: The Child's Conception of Geometry ° TB/1146
JOHN H. SCHAAR: Escape from Authority: *The Perspectives of Erich Fromm* TB/1155

Sociology

JACQUES BARZUN: Race: *A Study in Superstition. Revised Edition* TB/1172
BERNARD BERELSON, Ed.: The Behavioral Sciences Today TB/1127
ABRAHAM CAHAN: The Rise of David Levinsky: *A documentary novel of social mobility in early twentieth century America. Intro. by John Higham* TB/1028
THOMAS C. COCHRAN: The Inner Revolution: *Essays on the Social Sciences in History* TB/1140
ALLISON DAVIS & JOHN DOLLARD: Children of Bondage: *The Personality Development of Negro Youth in the Urban South* || TB/3049
ST. CLAIR DRAKE & HORACE R. CAYTON: Black Metropolis: *A Study of Negro Life in a Northern City. Revised and Enlarged. Intro. by Everett C. Hughes* Vol. I TB/1086; Vol. II TB/1087
EMILE DURKHEIM et al.: Essays on Sociology and Philosophy: *With Analyses of Durkheim's Life and Work.* || *Edited by Kurt H. Wolff* TB/1151
LEON FESTINGER, HENRY W. RIECKEN & STANLEY SCHACHTER: When Prophecy Fails: *A Social and Psychological Account of a Modern Group that Predicted the Destruction of the World* || TB/1132
ALVIN W. GOULDNER: Wildcat Strike: *A Study in Worker-Management Relationships* || TB/1176
FRANCIS J. GRUND: Aristocracy in America: *Social Class in the Formative Years of the New Nation* TB/1001
KURT LEWIN: Field Theory in Social Science: *Selected Theoretical Papers.* || *Edited with a Foreword by* Dorwin Cartwright TB/1135
R. M. MACIVER: Social Causation TB/1153
ROBERT K. MERTON, LEONARD BROOM, LEONARD S. COTTRELL, JR., Editors: Sociology Today: *Problems and Prospects* || Vol. I TB/1173; Vol. II TB/1174
ROBERTO MICHELS: First Lectures in Political Sociology. *Edited by Alfred De Grazia* || ° TB/1224
BARRINGTON MOORE, JR.: Political Power and Social Theory: *Seven Studies* || TB/1221
BARRINGTON MOORE, JR.: Soviet Politics—The Dilemma of Power: *The Role of Ideas in Social Change* || TB/1222
TALCOTT PARSONS & EDWARD A. SHILS, Editors: Toward a General Theory of Action: *Theoretical Foundations for the Social Sciences* TB/1083
JOHN H. ROHRER & MUNRO S. EDMONSON, Eds.: The Eighth Generation Grows Up: *Cultures and Personalities of New Orleans Negroes* || TB/3050
ARNOLD ROSE: The Negro in America: *The Condensed Version of Gunnar Myrdal's* An American Dilemma TB/3048
KURT SAMUELSSON: Religion and Economic Action: *A Critique of Max Weber's* The Protestant Ethic and the Spirit of Capitalism. || ° *Trans. by E. G. French. Ed. with Intro. by D. C. Coleman* TB/1131
PHILIP SELZNICK: TVA and the Grass Roots: *A Study in the Sociology of Formal Organization* TB/1230
GEORG SIMMEL et al.: Essays on Sociology, Philosophy, and Aesthetics. || *Edited by Kurt H. Wolff* TB/1234
HERBERT SIMON: The Shape of Automation: *For Men and Management* TB/1245
PITIRIM A. SOROKIN: Contemporary Sociological Theories. *Through the First Quarter of the 20th Century* TB/3046
MAURICE R. STEIN: The Eclipse of Community: *An Interpretation of American Studies* TB/1128
FERDINAND TÖNNIES: Community and Society: *Gemeinschaft und Gesellschaft. Translated and edited by Charles P. Loomis* TB/1116
W. LLOYD WARNER & Associates: Democracy in Jonesville: *A Study in Quality and Inequality* TB/1129
W. LLOYD WARNER: Social Class in America: *The Evaluation of Status* TB/1013

RELIGION

Ancient & Classical

J. H. BREASTED: Development of Religion and Thought in Ancient Egypt. *Introduction by John A. Wilson* TB/57
HENRI FRANKFORT: Ancient Egyptian Religion: *An Interpretation* TB/77
G. RACHEL LEVY: Religious Conceptions of the Stone Age *and their Influence upon European Thought. Illus. Introduction by Henri Frankfort* TB/106
MARTIN P. NILSSON: Greek Folk Religion. *Foreword by Arthur Darby Nock* TB/78
ALEXANDRE PIANKOFF: The Shrines of Tut-Ankh-Amon. *Edited by N. Rambova. 117 illus.* TB/2011
H. J. ROSE: Religion in Greece and Rome TB/55

Biblical Thought & Literature

W. F. ALBRIGHT: The Biblical Period from Abraham to Ezra TB/102
C. K. BARRETT, Ed.: The New Testament Background: *Selected Documents* TB/86
C. H. DODD: The Authority of the Bible TB/43
M. S. ENSLIN: Christian Beginnings TB/5
M. S. ENSLIN: The Literature of the Christian Movement TB/6

JOHN GRAY: Archaeology and the Old Testament World. *Illus.* TB/127
JAMES MUILENBURG: The Way of Israel: *Biblical Faith and Ethics* TB/133
H. H. ROWLEY: The Growth of the Old Testament TB/107
D. WINTON THOMAS, Ed.: Documents from Old Testament Times TB/85

The Judaic Tradition

LEO BAECK: Judaism and Christianity. *Trans. with Intro. by Walter Kaufmann* JP/23
SALO W. BARON: Modern Nationalism and Religion JP/18
MARTIN BUBER: Eclipse of God: *Studies in the Relation Between Religion and Philosophy* TB/12
MARTIN BUBER: The Knowledge of Man: *Selected Essays. Edited with an Introduction by Maurice Friedman. Translated by Maurice Friedman and Ronald Gregor Smith* TB/135
MARTIN BUBER: Moses: *The Revelation and the Covenant* TB/27
MARTIN BUBER: Pointing the Way. *Introduction by Maurice S. Friedman* TB/103
MARTIN BUBER: The Prophetic Faith TB/73
MARTIN BUBER: Two Types of Faith: *the interpenetration of Judaism and Christianity* ° TB/75
ERNST LUDWIG EHRLICH: A Concise History of Israel: *From the Earliest Times to the Destruction of the Temple in A.D. 70* ° TB/128
MAURICE S. FRIEDMAN: Martin Buber: *The Life of Dialogue* TB/64
LOUIS GINZBERG: Students, Scholars and Saints JP/2
SOLOMON GRAYZEL: A History of the Contemporary Jews TB/816
WILL HERBERG: Judaism and Modern Man TB/810
ABRAHAM J. HESCHEL: God in Search of Man: *A Philosophy of Judaism* JP/7
ISAAC HUSIK: A History of Medieval Jewish Philosophy JP/3
FLAVIUS JOSEPHUS: The Great Roman-Jewish War, *with* The Life of Josephus. *Introduction by William R. Farmer* TB/74
JACOB R. MARCUS The Jew in the Medieval World TB/814
MAX L. MARGOLIS & ALEXANDER MARX: A History of the Jewish People TB/806
T. J. MEEK: Hebrew Origins TB/69
C. G. MONTEFIORE & H. LOEWE, Eds.: A Rabbinic Anthology. JP/32
JAMES PARKES: The Conflict of the Church and the Synagogue: *The Jews and Early Christianity* JP/21
PHILO, SAADYA GAON, & JEHUDA HALEVI: Three Jewish Philosophers. *Ed. by Hans Lewey, Alexander Altmann, & Isaak Heinemann* TB/813
HERMAN L. STRACK: Introduction to the Talmud and Midrash TB/808
JOSHUA TRACHTENBERG: The Devil and the Jews: *The Medieval Conception of the Jew and its Relation to Modern Anti-Semitism* JP/22

Christianity: General

ROLAND H. BAINTON: Christendom: *A Short History of Christianity and its Impact on Western Civilization. Illus.* Vol. I TB/131; Vol. II TB/132

Christianity: Origins & Early Development

AUGUSTINE: An Augustine Synthesis. *Edited by Erich Przywara* TB/335
ADOLF DEISSMANN: Paul: *A Study in Social and Religious History* TB/15
EDWARD GIBBON: The Triumph of Christendom in the Roman Empire *(Chaps. XV-XX of "Decline and Fall," J. B. Bury edition).* § *Illus.* TB/46
MAURICE GOGUEL: Jesus and the Origins of Christianity. ° *Introduction by C. Leslie Mitton*
Volume I: *Prolegomena to the Life of Jesus* TB/65
Volume II: *The Life of Jesus* TB/66
EDGAR J. GOODSPEED: A Life of Jesus TB/1
ADOLF HARNACK: The Mission and Expansion of Christianity *in the First Three Centuries. Introduction by Jaroslav Pelikan* TB/92
R. K. HARRISON: The Dead Sea Scrolls: *An Introduction* ° TB/84
EDWIN HATCH: The Influence of Greek Ideas on Christianity. § *Introduction and Bibliography by Frederick C. Grant* TB/18
ARTHUR DARBY NOCK: Early Gentile Christianity and Its Hellenistic Background TB/111
ARTHUR DARBY NOCK: St. Paul ° TB/104
ORIGEN: On First Principles. *Edited by G. W. Butterworth. Introduction by Henri de Lubac* TB/310
JAMES PARKES: The Conflict of the Church and the Synagogue: *The Jews and Early Christianity* JP/21
SULPICIUS SEVERUS et al.: The Western Fathers: *Being the Lives of Martin of Tours, Ambrose, Augustine of Hippo, Honoratus of Arles and Germanus of Auxerre. Edited and translated by F. R. Hoare* TB/309
F. VAN DER MEER: Augustine the Bishop: *Church and Society at the Dawn of the Middle Ages* TB/304
JOHANNES WEISS: Earliest Christianity: *A History of the Period A.D. 30-150. Introduction and Bibliography by Frederick C. Grant* Volume I TB/53
Volume II TB/54

Christianity: The Middle Ages and The Reformation

JOHN CALVIN & JACOPO SADOLETO: A Reformation Debate. *Edited by John C. Olin* TB/1239
JOHANNES ECKHART: Meister Eckhart: *A Modern Translation by R. B. Blakney* TB/8
DESIDERIUS ERASMUS: Christian Humanism and the Reformation: *Selected Writings. Edited and translated by John C. Olin* TB/1166
ÉTIENNE GILSON: Dante and Philosophy TB/1089
WILLIAM HALLER: The Rise of Puritanism TB/22
HAJO HOLBORN: Ulrich von Hutten and the German Reformation TB/1238
JOHAN HUIZINGA: Erasmus and the Age of Reformation. *Illus.* TB/19
A. C. MCGIFFERT: Protestant Thought Before Kant. *Preface by Jaroslav Pelikan* TB/93
JOHN T. MCNEILL: Makers of the Christian Tradition: *From Alfred the Great to Schleiermacher* TB/121
G. MOLLAT: The Popes at Avignon, 1305-1378 TB/308
GORDON RUPP: Luther's Progress to the Diet of Worms ° TB/120

Christianity: The Protestant Tradition

KARL BARTH: Church Dogmatics: *A Selection* TB/95
KARL BARTH: Dogmatics in Outline TB/56
KARL BARTH: The Word of God and the Word of Man TB/13
RUDOLF BULTMANN et al.: Translating Theology into the Modern Age: *Historical, Systematic and Pastoral Reflections on Theology and the Church in the Contemporary Situation. Volume 2 of* Journal for Theology and the Church, *edited by Robert W. Funk in association with Gerhard Ebeling* TB/252
WINTHROP HUDSON: The Great Tradition of the American Churches TB/98
SOREN KIERKEGAARD: Edifying Discourses. *Edited with an Introduction by Paul Holmer* TB/32
SOREN KIERKEGAARD: The Journals of Kierkegaard. ° *Edited with an Introduction by Alexander Dru* TB/52
SOREN KIERKEGAARD: The Point of View for My Work as an Author: *A Report to History.* § *Preface by Benjamin Nelson* TB/88

SOREN KIERKEGAARD: The Present Age. § *Translated and edited by Alexander Dru. Introduction by Walter Kaufmann* TB/94
SOREN KIERKEGAARD: Purity of Heart TB/4
SOREN KIERKEGAARD: Repetition: *An Essay in Experimental Psychology. Translated with Introduction & Notes by Walter Lowrie* TB/117
SOREN KIERKEGAARD: Works of Love: *Some Christian Reflections in the Form of Discourses* TB/122
WALTER LOWRIE: Kierkegaard: *A Life* Vol. I TB/89
Vol. II TB/90
JOHN MACQUARRIE: The Scope of Demythologizing: *Bultmann and his Critics* TB/134
PERRY MILLER & T. H. JOHNSON, Editors: The Puritans: *A Sourcebook of Their Writings* Vol. I TB/1093
Vol. II TB/1094
JAMES M. ROBINSON et al.: The Bultmann School of Biblical Interpretation: New Directions? *Volume 1 of* Journal of Theology and the Church, *edited by Robert W. Funk in association with Gerhard Ebeling* TB/251
F. SCHLEIERMACHER: The Christian Faith. *Introduction by Richard R. Niebuhr* Vol. I TB/108
Vol. II TB/109
F. SCHLEIERMACHER: On Religion: *Speeches to Its Cultured Despisers. Intro. by Rudolf Otto* TB/36
PAUL TILLICH: Dynamics of Faith TB/42
EVELYN UNDERHILL: Worship TB/10
G. VAN DER LEEUW: Religion in Essence and Manifestation: *A Study in Phenomenology. Appendices by Hans H. Penner* Vol. I TB/100; Vol. II TB/101

Christianity: The Roman and Eastern Traditions

DOM CUTHBERT BUTLER: Western Mysticism: *The Teaching of Augustine, Gregory and Bernard on Contemplation and the Contemplative Life* § ° TB/312
A. ROBERT CAPONIGRI, Ed.: Modern Catholic Thinkers I: *God and Man* TB/306
A. ROBERT CAPONIGRI, Ed.: Modern Catholic Thinkers II: *The Church and the Political Order* TB/307
THOMAS CORBISHLEY, S. J.: Roman Catholicism TB/112
CHRISTOPHER DAWSON: The Historic Reality of Christian Culture TB/305
G. P. FEDOTOV: The Russian Religious Mind: *Kievan Christianity, the 10th to the 13th Centuries* TB/70
G. P. FEDOTOV, Ed.: A Treasury of Russian Spirituality TB/303
DAVID KNOWLES: The English Mystical Tradition TB/302
GABRIEL MARCEL: Being and Having: *An Existential Diary. Introduction by James Collins* TB/310
GABRIEL MARCEL: Homo Viator: *Introduction to a Metaphysic of Hope* TB/397
GUSTAVE WEIGEL, S. J.: Catholic Theology in Dialogue TB/301

Oriental Religions: Far Eastern, Near Eastern

TOR ANDRAE: Mohammed: *The Man and His Faith* TB/62
EDWARD CONZE: Buddhism: *Its Essence and Development.* ° *Foreword by Arthur Waley* TB/58
EDWARD CONZE et al., Editors: Buddhist Texts Through the Ages TB/113
ANANDA COOMARASWAMY: Buddha and the Gospel of Buddhism. *Illus.* TB/119
H. G. CREEL: Confucius and the Chinese Way TB/63
FRANKLIN EDGERTON, Trans. & Ed.: The Bhagavad Gita TB/115
SWAMI NIKHILANANDA, Trans. & Ed.: The Upanishads: *A One-Volume Abridgment* TB/114
HELLMUT WILHELM: Change: *Eight Lectures on the* I Ching TB/2019

Philosophy of Religion

NICOLAS BERDYAEV: The Beginning and the End § TB/14
NICOLAS BERDYAEV: Christian Existentialism: *A Berdyaev Synthesis. Ed. by Donald A. Lowrie* TB/130
NICOLAS BERDYAEV: The Destiny of Man TB/61
RUDOLF BULTMANN: History and Eschatology: *The Presence of Eternity* ° TB/91
RUDOLF BULTMANN AND FIVE CRITICS: Kerygma and Myth: *A Theological Debate* TB/80
RUDOLF BULTMANN and KARL KUNDSIN: Form Criticism: *Two Essays on New Testament Research. Translated by Frederick C. Grant* TB/96
MIRCEA ELIADE: The Sacred and the Profane TB/81
LUDWIG FEUERBACH: The Essence of Christianity. § *Introduction by Karl Barth. Foreword by H. Richard Niebuhr* TB/11
ADOLF HARNACK: What is Christianity? § *Introduction by Rudolf Bultmann* TB/17
FRIEDRICH HEGEL: On Christianity: *Early Theological Writings. Ed. by R. Kroner & T. M. Knox* TB/79
KARL HEIM: Christian Faith and Natural Science TB/16
IMMANUEL KANT: Religion Within the Limits of Reason Alone. § *Intro. by T. M. Greene & J. Silber* TB/67
JOHN MACQUARRIE: An Existentialist Theology: *A Comparison of Heidegger and Bultmann.* ° *Preface by Rudolf Bultmann* TB/125
PAUL RAMSEY, Ed.: Faith and Ethics: *The Theology of H. Richard Niebuhr* TB/129
PIERRE TEILHARD DE CHARDIN: The Divine Milieu ° TB/384
PIERRE TEILHARD DE CHARDIN: The Phenomenon of Man ° TB/83

Religion, Culture & Society

JOSEPH L. BLAU, Ed.: Cornerstones of Religious Freedom in America: *Selected Basic Documents, Court Decisions and Public Statements. Revised and Enlarged Edition* TB/118
C. C. GILLISPIE: Genesis and Geology: *The Decades before Darwin* § TB/51
KYLE HASELDEN: The Racial Problem in Christian Perspective TB/116
WALTER KAUFMANN, Ed.: Religion from Tolstoy to Camus: *Basic Writings on Religious Truth and Morals. Enlarged Edition* TB/123
JOHN T. MCNEILL: A History of the Cure of Souls TB/126
KENNETH B. MURDOCK: Literature and Theology in Colonial New England TB/99
H. RICHARD NIEBUHR: Christ and Culture TB/3
H. RICHARD NIEBUHR: The Kingdom of God in America TB/49
RALPH BARTON PERRY: Puritanism and Democracy TB/1138
PAUL PFUETZE: Self, Society, Existence: *Human Nature and Dialogue in the Thought of George Herbert Mead and Martin Buber* TB/1059
WALTER RAUSCHENBUSCH: Christianity and the Social Crisis. ‡ *Edited by Robert D. Cross* TB/3059
KURT SAMUELSSON: Religion and Economic Action: *A Critique of Max Weber's* The ˉrotestant Ethic and the Spirit of Capitalism. || ° *Trans. by E. G. French. Ed. with Intro. by D. C. Coleman* TB/1131
TIMOTHY L. SMITH: Revivalism and Social Reform: *Protestantism on the Eve of the Civil War* TB/1229
ERNST TROELTSCH: The Social Teaching of the Christian Churches ° Vol. I TB/71; Vol. II TB/72

NATURAL SCIENCES AND MATHEMATICS

Biological Sciences

CHARLOTTE AUERBACH: The Science of Genetics Σ TB/568
MARSTON BATES: The Natural History of Mosquitoes. *Illus.* TB/578
A. BELLAIRS: Reptiles: *Life History, Evolution, and Structure. Illus.* TB/520

LUDWIG VON BERTALANFFY: Modern Theories of Development: *An Introduction to Theoretical Biology* TB/554
LUDWIG VON BERTALANFFY: Problems of Life: *An Evaluation of Modern Biological and Scientific Thought* TB/521
HAROLD F. BLUM: Time's Arrow and Evolution TB/555
JOHN TYLER BONNER: The Ideas of Biology. Σ *Illus.* TB/570
A. J. CAIN: Animal Species and their Evolution. *Illus.* TB/519
WALTER B. CANNON: Bodily Changes in Pain, Hunger, Fear and Rage. *Illus.* TB/562
W. E. LE GROS CLARK: The Antecedents of Man: *Intro. to Evolution of the Primates.* ° *Illus.* TB/559
W. H. DOWDESWELL: Animal Ecology. *Illus.* TB/543
W. H. DOWDESWELL: The Mechanism of Evolution. *Illus.* TB/527
R. W. GERARD: Unresting Cells. *Illus.* TB/541
DAVID LACK: Darwin's Finches. *Illus.* TB/544
J. E. MORTON: Molluscs: *An Introduction to their Form and Functions. Illus.* TB/529
ADOLF PORTMANN: Animals as Social Beings. ° *Illus.* TB/572
O. W. RICHARDS: The Social Insects. *Illus.* TB/542
P. M. SHEPPARD: Natural Selection and Heredity. *Illus.* TB/528
EDMUND W. SINNOTT: Cell and Psyche: *The Biology of Purpose* TB/546
C. H. WADDINGTON: How Animals Develop. *Illus.* TB/553
C. H. WADDINGTON: The Nature of Life: *The Main Problems and Trends in Modern Biology* TB/580

Chemistry

J. R. PARTINGTON: A Short History of Chemistry. *Illus.* TB/522
J. READ: A Direct Entry to Organic Chemistry. *Illus.* TB/523
J. READ: Through Alchemy to Chemistry. *Illus.* TB/561

Communication Theory

J. R. PIERCE: Symbols, Signals and Noise: *The Nature and Process of Communication* TB/574

Geography

R. E. COKER: This Great and Wide Sea: *An Introduction to Oceanography and Marine Biology. Illus.* TB/551
F. K. HARE: The Restless Atmosphere TB/560

History of Science

W. DAMPIER, Ed.: Readings in the Literature of Science. *Illus.* TB/512
A. HUNTER DUPREE: Science in the Federal Government: *A History of Policies and Activities to 1940* TB/573
ALEXANDRE KOYRÉ: From the Closed World to the Infinite Universe: *Copernicus, Kepler, Galileo, Newton, etc.* TB/31
A. G. VAN MELSEN: From Atomos to Atom: *A History of the Concept* Atom TB/517
O. NEUGEBAUER: The Exact Sciences in Antiquity TB/552
H. T. PLEDGE: Science Since 1500: *A Short History of Mathematics, Physics, Chemistry and Biology. Illus.* TB/506
HANS THIRRING: Energy for Man: *From Windmills to Nuclear Power* TB/556
LANCELOT LAW WHYTE: Essay on Atomism: *From Democritus to 1960* TB/565
A. WOLF: A History of Science, Technology and Philosophy in the 16th and 17th Centuries. ° *Illus.* Vol. I TB/508; Vol. II TB/509
A. WOLF: A History of Science, Technology, and Philosophy in the Eighteenth Century. ° *Illus.* Vol. I TB/539; Vol. II TB/540

Mathematics

E. W. BETH: The Foundations of Mathematics: *A Study in the Philosophy of Science* TB/581
H. DAVENPORT: The Higher Arithmetic: *An Introduction to the Theory of Numbers* TB/526
H. G. FORDER: Geometry: *An Introduction* TB/548
GOTTLOB FREGE: The Foundations of Arithmetic: *A Logico-Mathematical Enquiry* TB/534
S. KÖRNER: The Philosophy of Mathematics: *An Introduction* TB/547
D. E. LITTLEWOOD: Skeleton Key of Mathematics: *A Simple Account of Complex Algebraic Problems* TB/525
GEORGE E. OWEN: Fundamentals of Scientific Mathematics TB/569
WILLARD VAN ORMAN QUINE: Mathematical Logic TB/558
O. G. SUTTON: Mathematics in Action. ° *Foreword by James R. Newman. Illus.* TB/518
FREDERICK WAISMANN: Introduction to Mathematical Thinking. *Foreword by Karl Menger* TB/511

Philosophy of Science

R. B. BRAITHWAITE: Scientific Explanation TB/515
J. BRONOWSKI: Science and Human Values. *Revised and Enlarged Edition* TB/505
ALBERT EINSTEIN et al.: Albert Einstein: Philosopher-Scientist. *Edited by Paul A. Schilpp* Vol. I TB/502 Vol. II TB/503
WERNER HEISENBERG: Physics and Philosophy: *The Revolution in Modern Science* TB/549
JOHN MAYNARD KEYNES: A Treatise on Probability. ° *Introduction by N. R. Hanson* TB/557
KARL R. POPPER: The Logic of Scientific Discovery TB/576
STEPHEN TOULMIN: Foresight and Understanding: *An Enquiry into the Aims of Science. Foreword by Jacques Barzun* TB/564
STEPHEN TOULMIN: The Philosophy of Science: *An Introduction* TB/513
G. J. WHITROW: The Natural Philosophy of Time ° TB/563

Physics and Cosmology

STEPHEN TOULMIN & JUNE GOODFIELD: The Fabric of the Heavens: *The Development of Astronomy and Dynamics. Illus.* TB/579
DAVID BOHM: Causality and Chance in Modern Physics. *Foreword by Louis de Broglie* TB/536
P. W. BRIDGMAN: The Nature of Thermodynamics TB/537
P. W. BRIDGMAN: A Sophisticate's Primer of Relativity TB/575
A. C. CROMBIE, Ed.: Turning Point in Physics TB/535
C. V. DURELL: Readable Relativity. *Foreword by Freeman J. Dyson* TB/530
ARTHUR EDDINGTON: Space, Time and Gravitation: *An Outline of the General Relativity Theory* TB/510
GEORGE GAMOW: Biography of Physics Σ TB/567
MAX JAMMER: Concepts of Force: *A Study in the Foundation of Dynamics* TB/550
MAX JAMMER: Concepts of Mass *in Classical and Modern Physics* TB/571
MAX JAMMER: Concepts of Space: *The History of Theories of Space in Physics. Foreword by Albert Einstein* TB/533
EDMUND WHITTAKER: History of the Theories of Aether and Electricity
Volume I: *The Classical Theories* TB/531
Volume II: *The Modern Theories* TB/532
G. J. WHITROW: The Structure and Evolution of the Universe: *An Introduction to Cosmology. Illus.* TB/504